D1239209

TAUNTON
COHANNET
A TOWN 1639. A CITY 1864.

JEREMY KEENAN

# THE TUAREG

PEOPLE OF AHAGGAR

ST. MARTIN'S PRESS
NEW YORK

 For information write:
St. Martin's Press Inc., 175 Fifth Avenue, New York, N.Y. 10010
Printed in Great Britain

Library of Congress Catalog Card Number: 77-77139
ISBN: 0-312-82200-6

First published in the United States of America in 1977

To Sandra, and Mark who was
born whilst Chapter Thirteen was being written
in a land where drought is also not
unheard of and where
elders also live on islands

# CONTENTS

# LIST OF PLATES

# LIST OF FIGURES

# PREFACE

Before going up to Cambridge I was fortunate in being able to spend ten months travelling through the Americas. During the course of these travels I found my interests being directed not so much to the 'new world' of the Manhattans and Hollywoods, but to the 'old world' of the Aztec, Mayan and Incan civilizations, and the desert regions of the south-west U.S.A., Mexico and the Atacama.

At Cambridge, where I read geography, my interest in desert regions was further stimulated by Mr A. T. Grove, and encouraged by my own supervisor at St John's College, Mr B. H. Farmer, who gave tacit support to my overly ambitious plans to do the Sahara, Kalahari and Middle East deserts in the space of a summer vacation! And so, in the summer of 1964, I set off for North Africa and the Sahara. It was not until eight years later, and under quite different conditions, that I was to visit the Kalahari.

The reason for not continuing my journey southwards from Tamanrasset, in the central Sahara, was because I was intrigued with the nomadic Tuareg of Ahaggar, with whom I had come into contact, and who were rumoured to be about to revolt against the newly independent Algerian government. In the following year I returned to the Sahara and spent four months with the Tuareg and travelling widely through Ahaggar.

My training as a geographer gave me a valuable understanding of the terrain and country in which I was travelling. But the longer I stayed with the Tuareg and the more I became aware of the critical conditions and difficulties which confronted them, so I realized that a training in social anthropology was an essential prerequisite for any serious study of their society. I am consequently indebted to Exeter University, and particularly Mr H. D. Munro and Professor Duncan Mitchell, head of the Department of Sociology, who allowed me, on graduating from Cambridge, to register for a Ph.D. in social anthropology.

Exeter University was generous in the facilities that it offered me, especially through the kindness of the trustees of the Devon War Memorial Scholarship Fund (Exeter University), who gave me considerable financial assistance. I am also indebted to the Royal Anthropological Institute of Gt Britain and Northern Ireland, which gave me a Horniman Scholarship, as well as the Worshipful Company of Goldsmiths, who gave me a very generous studentship. The financial assistance given by these bodies enabled me to pursue postgraduate research among the Tuareg for four years.

I would also like to express my thanks to Professor Ernest Gellner, not only for examining my Ph.D. thesis, but for much valuable comment and advice. Debts of gratitude are also due to various colleagues who have worked among the Tuareg, particularly Johannes Nicolaisen, Marceau Gast and André Bourgeot.

In addition, I would like to take this opportunity to thank M. Barrère, Mr and Mrs Baggott, the Frères at Assekrem (Antoine, Henrique, Jean-Marie and Louis Pilate), M. Laporte, and Mr and Mrs Johnson of the British Embassy in Algiers, all of whom offered me hospitality, kindness and valuable advice on many occasions while I was in Algeria.

In all parts of Algeria I was met and received with warmth and kindness. I cannot thank by name all the Algerians who have befriended me, for they are many, but I must thank them for the insight that they have given me into their country and the sympathy and love for it which they have imparted to me.

Above all, however, I am indebted to the Kel Ahaggar about whom this book is written. For the same reasons that many of the living Tuareg mentioned in the text have been given pseudonyms, so it is not in their interest that I list publicly the names of all my informants, interpreters and friends, without whose help this work could not have been undertaken. If they are never able to read this book, or even if they do not agree with all that I have said, I hope they will accept it as being written in gratitude to them, for they gave me much for very little in return.

Finally, I would like to thank those who have laboured in the preparation of the manuscript, namely Ms Arlene Guslandi, who typed two drafts of it, Professor David Hammond-Tooke, who kindly read and commented on the drafts, and my wife, Sandra, whose faith in it has always been greater than mine.

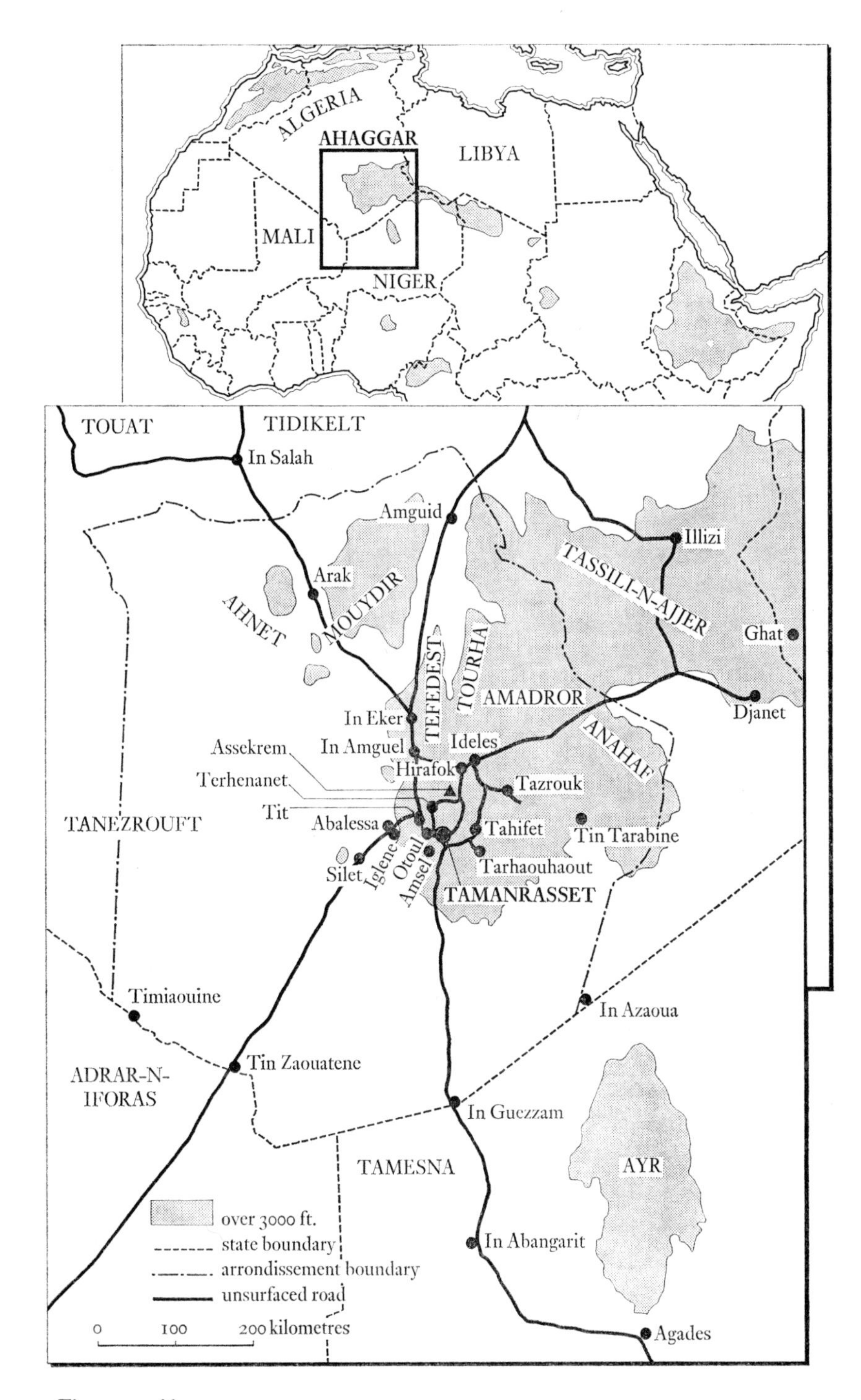


Figure 1 Ahaggar.

# INTRODUCTION

More or less in the centre of the Sahara, in fact just a little towards the west, and astride the Tropic of Cancer, is the vast mountainous area of Ahaggar.[1] Like a colossus the massif dominates the central Sahara, barring the outside world and challenging it to violate its defences. Covering nearly half a million square kilometres – almost the size of France – Ahaggar is geologically, climatically and botanically an island in the Sahara. On nearly all sides the various Tassili escarpments of uplifted and tilted palaeozoic rocks form an imposing wall.

The entrance to Ahaggar is perhaps most spectacular from the north, along the Amguid or better known Arak routes. From the Atlas regions, the road passes through the Mzab, the plateau of Tademait, and the oasis of In Salah in the low-lying and sandy depression of Tidikelt. On leaving In Salah the formless horizon gradually merges into the dark and often hazy outline of the Tassili escarpment. As the road approaches the escarpment and then runs parallel to it, almost within touching distance, the rock face towers hundreds of feet above and the impenetrability of Ahaggar seems absolute. Just when it seems that the wall will never part and admission be forever denied the road suddenly swings to the left into the gorges of Arak. The rock face closes in on both sides and tamarisk trees and a dense mat of rushes cover the valley floor. Barbary sheep[2] may be seen perched perilously on the uppermost crags, and the old Foreign Legion fort, like a hidden Pueblo city, provides a fitting back-cloth to 'Beau-Geste'.

The entry to Ahaggar is certainly dramatic; once through the gorges onto the uplifted plateau of Ahaggar itself, the landscape assumes an almost lunar perspective with the Precambrian granites, bared to erosion for 600 million years, forming weird and fascinating formations. Various ranges break the skyline: initially Mouydir (Immidir); then Tefedest to the east and Ahnet further away to the west; and finally, about two hundred kilometres south of Arak, the eastern skyline becomes dominated by Atakor, the central mountains of Ahaggar, which rise to almost ten thousand feet in Mount Tahat – the highest point in Algeria.

The most important period regarding the present morphology of the landscape was the late Tertiary and early Quaternary, when the now extinct volcanoes first became active. The present structure of Atakor is thus characterized by a series of basalt lava flows, and more chaotic phonolitic extrusions of the Mount Pelée type overlying the uplifted crystalline basement. These recent volcanic extrusions are the dominant feature of Atakor and explain many of the geomorphological features that have resulted since the late Tertiary. In many cases the lava flows have completely obliterated the pre-existing drainage pattern so that the present rejuvenated system is often discordant to it, and partially superimposed on the crystalline base. There is an almost complete absence of soil in these mountains, except in the lower valleys (*oueds*) where parts of the lower (neolithic) terrace have been preserved from erosion, and thus provide the limited cultivable land in Ahaggar. Water, however, is relatively abundant. The impermeable crystalline base and the discordancy of much of the drainage system make for numerous natural rock water-holes (*agelmam*/*gueltas*), which, although not often more than a few feet in depth, are rarely dry and consequently of great importance to the nomadic Tuareg tribesmen, the Kel Ahaggar,[3] who live in these mountains.

The main dirt road that leads south from Arak to the administrative centre of Tamanrasset, and then on to the Niger frontier, does not pass through Atakor, but skirts the foothills to the west, so that apart from the former French atomic base at In Eker, and the near-by village of In Amguel, it is possible for the traveller to pass through this intriguing country with little or no awareness of any human life, until the small cultivation centres of Tit and Otoul, forty and twenty kilometres north of Tamanrasset, indicate that people do derive some sort of livelihood from this country. From this road one can gaze across the broken foothills to the stark beauty of the rugged peaks of Atakor. But whatever feelings of desolation, foreboding and possibly even fear these mountains may evoke in the stranger, they are protective and familiar to the Kel Ahaggar.

The mountains of Atakor, and those of the other ranges, are not just physical features with names on a map, but reflect the social order and values of the Kel Ahaggar who live among them. They have not only names but are usually male or female and related by various mythological kinship ties. Mount Tahat, for example, is the wife of Ilaman, the needle-shaped plug that protrudes hundreds of feet above the surrounding red-coloured granites and grey-purple cappings of basalt lava. Their marriage, however, has not been devoid of jealousies and upheavals. Mount Amjer, just a little further to the west, once quarrelled with Ilaman over Tahat and struck him a heavy blow with his sword, which resulted in Ilaman's 'shoulder' and the start of a spring beneath the peak. But while Amjer's amorous advances were directed to Tahat, Mount Tioueyin was in love with Amjer. Rebuffed by Amjer's refusal to leave his position close to Tahat, Tioueyin left[4] in a fit of jealousy and anger and headed in a south-westerly direction towards Mali, only coming to a stop in her present position alongside the Oued Amded near Silet, about 150 kilometres south-west of the centre of Atakor. Mount Iherhe, whose site near Ilaman is now marked by a depression, left to follow Tioueyin and on arriving in the Oued Amded region began to court her; the small crater to the north of the Silet track known as Tegit-n-Iherhe is the mark left by Iherhe before he finally moved to his present position just behind Tioueyin.

The first European to gain a deep understanding of the Tuareg, and an appreciation of the incontestable beauty of these mountains, was probably the French priest Charles de Foucauld, who entered Ahaggar after the initial pacification by the French at the beginning of this century. Against the advice of his long-standing friend Colonel (later General) Laperrine, who was largely responsible for the French presence at that time, Foucauld built his hermitage on the summit of Mount Assekrem in the very heart of Atakor and among his Tuareg friends. In his diary he described his crude stone 'hermitage' as 'a beautiful place in which to worship the creator', and in a letter wrote, 'I am completely alone . . . on the summit of a mountain which towers above all others . . . the view is wonderful, comprising the whole Hoggar massif which falls away from the north to south to the endless expanse of desert. In the foreground one has the strangest medley of mountain peaks, pinnacles and phantastically stratified rocks.'[5] Foucauld's feelings are easily understood even in our more secular lives, but though he was alone on his summit one must not suppose there was no human life there, for graves, old camp sites, stone cairns, rock enclosures for the protection of kid goats, and well-worn camel tracks all testify to long habitation.

To the accustomed ear the unmistakable haunting cries and whistles of women tending goats somewhere in the distance waft upwards and echo from the surrounding valley sides. Dozens of slowly moving little black dots, each answering to its own particular call, can be descried on the rock-strewn slopes as the herd moves in search of pasture and water.[6]

Somewhere, probably not more than an hour or two away, is a camp – perhaps three or four tents perched above the valley floor and half-hidden in the lee of a protecting outcrop.

In Ahaggar many strange feelings and emotions would take hold of me while travelling alone on foot through the mountains, lying huddled into the stony ground in the cold night air, listening to the howls of jackals, the calming of the wind, and counting the stars like sheep in my discomfort. But in this emptiness there was a solace, the peace of loneliness that made me reluctant to enter the camps, for the intimacy of loneliness was greater than that found amidst the security of people. At the end of a journey I would stop on the hillside some way from the camp, take the weight of belongings off my shoulders and sit looking at the little centre of human habitation below me. There in the camp was food, warmth from the cold nights and friends whose understanding of me grew as mine did of them. But the crossing of that final threshold into the camp, to meet the bustle and talk, the end of privacy, was a passage of reluctance. It was not the embarrassment of foreignness, but the embarrassment of knowing, not so much what had gone before, for that they were to teach me, but the present and the wider horizons that lay beyond their experience. As I have dwelt now in the beginning of this book on the mountains rather than their people, so I would linger that one moment longer in the open space before entering the camp. For the more I was to learn from them about the past the more I became aware of the present as both the end and beginning of a way of life, and all transitions have their moments of sadness and regret.

There above the camps stood the mountain peaks, resolute, measuring their existence in millennia, and giving sanctuary not only to the eagles and other birds of prey who lodged in their crags but also to the Kel Ahaggar, who looked on them as part of their mythological past, of time immemorial, and with affection. But the existence of the camps could no longer offer the same permanence. Their hearths and awnings no longer gave the security that had been theirs for centuries, but rather sadness, and only a brief respite from the fate that now threatened them.

The Tuareg are commonly described as Berber-speaking nomadic stockbreeders. But, during the last few years, particularly since the early 1960s, the number of nomadic camps in Ahaggar has been dwindling, and most of those that remain can hardly be called 'nomadic' in the true sense of the word. Several years of insufficient rainfall and pasture, in conjunction with the socialist policies of a newly independent Algerian government (1962), have forced the Tuareg of Ahaggar to consider new means of existence. The last decade or so has thus been a period in which they have undergone radical change. After sixty years of 'protection' under French colonial rule, from 1902 to 1962, they have been obliged, as it were, to enter the twentieth century, but without grace and dignity, and perhaps that is the sadness of it all.

Although Tuareg are found extensively in southern Algeria, Niger, Mali, south-west Libya and a few other peripheral areas, they have not at any time formed a single politically united kingdom, state, or federation, but comprise several major groups which seem to correspond to politically autonomous units or federations. Nicolaisen recognized eight such groups, namely:[7]

1 *Kel Ahaggar* In the Ahaggar massif, the mountains of Atakor, Ahnet, Immidir (Mouydir) and Tefedest, and the surrounding lowlands. Certain tribes or sections of tribes of the Kel Ahaggar live in the plains of Tamesna, between the massifs of Ayr and Adrar-n-Iforas, particularly around I-n-abangerit and Tegidda-n-tesemt.

2 *Kel Ajjer* In the mountains of the Tassili-n-Ajjer to the north-east of Ahaggar in the eastern Algerian Sahara. They extend into Libya and northwards into Tripolitania and the Great Eastern Erg around Ghadames.

3 *Kel Adrar* In the mountains of Adrar-n-Iforas to the south-west of Ahaggar.

4 *Kel Ayr* In the mountain massif of Ayr and the plains to the west and south-west.

5 *Kel Geres* (*Gress*) South of the Kel Ayr in the plains around Tessawa. Late in summer they may move northwards to watering places in southern Ayr.

6 *Iwllemmeden Kel Dennek* (E. Iwllemmeden) In the plains around Tawa. At the end of the rains they move north to In Gal in the country of the Kel Ayr.

7 *Iwllemmeden Kel Ataram* (W. Iwllemmeden) In the plains around Meneka and along the Niger.

8 *Kel Tademaket* Comprising several tribes and groups of tribes around Timbuktu and Lac Faguibine. The Tengerregif and Kel Inteser are important among these groups. After about AD 1800, the Kel Tademaket were subjected to the Iwllemmeden Kel Ataram.

The two groups, Kel Ahaggar and Kel Ajjer, are usually referred to as the Northern Tuareg, while the remaining groups comprise the Southern Tuareg. Henri Lhote, with reference to the 1933–8 census material, gave the total number of Tuareg as 240,000 during that period and 300,000 in 1950,[8] although Nicolaisen considered that this latter figure was almost certainly too high.[9]

The meaning of the word Tuareg gives rise to considerable confusion, especially as the Tuareg do not in fact refer to themselves by this term. The name derives from an external or foreign and not an indigenous system of classification, so that our usage of the term relates in no way to the various social groupings and stratifications within Tuareg society, or even the Tuareg's own concepts of entity and self-designation. The word *Tuareg* is of Arabic origin (*tareq*; pl. *tuareg*) and according to Duveyrier, who travelled extensively in the country of the Northern Tuareg during the middle of the nineteenth century, though without actually penetrating Ahaggar itself, the Arabic meaning of the term is 'les abandonnés de Dieu', which was explained to him by his Tuareg informant: 'parce que nous avons pendant longtemps refusé d'adopter la religion des Arabes'.[10]

This meaning of Tuareg belongs to the Arabic system of classification based on religious criteria, which seems to have become prominent during the expansion of Islam into the central Sahara sometime around the eleventh century AD. To these earliest protagonists of Islam the land of Ahaggar seems to have been virtually unknown, and regarded as a particularly inhospitable, stony and mountainous desert inhabited by pagans. Historically, this denomination merely reflects the theocentric ideology of Islam during the first centuries of this millennium, and the opposition between believer and non-believer – or, in this case, between Arab and Tuareg.[11] The irrelevance and archaism of this system of classification is demonstrated by the Tuareg's subsequent islamization and, perhaps ironically, by their adoption of the same theocentric criteria in their classification of other peoples. The Arabic term for infidels or non-Moslems, *kafir* (pl. *kufar*), has been adopted by the Tuareg in its berberized form, *akafar* (pl. *ikufar*), as a generalized designation of all non-Moslems.

To avoid any further ambiguity resulting from the use of the word Tuareg, it is convenient to use the term *Kel Ahaggar* (people of Ahaggar) for the Tuareg of Ahaggar. Although this term also cuts across the indigenous terminology of the social groupings within Ahaggar society, it is not only unambiguous in its geographical reference but is used as a general form of self-designation by the people themselves, particularly when they are outside Ahaggar. When in Niger or Tidikelt, for example, and confronted with the question of 'Who are you?' or, in other words, 'To what "tribe" do you belong?' a Tuareg from Ahaggar will usually reply, 'I am a Kel Ahaggar.'

With the increased facility of Saharan transport over recent years, Ahaggar has become an increasingly active tourist area. Various safari-type companies grew in profusion during the later 1960s, catering for the more 'interested' tourist, or traveller, who has come, not so much to see the sun or just get away from it all, but to see and explore something of the central Sahara – the Tuareg tribesmen and the Hoggar mountains. But the conceptions that many of these visitors hold about the almost legendary and romantic 'blue-veiled desert warriors' often devolve into feelings of disillusion or surprise after their arrival in Ahaggar.

The reasons for this are twofold: firstly, Ahaggar has been part of the Algerian Revolution, not so much during the war of independence (1954–62) itself, which hardly touched the southern parts of the country, but during the decade since independence when Algerian socialism, in conjunction with certain ecological factors, has greatly accelerated the processes of change that were emergent during the last few years of French colonial rule. For example, it is now difficult to identify the once noble Tuareg warrior, especially when he may be seen, not in his flowing robes and indigo-coloured veil, and mounted on a white riding camel, but in an old army greatcoat and driving a large municipal truck through the high street of Tamanrasset, the administrative centre of Ahaggar (pop. 1966: 4,500).[12] Secondly, there have been very few objective studies of the Tuareg in recent years, with the result that many misconceptions have arisen and been reproduced in much of the more popular and accessible literature.[13]

But why should the visitor have such feelings for this region? What is there in Ahaggar or about the Tuareg there that conjures up such romantic appeal? Indeed, one might ask why it is, when the Kel Ahaggar number only about 5,000 compared with the 200,000–300,000 other Tuareg in the Sudanese regions of Niger and Mali, that they should have received so much more attention than the far more numerous southern groups. This anomaly cannot be attributed entirely to greater academic interest in the Northern Tuareg, although this is partly true. Rather it seems to be associated with the almost legendary and certainly romantic image that has grown up around them.

It is neither easy to describe this 'image' nor to account for its development, although it seems to have had much to do with the Northern Tuareg's warring activities prior to and during the period of French exploration and colonial expansion in the Sahara during the nineteenth and early twentieth centuries. During the short period of thirty-seven years, from 1880 to 1917, the Kel Ahaggar became something of a household name in France, introduced to a shocked and incredulous French public after the almost complete annihilation of Colonel Flatters's column of ninety men in 1881 as it pushed southwards into Ahaggar to reconnoitre a route for the projected trans-Saharan railway.

This massacre shocked France and effectively checked all further attempts at penetration into Ahaggar for twenty years, until the battle of Tit in 1902, at which the Kel Ahaggar showed remarkable ferocity and courage in the face of immeasurable military superiority. Following this 'pacification' the Kel Ahaggar showed great diplomatic skill in engineering a treaty with France, and only a few years later (1907), with France's position in Ahaggar still tenuous, the *Amenukal* (supreme chief) Moussa ag Amastane was awarded the Légion d'Honneur for daring reprisal raids against the Kel Ajjer[14] 'in the service of France'. At a time when France was in need of heroes, the activities of men such as General Laperrine and Charles de Foucauld captured the imagination of the French public; while Laperrine established the presence of France in the central Sahara, Charles de Foucauld attempted to establish the Roman Catholic Church among these violent warriors. But the Kel Ahaggar were not readily pacified. In 1916 Foucauld was treacherously murdered; a few months later a French patrol received severe casualties at the hands of the Dag Rali – an old Dag Rali woman once recounted this great victory to me and laughed uproariously on remembering how she watched the few French stragglers staggering back through the mountains and eating *tahle* (a thorny shrub) like camels! With the Turkish-backed Senussi uprising of 1916–17 spreading through the Sahara, at a time when France's commitments on the European front were severely stretched, the loyalty of the Kel Ahaggar became crucial to France's continued presence in the region. Many Kel Ahaggar joined the Senussi cause and French Saharan forces had to be reinforced at the expense of the European front, and it is interesting to reflect on what might have happened if Moussa ag Amastane, the supreme chief of the Kel Ahaggar, had not remained loyal to France when even his own kinsmen were defecting.

With the final pacification in about 1920, and the firm establishment of a French military administration in Ahaggar, the general policy towards the Kel Ahaggar was one of paternalistic *laissez-faire* – although not entirely without ulterior political motives. It is probably true to say that a certain *rapprochement* existed throughout the French period – a degree of sentimentality and perhaps even psychological identification with the Tuareg on the part of the French, which can be best understood in the feelings underlying De Gaulle's *Dunkerque to Tamanrasset.* The word Tuareg itself seems to conjure up something more than just a nomadic herdsman or caravaneer.

This 'image', particularly the more romantic aspect of it, has gained from their formidable appearance. A 'noble' Tuareg mounted on an elaborately caparisoned white riding camel, with his flowing robes, sword (*takouba*), riding whip, and indigo-coloured veil completely covering his head apart from a narrow slit around the eyes, is indeed an impressive and overwhelming sight. But it is essentially the veil that has given the Tuareg a particular identity, reflected in numerous European references such as Rodd's classic *People of the Veil*[15] and as expressed in their own self-designation as *Kel Tagelmoust* (people of the veil), and the Arabic counterpart, *El Molathemine* or *Ahl el Litham.*

My first visit to Ahaggar was in 1964, less than two years after Algerian independence, and at the beginning of what was to be a period of radical social change in Ahaggar. During the following few years Kel Ahaggar society was to experience a social revolution, which has been described by some observers as 'the ruination or destruction of traditional Tuareg society'. I should therefore explain why it is, when the original object of my investigations among the Kel Ahaggar was to observe and analyse these changes, that this book is concerned for the most part with an historical reconstruction and analysis of traditional society.

It was not my intention to write a history of the Kel Ahaggar. That this has been the case, or, rather, that I should have adopted a predominantly historical perspective, was necessitated by the nature of my inquiry and the questions that it raised.

The first and most important of these questions concerned the nature of the society that existed prior to Algerian independence. In other words, what was this so-called 'traditional' society that Algeria is alleged to have destroyed?

There are in the order of 1,000 published works on the Tuareg. We might therefore expect to have a reasonable knowledge of the general structure and organization of Tuareg societies. This, however, is not the case. When we look at the documentary accounts of pre-colonial or 'traditional' society,[16] as it existed during the period prior to the French conquest of Ahaggar in 1902, and perhaps for the following ten or fifteen years when French control of the region was still tenuous, we are almost entirely dependent on the dictionary of Charles de Foucauld, compiled between about 1908 and 1916; on the explorations of the French geographer Henri Duveyrier, published in 1864; and on the six months' reconnaissance of Maurice Benhazera, published in 1908. Our analysis of traditional society, prior to the colonial period, thus raises many questions which must inevitably remain unanswered.

Such a state of affairs is not at all surprising. What is surprising is that this difficulty is not confined to the pre-colonial period. The large corpus of literature compiled during the colonial period poses more questions than it answers, and has been the main reason for the perpetuation of so many misconceptions about Tuareg societies.

Tuareg societies are characterized, perhaps above all else, by their rigid class structure. The basic class division was between 'nobles' (Ihaggaren) and 'vassals' (Imrad or Kel Ulli). There were other classes, such as the slaves, whom we shall introduce later. The Ihaggaren (nobles) comprised a warrior aristocracy. Through their control over camels and their rights to certain specialized arms such as the *takouba* (double-bladed sword), they controlled the means of physical force, the ultimate sanction to their political dominance.

In traditional times, at least from the middle of the eighteenth century until the beginning of this century, there were three major Ihaggaren descent groups (*tawsatin*, sing. *tawsit*)[17] in Ahaggar; namely the Kel Rela, the Taitok and the Tegehe Mellet. Over the last two or three generations, however, both the Taitok and the Tegehe Mellet have dwindled in both political and numerical importance with the result that the Kel Rela have effectively comprised the totality of Ihaggaren in Ahaggar throughout most of this century. Today the Kel Rela number about 275 individuals; the Taitok, by the end of the 1960s, did not number more than about thirty individuals in Ahaggar,[18] while the Tegehe Mellet are now quite insignificant.

The Imrad or Kel Ulli (vassals), who are 'pure Tuareg' in the racial and ethnic sense, have always been numerically the largest group among the Kel Ahaggar,[19] outnumbering the Ihaggaren in the ratio of about eight to one. Their political subordination to the Ihaggaren was expressed in the payment of certain tributary dues and various other exactions levied upon them. The term Imrad is not used frequently by the Kel Ahaggar themselves because of its pejorative overtones and implication of a socially inferior position. The Ihaggaren particularly, who until fairly recently were dependent on their Imrad for many services, and consequently did not want to insult them by referring to their inferior status, use the term Kel Ulli, meaning literally 'the people of the goats', as a more common term of reference. This term is also preferable to us, for not only does it avoid the insinuation of a status which they no longer possess, but it refers explicitly to their predominant economic activity of goat-breeding and their position in the overall process of production.

The Ihaggaren were the dominant class, a warrior aristocracy, living off the surplus labour expropriated from their Kel Ulli, their slaves, and various other dependent and subordinate groups. To understand the nature of this class division, and the changes that have taken place in the relations between these two main classes, the Ihaggaren and the Kel Ulli, particularly over the last hundred or so years, it is imperative that we understand the social relations of production through which this surplus labour was appropriated. The main institution through which this appropriation was effected, and through which the diverse economic activities and interests of these two classes were integrated within the overall economy, was the relationship known as *temazlayt*. And yet, as far as I am aware, this crucial relationship, which is fundamental to our understanding of the Kel Ahaggar from the earliest times to the present, has received no mention in any publication, apart from a brief entry in Foucauld's dictionary, until the publication of Johannes Nicolaisen's fieldwork in 1963. By that time it was too late. The relationship had ceased to exist in anything like its traditional form and, as Nicolaisen himself stressed, was consequently difficult to describe.

Similarly, a common assumption running through this literature is that the Kel Ahaggar share a common social system. While this is true at the ideational or cultural level, it is certainly not true at the level of social reality, for, as will be seen, the Ihaggaren and Kel Ulli have manipulated the rules of descent, through their different marital strategies, to the extent that while the social organization of the nobility, in terms of succession, inheritance, residency, group membership and so forth, is effectively matrilineal, that of the vassals, in practice, is predominantly patrilineal.

At a less serious level we may note that an article, published in the early 1950s by a highly decorated and prominent 'Saharien', described the Tuareg quite categorically as 'a People who don't dance'! And yet, at the Pan-African Congress, less than two decades later, a 'troupe' of Tuareg danced quite splendidly in the streets of Algiers.

Two further misconceptions that abound throughout most of the literature are, firstly, that traditional or pre-colonial society was in some way static, or 'timeless', without any internal dynamic. As we shall see, noble–vassal relations had already undergone considerable changes during the latter part of the last century, while there is sufficient evidence to suggest that Ahaggar society was on the verge of a 'class revolution' at the time of the French arrival. Secondly, many writers have tended either to assume that France more or less preserved Ahaggar society in its 'traditional' form or to underplay the changes ensuing from pacification. We cannot therefore talk about Algeria destroying traditional society, for 'traditional' society, as it existed during the last century, had already undergone considerable transformations prior to the end of the colonial period.

A complete reanalysis of Ahaggar society as it existed prior to and during the period of French colonial rule is therefore necessary, not only to clarify many of these misconceptions, but also to enable us to understand the nature of the society that existed at the time of Algerian independence.

A second and closely related reason for adopting this historical approach is that it enables us to provide satisfactory explanations for certain processes and phenomena of social change that have occurred during the last decade and that would otherwise remain problematical. The two main determinants of change during this period have been the coercive implementation of Algerian government policies and the incidence of drought. However, the fact that the two main classes (nobles and vassals), and to a lesser degree certain constituent groups within these classes, have tended to perceive, and respond to, the overall situation confronting them in quite noticeably different ways can only be understood and explained in terms of their respective concrete situations, and their different cognitive systems and associated definitions of social reality, which for the most part have been historically determined.

Thus, while the object of the book is to explain the processes of change that have taken place amongst the Kel Ahaggar during the last decade or so, it is, in effect, an historical analysis of change from the earliest traditional times, through the colonial period, to the present.

Throughout this analysis, however, the common thread, indeed, the central focus, is that of class structure and conflict. Such a focus is not limited in its perspective of the total society, for the concept of classes is a 'totalizing' concept – not only must one refer to all aspects of social reality in order to define it,[20] but no aspect of social reality can be referred to or defined without it. As Terray commented in his introduction to his analysis of the Abron kingdom in West Africa, 'If history may be regarded as the history of class confrontation, it is because class is, as it were, the place where the various dimensions of social life – economic, political, ideological – intersect.'[21]

In short, such an analysis of the Kel Ahaggar is the story of how a proud warrior aristocracy, which dominated much of the central Sahara and gained an honourable peace with France, has finally had to bow ignominiously to the egalitarianism of the Algerian Republic.[22]

# ONE
# THE EARLY HISTORY OF THE TUAREG AND THE ORIGINS OF THE CLASS DIVISION

The two Northern Tuareg groups, the Kel Ajjer and the Kel Ahaggar, did not emerge as separate, politically independent groups until about 1660. Before that time, the Tuareg, who inhabited the extensive area between Ghat on the present Libyan frontier and Tin Zaouaten on the Mali frontier, which included the mountainous regions of Ajjer, Ahaggar and the Adrar-n-Iforas, were ruled by the Imenan, whose chiefs held the title of 'Sultan'. The Imenan lived at Ghat and Djanet, which is now the administrative centre of the Ajjer region, and commanded all the Tuareg throughout this vast area. They were *cheurfa*, that is descendants of the Prophet, and, even today, although completely fallen from power and few in number (only about six), all Tuareg still recognize their religious status.[1, 2]

The title of *cheurfa* must have commanded considerable respect and led to their elevation into something of a royalty, their considerable authority being legitimized by their religious status. They had a personal bodyguard of slaves, the Iklan-oui-n-Tawsit, and their authority was symbolized, as it is among other Tuareg chiefs today, by a large hemispherical drum (*ettebel*).

The Imenan ravaged the land through numerous wars, until, under the rule of the sultan Goma, their tyranny and exactions on the population finally became so intolerable that the noble Tuareg threatened to overthrow them. Goma, realizing the danger, and in an attempt to appease them and gain their co-operation, divided the land into hereditary fiefs to be inherited matrilineally among the noble Tuareg. In spite of Goma's attempt at appeasement, he was assassinated by Biska of the noble Uraren, and authority was transferred to Mohammed ag Tinekerbas of the Uraren of Niger, who had come to help the Northern Uraren in their struggle against tyranny.

With the overthrow of the Imenan dynasty, and the transfer of power to the Uraren, we see the division of the Northern Tuareg, who had formerly been unified under the Imenan sultans, into two separate and independent groups, the Kel Ajjer and the Kel Ahaggar.

The early history of the Northern Tuareg, prior to the overthrow of the Imenan dynasty and the secession of the Kel Ahaggar around the middle of the seventeenth century, is virtually unknown. Questions regarding the origin and early history of the Tuareg must therefore remain largely speculative, for we are dependent on only a few scant references in the writings of certain Greek, Roman and Arab historians, and the Tuareg's own legendary and mythological accounts of their origins. Nevertheless, when we explore these two lines of inquiry, there is one fact which stands out, namely that both the documentary sources and the Tuareg's own conceptions of their origin focus on the division of Tuareg societies into nobles and vassals. Let us look first at the historical evidence for the origin of this division.

Greek and Roman documentary sources, such as Herodotus, Strabo, Pliny and especially Ptolemy, although very confusing, provide sufficient names to suggest that the populations which we now call Tuareg had almost certainly reached the Sudanese regions between the Niger bend and Chad 1,800 years ago.[3]

Between the time of Pliny and Ptolemy in the first and second centuries AD and the secession of the Kel Ahaggar from the Imenan sultans we thus have a span of about 1,500 years in which we are almost entirely dependent on the writings of a few Arab historians such as Ibn Abdal-H'Akam (ninth century), Ibn Haukal (tenth century), El Bekri (eleventh century), Edrisi (twelfth century), Ibn Batutah, Ibn Khaldoun (fourteenth century), and Leo Africanus (sixteenth century).[4]

These Arab writers give us a very sketchy picture of the central Sahara during these centuries. Certainly, by the time of the first Arab invasions into the Fezzan in AD 666–7, we know that the indigenous population included various groups of the 'veiled Sanhadja' Berbers who, according to Ibn Khaldoun, formed the major part of the population in West Africa and comprised about a third of the entire Berber race. Originally they occupied almost all the Mediterranean coast and, according to Ibn Khaldoun, had travelled across the region which separated the land of the Berbers from the land of the Blacks, that is to say the central plateau of the Sahara between the Mediterranean regions and the Niger bend, since time immemorial (many centuries before Islam). Among the various groups of veiled Sanhadja, or Western Berbers, listed by Ibn Khaldoun[5] as living in the desert since 'immemorial times', we find the Lemta living in the desert south of the Arab Riah tribe in eastern Algeria; the Targa living south of the Arab Sulayim tribe in Ifrikia, that is in Tunisia and the adjacent parts of Tripolitania; and the Guedala, whose last remains, as suggested by Heinrich Barth, may have been the Igdalen or Iguedal, living around In Gal in southern Niger.[6]

Ibn Khaldoun's writings, in the fourteenth century, indicate that the country of the Northern Tuareg was inhabited at that time by two main groups of Tuareg known as the Lemta and the Targa. Leo Africanus, writing in the sixteenth century, also states that these two groups, the Lemta and the Targa, not only inhabited the areas indicated by Ibn Khaldoun[7] but also occupied the country to the south of the Northern Tuareg's present territory. This means that Ayr formed part of the territory of the Targa group – a point which may give support to Barth's suggestion regarding the Igdalen.[8]

Although the words Targa and Lemta no longer exist as names of Tuareg groups, there is agreement among most writers that they were two of the main Berber, or 'Tuareg', groups occupying the general territory of the Northern Tuareg at the time of the Arab invasion into the central Sahara, and it is interesting to note that they are mentioned not only by Arab writers but are also marked on European maps in the sixteenth and seventeenth centuries. On Ortelius's *Africae Tabula Nova* in 1570 we find the word Targa located in the central or southern part of the Sahara; we find the word Targa in the northern Sahara, and the word Lemta in the south-east central Sahara on Blaeu's *Africae Nova Descriptio* (1665),[9] and both names on the map produced by Dapper in 1670.[10, 11]

The association between the words Tuareg and Targa would seem obvious, and it is reasonable to suggest that the word Tuareg was used by the Arabs to refer to Berber populations of the Tripolitanian Sahara. Both Maurice Benhazera and Charles de Foucauld accept this meaning of the word Tuareg, and it is interesting to note that the Kel Ahaggar, at the time of Foucauld's writing (the beginning of this century), still referred to the Fezzan region of southern Libya as Targa.

The origin of the word Ahaggar is even more pertinent. Foucauld considers that the word Hawwara is identical with Ihaggaren (sing. Ahaggar), for the letter *w*, when redoubled, will, as a rule, change into *gg*, and *w* very frequently permutes with *g*.[12] He suggests that the Berber tribe of the Houara (Hawwara), whose name has changed into Ahaggar, emigrated from the Fezzan towards the mountainous massif which took its name, conquered it, reduced the indigenous Berber population to the state of 'plebian vassals' (*amerid*, pl. *imrad*)[13] or Kel Ulli, and that their name became synonymous with 'noble' as they were the conquering and sovereign tribe which spread out and subjected the whole region to its domination.[14]

This hypothesis, which has been accepted by more recent writers such as Nicolaisen,[15] was in fact advanced much earlier by Ibn Khaldoun.[16] Ibn Khaldoun described the Hawwara as nomads and sedentary people living predominantly in the regions of Tunisia, Tripolitania and Cyrenaica, but with some tribes belonging to the Hawwara groups found outside this area, both to the east and west. According to Ibn Khaldoun, the Hawwara were conquered by the Arabs as early as the ninth century, and at the time of his writing in the fourteenth century were completely dominated by Arabs, being vassals of the Arab Beni Sulayim tribe. They were fully arabized Berbers, speaking Arabic and culturally indistinguishable from their Arab conquerors. Not all the Hawwara, however, were arabized in this way, for some of the pastoral Hawwara moved southwards at a very early date and settled close to the Lemta. Ibn Khaldoun actually considered that the descent of these people from the Hawwara was indicated by their name Heggar, the *w* in Hawwara having changed into something between a soft and a guttural *k*.[17, 18]

Other Arab writers confirm the presence of Hawwara pastoralists in southern Tripolitania at an early date, but the time of their southwards migration into the Fezzan is uncertain. Ibn Abdal H'Akam notes the continued presence of the Hawwara in southern Tripolitania around AD 745 and their involvement in the 'Ibadite schism', and it seems possible that their movement southwards took place at that time, although other Arab writers suggest that the migration may not have taken place until later, around AD 1050, as a consequence of the Hilalian invasion into the Fezzan.

The so-called Hilalian invasion of North Africa, beginning in the eleventh century, certainly caused far greater upheaval among the populations, not only in the Sahara but in all North Africa, than the initial Arab conquest three centuries earlier. In the Maghreb, to the north of the Sahara, these invasions marked the decline in the relative rural prosperity built up under the Pax Romana and the reversion to the dominance of nomadic herdsmen. The history of North Africa, throughout the Roman period, during the various Arab invasions, and in the colonial period, is reflected in the shifting 'frontier' between nomadic herdsmen and settled farmers. Even among the original Berber population of North Africa, prior to the Roman occupation, there was strife between these two irreconcilable ways of life, with the nomadic herdsmen usually maintaining dominance and restricting the settled farmers to the mountainous areas. The presence of Rome and her well-guarded frontiers ('limes') held the nomads back and enabled the expansion of Berber farmers. The Arab conquest of North Africa in the seventh and eighth centuries did not destroy this relative rural prosperity, for the nomads remained more or less restricted to the south of the old 'limes', while the invading Arabs, or arabized Berbers, settled for the most part in the cities (or built new ones). For three centuries the Arab empire was a flowering reincarnation of the Roman.[19] The Berber tribes were gradually converted to Islam in increasing numbers – a process which was facilitated by their never having been 'too difficult' in matters of religion.[20] by the attraction of loot from the conquest of Spain and by the Moslem's exemption from certain taxes.

Between the eleventh and fourteenth centuries, however, there was a great nomadic revival. Arab tribesmen, moving westwards, attached themselves to the nomadic Berber tribes to the south of the old 'limes', among whom arabization (the adoption of Islam and Arabic customs) was far more complete than among the Berber farmers, who had been converted earlier; beginning in the eleventh century, the hordes of Beni Hilal, Beni Sulayim and Makil moved northwards into the settled Berber countryside. The nomadic 'frontier' was pushed forwards; villages disappeared, and the settled population retreated into the protection of the mountains (e.g. Kabylia, Aures).

While the Hilalian invasion laid the pattern of things to come in the Maghreb until French colonization in the nineteenth century, the consequences of this invasion for the Saharan populations are less well known, but probably no less great. The various Tuareg groups were almost certainly pushed further south by the invading Arab nomads, although Tuareg territory was by no means overrun; indeed, it seems that a frontier of sorts may have stabilized between the invading Arab pastoralists and the Tuareg groups to the south. In Ibn Khaldoun's time this frontier appears to have run through the sand areas of the Eastern and Western Ergs, but while the Arabs undertook raids against the Tuareg groups, they also suffered severe losses from the constant reprisal attacks of the Tuareg.[21] Capot-Rey states that not only were the Tuareg able to defend most of their territory, but they were also able to assimilate certain Arab tribes,[22] while Nicolaisen mentions that contact between Arabs and Tuareg has always led to the adoption of Tuareg cultural traits by many Arab pastoralists (e.g. the powerful Arab tribe of Ulad Ba Hammu of Tidikelt).[23]

The fragmentary picture presented to us by the Arab authors of the Middle Ages tends to suggest that the Hilalian invasions caused a considerable upheaval among the Saharan populations, and it seems quite feasible to suggest that the migration of the Hawwara from the Fezzan towards Ahaggar took place around AD 1050, as a consequence of the Hilalian invasion of the Fezzan, and that the Saharan massifs of Tassili, Ahaggar and Ayr may have become impregnable refuges into which the Arab invaders dared not venture.

It is reasonable to suppose that the division of Kel Ahaggar into nobles (Ihaggaren) and vassals (Imrad or Kel Ulli) stemmed from this migration of the Hawwara Berbers into Ahaggar and the subjection of an indigenous Berber population to their sovereignty.

The fundamental characteristic of this division was that the nobles were camel breeders while the vassals were goat breeders. It is only since the middle of the last century, and possibly even a little later, that vassals have acquired possession of many camels of their own. For much of the last century they possessed few camels, and it seems that in earlier times they may have possessed none at all. The vassals, as their name Kel Ulli tells us, involved themselves almost exclusively in goat breeding.

Nicolaisen suggests that this structural division arose from two distinct cultures meeting each other in the desert – a camel-breeding culture of a Berber-speaking people, and a goat-breeding culture of an ancient Berber-speaking population, which now constitutes the Kel Ulli (Imrad) or vassal class.[24] He considers that the first invasion of pastoral camel-breeding Berbers almost certainly began sometime during the first centuries of the Christian era, but that further immigrations of 'noble' camel-breeding Tuareg have taken place in Islamic times due to the pressure from Arab Bedouins in the north.[25] It is reasonable to suppose that these further immigrations to which Nicolaisen refers might have been those of the Hawwara Berbers around the eleventh century.

Although the Kel Ahaggar's conceptions of their origin and ancestral history throw no further light on what we have already said, they provide strong validation for the class division and the supremacy of the Ihaggaren. Their conceptions centre mostly around the legendary queen Tin Hinan and her companion Takama. Tin Hinan, a noble woman of the Beraber tribe, is alleged to have travelled in company with her slave-girl, Takama, from Tafilalet in Morocco to Ahaggar, where they both eventually died. Tin Hanan is reputed to be buried in the well-known tomb on the bank of the Oued Tiffert near Abalessa, close to its confluence with the Oued Abalessa, and Takama in a smaller tomb about 200 metres away. After

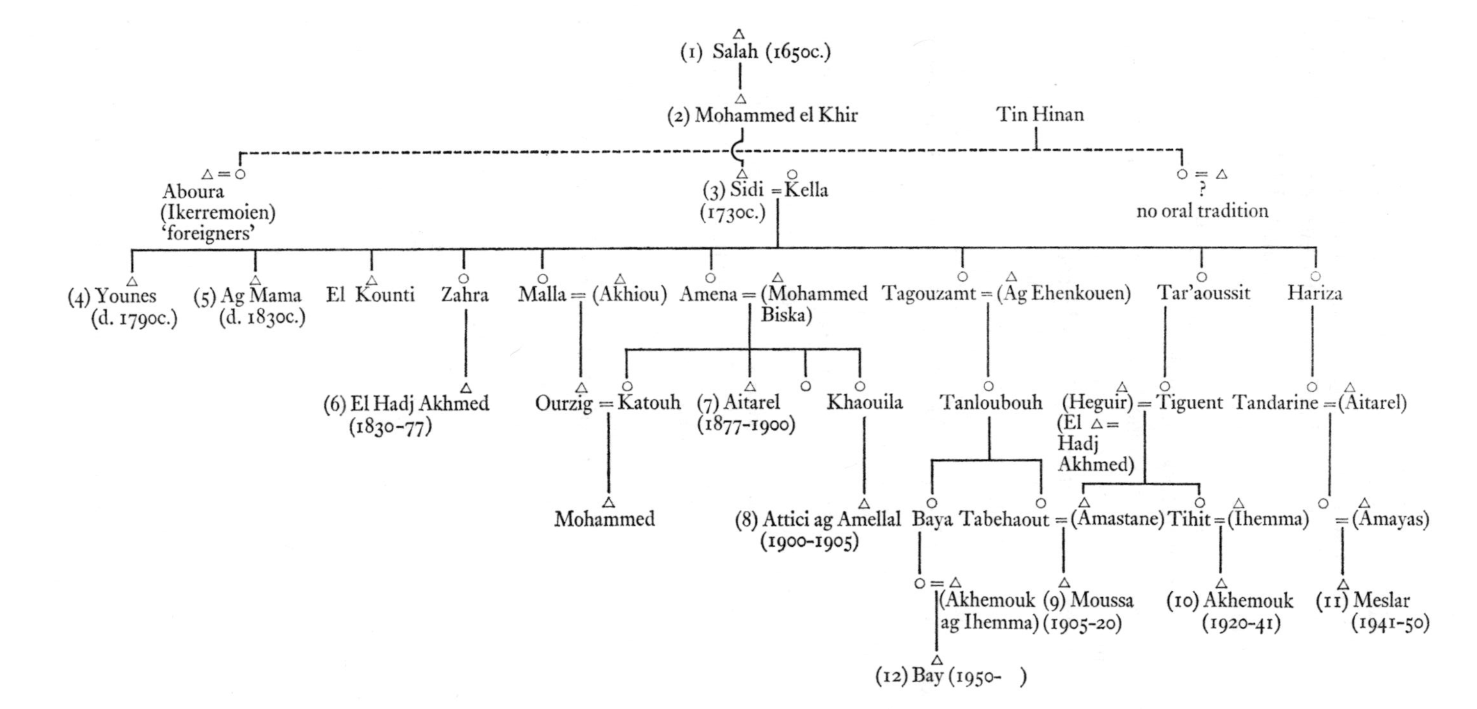


**Figure 2** Genealogical basis of Tin Hinan myth, order and descent of Ahaggar Amenukals.

B

arriving in Ahaggar Tin Hinan had a daughter, Kella, from whom the noble Kel Rela and Taitok 'descent groups' (*tawsatin*, sing. *tawsit*)[26] claim descent, while Takama had two daughters from whom the vassal descent groups of the Dag Rali (and Kel Ahnet) and Ait Lowayen are alleged to descend. Kella, we know, married Sidi ag Mohammed el Khir, the third Amenukal (supreme chief) of Ahaggar, a little before 1750, and is thus an historical person. Her relationship to the legendary queen, Tin Hinan, is based, however, not on history but myth.

The generally accepted mythological relationship is that Kella was the daughter of Tin Hinan. An elder daughter married a certain Aboura of the Ikerremoien *tawsit* (descent group) from the south. As a foreigner his descendants had no right to the sovereignty (*ettebel*) of Ahaggar and there is no further record of them. Similarly, there is no oral tradition of the descendants of Tin Hinan's younger daughter. The genealogical basis of this myth and the resulting descent of the Amenukals of Ahaggar is shown in Fig 2.

A variation of this myth is that Tin Hinan had three daughters,[27] who bore the names of animals: Tinhert (antelope), the ancestress of the Inemba section; Tahenkot (gazelle), the ancestress of the Kel Rela; and Tamerouelt (doe-rabbit), the ancestress of the Iboglan. Kella was apparently the great-granddaughter of Tahenkot in the maternal line. In a recent discussion[28] André Bourgeot suggested that the first three Amenukals (or four?) descended patrilineally in the Iboglan section until Sidi ag Mohammed el Khir married Kella, who was apparently a matrilineal descendant of Tahenkot. The question of the patrilineal succession of these early Amenukals will be discussed later.

Both these variations agree that Kella descended matrilineally from Tin Hinan, and historically we know that she was the wife of Sidi ag Mohammed el Khir just before 1750. Whether she was the daughter, granddaughter, great-granddaughter, etc., of Tin Hinan is thus largely irrelevant and purely of mythological interest, for the alleged tomb of Tin Hinan has been excavated[29] and is unquestionably pre-Islamic and dates from about the fourth century AD. The discrepancy between the mythological relationship and archaeological evidence is thus not a matter of an occasional generation, but about fourteen centuries!

Several aspects of the Tin Hinan myth, and its variations, appear to have been created to justify the class division and supremacy of the Ihaggaren in Kel Ahaggar society. For example, while most Kel Ahaggar, both nobles and vassals, recognize that the descendants of Tin Hinan are nobles and those of Takama are vassals, most vassals claim that Takama was the younger sister of Tin Hinan and not her slave-girl. This variance is undoubtedly related to the justification of the division between nobles and vassals, for in traditional times it seems that the vassals may have recognized the superior position of the nobles in terms of the respectful relationship of a younger sister towards an elder sister, while the nobles may have justified the division in terms of the relationship between master and slave-girl.

Similarly, a further variation, recorded by Lehureaux, which gives justification to the traditional social structure of Ahaggar society is as follows: 'Tin Hinan came from Tafilalet to Ahaggar riding on a white camel and accompanied by her faithful companion Takama and a certain number of slaves.[30] From their homeland, the country of the Beraber, they had brought with them many loads of dates and millet. But the road to Ahaggar was a very long one, and the caravan became seriously threatened by hunger. However, one day Takama discovered a great many ant-hills, and assisted by the slave-women she collected all the seeds which the ants had stored. Takama gave these seeds to Tin Hinan, who remained sitting on her camel as she was of noble descent. By means of these seeds the caravan was able to arrive in Ahaggar. In order to commemorate this event the Dag Rali and the Kel Ahnet, who descend from Takama, each year give a fixed tribute of seeds or dates to the noble Tuareg, who descend from Tin Hinan.'[31] In this version we see the reference to a white riding camel, a symbol of prestige and status, and also what appears to be a justification for the annual tributes and certain other obligations of the vassals to the nobles which will be discussed more fully later.

Furthermore, although there is general agreement in most recorded versions of the myth that Tin Hinan was a Moslem, the mention of her faith is almost certainly attributable to political motives, for, as Gabriel Camps has suggested, the dominance of the noble Kel Rela in Ahaggar is fairly recent and the attachment of a Moslem princess to their relatively scant pedigree would have exalted their prestige and status considerably.

There is some dispute about which Kel Ahaggar groups are descended from Tin Hinan. The noble Kel Rela and Taitok descent groups, which are related matrilineally, both claim undisputed descent from Tin Hinan, but the descent of the two other descent groups, the Tegehe-Mellet and Kel-Ahem-Mellen, is ambiguous. According to Benhazera, both descend from Tin Hinan, for he records that the Kel-Ahem-Mellen told him that they descend from the Ait Kebbach, of the Beraber tribe.[32] This, however, conflicts with the information of both Foucauld[33] and Nicolaisen,[34] which suggests that these two did not descend from Tin Hinan.

However, as regards the present relationship of Ahaggar descent groups, it is of little importance, since both the Tegehe-Mellet and Kel-Ahem-Mellen have dwindled, politically and numerically, to the extent that there are now scarcely more than a handful of individuals in Ahaggar who claim membership of them.

Of the Kel Ulli descent groups, the oldest, the Imessiliten, which now constitutes the Dag Rali and the Kel Ahnet, and the Ait Lowayen, all claim descent from Takama's youngest daughter. The Ihadanaren, who belong to the Kel Ajjer, also claim descent from Takama through her eldest daughter, and although regarded as noble among the Kel Ajjer, they have no vassals. The important Kel Ulli descent groups of the Aguh-en-tehle and the Tegehe-n-Efis do not claim descent from Takama, but recognize their relatively recent arrival in Ahaggar and claim that they came originally from the In Gal and Ayr regions to the south.

A further tradition which, according to Nicolaisen, is widely known in Ahaggar is that all Tuareg have a common origin as they descended from a woman named Lemtuna, who was also the ancestress of certain Berbers living around Ghadames in Tripolitania. Most Berbers of Morocco descend from Lemtuna's sister, who became the ancestress of the Beraber.[35]

How does the Tin Hinan legend fit our ideas about the meeting of a camel-breeding culture and a goat-breeding culture, the pre-existence of an indigenous pagan people and the invasion of the Hawwara?

The legend of Tin Hinan claims that when the two women arrived in Ahaggar they found it almost uninhabited except for a pagan people called Isebeten who were goat-breeders and hunters living in the mountainous parts of the country. The tradition of the Isebeten is in fact widely respected among the vassals, especially the Dag Rali; they claim that the oldest inhabitants of Ahaggar were a people called the Isebeten who were pagan, lived in caves in the mountains, and subsisted mainly by hunting and goat-breeding. Numerous prehistoric archaeological findings testify to the existence of such a people, and the Dag Rali, who inhabit the highest mountainous area of Atakor, regard themselves as the oldest inhabitants of Ahaggar and claim that they were very closely related to, or descend directly from, the Isebeten.

The idea of a camel-breeding culture meeting a goat-breeding culture, as suggested by Nicolaisen, finds some support both in the tradition of the Isebeten, which claims that they were conquered by the ancestors of the nobel Tuareg who came to Ahaggar at a later date and introduced the camel, and in an expanded version of the Tin Hinan myth recorded by Foucauld.[36] After the immigration of Tin Hinan and Takama to Ahaggar, their descendants, who constituted the Kel Rela, Dag Rali and Ait Lowayen, lived alone in Ahaggar for a very long time. They were few in number, had no camels, subsisted mainly by goat-herding and hunting, and never travelled outside Ahaggar – having no knowledge of such places as Tidikelt, Ayr, and Adrar-n-Iforas. It then happened that the two noble 'tribes'[37] of Kel-Ahem-Mellen and Tegehe Mellet penetrated into Ahaggar and conquered and burnt down the agricultural settlement of Ennedid, the centre of the Dag Rali. The Dag Rali then assembled at the village of Tahart to fight their invading enemies. They succeeded in killing most of the Kel-Ahem-Mellen and Tegehe Mellet, and took their camels; from this time onwards the Ahaggar Tuareg became camel-breeders, began to travel outside Ahaggar, and grew in number.[38]

Nicolaisen considers that the noble descent groups[39] that are now dominant in Ahaggar, that is the Kel Rela (and Taitok), who claim descent from Tin Hinan, are not the oldest noble Tuareg of that area. He suggests that the descent groups which are said to descend from Tin Hinan were in fact Islamic when they migrated to Ahaggar, and they were not the first noble Tuareg in the north. The first noble Tuareg, who probably introduced the camel and set up the initial class division, probably belonged to the Lemta group. Foucauld says that the word Tuareg has two distinct meanings to the Arabs of Tidikelt: namely, 'noble Tuareg' and 'Tuareg of all classes'. Furthermore, he adds that the word Ilemtiyen means the same to the Berber-speaking population of Touat and Tidikelt as the word Tuareg to the Arabs of the same area, and that the name Ilemtiyen is used for a small tribe of Tuareg living in the Kel Ajjer territory.[40] Today, the Ilemtiyen, who are noble by descent, are very few in number and live as cultivators near Ghat; Nicolaisen records that Bay, the present Amenukal of Ahaggar, told him that the Ilemtiyen were not related to the Tin Hinan tribes but descended from an ancestress named Lemta.[41] The only people in Ahaggar who may have descended from these earlier noble camel-breeders are the Ikadayen; they are very few in number and now live as cultivators around the village of Tit (40 kms north of Tamanrasset), and it is interesting to note that they are referred to as 'only a little Ihaggaren', or 'Ihaggaren but not true Ihaggaren'.[42]

Our lack of detailed knowledge of the Tuareg prior to the secession of the Kel Ahaggar around 1650 inevitably limits our reconstruction of their earlier history to a very fragmentary and somewhat speculative picture. Furthermore, we must remain sensitive to the fact that the Kel Ahaggar's own conceptions of their origins and early ancestry are only orally transmitted histories, merging into the realm of mythology, and inevitably subject to the distortions and manipulations that are made to validate and justify the current socio-political order.

Nevertheless, there is sufficient evidence to believe that the noble–vassal division is long-standing, stemming, at the latest, from the immigration of certain camel-breeding Hawwara into the central Saharan massifs of Ajjer and Ahaggar sometime around the eleventh century.

# TWO
# THE DIVISION OF THE KEL AHAGGAR INTO THREE DRUM GROUPS

We know very little about the Kel Ahaggar at the time of their secession from the Kel Ajjer. No longer obeying any religious authority, it appears that a state of anarchy developed amongst them, with almost indiscriminate pillaging of surrounding areas, especially the oases of Touat to the north of Ahaggar and the territory of the Arabic Kunta tribe to the west of Ahaggar and in southern Mauretania and the Adrar-n-Iforas, among whom the influence of the *cheurfa* remained particularly strong.

Although the Kunta were undoubtedly anxious and concerned at the overthrow of the Imenan, they could quite reasonably rest assured that the Kel Ahaggar, if left to themselves to continue their internal struggle for power, would gradually become weakened. The prolonged war among the Kel Ahaggar eventually ended when one of them, by the name of Salah, took power and made peace with the Kunta marabout Sidi Mohammed ben Abderrahmane ben Abi Naama. Salah's son, Mohammed el Khir, who succeeded him, continued the good relations with the Kunta marabouts, including the Sheikh Mokhtar ben Ahmed ben Bubeker, to whom he returned much of the booty which had been pillaged on earlier Kel Ahaggar raids. The Kunta, however, in spite of the Sheikh's efforts to dissuade them, sought revenge on the Kel Ahaggar and saw their opportunity in the considerably weakened state of the Kel Ahaggar after their prolonged struggle for power. But the Kunta underestimated the Kel Ahaggar's fighting ability. They were soundly defeated (*c.* 1755) and obliged to pay an annual tribute to the Kel Ahaggar of eight she-camels; which continued for about 150 years until their submission to the French authorities at the beginning of this century.[1]

Salah took the title of Amenukal (supreme chief), which had formerly been held by the Imenan.[2] There is some confusion over the original meaning of the word Amenukal. Nicolaisen states that the Amenukal is a title used for supreme and independent chiefs of large political units.[3] Duveyrier, Lhote and Blanguernon all refer to the Amenukal as the owner of the land,[4] while Foucauld merely defines the term as 'the title of a chief who is not subjected to any other chief'.[5] According to K. G. Prasse, Amenukal is probably a composite of *amenu* and (*a*) *kal*, meaning literally 'amenu of the country'.[6] Nicolaisen, following Prasse, writes, 'The first part may be the now extinct singular of "Imenan", the original meaning of which is unknown (princes?); this agrees with Foucauld's statement that normally "Amenukal" is used as the singular of Imenan, meaning "iyen-dar-Menan" – "one of the Imenan tribe" (Prasse verbal information).'[7]

Salah was succeeded by his son Mohammed el Khir, who was succeeded in turn by his son Sidi. Succession to political office amongst the Kel Ahaggar is determined by matrilineal descent, and it is not easy to explain why the first three Amenukals following Salah (also Sidi's son) should have succeeded their fathers. We do not know whether succession during the Imenan period was matrilineal, although there is some slight evidence to suppose that this may have been the case. On the other hand, it is possible that these first Amenukals of Ahaggar were influenced by Arab religious leaders in neighbouring areas. This seems unlikely in view of the degree of pillaging that the Kel Ahaggar inflicted on these peoples, although it is reasonable to suppose that a degree of compliancy on the part of the Amenukals would have provided them with a certain amount of religious status and prestige, and consequently a greater legitimization of their tenuous authority.

The reign of Sidi ag Mohammed el Khir, spanning the middle of the eighteenth century, effectively marks the beginning of our analysis of Kel Ahaggar society, for the society with which we are familiar, in terms of its territorial arrangements, political groupings and divisions, was established during his reign.

At the time of Sidi ag Mohammed el Khir's succession, the dominant 'nobility' in Ahaggar were the Tegehe-n-ou-Sidi. The less important noble descent groups (*tawsatin*) were those of the Kel Rela, Taitok and Tegehe Mellet.

From the writings of Duveyrier and, more specifically, Benhazera, we know that the chiefs of the Taitok and the Tegehe Mellet made repeated demands to the Amenukal, Sidi ag Mohammed el Khir, that they should have their own vassals, and political control over them independent from that of Sidi. Although Benhazera does not mention the Kel Rela in this context, we must presume that they were also involved.

It seems, from Benhazera's writings, that all the vassal descent groups were under the direct authority and command of the Amenukal, and that the other nobles, or at least the Taitok and Tegehe Mellet, had no vassals of their own. One gathers that the Taitok and Tegehe Mellet were subordinated to the Tegehe-n-ou-Sidi and the authority of the Amenukal. If this was in fact the case we thus see a political system comprising a supreme centralized authority, the Amenukal, belonging to the Tegehe-n-ou-Sidi, with all the vassal descent groups directly under his command, and with the other noble descent groups in some way secondary or ranked subordinately to the Tegehe-n-ou-Sidi. Benhazera does, however, make reference to the *tobol* (*ettebel*: political authority, sovereignty) of the Kel Rela at this time, which leads us to suppose that they may have had slightly more influence and political autonomy than the Taitok and Tegehe Mellet, and that they may have had a few vassals of their own.

Sidi yielded to the demands of the Taitok and Tegehe Mellet and completely reorganized the political groupings in Ahaggar. He divided the vassals between the Kel Rela, Taitok and Tegehe Mellet, and granted them political autonomy and control over them, thus creating the three more or less politically independent groups (drum groups – *ettebel*) which existed in Ahaggar, with only slight modifications, until this century. Benhazera finds confirmation of this political realignment in the statement of Aitarel, the Amenukal between 1877 and 1900, that the Tegehe-n-ou-Sidi was the back (*arouri*), and the Kel Rela, Taitok and Tegehe Mellet the sides (*ir'erdechane*), but that the back lost its strength to the sides.[8]

In this division Sidi ag Mohammed el Khir kept the command of the Kel Rela drum-group for himself, which leads us to ask: What was the relationship between the Kel Rela and the Tegehe-n-ou-Sidi, and what happened to the Tegehe-n-ou-Sidi? We do not know the answer to either question, except that the Tegehe-n-ou-Sidi seem to have just disappeared, at least in name. They certainly no longer existed at the time of Benhazera's travels, for he states that 'they dissolved into other tribes'. The question is made even more intriguing by the statement of Brahim oult Sidi to Duveyrier, namely that 'Kel Rela; they are the Ebna Sid, that is to say, the sons of their fathers, whose ancestor was the Sultan El Aloui'.[9] Not even Benhazera was able to elucidate this statement for he merely asked whether this meant that the Kel Rela were in fact the sons of Sidi ag Mohammed el Khir of the Tegehe-n-ou-Sidi. The question remains unanswered, and open to speculation.

We thus see, around 1755, the division of the Kel Ahaggar into three territorially compact and more or less politically autonomous drum groups. Each drum group comprised one noble descent group (*tawsit*) from which the drum group took its name, and a varying number of subordinate vassal descent groups.

The composition of these three drum groups after this division is shown in Fig. 3.

Figure 3 Composition of Kel Ahaggar drum groups around the mid-eighteenth century.

| | KEL RELA | TAITOK | TEGEHE MELLET |
|---|---|---|---|
| Ihaggaren | Drum Chief: Sidi ag Mohammed el Khir, with title of Amenukal of Ahaggar | Drum Chief: Amer el Hadj | Drum Chief: Khelba (&) ? ag Ser'ada |
| Kel Ulli | Dag Rali<br>Aguh-en-tehle<br>Iklan Tawsit<br>Ibettenaten | Kel Ahnet<br>Tegehe-n-Efis | none* |
| Isekkemaren | Kel Immidir†<br>Kel Tazulet<br>Kel Amguid<br>Kel Tefedest<br>Iheyewan Hada<br>Kel In R'ar<br>Irregenaten | Kel In Tunin<br>Iouarouaren<br>Ikoutessen<br>Ikechchemaden (now with Dag Rali) | Kel Ohet<br>Kel Terourirt<br>Kel Tourha |

* The Ait Lowayen (Kel Ulli), who were later to become firmly attached to the Kel Rela, were at this time divided, with one section attached to the Tegehe Mellet and another to the small noble descent group of the Kel Ahem Mellen.

† And Iselamaten. Tegehe-n-Selama.

The Kel Ulli were numerically the largest class in Ahaggar, outnumbering the Ihaggaren in the ratio of about eight to one.[10]

The Isekkemaren are a vassal class that is only found among the Northern Tuareg, particularly the Kel Ahaggar. They are not as important numerically as the Kel Ulli, but nevertheless outnumber the Ihaggaren in the ratio of about four to one. It is generally recognized that they are descended from unions between Arab men and Tuareg women, at a time when the Northern Tuareg made occasional alliances with Arab tribes, or tribes of mixed origin, in exchange for certain land rights in Ahaggar.

They came from Touat and Tidikelt to the north of Ahaggar, where they had settled about 800–900 years ago, probably after leaving Es Souk.[11] They were brought into Ahaggar before the overthrow of the Imenan and the secession of the Kel Ahaggar, assimilated culturally and incorporated into the Ahaggar 'federation' (*tegehe*). According to the 1948–9 census, they numbered about 1,400, about 1,000 less than the Kel Ulli. Their status is ambiguous. Although they could be regarded as vassals in the same way as the Kel Ulli, in terms of their political subordination and various economic rights and obligations, their socio-political status and economic relationship with the nobles was slightly different from that of the Kel Ulli. Although some observers have considered the Isekkemaren to be 'superior vassals', in that they were attached directly to the drum chief of their drum group, and do not appear to have been tied to any other nobles through *temazlayt* relationships (see Ch. 3) in the same way or to the same extent as the Kel Ulli, they were generally referred to by both Ihaggaren and Kel Ulli in slightly disparaging terms, not so much because of their mixed descent but because of their propensity for trading rather than warfare and raiding, with the consequent inference that they were weak. Isekkemaren also tended to be poorer than most Kel Ulli in terms of their general resources, which partly explains their greater readiness to sedentarize in recent years.

Two other descent groups which are often thought similar in both origin and status to the Isekkemaren are the Ibettenaten and the Irregenaten (see Fig. 3). The Ibettenaten, however, do not seem to have descended from mixed marriages, for most statements agree that they were once Ihaggaren, but that one of their ancestors killed a Kel Rela, after which they were driven out of Ahaggar, defeated, and reduced to vassal status. They settled mainly in the Adrar-n-Iforas around Bou-Djebiha to the south-west of Ahaggar, but sometimes moved back as far as the limits of Ahaggar.[12] The Irregenaten, on the other hand, do descend from mixed marriages between Arab men from the south and Tuareg women of the Ibettenaten, and were assimilated into the Kel Rela drum group with the same status as the Isekkemaren. Their allocation of land rights, like the Isekkemaren, was on the periphery of Ahaggar along the western and south-western limits between the south-east of the Ahnet massif and the north of the Adrar-n-Iforas. In fact, it seems likely that the Isekkemaren's allocation of land rights in these peripheral and marginal areas may have been designed to provide the Kel Ahaggar, or, more specifically, the Ihaggaren and their Kel Ulli, with a 'buffer' zone.

The division of the various vassal descent groups between the three noble descent groups, as shown in Fig. 3, was in response to the latter's demands for their own drum groups independent from that of Sidi ag Mohammed el Khir and the Tegehe-n-ou-Sidi. However, it does not need more than a cursory glance at Fig. 3 to see that the division of vassal descent groups between the Kel Rela, Taitok and Tegehe Mellet favoured the Kel Rela and gave them overwhelming dominance in Ahaggar. In purely numerical terms, the Kel Rela obtained about 70 per cent of both the Kel Ulli and the Isekkemaren. This dominance was also reflected in the territorial division of Ahaggar between the three drum groups, with the Kel Rela taking the central region of Ahaggar, and the Taitok and Tegehe Mellet being allocated the regions to their west and east respectively. This territorial division seems to have been based on strategic considerations, with the Tegehe Mellet acting as a buffer against the Kel Ajjer, and the Taitok acting as a buffer against the Kunta and other tribes to the west. Furthermore, the Kel Rela's central position would have reduced the effectiveness of any possible military alliance between the Taitok and Tegehe Mellet against them.

Sidi's division thus established the Kel Rela as the dominant and most powerful noble descent group in Ahaggar. After appeasing the initial demands of the Taitok and Tegehe Mellet, Sidi no doubt felt that he could live in peace, but this was not to be, for it was not long before the Taitok began to feel that they had been treated unjustly in the division and that the Kel Rela had benefited disproportionately. Amer El Hadj, the Taitok drum chief, was well aware that the forces at his disposal were insufficient to fight Sidi ag Mohammed el Khir and the Kel Rela, and he turned towards the Tuareg of Ayr in the south to solicit their assistance. With the help of the Kel Ayr, the Taitok raided the Kel Rela in the Oued Arak. This raid must have been quite successful, for Amer el Hadj soon returned at the head of ninety Taitok to attack Sidi ag Mohammed el Khir himself, but he underestimated the forces of the Kel Rela and was heavily defeated by Sidi at Ifetessen. Sidi kept hostages to enforce peace, and, to ensure a final reconciliation, he married his two sons Younes and Ag Mama to daughters of the Taitok.

Sidi ag Mohammed el Khir died soon after this event and the succession of a new Amenukal, Younes, provided the Tegehe Mellet with an opportunity to complain about Sidi's division. Their main complaint, it seems, was that they lacked dates, which came from the oases of Touat and Tidikelt, the vital caravan routes to which were controlled by the Kel Rela. And so, only just after dispelling the Taitok danger, the Kel Rela found themselves threatened once again. Like the Taitok, the Tegehe

Mellet were not strong enough to fight the Kel Rela on their own, and they sought the assistance of the Arabic Chaamba tribe, who were feared and long-standing enemies of the Tuareg, particularly the dominant Kel Rela. Confronted by this formidable allied force, Younes adopted a scorched earth policy, retreating deeper into the mountains of Ahaggar as the Chaamba and Tegehe Mellet plundered and pillaged everything before them. Finally, as the invaders were returning with their booty, Younes found his awaited opportunity and launched a surprise counter-attack in the dark of night which completely routed the combined force.

After overcoming these successive threats from the two other drum groups, and thus establishing themselves as the central and dominant force in Ahaggar, the Kel Rela felt it was time to turn their attention to resolving their long-standing quarrel with the Kel Ahem Mellen, who at that time consisted of two sections, the Tegehe-n-Essakal and the Tegehe-n-Egali. The nature of this dispute is not clear. Benhazera tells us that the Tegehe-n-Essakal had been enemies of the Kel Rela for a long time, since before the death of Sidi ag Mohammed el Khir, by which time they had already moved north to settle more or less permanently among the Arab tribes around In Salah in Tidikelt. It is not known why they emigrated from Ahaggar, but the main reason for the Kel Rela's wrath was that they had taken with them certain Isekkemaren, possibly the Kel Tefedest, who were attached to the Kel Rela drum group. The Kel Ahem Mellen sought the support of the Ulad Ba Hammu and the Ulad Mokhtar, the Arab tribes among whom they had settled, but once more the military superiority of the Kel Rela was decisive. The Kel Ahem Mellen and their Arab allies were defeated and the dissident Isekkemaren returned to the Kel Rela drum group.

And so, after a period of anarchy, about which we know very little, the Kel Rela overcame the challenges of the other drum groups to become the dominant power in Ahaggar, although, as we shall see presently, their pre-eminence was to be disputed throughout much of the nineteenth century.

# THREE
# NOBLE–VASSAL RELATIONS

This summary history of the secession of the Kel Ahaggar, and the division and establishment of their various constituent groups within the general political structure of the drum groups, raises several pertinent questions. In particular, we have not explained the fundamental basis of the class division between nobles and vassals, and why control over vassals was of such importance to the nobility. As we have seen, the central and recurring theme of the Tegehe Mellet's and Taitok's complaints, and indeed, the whole basis of the redivision of the Kel Ahaggar into the constituent drum groups, was the nobles' desire to have vassals of their own, under their direct control, in the form of territorially and politically independent and autonomous drum groups.

The origin of this noble–vassal division stems from the invasion or immigration into Ahaggar of a camel-breeding people at some time, or times, in the distant past. The arrival of a camel-breeding people in Ahaggar would, I believe, have had far-reaching implications. It would almost certainly have led to a substantial increase in the total population, whose self-sufficiency, in terms of subsistence, could probably no longer be guaranteed by the internal resources of Ahaggar.

The subsistence base of the indigenous population, consisting primarily of goat products, supplemented by a certain amount of hunting and the collection of wild grains and other plants, must necessarily have been one of self-sufficiency. On what grounds then do we presume that the arrival of a camel-breeding population destroyed a self-sufficient subsistence base within Ahaggar? At the time of the French arrival the Kel Ahaggar were critically dependent on various 'external' resources, such as dates, cereals, caravan dues, etc., and there is no reason to believe that this was otherwise in earlier times.

Increased productivity within Ahaggar, to accommodate this population increase, could have been achieved through several means. Firstly, camel-breeding could have been extended to the Kel Ulli, with the idea of developing, or rather diversifying, the pastoral subsistence base. It is doubtful, however, whether the arrival and the subsistence utilization of camels would have provided a sufficient increase in pastoral productivity to offset the overall population increase. The productive capacity of goats, in terms of subsistence, exceeds that of camels quite considerably. Goats are more resilient to the climatic exigencies of Ahaggar, primarily because their relatively short gestation period enables a goat herd, decimated by drought, to be re-established within twelve months or so after good rains and the regeneration of pasture. Whereas goats may have four kids in a year, with each one fully grown for mating within twelve months, camels can give birth only once every two years. Camels do provide an important source of milk, but, unlike goats, they are not a practical source of meat, as the amount of meat per animal is far in excess of immediate household needs and is not well-suited to preservation.[1] But even if such an extension could have increased pastoral productivity sufficiently, it would have been at the cost of threatening the domination of the Ihaggaren. The camel provided the Ihaggaren with an efficient means of transport, which, in conjunction with their use of arms, enabled them to establish and maintain their dominance over Ahaggar and neighbouring regions. The extension of the camel to the Kel Ulli would merely have provided them with the means of challenging or overthrowing the Ihaggaren. From our knowledge of nineteenth-century conditions, we know that the Ihaggaren retained exclusive control over the camel until quite recently, and it is erroneous to think that the arrival of a camel-breeding people in Ahaggar led to camel pastoralism becoming a widespread and generalized activity among all sections of the population.

Secondly, it might be suggested that productivity could have been increased by Ihaggaren possessing their own goat herds. This, however, would have been impractical in terms of the constant attention required by goat herds; their relative immobility; the Ihaggaren's preoccupation with raiding; and the presumably insufficient labour resources. There is, of course, the possibility that goat-breeding among the Kel Ulli could have been increased. We must conclude, however, that goat-breeding would already have been maximized within the constraints of either ecological conditions or labour resources, and that if any further increase was possible ecologically it would have required a considerable increase in labour resources.

Alternatively, productivity could have been increased through the exploitation of certain 'external' resources – notably by trading, raiding, and the imposition of protection dues on neighbouring peoples and passing caravans.

We can thus see the conditions that led to the development of slavery in Ahaggar. Raiding southwards into Sudanese regions to capture slaves, whom we shall consider in more detail later, was the logical means of increasing labour resources. We can also see the political and economic constraints that gave rise to, and maintained the system of, class specialization between Ihaggaren and Kel Ulli. While the Kel Ulli preoccupied themselves predominantly with goat-breeding, the Ihaggaren's exclusive control over camels and certain specialized arms (e.g. *takouba* – double-bladed sword) enabled them to maintain themselves as a warrior class, raiding outwards from Ahaggar and establishing domination over the vital oases of Touat and Tidikelt to the north, neighbouring Arab nomads (e.g. the Kunta), and the trans-Saharan caravan routes that passed east and west of Ahaggar.

These considerations, it must be admitted, are largely speculative. What is quite evident, however, is that the dominance of the Ihaggaren, and the associated class division, could not have been maintained if the Ihaggaren had not retained exclusive control over the camel, for it was the camel that provided them with the basis of physical control and military dominance, both over the peoples within Ahaggar and over many surrounding areas. What is also evident is that camels do not provide a sufficient subsistence base. Neither was the nature of the Ihaggaren's raiding exploits orientated exclusively towards subsistence needs. As we shall see presently, many of their raiding exploits were associated with the internal struggle for power between the noble descent groups themselves, and were often directed towards the acquisition of camels, which might be found among neighbouring or quite distant peoples; these peoples thus found themselves unwittingly and innocently embroiled within the internal feuds and struggle for power of the Kel Ahaggar nobility.

The protection dues paid by these peoples, the raids on surrounding areas, and the control established over passing caravans did not, I believe, provide the nobility with a regular source of income in the form of subsistence goods. On the contrary, not only does this source of income seem to have been relatively intermittent, but it comprised, in large part, luxury and non-subsistence goods, in the form of camels, merchandise and various material artefacts, which may have been in short supply or unobtainable within Ahaggar, but which also circulated within the prestige rather than subsistence spheres. The Kel Ahaggar's trading links with the oases of Touat and Tidikelt to the north, which provided them with dates and certain cereals, do appear to be long-standing. We know very little about the details of this trade in earlier times, when it may well have been fairly intermittent, depending on the extent to which the Kel Ahaggar, through their nobility, could maintain or exert military control over these regions. In more recent times this trade seems to have been carried on predominantly by the Isekkemaren. Whether this was always the case is not clear, but we can assume quite safely that it was at all times beneficial to the Ihaggaren, since they were able to claim tributary and protection dues. This, however, was not the case with the southbound caravans to Niger. These caravans, which traded locally mined salt for millet, and which came to provide Ahaggar with the bulk of its cereal requirements, are of recent origin. The first such caravan was in 1896, and it was not until the 1920s that they became a regular annual event. However, what is most significant about this caravan trade is that it was organized and undertaken almost exclusively by the Kel Ulli, after they had gained possession of their own camels, and after the cessation of warfare and raiding, and was consequently of little direct benefit to the Ihaggaren.

The real significance of the Ihaggaren's external raiding to the economy of Ahaggar as a whole is that it provided something of an insurance mechanism in times of hardship and need. From our rather tenuous and limited knowledge of these earlier times, it appears that such raiding increased in incidence following periods of physical conflict among the Kel Ahaggar themselves, when certain groups would need to recuperate livestock losses, or following periods of drought when hardship and famine threatened.

For reasons that have already been suggested, the nobles could not have engaged extensively in goat-breeding. And yet, it was goats, through their various milk products, meat, and various material artefacts such as skins for clothes, tents, water-bags and so forth, that provided the basis of the Kel Ahaggar's subsistence needs. We can thus see the importance of the Kel Ulli to the Ihaggaren, for without guaranteed access to these goat products the Ihaggaren could not have maintained themselves as a specialized and dominant warrior class. We can now understand the basis of the Tegehe Mellet's and Taitok's grievances against the Kel Rela, and the initial complaints of the nobles against Sidi ag Mohammed el Khir that they should have their own vassals independent of Sidi and the Tegehe-n-ou-Sidi.

The means by which the Ihaggaren assured themselves of access to goat products, or, to be more specific, the mechanisms through which they appropriated the surplus labour of their vassals, were the 'formal' political ties of domination and subordination established within the drum group, and the more 'informal' and less rigidly structured ties of the *temazlayt* relationship.

Let us look first of all at the way in which these relations of production were expressed within the 'formal' political structure of the drum group.

## Political Structure of the Drum Group

The drum group, as we have seen, comprised one noble descent group and a number of subordinate Kel Ulli and Isekkemaren descent groups. The subordination of the Kel Ulli and Isekkemaren descent groups was expressed in an annual tributary payment of allegiance to the drum chief (*amrar*) known as *tiwse*. Although this payment was fixed for each group, the amount paid, in practice, seems to have fluctuated from year to year depending on the condition of livestock (particularly goats), pasture and other resources. There is also considerable evidence for believing that the payment of *tiwse* was often made with difficulty, and at times seems to have caused a certain amount of hardship.

As *tiwse* payments were officially abolished by the administration in 1960[2] it is difficult to comment in any great detail on the nature of these payments. Fortunately, however, the studies of Benhazera (1908), Lhote (1955) and Nicolaisen (1963) record the payments made by the two Kel Ulli descent groups of the Dag Rali and Aguh-en-tehle in earlier times.[3]

### *Aguh-en-tehle* tiwse *Payments*

According to Nicolaisen,[4] Aguh-en-tehle *tiwse* payments were made separately by the three sections, Kel Tarhaouhaout, Isandan and Kel Arefsa, with the total comprising 1,200 kgs. of millet,[5] nine goats and thirty-one kgs. of butter, in exchange for which they received eight metres of cotton.

Lhote's account is approximately the same:[6] twelve bags of dates or millet, six containers of butter and ten goats. This is a slight increase on the amount recorded by Benhazera,[7] who states that the payment consisted of six bags of dates or millet, four containers of butter and six goats. The increase may well have arisen from the greater wealth of the Kel Ulli after French pacification, resulting particularly from their Harratin-cultivated gardens, their substantial caravan trade to Niger, and possibly the cessation of raiding, which may have contributed to the increase in herd sizes.[8]

### *Dag Rali* tiwse *Payments*

The accounts of Benhazera,[9] Lhote,[10] and Nicolaisen[11] give the payment as approximately: ten bags of millet, six containers of butter, and the use of ten goats (in earlier times it may have been twenty goats). The payment of the grain was made individually by the four main sections, who each gave three bags to the Dag Rali chief, who kept two for himself before paying the ten to the Amenukal.

In the Kel Rela drum group, *tiwse* payments were not paid exclusively to the Amenukal (drum chief); there are a few instances of vassal descent groups, or sections of descent groups, paying their *tiwse* to other prominent Kel Rela. For example, Marli ag Amayas, the Khalifa (appointed deputy)[12] and brother-in-law of the present Amenukal, Bay ag Akhemouk (1950– ), received an annual *tiwse* payment from the Ait Lowayen, which was made with respect not to his office of Khalifa but to his position as head of the Inemba Kel Emerri section of the Kel Rela, which traditionally had the right to this payment. Similarly, according to Benhazera,[13] one section of the Irregenaten paid *tiwse* to Mohammed ag Ourzig, others paid to Sidi ag Othman (grandson of El Hadj Akhmed, living at Tazrouk) and Attici ag Amellal, while the small Ulad Mouima section made payments to Baba ag Tamaklast.[14] This fragmentation of the Irregenaten's *tiwse* payments may have originated at the time of the dispute (see Chs. 4 and 5) between Mohammed ag Ourzig and Attici, both of whom were 'elected' as Amenukals in 1900, and, as such, claimed *tiwse* payments. It seems that these particular payments continued until quite recently, for Lhote[15] mentions that the Irregenaten paid *tiwse* to the descendants of Mohammed ag Ourzig as well as the descendants of the Inemba. A further instance of payments being made to other important Ihaggaren is mentioned by Nicolaisen.[16] He states that the Kel Rela Khalifa in Tamesna (Iboglan section) told him that he had rights to *tiwse* payments from the Isandan section of the Aguh-en-tehle, but that as he was living outside Ahaggar these payments were now made to the Amenukal.

It seems that these particular *tiwse* payments are the legacies of past political attachments or groupings, such as those ensuing, albeit perhaps temporarily, from the chaotic state of affairs that gave rise to the 'election' of two Amenukals at the same time in 1900, or possibly even from earlier times prior to the division of the Kel Ahaggar in the reign of Sidi ag Mohammed el Khir and of which we know nothing. In any case, there is no evidence to suggest that these particular Kel Rela held any formal political authority over the vassals from whom they received *tiwse*. Such authority was vested solely in the drum chief, who was the 'owner' of all the land of the drum group, its supreme judicial authority, and its supreme military commander.

This annual payment of tribute must be distinguished from another kind of payment, also known as *tiwse*, which was made by whole groups of Tuareg outside Ahaggar, and other neighbouring tribes, to both the drum chiefs and certain prominent Ihaggaren as a protection against being raided by them. This form of *tiwse* does not seem to have been large. According to Nicolaisen,[17] the Kel Adrar (Iforas) gave annually a skin tent and a camel to the Amenukal of Ahaggar, while a similar payment is said to have been made by the Kel Tedale of northern Ayr. *Tiwse* of this kind, which might aptly be called 'protection money', did not involve any of the rights and obligations incurred through the political allegiance of groups within the drum group. In fact, groups outside Ahaggar were frequently raided in spite of their *tiwse* payments.

### '*Ownership*' *of the Land*

The three drum groups formed territorial units which were subdivided into the specific territories of the subordinate descent groups within the drum group. Vassal descent groups, which, it might be added, were predominantly endogamous, were thus clearly defined both in terms of their cognatic descent and the territory over which they held 'tenant' rights and in which their members lived. The nobles, on the other hand, held rights over the entire territory of their respective drum groups.

Within the drum group, the drum chief was the 'owner' of all the land, but not in the modern sense of the word. He could not, for instance, sell or transfer even the smallest portion of land; this was quite incompatible with any system of private land ownership under civil law and, not surprisingly, gave rise to an unresolved conflict with French statutory law. Rather, the drum chief exercised a sort of sovereignty, acting not so much as a trustee or representative but more by eminent right, and accordingly divided the various rights of tenure among his subjects. No one could enjoy any rights to the land without the explicit or implicit authorization of the drum chief, in return for which he paid an annual land-rent known as *ehere-n-amadal*, which means literally 'the wealth' or 'fortune of the land'. What was significant about this payment, in contrast to *tiwse* payments, is that it was paid only to the drum chief, and not to any other nobles. Neither the heads of the various Kel Rela sections (or any other noble descent group sections), nor *temazlayt* masters, whom we shall consider presently, had any rights to land-rent. Similarly, any caravans passing through the territory of the drum group paid dues to the drum chief and not to the tenants of the sub-areas through which they passed.

For the cultivators who came into Ahaggar in increasing numbers after the middle of the last century, this land-rent constituted a real levy. For the Kel Ahaggar, however, it was largely symbolic and minimal in amount. As in the case of *tiwse* payments, this land-rent has been officially abolished, but Nicolaisen has recorded details of the annual payments made by the Dag Rali and Aguh-en-tehle during the 1950s.[18] His findings are reproduced in Appendix II, and it can be seen that the total land-rent of six donkeys and five goats paid by the Aguh-en-tehle was relatively small compared with their *tiwse* payments.

Territorial rights were held corporately by the various Kel Ulli and Isekkemaren descent groups, with the 'tenant' rights being vested in the 'chief' (*amrar*) of the descent group. In the case of the vassal descent groups the translation of *amrar* as 'chief' is misleading,[19] for the *amrar* of subordinate descent groups was more of a headman than a chief, in that he held little or no judicial, political or military authority over his descent group. His position was more that of a representative, responsible to the drum chief for such things as the collection and payment of the various tributary dues and so forth, and wielding little formal political authority in his own right. In most vassal descent groups, territorial rights were subdivided between the specific 'sections', which formed local residency groups within the descent group itself; each of these held corporate rights over its specific sub-areas, with the tenant rights vested in the section headman. Each of the sections, whose structure will be examined later (Ch. 7), was responsible for paying its own land-rent to the chief of the descent group, who was in turn responsible for the descent group's overall payment to the drum chief.

Although the drum chief, as owner of the land, held the right to revoke land rights, these rights, in practice, were almost absolute and not readily revoked. Only for serious reasons, such as refusal to pay land-rent, which was tantamount to revolt, or actual physical revolt, might the drum chief revoke land rights and expel the dissidents from the drum group. Such an incident has never occurred in any of the drum groups,[20] so that, in practice, the land rights of Kel Ulli and Isekkemaren descent groups were effectively permanent. In fact, this permanency was reflected in areas being referred to by the name of the descent group (or section) which held rights over them (e.g. 'amadal-oua-n-Dag Rali' – 'land of the Dag Rali'), and by many descent groups taking the name of the area over which they held land rights (e.g. Kel Tefedest, Kel Tourha, etc.).

The most valuable asset of a descent group, and the drum group as a whole, was its livestock. Consequently, as we might expect, the various rules governing land rights were orientated towards the needs of livestock. In principle, a descent group held grazing rights only over its own territory, and could only graze its animals in another territory with the specific authorization of the tenant of that area, or the drum chief himself. After a long period of drought, an entire descent group might move temporarily into another territory, on the understanding that its members did not hunt or cause damage, particularly to trees. Similarly, when a particular region had been favoured by abundant rainfall, the tenant holding rights over that region could declare it a forbidden grazing area to protect the growth of good pasture, and no one, including the members of his own descent group or section, could enter the area. After a few weeks the ban was lifted and the pasture made available to anyone, providing they conformed to the rules governing damage to trees and hunting.

These rules were extremely flexible. Livestock grazed in another territory did not incur any form of payment from their owners, except in the event of their entering protected pasture areas. Similarly, livestock in transit through an area could graze according to their needs. However, in all cases, the drum chief, as owner of the land and the supreme judicial authority of the drum group, held the power of arbitration and could intervene at any time and at his own discretion to preserve the overall interests and needs of livestock and grazing within the entire drum group. In the event of any breach of these rules, the sole judicial authority was the drum chief. He alone could impose indemnities, which were paid directly to him and not to the aggrieved tenant.

Rights over water were non-existent. Animals are watered at wells dug in the *oueds* (valleys) and the fairly abundant natural rock water-holes (*gueltas, agelmam*), which were free to all.

Rules concerning products of special value, such as trees and wild animals, were equally simple. The tenant held rights to all wood and living trees in his area. The collection of wood, within reason, was acceptable, although the use and cutting of living trees was subject to the tenant's authorization, without which an indemnity (payable to the drum chief) could be claimed. Rules governing hunting do not seem to have been so explicit. Game, particularly barbary sheep, was a valuable asset of many sub-areas over which the tenant held certain rights.[21] In principle, game could only be hunted by the occupants of a territory, but in practice this rule seems to have been extremely flexible, with barbary sheep being hunted more or less anywhere by anyone, and the tenant only having rights to specific parts of animals or a portion of the game caught in his territory. It seems that it was only the Dag Rali who held exclusive rights over hunting in their territory, and only in the case of systematic hunting in another's territory did complaints arise.[22, 23]

### *The Concept of* Ettebel

This is a convenient point, before leaving our analysis of the drum group, to elaborate on the concept of *ettebel*, for it arises, in contexts other than that of the drum group, in subsequent chapters. We should also consider the concept of *ettebel* before looking at the *temazlayt* relationship, for unlike the various dimensions of noble–vassal relations which we have considered so far, particularly in the context of the drum group, *ettebel* was never used, as far as I am aware, in the specific context of the *temazlayt* relationship that existed between the Ihaggaren and their Kel Ulli.

The *ettebel* (Arab *tobol*) is a large hemispherical drum, often measuring more than half a metre in diameter and forty or more centimetres in height. The *ettebel* (drum) is the symbol of authority or sovereignty of all the principal chiefs, particularly the Amenukal, whose drum, which was the largest, symbolized his authority over the entire federation (*tegehe*) of the Kel Ahaggar. In the past, when raiding and warfare were widespread, the sound of the drum was the signal for war, and on hearing it all warriors had to join their chief.[24]

However, the word *ettebel* has many meanings. It is the word used, as we have seen, to describe the drum group, but its many other related meanings can be best understood by reference to specific examples, for the word denotes not only 'authority' and 'sovereignty', but also the notion of 'belonging' in the context of group membership and descent, and the various political, economic and social rights and obligations incumbent in that particular position of belonging.

We can thus talk of having *ettebel* (sovereignty) over one or several groups; for example, a noble may have *ettebel* over several noble (Ihaggaren) and vassal (Kel Ulli) groups, as in the case of the Amenukal, or perhaps a drum chief who has several Kel Ulli descent groups within his drum group. In the same way we can talk about an individual noble or vassal having *ettebel* over his own particular descent group or just a descent group section. In this sense one can say that someone *is* the *ettebel*, and that he *has* the *ettebel*. For example, in Tamahak, the language of the Kel Ahaggar, one could say 'Moussa il ettebel n Ahaggar', which means literally, 'Moussa *has* the sovereignty (sovereign power) of Ahaggar', and amounts to the same thing as 'Moussa iemous ettebel n Ahaggar', which means more specifically that Moussa *is* the sovereign (supreme chief) of Ahaggar.[25] In this instance the term *ettebel* is used to mean the chieftainship or, more, specifically, the authority of a chief, whether at the level of a particular section, descent group (*tawsit*), drum group or the entire *tegehe*, as in the case of the Amenukal, and embodying the judicial, political and military authority incumbent on that specific level of chieftainship. In the same context, however, it also refers not only to the authority of a chief but, by implication, to the authority of the whole *tawsit*, as in the case of a noble *tawsit*, such as the Kel Rela, having sovereignty over Kel Ulli *tawsatin*; here one refers to the *ettebel* of the Kel Rela, for at least theoretically the chief holds his authority only as the representative of his particular *tawsit* or drum group.

With a slightly different meaning, *ettebel* also refers to the situation where a particular group, not necessarily belonging to the drum group, or even the *tegehe* for that matter, paid dues to the Amenukal or another drum chief in receipt of the guarantee that it would not be raided by any of that chief's subjects. The group paying the due, or more appropriately the 'protection money', became part of the *ettebel* of that chief or group. Examples of this were the Kunta and Berabich tribes, who both paid such dues to the Kel Rela prior to French pacification and so became part of the Kel Rela *ettebel*.

In these examples we see a slightly more subtle distinction in the meaning of *ettebel*. In the first case *ettebel* refers to the drum group as a specific political structure, embodying all the various political ties of subordination and dependency between the Ihaggaren, Kel Ulli and Isekkamaren *tawsatin* within that drum group. In the second case the concept of *ettebel* refers more to the 'following' or 'entourage' of a particular group or chief, not necessarily as part of a drum group, but within a wider context, whereby neighbouring tribes, such as the Kunta and Berabich, attached themselves to a drum group or chief in a more transient and loosely defined relationship than that between the internal groups; they did not acquire political rights within the drum group and could be considered more as an appendage than a part of it, contributing to its overall wealth but having no other rights than the tenuous guarantee of protection.

The term *ettebel* is probably used most frequently in the expression *agg ettebel*, or in the case of a woman *oult ettebel*, which translated literally is 'son (or daughter) of the sovereignty'. When someone is described in this way (as being *agg ettebel*), it really means that they belong to a particular *tawsit* or section within that *tawsit* which has *ettebel*, or in other words suzerainty over other groups. For example, all the members of the Kel Rela, Taitok and Tegehe Mellet are said to be *agg ettebel* since all three have *ettebel* over various Kel Ulli and Isekkemaren. These three *tawsatin* are consequently considered as Ihaggaren, or noble of the highest order, in contrast to the other smaller noble groups such as the Ikadayen, who have no Kel Ulli or drum group of their own, and are therefore not regarded as *agg ettebel*, but as 'second class nobles'. Thus, to refer to a man or woman as *agg* or *oult ettebel* in this context is merely a way of saying that they belong to one or other of these three noble *tawsatin*, although today, when all the Ihaggaren except the Kel Rela have been dissipated, it is just another way of saying that someone is noble, with the inference that he belongs to the Kel Rela.

A further meaning of *agg ettebel*, which we shall discuss in detail later, concerns an individual's lineage membership and his right of succession to chieftainship, and is almost synonymous with 'descent'. In this sense a man is said to be *agg ettebel* when he belongs to one of the matrilineages from which the chief must be chosen according to customary law. Among all Kel Ahaggar *tawsatin*, whether Ihaggaren, Kel Ulli or Isekkemaren, succession to the chieftaincy is usually restricted to certain matrilineages within the *tawsit*, the members of which are said to be *agg ettebel*, or *oult ettebel* in the case of a woman. This reference to women does not infer that women can succeed to the chieftaincy, but rather that since succession, as well as descent group membership, is reckoned matrilineally, a woman's descent is of crucial significance, particularly among the Ihaggaren; for power, in the form of access to chieftaincy and other related political rights, is transmitted through the *agg ettebel* matrilineages.

To be *agg ettebel* is to have the hallmark of pedigree, and to be 'in line', or at least eligible, for succession; not surprisingly it is often the subject of 'gossip', especially with reference to the Kel Rela, for whom such matters are all-important. One of the most interesting references to *agg ettebel* in recent years, which I frequently heard in the camps and around Tamanrasset, centred on the power struggle between the present Amenukal Bay ag Akhemouk and his half-brother Hadj Moussa. During the years immediately following Algerian independence all sorts of bizarre rumours circulated about the possibility of Hadj Moussa replacing his half-brother Bay as Amenukal. During the upheaval of these few years many Kel Ahaggar saw Hadj Moussa as their spokesman and representative in Tamanrasset and considered him as their effective political leader. He did at least live in Tamanrasset and was in more or less permanent contact with various government elements in his official position as President of the special council, which had been created after independence and lasted until the municipal elections in 1966. Bay, on the other hand, had no official position in the new local administration or government, except as an honorary Vice-President of the Republic of Algeria, a position which in effect was merely a 'pensioning off'. Furthermore, he lived about 100 kilometres away from Tamanrasset and was consequently removed from the centre of administration and disputations. But, whatever the respective merits of Hadj Moussa and Bay, and whatever the influence of certain external forces agitating for the displacement of the Amenukal, the Kel Ahaggar were fully aware that Hadj Moussa, because his mother was not *oult ettebel*, was himself not *agg ettebel*, and could consequently never replace his half-brother as Amenukal.

On many occasions I heard Bay being referred to simply as the *ettebel* in contradistinction to Hadj Moussa, who had no *ettebel*.

## Temazlayt Relations

The word *temazlayt* derives from the root *ezli*,[26] meaning to set aside a special portion or share, and refers specifically to the tribute given to the Ihaggaren by the Kel Ulli for their protection. The *temazlayt* was, as Gast has defined it,[27] a 'contract of protection'.

In early times, probably prior to the second half of the last century, the Kel Ulli owned few, if any, camels. They were, as their name tells us, goat-breeders, and their goat herds provided both themselves and the Ihaggaren not only with numerous food products (milk, cheese, butter, etc.), but the materials used in the manufacture of many essential artefacts (clothes, tents, various types of rope and cord, etc.). The Kel Ulli were the main producers, and as such had to suffer the exactions of the Ihaggaren and other groups within the *tegehe* as well as foreign raiders. In the latter instance it was the responsibility of the Amenukal to ensure the defence of the *tegehe*, but it seems that he was often powerless to settle or prevent raids that went on within Ahaggar. Consequently, the Kel Ulli, without camels and such specialized arms as the *takouba* (sword), were obliged to turn to the Ihaggaren for their protection. It was for this reason, as Gast says, that the Kel Ulli would choose a warrior from among their nobility to protect them personally, in return for which they gave him a special tribute in kind – the *temazlayt*.

It was therefore in the interest of this 'secondary suzerain' to defend the wealth and resources of the Kel Ulli who gave him *temazlayt* in the same way that it was in the Amenukal's interest to defend, with the aid of the nobility, the wealth of Ahaggar against foreign raiders.

Gast concludes his note by saying that the *temazlayt* institution assured the balance of the overly aggressive internal forces with respect to the productive resources of the Kel Ulli. Each group of Kel Ulli, or productive unit, thus had its protector at the local level, while in the event of large foreign raids all the warriors of the drum group or *tegehe* would join together, on the command of the Amenukal, in what could be regarded as the national defence.[28]

Although the need for protection was undoubtedly great and may well have been the fundamental reason for the original instigation of the *temazlayt*, the relationship was, I believe, more functionally diverse. It is also possible, considering Nicolaisen's comments on the *temazlayt*, that the relationship was structurally less *ad hoc* than the foregoing implies.

According to Nicolaisen,[29] *temazlayt* relationships were structurally akin to the drum group in that they were matrilineally organized. By this he means, if I interpret him correctly, that membership of a *temazlayt* group and succession to its leadership, like *tawsit* membership and succession to political office within the drum group, were determined according to matrilineal principles of descent. The *temazlayt* group, as described by Nicolaisen, seems to have consisted of a small noble matrilineage and a larger matrilineage of Kel Ulli. He also recognized that the noble matrilineage would not necessarily correspond to what he called the 'matrilineal core of a (*tawsit*) section', for in the case of the Kel Rela there appear to have been more *temazlayt* leaders than there were *tawsit* sections.[30] The Kel Ulli matrilineage on the other hand may have corresponded to an entire *tawsit* section.

The extent to which the nobles' *temazlayt* rights over Kel Ulli were held corporately by the 'small noble matrilineage' to which Nicolaisen refers is questionable. Although *temazlayt* rights over Kel Ulli were vested in an individual, the *temazlayt* leader, it seems that these rights may also have been shared by some of his matrilineal kin. Nicolaisen is not explicit on this point, and we can only conclude that the degree to which these rights were held in any corporate sense by the noble matrilineages concerned must inevitably have contained an element of ambivalence, for the predominance of *tawsit* endogamy provides the individual with considerable latitude of choice in the manipulation of his descent and the reckoning of kinship relations. He does, however, state quite specifically that a noble Tuareg who held such rights over certain vassals would be succeeded (as *temazlayt* leader) by a maternal (he presumably means matrilineal) kinsman, and that in a group of vassals rights and obligations would usually follow matrilineal rules.

These observations on the structural organization of *temazlayt* relations must be regarded with considerable caution, particularly in view of the fact that the traditional form of the relationship, as Nicolaisen himself points out, had disintegrated many years before he carried out his investigations in the field. Nevertheless, they do provide a reasonable indication that:

1 The relationship was clearly defined in its social structure and organization.
2 The relationship was of a fairly permanent and lasting nature.
3 The Kel Ulli's 'choice' of a protector, except perhaps in exceptional circumstances, may have centred more on the choice of a successor as *temazlayt* leader from within the specific noble matrilineage.

These observations become particularly significant when we shift our attention from 'protection' and focus instead on the wider dimensions of the social system as a whole, particularly the relations of production between the Ihaggaren and the Kel Ulli.

Goats were the main productive resource of the Kel Ahaggar and without assured access to their products the Ihaggaren could not have maintained themselves as a specialized warrior class. Various means of assuring this access may be suggested:

1 The Ihaggaren could have possessed their own goat herds.
2 They could have relied on raiding goats from the Kel Ulli.
3 They could have established or gained control over some form of exchange with the Kel Ulli.

The first of these alternatives was virtually impossible, as goats require permanent attention and could obviously not have been taken on raiding expeditions. Neither would it have been desirable or practical to leave them in the care of their slaves who were used primarily for tending their camels.

Raiding Kel Ulli, particularly of other drum groups, seems to have been fairly common, but usually only during feuds between the drum groups. Raiding within the *tegehe*, however, was an essentially negative process, for even if neither men nor animals were killed, it merely resulted in an overall redistribution of productive resources within the *tegehe*. The long-term result of such continuous action would probably have led to the ultimate dissolution of the *tegehe* in a state of anarchy.

It is to the third of these alternatives that we must turn our attention. The vassals' various tributary payments within the political framework of the drum group were, as we have seen, one means whereby the Ihaggaren maintained a certain measure of appropriation over their produce. However, when we consider the amount of these payments, it is unlikely that they contributed the major part of the Ihaggaren's subsistence needs; though in the years following French pacification, when many of the nobles' traditional activities, such as raiding, and the *temazlayt* relationship on which they were dependent for much of their subsistence dwindled or disintegrated, these tributary payments became of considerably greater importance.[31]

The primary means whereby the Ihaggaren gained control over access to goat products was through the *temazlayt* relationship. The obligation of the *temazlayt* leader to protect the Kel Ulli in his *temazlayt* group, or groups, was, I believe, merely the most overt feature of an institutionalized relationship through which the Ihaggaren were able to appropriate sufficient surplus labour from their vassals to meet their subsistence needs. In this respect the relationship was the fundamental means whereby the diverse economic activities of the two classes were integrated within an overall 'pastoral-cum-raiding' economy.[32]

The form of this appropriation, or rather the 'unequal' exchange basis of the *temazlayt* relationship, can be seen in the nature of the various rights and obligations of the two parties.

The rights of the *temazlayt* leader were quite different from those of the drum chief. He had no judicial authority over his Kel Ulli, neither could he summon them to war or raid unless they were interested. Furthermore, if the Kel Ulli did undertake raids, either on their own or under the leadership of their *temazlayt* leader, half the booty was given as tribute (*aballag*) to the drum chief. The rights of the *temazlayt* leader were essentially of an economic nature. *Temazlayt* payments provided the nobility with valuable goat-breeding products, while the associated but more generalized institution of *tamekchit*,[33] whereby Ihaggaren could claim food from the Kel Ulli, enabled them to obtain more or less anything they needed for their subsistence. Ihaggaren would consequently camp close to their Kel Ulli, who were obliged to feed and provision them.

The Kel Ulli, however, received certain compensations, not least of which was the assurance of protection. As Ihaggaren were frequently away raiding or roaming over more distant parts, they kept few livestock in their camps. Instead, they would leave most of their animals in the care of their Kel Ulli, who then had certain usufruct rights over them. The more important of these rights was that they could 'borrow' the Ihaggaren's camels for their own caravan or raiding expeditions, for which they gave a tribute (also known as *aballag*) consisting of half of the booty remaining after the drum chief had received his share.

The extent to which the Ihaggaren could make demands on their Kel Ulli is not altogether clear. Through the *tamekchit* relationship, the Kel Ulli were obliged to afford hospitality to the Ihaggaren in the form of food, while the *temazlayt* seems to have entailed several more generalized obligations, in the form of various 'services', in addition to the actual *temazlayt* payment itself. Duveyrier mentions that when in need of riding camels, the Ihaggaren could freely take them from their Kel Ulli.[34] Nicolaisen also mentions that if Kel Ulli had milk-yielding camels, the Ihaggaren could claim them until the milk-yield stopped.[35] This may have been the case, but it seems more likely, particularly as Kel Ulli owned few, if any, camels in earlier times, that many of these animals were in fact owned by the Ihaggaren, but had been left in the care of their Kel Ulli. Their 'taking' may thus have been only a temporary loss of usufruct rights.[36]

Although the rights of the Ihaggaren appear to have been extensive, it should be stressed that it was in the interests of the Ihaggaren to ensure that their Kel Ulli were rich and well protected, for they were dependent on them to a very large extent for much of their subsistence, and in the case of persistent or excessive demands, the Kel Ulli always held the right to refuse their requests.

Furthermore, in the case of the individual *temazlayt* group, the over-exploitation of the Kel Ulli would have been disadvantageous to the Ihaggaren, for, bearing in mind the initial comments about 'choosing' a protector, it is conceivable that the Kel Ulli could have reinforced their right of refusal by turning to another noble for protection.

### *'Communicators' and Communication Networks*

One feature of Ihaggaren–Kel Ulli relations during these traditional times that is perhaps a little surprising, particularly when we consider the potential areas of conflict between the two classes, is the question of why there appears to have been relatively little open conflict between them within any of the drum groups.[37]

Such a question does not so much concern the 'formal' means of conflict resolution in terms of the judicial system, but rather the underlying mechanisms, which appear to have maintained a surprisingly high degree of cohesion and solidarity between the classes within the drum groups.

One could suggest several such mechanisms: namely, the recognition of a mythical or real common ancestor or origin; marital alliances between the classes; inter-class 'joking relations', etc. The first two of these suggestions can be discarded without further ado. Few Ihaggaren and Kel Ulli descent groups recognize a common origin, while inter-class marriages, as we shall see, were almost unknown.

A form of 'joking relationship' (*tehandezzit*) seems to have existed, and still does exist, in what is perhaps a slightly modified form, between most people of different classes. The separateness of the classes was thus emphasized, while their divergent political interests and necessary economic interdependence could be interpreted in terms of 'social disjunction' and 'social conjunction' respectively.[38] Generally speaking there was a degree of 'joking' between Ihaggaren and Kel Ulli, and between both these classes and the Isekkemaren. Although joking between classes appears to have been symmetrical, it is important to note that the intensity of the joking varied between certain *tawsatin*. Within the Kel Rela drum group, for example, there was a particularly strong joking relationship between the Aguh-en-tehle and the Isekkemaren.[39] The Aguh-en-tehle also had a very intense joking relationship with the Kel Rela and frequently indulged in sham fights (*tebillant*) with them. In the case of the Dag Rali, however, such joking with members of other classes was comparatively slight, and their relationship with the Kel Rela seems to have bordered more on formality.

The greater intensity of joking between the Aguh-en-tehle and the Kel Rela may be explained, as Nicolaisen has suggested,[40] by the latter's more recent arrival in Ahaggar than other Kel Ulli *tawsatin*, notably the Dag Rali, who regard themselves as the oldest inhabitants of Ahaggar.

As a result of the *temazlayt* and *tamekchit* relationships the Ihaggaren often lived in close contact with their Kel Ulli. The joking relationship may have functioned to reduce potential conflict between them, and thus have been a contributory factor in enabling the two classes to co-exist in a relatively harmonious state.

Joking relationships, however, do not provide us with more than a secondary and extremely questionable explanation. Instead, I think it is more worth-while to consider the one fundamental role that the Ihaggaren have played, in different structural contexts, from these traditional times, throughout the period of French occupation, to the present – namely, that of 'communicators'.

To understand this role in traditional society it is perhaps useful for us to take a 'bird's-eye view' of Ahaggar!

The vast area of Ahaggar was divided into the territories of the three drum groups, within which each Kel Ulli *tawsit* held extensive territorial rights over thousands of square kilometres. Their camps, dotted sparsely over their respective territories, varied in size according to pastoral conditions. If pasture was exceptionally good a whole *tawsit* section, comprising anything up to about twenty tents and eighty individuals, might camp together for some time, although under normal conditions most camps (*ariwan*) would consist of about two to seven tents; while in severe conditions camps would split into even smaller units to eke out pasture. Though the size of these camps fluctuated considerably, their movements were relatively small, being confined to their specific *tawsit* territories or sectional sub-areas within that territory, and often being little more than a shift from one major valley to the next. Only in exceptional cases of pastoral impoverishment or abundant rainfall in a specific area might they migrate temporarily out of their own territories.

Ihaggaren, by contrast, with their riding camels and territorial rights over the entire territory of the drum group, roamed extensively throughout Ahaggar and farther afield, and were often away from the territories of their drum groups for long periods, for a successful warrior enhanced the material wealth of both his own immediate family and *temazlayt* groups, as well as his influence and prestige within the political élite. When they were not away from their drum groups they tended to camp near their Kel Ulli, particularly those with whom they had *temazlayt* relations, and upon whom they depended largely for food and other supplies. We can assume that their duration of stay with any one group of Kel Ulli was determined largely by the condition of the goat herds and the amount of food available, and may have ranged from a few weeks to an entire season. But it was obviously not in the interests of the Ihaggaren to burden their Kel Ulli excessively, and once they had outstayed their welcome we can picture them moving off to camp alongside other Kel Ulli with whom they had *temazlayt* relations.

From our 'bird's-eye view' we can thus see that the Kel Ulli camps were relatively static, moving from time to time over fairly small distances within their specific *tawsit* territories. Beyond this limited range of movement were the rovings of the Ihaggaren, criss-crossing as it were the entire territory of the drum group; camping alongside one group of Kel Ulli for a time and then moving on to another.

This territorial arrangement of the two classes, their geographical movements and their social relationship lead us to speculate on the function of these 'comings together' or 'points of union', particularly in the context of the *temazlayt* relationship,[41] in terms of a communications network.

Kel Ulli descent groups were well-bounded in so far as they were both territorially compact and predominantly endogamous.[42] Nomadism, as we have seen, tended to be 'in the small', while even at the individual level there was probably little reason or necessity to travel much beyond their own territory. The predominance of *tawsit* endogamy tended to restrict their network of kinship and affinal ties geographically and consequently provided few 'social' reasons for venturing farther afield; while their economic activities, particularly before the introduction of agriculture[43] and the development of caravan trade to Damergou,[44] were also fairly localized. The 'informal', casual, or day-to-day contact between individuals of different Kel Ulli *tawsatin* would thus have been limited by the probable infrequency of their social interaction.

Ihaggaren, on the other hand, with their greater mobility, extensive travels throughout the country, and necessary political interest in both 'home' and 'foreign' affairs, were the main disseminators of information, news and gossip. They were the main channels of communication in a network whose nodes were the camps of those Kel Ulli with whom they held *temazlayt* and *tamekchit* relations, for it was at these 'points of union' that the two classes came together and lived temporarily alongside each other.

We can thus see the Ihaggaren acting as 'communicators' between the various groups and parties of Ahaggar society. When they joined their Kel Ulli they undoubtedly brought news of what was happening in other parts of the country; news of distant pastures, raids, the Amenukal, movements of other groups and so forth. Because individual Ihaggaren had no administrative or judicial authority over their Kel Ulli, except in certain specific roles within the formal political structure of the drum group, the *temazlayt* group provided an arena in which such matters could be discussed impartially and informally. Through this particular form of relationship with the Kel Ulli the Ihaggaren were consequently in a position to advise the Amenukal (or drum chief) of the activities, attitudes and general state of affairs among the Kel Ulli, and vice-versa, and in a way acted as informal or unofficial go-betweens for the various levels of the social and political hierarchy.

In addition to its economic function, the *temazlayt* relationship thus seems to have constituted an important informal, underlying, or interstitial structure within the political system. By affording the means through which disputes or conflicting interests could be discussed informally and possibly resolved outside the formal administrative and judicial machinery, the *temazlayt* relationship may have constituted an important mechanism in the maintenance of cohesion and solidarity within the drum group.

# FOUR
# THE DISTRIBUTION AND CHANGING BALANCE OF POWER

Two questions about traditional Kel Ahaggar society, which we cannot answer easily, concern the nature and the extent of the authority held, on the one hand by the drum chiefs and on the other by the Amenukal, both ideally and in practice, over the drum groups and the *tegehe* (federation of Ahaggar) respectively. The consideration of these two questions throws light on the internal conflicts and dynamics of Kel Ahaggar society in the form of changing noble–vassal relations, and the struggle and competition for power both between individual nobles within the same descent groups (e.g. Kel Rela) and between the noble descent groups themselves. It also highlights the misconception, inherent in so much of the literature, that traditional society, prior to the French conquest, was in some way static or changeless.

Let us look first at the nature and extent of the drum chief's authority within his drum group. The drum chief was the supreme judicial authority of the drum group. There was no hierarchical system of courts; neither subordinate chiefs or headmen, *temazlayt* masters nor any other noble held any formal judicial authority. All legal sanctions were imposed by the drum chief himself, usually in the form of indemnities, which were paid to the drum chief and not the aggrieved party.[1] Similarly, the drum chief held the sole authority to summon all the members of his drum group, both nobles and vassals, to war, as distinct from incidental raiding.[2]

It would thus seem that the drum chief's authority was not only absolute but almost limitless. However, the question we must ask is what sort of constitutional checks, if any, limited this authority and enabled the subordinate members of the drum-group to maintain some balance of power. The question relates specifically to the extent to which the drum chief was 'elected' to office, and, related to this, the question of whether or not he could be dismissed from office, and also to the question of the existence of some sort of advisory or governing council.

In all descent groups, both noble and vassal, the chief (or headman) had to succeed from within certain matrilineages which were referred to as *agg ettebel.* From within these *agg ettebel* matrilineages, the right to succeed was transmitted adelphically through the line of brothers, thereafter through the line of mother's sisters' sons (in order of genealogical seniority), and finally through the line of sisters' sons. However, most references to the traditional political system of the Kel Ahaggar state that the drum chief was elected to office by the chiefs of the Kel Ulli descent groups within his drum group. In other words, authority, if we are to believe these references, was delegated to the drum chief by the chiefs of the subordinate descent groups. Furthermore, most of these references agree that these same subordinate chiefs could dismiss the drum chief from office if dissatisfied with his performance. I should also add that most statements given to me by the Kel Ahaggar, particularly the vassals, give qualified support to these references. In other words, it would appear that the drum chief, although succeeding from the *agg ettebel* matrilineages of the noble descent group, was effectively nothing more than the delegated representative authority of the drum group as a whole. Further confirmation of this conclusion may be seen in the emphasis which most of these references give to the fact that the Amenukal was ritually installed in office by one of his Isekkemaren.[3]

However, after examining these references and statements carefully, and considering them in relation to certain known facts, I am inclined to believe neither that the drum chief was in any way 'elected' by his subordinate Kel Ulli, nor that they could dismiss him from office, at least until towards the end of the last century.

Certainly, there is evidence to show that the Kel Ulli were involved in the choice of successors during this century. The letter of Boukhelil ag Douka to the French authorities in 1920,[4] notifying them of the death of the Amenukal Moussa ag Amastane and the 'election' of Akhemouk ag Ihemma, indicates that all the Kel Ulli chiefs, without exception, were present at the council (*djemaa*) to 'elect' the new Amenukal.[5]

However, as I have already mentioned, traditional society had undergone significant changes, particularly in noble–vassal relations, prior to French pacification. In the distant past, the control over the use of physical force was held exclusively by the Ihaggaren. And yet, at the time of the French arrival in Ahaggar at the beginning of this century, the Kel Ulli (vassals) had come to own their own camels and carry the same weapons as the Ihaggaren. They were, as the French themselves commented, 'warriors in their own right'.

The evidence for the original division in the control of physical force between the nobles and the vassals, and its apparent transformation, is remarkably contradictory. There is no doubt that by the beginning of this century all adult men in Ahaggar carried the *takouba* (sword).[6] As far as earlier literary sources are concerned we find that Duveyrier, writing in the middle of the last century, is quite emphatic that the Kel Ulli carried the same weapons as the Ihaggaren and were equally capable warriors.[7] On the other hand, the German explorer Heinrich Barth, who visited the Kel Ajjer at about the same time as Duveyrier, recorded that the vassals had no rights to possess iron spears and swords.[8] This same contradiction is found among more recent commentators. Lhote, for example, states that it was only recently, and with reluctance, that the Ihaggaren yielded the right to carry the *takouba* to the Kel Ulli.[9] Nicolaisen, for his part, regards Barth's observations as spurious, and states that all Tuareg confirmed to him that in the past noble and vassal Tuareg did not differ in regard to weapons![10]

The contradiction could not be more blatant, and I can throw little light on the confusion except to try and clarify what is meant by 'recently' and 'in the past'. Few Kel Ahaggar are able to remember many details of events before the time of Moussa ag Amastane (Amenukal 1905–20), and although most Kel Ahaggar have assured me that the Kel Ulli were also great warriors, recounting their exploits during the Senussi revolt (1916–17), and even their participation in the Ajjer war (1875–8), such verbal information reaches particularly shaky ground by the middle of the last century. If we accept that the Ihaggaren once formed a specialized class of warriors, with exclusive rights over certain weapons – and this does not seem to be in doubt – then we must ask at what time, and under what circumstances, the Kel Ulli gained rights over these weapons.

My own opinion, which is extremely speculative, is that this development may have begun during the latter half of the eighteenth century, at some time after the division of the Kel Ahaggar into three drum groups. Before this division the Ihaggaren may have held exclusive rights over these weapons, but with the division of the Kel Ahaggar into three drum groups, the imbalance of power between them, and the need to control and protect their respective territories and resources, not only from foreigners but from the other drum groups, the nobility may have yielded the right of the *takouba* to their vassals in order to make them a more effective auxiliary force within the drum group. When we look back (see Ch. 5) at the more or less continuous conflict that existed between the three noble descent groups during the last century in their struggle for overall domination of Ahaggar, this seems like an obvious and logical strategy. If it was the case, then Lhote's 'recently' may have referred to the later eighteenth century. This would also conform with Duveyrier's statement that all Kel Ulli carried the same weapons as the Ihaggaren at the time of his visit to the Kel Ajjer. However, with regard to Duveyrier's observations, we must bear in mind that he did not actually enter Ahaggar. Most of his time was spent with the Kel Ajjer, whose nobility may well have yielded the right to the *takouba* to their vassals earlier than the Kel Ahaggar.

However, the Kel Ulli's acquisition of specialized weapons is only part of the answer. In this vast, sparsely populated region, warfare usually took the form of raids, with success often dependent on speed and cunning rather than sheer weight of numbers. Raiding parties usually numbered only a few dozen (or less) specialized, well-armed, mounted men, and booty consisted mostly of livestock, particularly camels, which could be driven off quickly.

In this form of warfare, the camel was paramount, giving ease of mobility over long distances and speed in both attack and withdrawal. The possession of camels, as much as arms, made the Ihaggaren a specialized warrior class, and was thus the determining factor in the control of physical force. Before the latter part of the eighteenth century, the Kel Ulli, according to Foucauld,[11] possessed no camels at all, while throughout the nineteenth century they possessed only a few of their own, riding camels in particular being the prerogative of the Ihaggaren. Gradually, the Kel Ulli acquired their own camels. We can only speculate on the process whereby the Kel Ulli came to possess camels. Wittingly or unwittingly the Ihaggaren were partly if not wholly responsible, for as it was in their interests for their Kel Ulli to be wealthy, they encouraged them to raid, both alongside them and on their own, with the camels left behind in their care. Through their raiding expeditions and such large-scale operations as the Ajjer war (1875–8; see Ch. 5), the Kel Ulli, in spite of giving much of the booty as tribute to both the Amenukal (or drum chief) and their *temazlayt* masters, were able to gain possession of their own camels.

This process may well have accelerated during the last generation or so of the last century, for during that period there was a general escalation of warfare and raiding, associated with the Kel Ahaggar's prolonged war against the Kel Ajjer, attacks against encroaching French patrols, and feuding between the drum groups themselves. These specific events will be examined in the next chapter. For the moment there is enough evidence to show that by the beginning of this century, and possibly even earlier, the Ihaggaren no longer held exclusive control over the means of physical force.

This transformation must undoubtedly have had important implications, especially as regards the extent to which the Kel Ulli held rights over, or were able to exert influence on, the succession and dismissal of the drum chief or Amenukal.

What evidence is there, in terms of specific successions, to clarify this question? We know very little of the detailed events surrounding successions amongst the Taitok and Tegehe Mellet. But in the case of Kel Rela successions, I believe there is sufficient evidence to suggest that the Kel Ulli's acquisition of camels and specialized arms was reflected, by the end of the last century, in their increased acquisition of political power and representation.

Amenukals of Ahaggar since Salah:*

| | | |
|---:|---|---|
| Mohammed el Khir | – | |
| Sidi ag Mohammed el Khir | – | |
| Younes ag Sidi | – | died about 1790 |
| Ag Mama ag Sidi | – | reigned to about 1830 |
| El Hadj Akhmed | – | 1830–77 |
| Aitarel | – | 1877–1900 |
| Attici ag Amellal | – | 1900–1905 |
| Moussa ag Amastane | – | 1905–20 |
| Akhemouk ag Ihemma | – | 1920–41 |
| Meslar ag Amayas | – | 1941–50 |
| Bay ag Akhemouk | – | 1950– |

We know nothing about the succession of Amenukals preceding Sidi ag Mohammed el Khir, except that each succeeded his father. However, on Sidi's death, the succession was disputed. The nature of the dispute is not entirely clear, but according to Benhazera, Sidi's wife, Kella, had an elder and a younger sister. The elder had married a certain Aboura of the Ikerremoien, whose son disputed the title with Younes (see Fig. 2). From Benhazera's notes, it appears that the Kel Rela nobility were the

* Mohammed el Khir, Sidi and Younes all succeeded their fathers. All subsequent Amenukals descended matrilineally from Kella, the last seven all descending from one or other of Kella's daughters (see Fig. 2).

decisive force in the matter, and their siding with Younes, on the grounds, it seems, that Aboura was an Ikerremoien from the south and hence a 'foreigner', decided the issue. There is no record of the Kel Ulli playing any part in this succession; it seems to have been determined solely by the nobility.

The succession of Ag Mama seems to have been quite straightforward. However, his reign produced an extraordinary, indeed a unique, situation in Ahaggar. Fortunately for us, Duveyrier not only travelled among the Northern Tuareg during this period (1859), but was held in some trust by Sheikh Othman, the brother of the new Amenukal, El Hadj Akhmed, who eventually succeeded Ag Mama, so that his insight into this episode in Tuareg history is one of the most valuable commentaries to have reached us from the last century.

The problem was that Ag Mama had evidently reached a very old age and his longevity was the cause for considerable consternation, not only in Ahaggar, but throughout much of the Sahara. He was, to use Duveyrier's expression, 'le doyen des centenaires du Sahara', and had been blind for a long time and quite incapable of governing. Although Duveyrier does not say so in so many words, he implies that Ag Mama was approaching an advanced state of senility. The need for a stronger authority was felt, not only among the Kel Ahaggar themselves, but as far afield as In Salah and Timbuktu, where there was concern for the security of the trade routes – as well as among neighbouring Tuareg, who were anxious to maintain the state of good relations that seems to have existed for most of the previous generation.

What could be done to overcome this alarming situation? Duveyrier devoted several pages to the consideration of this question, in the course of which he gives us a valuable insight into certain affairs. His most revealing statement is that it was contrary to the laws of the country to initiate a successor while the Amenukal was alive,[12] which is in direct contradiction to all later references and statements on the Kel Ahaggar's political system regarding the rights of the Kel Ulli to dismiss the Amenukal (or other drum chiefs) from office. The immediate conclusions to be drawn from this apparent contradiction are that either Duveyrier was incorrect or that a fairly radical change in the political system occurred between the time of Duveyrier's visit and the arrival of the French some forty or so years later.

The second of these conclusions is, I believe, correct, for as we have seen there is sufficient evidence to suggest that the Kel Ulli became a more significant force in Ahaggar during the latter part of the century. Nevertheless, the possibility of Duveyrier being mistaken, or 'misled', cannot be discounted altogether. At the time of his visit, the Northern Tuareg were aware of the French presence in the northern parts of the country. Sheikh Othman, of the Kel Ajjer, had in fact accepted an invitation from the Governor-General of Algeria to visit Algiers in 1855. The Kel Ahaggar, however, remained hostile to any such diplomatic advances by the French, and, for reasons of safety, Duveyrier did not enter Ahaggar, but remained in Ajjer territory, where he was accompanied by Sheikh Othman. His main sources of information were presumably Sheikh Othman himself, certain Kel Ajjer nobles and various other nobles, presumably Kel Rela (Sheikh Othman's brother, El Hadj Akhmed, was a Kel Rela through matrilineal descent), with whom he came into contact outside Ahaggar. There is little evidence to show that he associated with vassals. In other words, most of his informants were close to the centre of power, and it is reasonable to assume that these more informed persons, like Sheikh Othman himself, were not only well aware of the French presence to the north but were probably well aware of their intentions further south. If this was so, it is unlikely that the Sheikh and other nobles would have gone to undue lengths to explain that the subordinate vassal chiefs held the right to dismiss the Amenukal from office – if, of course, they did in fact hold this right – for such information could well have weakened the bargaining power of the respective Amenukals with their imminent adversaries, the French. Neither does it seem likely that the proud, arrogant nobles would have eagerly given such recognition to their vassals and confided to a stranger that the authority of the Amenukal was effectively delegated to him by his subordinate chiefs. If Duveyrier had been able to enter Ahaggar and talk with Kel Ulli, he might have heard another side of the story. But, even if the Kel Ulli did hold this right, it is impossible to imagine how they could have enforced it at that time, for the enforcement of whatever rights the Kel Ulli may have held in this respect was effectively denied by the Ihaggaren's almost exclusive control of the use of physical force. Furthermore, if the nobility held exclusive control over the use of physical force at that time, there seems no logical reason for them to concede such political power to their vassals.

Duveyrier's comments do in fact suggest that the vassals had little or no say or influence in the matter of 'electing' the Amenukal. His statement, that to find a successor to Ag Mama, by right of descent, while he was still alive would almost certainly ignite a civil war between all the Kel Rela families and the others who had married sisters, or even nieces or grandnieces of the living chief, implies that the establishment of a successor was 'fought out' amongst the nobility themselves.

Whether or not it was contrary to the law of the country, it was decided to find a successor to Ag Mama while he was still alive. But this presented a great difficulty, for the number of Ag Mama's matrilineal kinsmen who had legitimate claims to the succession was considerable. Our rather sketchy genealogical data of this period makes it difficult to know the exact number of legitimate claimants, but there were certainly ten matrilineal nephews (sisters' sons), probably all living at the time, which gives some indication of the enormity and delicacy of the problem. The threat of civil war was very real.

The difficulty was overcome, as Duveyrier explains, by miraculously finding the three important conditions for succession in such circumstances united on the head of one man, El Hadj Akhmed, the brother of Sheikh Othman and a member of the Iforas tribe of the Ajjer confederation, but who belonged to the Kel Ahaggar and the Kel Rela through his mother. As a marabout he was respected; as a stranger, or outsider, his succession destroyed local rivalries; and, as the son of one of Ag Mama's sisters, his succession conformed to the traditional rules of matrilineal descent. It was a wise choice and at least a provisional solution to the problem, and in order to ratify it the marabout, Sidi el Bakkey of Timbuktu, sent one of his brothers to the spot.

Here again, Duveyrier's final comment on the situation, that God alone knew what rival claims would be thrust forward on the eventual death of Ag Mama, is a further indication that the Kel Ulli played little effective role in choosing, or in any way 'electing', a successor.

It seems that God was wise, or merciful to El Hadj Akhmed, for we have little further record of Ag Mama and we can only assume that, by the time of his death, El Hadj Akhmed had gained sufficient respect and authority to overcome the likelihood of civil war amongst the Kel Rela.

The succession of Aitarel seems to have been quite straightforward. There does not appear to have been any rival claimant on the grounds of descent, and Aitarel succeeded as the son of El Hadj Akhmed's mother's sister.

It is not until the death of Aitarel in 1900 (see Ch. 5) that we come across any concrete evidence of the Kel Ulli exerting a real influence in 'electing' an Amenukal. By that time the Kel Ulli were, as the French noted on their arrival in Ahaggar two years later, equally capable warriors.

The various literary references, and the statements of the Kel Ahaggar themselves, with regard to this question of the Kel Ulli's role in 'electing' the drum chief and their right to dismiss him from office, refer, I believe, to the period subsequent to, and including, the succession to Aitarel in 1900, and not to traditional society as it existed before the latter part of the nineteenth century; for the evidence that we have, albeit fragmentary, indicates that the Kel Ulli's political power, in terms of their ability to 'elect' and dismiss the drum chief, was minimal.

## The Djemaa

The question of checks on the drum chief's authority concerns the function, and even the existence, in these earlier times, of an advisory or governing council. Henri Lhote states that the decision of the Amenukal only carried his full authority if it was approved by an assembly of notables called the *arollan*, which consisted of important chiefs and nobles.[13] Unfortunately, Lhote tells us no more about this *arollan*, nor have I come across any other reference to it among the Kel Ahaggar, though in Ayr, and among the Kel Gress (Southern Tuareg), the word *arolla* (pl. *irollan*) is the title of a chief of a specific group of tribes.

Lhote seems to be referring to the period after French pacification, when there was effectively only one drum chief in Ahaggar, namely the Amenukal. We must assume, however, that in traditional times, each drum group had what Lhote refers to as an *arollan*. If the Amenukal's decisions were in fact subject to the approval of such a council, as Lhote states, then this council would have acted as a major check on his power. However, I do not believe that that was the case. Nearly all Kel Ahaggar with whom I have discussed this question have told me that the 'word of the Amenukal was sufficient authority', although he could, of course, consult any other important or knowledgeable persons. My own opinion is that such a council (*djemaa*), which Lhote calls an *arollan*, never had any sort of corporate existence, and seems to have been more of an *ad hoc* assembly, comprising most of the more powerful and influential nobles, subordinate chiefs and headmen, and other important or knowledgeable persons such as marabouts (religious men), and which provided the only machinery for settling disputes or discussing matters of concern to the drum group.

The role of the *djemaa* among the Kel Ahaggar seems to have been very similar to what it is amongst other Berber groups, especially in the Atlas regions. In this respect, the comments of Ernest Gellner are particularly interesting, for he considers that many of the accounts of *djemaas* given in the French literature have overstressed their role, and have given the impression that the *djemaas* have some kind of corporate existence. This, I believe, is especially true of Lhote's account of the *arollan* (*djemaa*). As Gellner notes among the Berbers of the Moroccan Atlas, 'They [*djemaas*] have no existence independently of the social group, the segments, of which they are the assemblies. They simply are the natural form of discussing and settling issues for groups which are reasonably egalitarian and which have no other machinery available to them.'[14]

The drum group, characterized as it was by the division between nobles and vassals, could hardly be regarded as egalitarian. However, the overall change in noble–vassal relations during the latter part of the last century and the early part of this century, in terms of the vassals' increased control over the use of physical force and their greater economic autonomy, shifted the balance of power within the drum group more in favour of the vassals. As we shall see in the next chapter, the succession of Moussa ag Amastane as Amenukal in 1905 was attributable, in large part, to the 'popular' support given to him by the Kel Ulli. Indeed, there can be no doubt that the voice of the Kel Ulli has carried more weight since the time of Moussa ag Amastane.

During this century, the *djemaa*, amongst the Kel Ahaggar, seems to have become fairly similar to that described by Gellner amongst the Berbers of the Atlas. But at no time does it seem to have had any formal or corporate existence, nor any real check, in a constitutional way, on the Amenukal's authority.

When we consider the means at the vassals' disposal in earlier times to enforce whatever political rights that they may have actually held, I think we can conclude, with reasonable surety, that their position in the drum group was one of almost total subordination. I can find no evidence to suggest that the vassals, prior to the latter part of the last century, held any effective political rights of the nature that we have discussed, or exerted influence over the drum chief through their participation in any form of council; I am inclined to believe that those references, both literary and oral, which infer the contrary relate to the social formation that existed around the turn of this century, and which was regarded by most French observers as 'traditional' rather than as the outcome of fairly radical changes that were taking place, or had taken place, during the previous generation or so.

# FIVE
# INTERNAL WARS AND CONQUEST BY FRANCE

When we look at the history of the Kel Ahaggar prior to French pacification, it would appear that the main checks on the power of the drum chiefs, particularly the Amenukal, were exercised not so much by the vassals as by the nobility themselves. Three general characteristics of Kel Ahaggar society prior to pacification were: the almost continual challenges by the Tegehe-Mellet and particularly the Taitok to the pre-eminent position of the Kel Rela; the tendency for rivalries and political factions to develop amongst the nobility within the drum group itself; and the consistency with which 'strong men' succeeded as Amenukal (drum chief of Kel Rela). We must be cautious in extending this last characteristic to the Taitok and Tegehe Mellet drum chiefs, for our knowledge of their personal qualities and the events surrounding their successions is inadequate. Nevertheless, when we consider the Amenukals of Ahaggar during this period, from the time of Ag Mama at the end of the eighteenth century to the death of Moussa ag Amastane in 1920, at the end of the period of French pacification – namely, El Hadj Akhmed, Aitarel, Attici and Moussa ag Amastane himself – it is clear that they were all 'strong men', characterized by physical strength and courage, wisdom and a sense of justice, although these last two qualities may be doubted in Attici's case. That men with such qualities should have succeeded with such regularity is not, I believe, a matter of historical contingency, but a product of the political system itself.

Rights to succession to political office were transmitted adelphically within the matriline, firstly through the line of brothers, followed by the line of mother's sisters' sons, and thereafter through the line of sisters' sons, so that there were usually several legitimate claimants to succeed. Not only did such a system provide a degree of flexibility, in that it offered legitimate means whereby a weak or ineffectual claimant could be passed over in favour of a more suitably qualified and popular claimant, thus giving some degree of explanation to the 'strong man' syndrome to which I have referred, but it also gave rise inevitably to rivalries and the development of political factions amongst the nobility themselves, and consequent succession disputes.

During the nineteenth century the extent to which the Amenukal, as supreme chief of the *tegehe* (federation of Kel Ahaggar), was able to exert his authority over the two other drum groups (Taitok and Tegehe Mellet) was often extremely limited. Throughout much of the period the two other drum groups not only acted more or less independently of any centralized authority but were bent on wresting the Kel Rela's pre-eminent position for themselves. Similarly, the extent of the Amenukal's authority over his own drum group (the Kel Rela) was often dependent on the existence and strength of opposition factions amongst the Kel Rela themselves.

The Taitok's and Tegehe Mellet's grievances against the Kel Rela stemmed from Sidi ag Mohammed el Khir's unequal division of the vassals between the three drum groups. As we have seen, both the Taitok and Tegehe Mellet, in turn, attempted to redress this state of affairs, and both were equally unsuccessful.

After their defeat at the hands of Younes, the Tegehe Mellet never again became sufficiently strong to challenge the Kel Rela. The Taitok, however, were not to lay down their arms in Ahaggar until stripped of their power (*ettebel*) by the French in 1918. Following the Taitok's initial defeat by the Kel Rela, Sidi ag Mohammed el Khir had shrewdly married his two sons, Younes and Ag Mama, to Taitok women as a means of long-term reconciliation.

Throughout the reigns of both Younes and Ag Mama the Taitok and Kel Rela lived in peace. But the Taitok's long-standing grievance about having received a disproportionate and unjust share of the 'spoils' of Ahaggar was simmering not far below the surface, and the difficulties involved in finding a successor to Ag Mama provided them with an opportunity of redressing, once and for all, the balance of power in Ahaggar.

The real danger to El Hadj Akhmed came not from the Kel Rela, as might have been expected in view of the number of rival claimants, but from the Taitok. The issue, or rather the excuse for renewed hostilities, was the rival claim of Ag Mama's son, Mohammed, who belonged to the Taitok *ettebel* and consequently had no legitimate claim to the title of Amenukal in terms of his descent. As far as the Taitok were concerned, however, it provided sufficient grounds, in spite of the intervening years of peaceful co-existence with the Kel Rela, to declare war on El Hadj Akhmed. The details of the many raids and counter-raids are lost to us. We simply know that the drum chief of the Taitok, Amastane ag Ourzig, eventually made peace with El Hadj Akhmed at Tit in Tidikelt.

After this peace, and frustrated in their ultimate object, the Taitok, under the leadership of Mohammed ag Mama, turned their attention to expanding their field of operations to the south of Ahaggar. Incorrigible raiders, they saw the means of recuperating their loss of camels at the hands of the Kel Rela in the organization of a great raid against the Tuareg of Ayr, who in turn came immediately to the Kel Rela to implore their protection. The Kel Rela caught the Taitok unawares and once again defeated them, at a place called Tarhebout. Mohammed ag Mama was wounded in the battle; two of his sister's sons, Ilou and Anaba, were killed; and the Taitok duly emigrated from Ahaggar to seek refuge in Ayr.

Mohammed ag Mama died from his injuries soon after their departure and was succeeded by Ibrahim ag Khemidou, his mother's sister's son. Ibrahim, however, was a weak and ineffectual man, without influence and the qualities of a great fighter that the Taitok idealized, and although he seems to have retained some of the drum chief's privileges, the effective leadership was taken over by Sidi ag Keradji, a man of Herculean strength, great courage and intelligence. Under such a leader, the Taitok could hardly be expected to remain peacefully in the mountains of Ayr, and once more they characteristically set out to make good their losses at the expense of the Iwllemmeden and Kunta, both of whom it seems were usually regarded as fair game for lucrative pickings. The raid against the Iwllemmeden seems to have been successful, but the Kunta, rather surprisingly, managed to kill two members of the Kel Ahnet who belonged to the Taitok drum group as well as a slave of an Iboglan encampment. We can only surmise how an Iboglan slave, one of the more important Kel Rela sections, became caught up in the skirmish. He was probably quite innocently tending Iboglan herds in the area, but the poor Kunta, in the innocence of self-defence, now faced the wrath of the powerful Iboglan as well as the aggrieved Kel Ahnet, and duly suffered great losses, first at the hands of the Kel Ahnet, who killed their chief, Mohammed Sr'ier, and then at the hands of the Iboglan, who not only inflicted several casualties but succeeded in pillaging a considerable number of their camels. Finally, the Taitok returned with a smaller raid of seven men, but they were all killed. Whether the Kunta feared revenge or merely saw this as an opportune moment to negotiate with the Taitok is not known, but under Mohammed Sr'ier's son, Bekkai, they went to Ayr to seek peace with the Taitok.

In spite of this series of raids and counter-raids sparked off by El Hadj Akhmed's succession, his rule, spanning almost two generations (1830–77), was something of a Golden Age in Ahaggar, for of all the qualities needed by an Amenukal he was above all wise. Almost his first action, while waiting for the death of Ag Mama, was to ensure, through the intercession of his brother Sheikh Othman, the Kel Ahaggar's security from their formidable enemies, the Chaamba. Duveyrier comments that, even if he had not re-established peace, order and harmony among all the tribes, he at least succeeded, through his conciliatory nature and the authority derived from his age and status as a marabout, in averting civil war and establishing better relations between the Kel Ahaggar and their neighbours. Through his wisdom, strength of character and respect, his reign was characterized by relative stability and an increase in the material prosperity of Ahaggar.

This prosperity derived not only from the security of the trade routes but also from the introduction of cultivation, which will be discussed in detail later; but the stability which enabled its introduction resulted almost entirely from the Amenukal's increased power and authority, for it was during El Hadj Akhmed's reign that we see the Amenukal achieving a position of centralized authority over Ahaggar, and the establishment of a unified political entity in contradistinction to three almost totally independent and autonomous drum groups.

The Tegehe-Mellet, it is true, never became sufficiently strong after their defeat at the hands of Younes to challenge the domination of the Kel Rela, but it was not until El Hadj Akhmed had effectively driven the Taitok into exile that he was in a position to consolidate his authority over Ahaggar. In this respect one might also mention that the gifts that Sheikh Othman brought to El Hadj Akhmed from the French government after his visit to Paris contributed to the consolidation of his authority, for, as Duveyrier remarked, such overt support from a foreign government, particularly one as powerful as France, would greatly enhance his prestige among the Tuareg populations.

The Taitok exile was not to last for long. Although Sidi's father, Keradji, had married a Taitok, he was a Kel Rela of importance. He was the first cousin (mother's sister's son) of El Hadj Akhmed, and the brother of Aitarel, who was to succeed El Hadj Akhmed as Amenukal of Ahaggar; it was Aitarel who used his influence on El Hadj Akhmed to allow the Taitok to return to Ahaggar – an act of 'clemency' that was a measure of his command over Ahaggar and brought about a period of peace and calm in the region.

The calm that settled over Ahaggar after the Taitok return must have seemed like the lull before the storm. Such peace could hardly have been expected to last amongst such inveterate warriors, for whom raiding and warfare were not just an economic imperative, or, as in the case of the Taitok, the means of reversing the balance of power, but an idealized way of life. The storm that broke over Ahaggar in 1875 was not of the usual pattern of raid and counter-raid between rival drum groups jostling for power and control over Ahaggar with the inevitable plundering of unsuspecting neighbours to recuperate their losses. For the first time the Kel Rela, Taitok, Tegehe Mellet and their best Kel Ulli, rose up in arms together against the Kel Ajjer in a war that was to drag on for three years. Internal feuds, grievances and petty bickerings were cast aside as the Kel Ahaggar united in common cause under the overall command of the Amenukal.

The cause of the war, its course and outcome were 'typically Tuareg', with all the ingredients of a medieval crusade – the tears of beautiful women, the chivalry and valour of noble warriors, the cunning of habitual raiders, and the final dissipation of energy when the initial cause has been lost as a mere triviality along the way.

To understand the cause of the war we must go back to the fall of the Imenan sultans in the seventeenth century. After their overthrow by the Uraren they were left with only a few vestiges of their former power: a few small Kel Ulli descent groups, namely the Kel Ahrir, the Ibettenaten, the Kel Tassili, and also the Iklan-oua-n-Tawsit, or what was left of their Negro guards. They also retained a tribute from the people of Mesrata, as well as certain passage rights on caravans going down to Ayr from Tripolitania.

After seizing power the Uraren had become all-powerful in Ajjer, and by 1875 there were no more than seven Imenan who held their traditional right to the title of Sultan, namely: Sheikh, Okha, Amma, Rezkou, Keneiss, El Mokhtar, and Amoud, with their few women whose reputation for beauty was renowned among all Tuareg. After fleeing from the Uraren they had settled with their few Kel Ulli in the oasis of Djanet, about three days' journey to the south-west of Ghat,[1] and nomadized in the territory adjoining Ahaggar.

We do not know whether it was greed, a matter of conscience or perhaps even embarrassment, but the Uraren were still jealous of the Imenan's shadow of power as reflected in their few remaining privileges and the arrogance of their noble origin, and were intent on provoking a quarrel which would lead to their ultimate humiliation and destruction. The Uraren began their strategy by slitting the throats of the cattle which the Imenan had sent to graze in the Oued Taharamet near Ghat, and it looked as if fighting would flare up, but the religious *cheurfa* and Ansar of Ghat,[2] and the Ilemtyen from the village of El Barkat in the Fezzan, intervened and managed to patch up a rather tenuous peace. This did not satisfy the Uraren, whose next step was to claim ownership rights over a well in Djanet at which the Imenan watered their cattle and donkeys. They also declared that they intended taking part of the tribute that the people of Mesrata paid to the Imenan. The Imenan ceded over the Mesrata issue but refused to compromise over the well. In the meantime, to provoke and embarrass the Imenan still further, the Uraren plundered the merchandise of the Tripolitanian caravans whose security was guaranteed by the Imenan. As far as the Imenan were concerned this action was the final straw and in desperation they broke camp and rode to Ahaggar to implore El Hadj Akhmed's help.

It must have been a piteous and moving sight to see the small band of Imenan, accompanied by their women, invoking their ancestral but long-lost heritage and pleading their case before the Kel Ahaggar. Indeed it was, for the tears and lamentations of such beautiful women filled the Kel Ahaggar with compassion and zeal to avenge their cause. Confronted by the unanimous outcry of Ahaggar, El Hadj Akhmed had no alternative but to write to Ikhenoukhen, the chief of the Kel Ajjer, protesting the cause of the Imenan and asking that justice be granted to their ancient sultans, but the letter met with a refusal to yield over either the disputed well or the question of the Tripolitanians' security.

The gauntlet had been thrown down and the entire *tegehe* rose up together: Kel Rela, Taitok, Tegehe Mellet and their best Kel Ulli, with the Imenan, came together as a combined force of about 650 men. It was an army, the entire fighting force of Ahaggar, united for the first time in the history of the *tegehe* under the authority of the Amenukal. El Hadj Akhmed, who was by then an old man, delegated the overall command of the expedition to Aitarel, his future successor, with Sidi ag Keradji, Aitarel's nephew, in command of the Taitok contingent.

The Kel Ahaggar rode on Ajjer, and as they approached Ghat the Kel Ajjer became less enthusiastic and may even have regretted rejecting El Hadj Akhmed's request. The Kel Ahaggar stopped short of the town and arrayed themselves in the Oued Tin Kaouia, about three hours from the town, where they were met by the *cheurfa* and Ansar, who came out from

Ghat to meet them in an attempt to avert bloodshed. The Kel Ahaggar agreed to wait for the decision of the Kel Ajjer, who by this time had barricaded themselves into the town and hidden their camels behind the little hill that overlooked it. Ikhenoukhen was in a difficult position; his bluff had been called, in so far as he was probably not expecting to be confronted by such an ominous force, but to cede to the proposals of the *cheurfa* would have incurred the ultimate shame. Rebuffed by Ikhenoukhen and deeply hurt by his rejection of their wise advice the *cheurfa* asked, as the religious guardians of the town, that the fighting should at least take place outside the town walls. Having failed to reach any sort of agreement with Ikhenoukhen they rode back to the Kel Ahaggar to forewarn them of their failure and declared their neutrality while hoping that this stubborn and foolish man would be defeated.

The drum sounded throughout Ghat, and 900 men assembled under Ikhenoukhen's command. Safi Ould el Hadj el Amine, the Sheikh of the town, who had offered his support to the Uraren, along with the townsmen and Harratin cultivators, assembled alongside the Uraren. The Kel Ahaggar, in the meantime, had moved out of the Oued to make their stand on a little hillock on which stood a solitary male date palm. The first shot seems to have been fired by the Kel Ahaggar as three scouts, including both Ikhenoukhen's son, Amma, and his sister's son, Yakhia, made a reconnaissance of the position. The shot merely wounded the horse of the third member of the party, a certain Ou-Fenait of the Imanr'assaten, and they returned unharmed to the town. Ikhenoukhen's force then left the town and advanced to a spot called Kalala, just short of the Kel Ahaggar's hillock, where they spent the night under the protection of watches. At dawn Aitarel sent an ultimatum to Ikhenoukhen, to choose either peace or war. But while they were negotiating a group of Taitok, who it might be added were the most impulsive and intolerant raiders and had always been the party most interested in the prospect of war, broke away from the main force under the leadership of Aziouel ag Ser'ada, and raided the Ajjer camels hidden behind the town.

Such treachery put an end to the negotiations, and although Aitarel, who had been constantly endeavouring to restrain his followers and settle the dispute without bloodshed, asked Sidi ag Keradji to return the booty, the Kel Ajjer were enraged beyond appeasement. In the afternoon they advanced provocatively towards the Kel Ahaggar, and with several of their best warriors in the front hurled clods of earth at the Amenukal – the supreme insult!

Insult met treachery and the battle began. The Ajjer soon yielded before the Kel Ahaggar's onslaught and were driven right back into the town itself with casualties of sixty nobles, thirteen Kel Ulli and three townsmen killed. It must have been an overwhelming victory for the Kel Ahaggar, for although several were wounded the only men killed, according to Benhazera, were: Ihemma, the father of Dassine, the 'belle' of Ahaggar; El Hamous ag Alemhok, the son of El Hadj Akhmed's sister; Ihemma ag Ibrahim, the brother of Beketa; and Ilbak ag Amellal, the brother of Attici and Anaba.

After such a resounding battle the Imenan cause must have seemed of secondary importance, but this was merely the first battle, the first round in a war that was to drag on for another three years. While the Kel Ahaggar retired to the little town of El Barkat the Kel Ajjer burned with desire for revenge – they had lost not only many warriors, but all their camels had been driven off by the Kel Ahaggar. After this humiliating and devastating experience even the stubborn Ikhenoukhen realized that the Uraren could never hope to revenge themselves against such formidable warriors without the support of a considerable military alliance.

In the company of Safi Ould el Hadj el Amine, Ikhenoukhen rode eastwards through the Fezzan to ask the Turkish Bey of Murzuk, Ali ben Mohammed, for the support of the Arabs in the Oued Chiata region. The Bey consented, but on the shrewd and farsighted condition that, if the campaign against the Kel Ahaggar was successful, the Turks would have the right to build a garrison in Ghat in case of their future need for defence. How could Ikhenoukhen and the Sheikh have been aware of the grand designs of the world powers? They accepted the Bey's condition, which must have seemed quite innocuous, especially when their immediate predicament gave them little bargaining power and few alternatives, and returned to Ghat with 400 Arabs recruited and armed by the Bey.

When Ikhenoukhen returned with his reinforcements the Kel Ahaggar were encamped near the Tassili-n-Ajjer, where there was good pasture. The combined force of Kel Ajjer and the Fezzan Arabs[3] found them after five days' ride from Ghat and inflicted a crushing defeat. There is no record of how many Kel Ahaggar were killed, except that the Imenan were virtually annihilated. El Mokhtar, Sheikh, Amma, Rezkou and Keneiss were killed, and Okha was taken prisoner. The only Imenan to escape the onslaught was Amoud, who was too young to fight and had remained behind in other Kel Ahaggar camps. The Kel Ahaggar lost almost everything; their camels, goats and sheep were all pillaged, and in their crippled condition they withdrew deep into the south of Ahaggar, where they licked their wounds and tried to recover sufficient strength to revenge themselves. Finally, after ten months, and with a massive force of 800 men, comprising all the groups of Ahaggar, they once more set off from Ahaggar to attack the Kel Ajjer. The Kel Ahaggar eventually came across the Ajjer settled at Tarat, between Ghadames and Ghat, and on seeing the Ahaggar force they took refuge on a mountain called Edjmidhan. The Kel Ahaggar surrounded the mountain and for ten days laid siege to it, watching from their camp fires without daring what would have been a suicidal assault.

We do not know whether Aitarel had visited the mountain on some earlier occasion, whether he had gained some secret information or just made a reconnaissance, but apparently, after ten days of siege, he remembered or found a circuitous path that led up the mountainside. That night the Kel Ahaggar lit their camp fires as usual, and at about midnight Aitarel set off with a hundred men to tackle the tortuous climb. At dawn the Kel Ajjer awoke to see the Kel Ahaggar lined in ambush against them. In startled desperation they struggled to build a defensive stone wall, but they had been taken completely off guard and hand-to-hand fighting started almost immediately. It was an overwhelming victory for the Kel Ahaggar. Over forty Kel Ajjer were killed and many others wounded. Revenge was complete, and having plundered the camels they returned triumphantly to Ahaggar.

This was not the end of the war. Although the Kel Ahaggar proposed peace the Uraren deliberately dragged out the negotiations to gain time to reorganize and once again avenge themselves. It was during this time that the Turks arrived in Ghat to set up their garrison in accordance with the conditions of their earlier agreement with Ikhenoukhen, who took the opportunity of their presence to ask for renewed support. The Turks refused, saying that they had kept their side of the agreement and that the Ajjer had in fact been victorious with their assistance; in short, all they could do was to lend arms. Ikhenoukhen was furious and wanted to tear down the Turkish flag that now hung over the town, but he eventually decided to accept the Turkish offer and sent out word for the Kel Ajjer to come together at a place called Ademer, between Djanet and the Tassili, in preparation for a further campaign against the Kel Ahaggar.

The Kel Ahaggar somehow received word of the gathering, and taking the initiative they attacked and defeated all the various groups before they were able to concentrate in force. For their part, the Kel Ajjer had in the meantime been successful in a few small raids against Isekkemaren, and the Amenukal, El Hadj Akhmed, had been killed in one of the small combats of which we have no detailed records. Aitarel, who succeeded as

Amenukal, was by this time tired of the continual war. Too many men had been killed and he wanted peace. After exchanging letters with Ikhenoukhen he sent an envoy[4] to the *cheurfa* and Ansar of Ghat, and together with a group of Isekkemaren they went in search of Ikhenoukhen, who was camped at Tadrart to the east of the town. The Kel Ahaggar held to the original demand that the Imenan should be treated justly, and on this condition peace was made in 1878. Okha was freed and a year later, after Aitarel had requested permission for his return to Djanet, he reconciled himself with the Kel Ajjer, but swore not to be buried amongst them and returned to Ahaggar to die. His tomb, and that of his sister, Taber'ourt, is at Tamanrasset.

And so the war that had raged back and forth for so long and dissipated the strength and resources of both federations came to an end, negatively it may seem, for although the Kel Ahaggar claimed to have won the cause for the sole surviving Imenan, it was something of a Pyrrhic victory.

## Conquest and Pacification by France

The successions of the next two Amenukals after Aitarel are particularly interesting in that the controversy surrounding the succession at the death of Aitarel was resolved by the 'appointment' of two Amenukals, while the succession of Moussa ag Amastane five years later was also unprecedented in that he succeeded not so much by virtue of his descent, but by 'popular choice' and the ratification of France. The extraordinary circumstances of these two successions were induced by two emergent forces in Ahaggar: the presence of France, whose penetration into the central Sahara in the late nineteenth century was threatening the independence of Ahaggar; and to a lesser extent the changing military and economic status of the Kel Ulli.

Although the Kel Ahaggar were involved after the Ajjer war with a more or less continuous series of raids on the populations of Ayr, the Iwllemmeden, the Berabich and the Chaamba, their attention during this period was focused more on the menacing advance of France into the central Sahara.

The French capture of Algiers in 1830 led eventually, after several bitter campaigns against Abdel Khader and other local 'resistance leaders', to Algeria being declared French in 1848. It was not until the end of the century, however, that there was any real penetration into Tuareg territory.[5]

France's first contacts with the Tuareg, at least in the Ajjer region, were reasonably amicable. Sheikh Othman had accepted the invitation of the Governor-General of Algeria to visit Algiers, while Duveyrier had stayed amongst them as an honoured guest in 1859 for several months and had gone so far as to advise the French government on the friendliness of the Tuareg. Nevertheless, this initial period of exploration was followed by a series of troublesome events, such as the killing of the Dutch explorer Miss Tinné, followed shortly afterwards by that of the Dourneaux-Duperné and Joubert expedition in 1874, and by 1880 no European had yet entered Ahaggar. At the time of the Ajjer war France was entertaining ambitious aspirations for her colonial territories. She even went so far as to consider the idea of negotiating with the Kel Ahaggar in the hope of preventing Ikhenoukhen's submission to the Turks, who were already well installed at Ghadames and who threatened her own designs.

France wanted to strengthen and consolidate her hold over her colonial territories, and the political atmosphere was one in which grandiose schemes and almost senseless reasoning had more than their fair share of expression. In particular she wanted a closer link with her Sudanese and West African territories and saw the answer in a trans-Saharan railway, a scheme proposed by M. Duponchel, an engineer who considered that it would save endless time in the transportation of goods. The fact that the Americans had succeeded in building a railway across their continent eleven years previously merely gave further impetus to the scheme, which from start to finish was a tragi-comedy.

The three possible routes for the railway were: (1) the route more or less followed by René Caillé in 1828 across the flat expanse of Tanezrouft to the west of Ahaggar; (2) from Laghouat to Ouargla, across some dangerous sand-tracts, and then through the unknown and precipitous Hoggar mountains; (3) the ancient caravan route across the Fezzan from Tripoli to Lake Chad.

The arguments in favour of the Hoggar route, which was chosen by M. de Freycinet, the Minister of Public Works and later Prime Minister of France, were based largely on Duveyrier's reported friendliness of the Tuareg towards the French, and the fact that the extension of French territory as far as Ouargla would enable supplies and assistance to be rendered more quickly and easily. In addition, M. de Freycinet also considered that the Tuareg would welcome these new facilities for trade, and totally ignored both the counsels of a commission that opposed any railway scheme on practical grounds, and the advice of the officers of the Bureaux des Affaires Indigènes, who pointed out that Tuareg preferred to raid rather than trade for their needs.

No consideration at all was given to such practicalities as to how the locomotive would be supplied with water, coal or wood in the midst of this barren desert.

The story of the expedition that left Laghouat in November 1880, under the command of Colonel Flatters, to survey a route through Ahaggar is one of the best known and most gruesome episodes in the history of the Sahara. The expedition consisted of ninety-two men: ten French army officers and engineers; forty-seven Arab soldiers of the Algerian Tirailleurs with two French N.C.O.s and two orderlies; and thirty-one Chaamba guides and cameleers. Colonel Flatters, who was a most unsuitable commander for such an expedition, had already written to the Amenukal, Aitarel, not so much asking for his permission to travel through Ahaggar as more or less announcing his intention to pass through the country regardless of the Tuareg. Aitarel's reply, stating that the column would not be allowed through Ahaggar, was brushed aside contemptuously and the arrogant colonel resolutely headed the column south. By the 10 January the Chaamba guides, who were already alarmed by the lack of definite news from Aitarel, received confirmation of the Tuareg's hostility towards them from a northbound caravan with whom they had made contact. Flatters, however, refused to heed the warnings of his guides, but as they pushed further south towards Ahaggar through the unknown and desolate country even his own officers begged him to show caution. On 25 January, with the black Tassili escarpment on the horizon, they were met by a mounted Tuareg bearing a letter from Aitarel stating that the rider had been sent on his authority to escort the column into Ahaggar. Flatters, naïvely unsuspicious of any treachery, became even more confident as seemingly friendly veiled warriors assured him of Aitarel's friendliness. Only the Chaamba, familiar with the ways of their traditional enemies, remained suspicious of this uncustomary friendliness, and, convinced that they were being led into a trap, begged Flatters to allow them to return home. Flatters refused, but, as they moved deeper into Ahaggar, condescended to post double sentries at night. Eventually, on 16 February, the column was made to change course, and after crossing a stony plain interspersed with patches of sand, they arrived, a little before midday, at a spot where recent rain had left a few pools of water. Here they made camp, but as there was insufficient water for the animals the Tuareg guides suggested that the colonel, with some of his officers and the cameleers, should leave the camp and take the animals to a place called Tadjemout, about two hours away, where there was ample water for the animals and their water-skins. Flatters agreed, and with the Tuareg guides the small party left the main body of men at the camp. His only precaution was to have himself covered by a rearguard of twenty Tirailleurs under an N.C.O.

The colonel had foolishly allowed the column to be divided, and even when one of the Tuareg guides told him that he had been betrayed he still refused to pay attention to the warnings. At the wells the animals were led away to drink and the small party rested in the shade of the tamarisk trees. But the peaceful scene did not last for long. Tuareg, waiting in ambush, charged down on the small party and slaughtered the entire group, hacking most of them to death with their swords, although not before several had fallen under the Frenchmen's desperate fire. The rearguard of Tirailleurs reached the crest of the hill overlooking the wells in time only to witness the final scenes of the massacre. The camels had already been driven off into the mountains and about 100 Tuareg, now armed with the rifles taken from the dead cameleers, had been left to guard the wells. In spite of such odds the N.C.O. in command held his ground, killing several Tuareg, until, with his ammunition running low and casualties mounting, he called off the attack. But with the sound of gunfire attracting ever-increasing numbers of Tuareg the retreat to the main camp was a hazardous business. Under constant harassment ten of the original party fought their way back to join their companions.

For the forty desperate survivors, now under the command of Lieutenant Dianeaux, there was no alternative but to face an almost impossible trek back to the nearest French post – 750 miles away to the north. With no transport each man would have to carry his own rifle, ammunition, water and food supplies, with little hope of replenishment and under constant harassment from the Tuareg shadowing their flanks. When the supply of rice was finished the men began to chew leather; two Saluki dogs accompanying the expedition were killed for meat, and a wild ass was shot and eaten raw.

In their desperate plight many of the Tirailleurs wanted to commit suicide, but the French maintained a degree of optimism which was raised when four stray camels were found and taken to relieve the men of their loads. The column was under constant surveillance from the Tuareg, who even came to sell a few mangey camels for exorbitant sums of money.

The little group of survivors pressed on northwards, but they were still to the south of Amguid, one of the major gorges leading northwards out of Ahaggar, and they knew that such a strategic site, with its abundant water supply, would not be left unguarded. Sure enough, when only a few hours from the gorge, they were approached by Tuareg. To their surprise they did not attack. Instead, one of them came forward and threw down two bags of crushed dates with the promise of sheep on the next day if their price was met.

The starving men had scarcely devoured more than a few mouthfuls when they collapsed on the ground, foaming at the mouth, and raving like maniacs. The crushed dates had been mixed with *efelehleh*,[6] an extremely poisonous plant, which when taken in small doses acts as a nervous stimulant, sending a person completely delirious. I am not certain, but believe this plant is found only in the region of Silet, about 150 kilometres to the west of Tamanrasset, and several hundred kilometres from Amguid. If this is true, it is further indication that the whole massacre was thoroughly planned well in advance. Fortunately, the Chaamba were suspicious of such generosity and did not touch the dates; they were consequently able to subdue their raving colleagues, some of whom had rushed off into the desert never to return, while others, including Lieutenant Dianeaux, in their delirium, were tearing off their clothes and shooting at each other.

Why the Tuareg did not attack their victims when they were in this helpless state is a mystery. We can only surmise whether it was an act of pure sadism, a desire to continue the game of cat and mouse and watch the drawn-out agony; whether it was to prevent any further loss of their own lives in open attack when the remainder of the booty would assuredly be theirs for the taking in a matter of time; or whether it was a carefully designed act of cruelty, which, when reported to the French authorities, possibly by a few 'permitted' survivors, would act as a deterrent against any further violation of their territorial sovereignty. There is of course the possibility, which we shall examine presently, that their action was coloured by intrigue within Ahaggar itself, and designed to vilify or accredit certain factional interests that were developing among the Kel Ahaggar.

The next ploy was to sell the column the promised sheep, but on the condition that responsible men were sent to negotiate the deal. Lieutenant Dianeaux, feeling that they would have some respect for the holy Mokhadem who had been attached to the mission, delegated him and three other men who had not been affected by the poisoned dates to act as emissaries.

The Tuareg were grouped on the edge of a cliff overlooking the Amguid gorge. As the Mokhadem and three Chaamba soldiers approached they were seized and bound, and lined up against the cliff in sight of their companions. The three Chaamba were decapitated in turn. Then, after a short pause, the Mokhadem was split in half from skull to hips with a heavy broadsword.

Lieutenant Dianeaux, although still semi-comatosed, realized that he could do nothing to avenge their deaths as the Tuareg were keeping well out of rifle range, and so ordered the remainder of his men to continue the advance to the precious water in the gorge. As they had suspected, it was heavily guarded and Lieutenant Dianeaux, much to his credit, led a well-organized attack which inflicted heavy casualties on the Tuareg and drove them out of the gorge. In battling to the water, however, Lieutenant Dianeaux gave his life, along with two other Frenchmen and one Tirailleur.

The command of the little group of stragglers now fell on Sergeant Pobeguin, a cavalry N.C.O., who was so ill that he had to be carried on an already overladen camel. Although most of the men were still suffering the effects of the poisoned dates, they somehow staggered relentlessly northwards. On 18 March, almost five weeks after the death of Flatters, they reached one of the camps they had set up in January, where they found the parched remains of a dead camel. The bones and dried skin were all that they now had left to eat, and although they had miraculously struggled this far they knew they could not reach safety unless they found more food.

What happened during the next two weeks reads in the official report like a horror story. Pobeguin, the only surviving Frenchman, was a dying invalid; discipline no longer existed, and each man was on his own. On 22 March several of the men left the camp on the pretext of hunting gazelles. Those who remained behind heard shots and when one of the hunters returned carrying meat it was soon recognized as the flesh of one of their companions, who had been killed and devoured by the starving men. Soon after this first act of cannibalism rifle shots were heard in the night, and at daybreak it was found that a soldier had killed two of his companions in a quarrel. Their flesh was rapidly devoured, and even Pobeguin joined his men in the meal. Cannibalism was now the accepted means of survival; the cook, Private Belkacem, in addition to the task of preparing the meat, took upon himself the role of official executioner. His companions were now specimens of professional interest, and on the following day he summarily executed and roasted two more men. In fear, all eyes stayed pinned on Belkacem, none daring to sleep even for a moment.

Pobeguin was still alive, but only just, and discussion now centred on whether to save him from further suffering and so render assistance to his companions. The thought of butchering a Frenchman elicited considerable discussion, particularly from El Madani, the last surviving Tirailleur

N.C.O., who retained his respect for a Frenchman of superior rank, but Belkacem settled the issue by shooting Pobeguin without further ado.

On the next day they at last came across a nomadic camp where they rested for two days before hiring camels to take them to Ouargla, and on 4 April, about two months after leaving the scene of Flatters's massacre, El Madani led eleven half-dead Chaamba into the town.

What were the motives of the Kel Ahaggar in this ugly episode? In spite of our meagre knowledge of the Tuareg at this time, there are certain pertinent facts which deserve comment. Although France's intentions were a threat to the independence of the Kel Ahaggar, the attack on the Flatters expedition was not organized by the whole *tegehe* as was the war against the Kel Ajjer. On the contrary, the massacre seems to have been the exclusive business of the Kel Rela and Tegehe-Mellet; the Taitok at that time were preoccupied elsewhere with counter-raids of their own. The Kel Ahaggar guarded their territorial sovereignty jealously and it is unlikely that any such expedition would have been allowed free passage through Ahaggar. Moreover, Flatters's route took him directly into the north of Ahaggar, the central territory of the Kel Rela, with perhaps a slight inclination towards that of the Tegehe-Mellet, rather than towards the Taitok territory to the west, which may be an additional reason for the Taitok's non-involvement. What does seem to be particularly relevant, however, is that the actual participants in the massacre seem to have represented an emergent faction within the Kel Rela. By 1900 Ahaggar was split by 'pro' and 'anti' French factions, and there is evidence to suggest that these movements began to organize themselves at the death of El Hadj Akhmed.

It is perhaps a little far-fetched to call El Hadj Akhmed a statesman, but his diplomacy and farsightedness had certainly brought relative peace and stability to Ahaggar. Even at the outbreak of the Ajjer war it seems that he had been reluctant to commit the Kel Ahaggar to battle and only yielded to the pressure of the *tegehe* as a whole. At his death, many of his qualities and much of his wisdom lived on in the person of Khyar ag Heguir, the leader and mentor, if we are to press the analogy, of what might be called the 'El Hadj Akhmed school', which was to be epitomized later in Moussa ag Amastane. Khyar was the son of Lella Tiguent, a granddaughter of Sidi ag Mohammed el Khir.[7] After the death of Khyar's father,[8] Lella Tiguent married El Hadj Akhmed, who took an exceptionally close interest in his stepson; so much so that Khyar grew up under the guiding eye of the great Amenukal and was closely associated with all matters of government. Khyar was very much the protégé of his stepfather, but although he was *agg ettebel* (through his mother), he was not directly in line to succeed to the position of Amenukal, which passed to El Hadj Akhmed's mother's sister's son, Aitarel.

Benhazera states that it was Khyar's ambition to become Amenukal of Ahaggar, and we know that he felt frustrated in this respect and was constantly opposed to Aitarel.[9] Frustration and jealousy no doubt contributed to Khyar's feelings towards Aitarel, but the opposition between them seems to have been more deep-rooted, stemming from a fundamental difference in policy. Khyar condemned the Flatters massacre and even went so far as to communicate his opinion to the French. It is doubtful whether this stance was made out of sheer antagonism towards Aitarel, for there are indications that Khyar might have been prepared to enter into negotiations with the French after the Ajjer war if he had been in command of Ahaggar. The extent to which he advocated a more conciliatory and diplomatic policy towards the French is not known, but any gesture of conciliation by Aitarel might have been regarded as giving weight to Khyar's policy and thus strengthening his position in Ahaggar. I am, of course, indulging in considerable speculation, but I suggest that Aitarel's decision not only to attack Flatters but to execute the attack in such a gruesome manner may well have been influenced by Khyar's opposition. An overwhelming victory over such a large and well-armed force of 'invading Christians', particularly if the number of casualties was relatively low, would have enhanced his position, not only through the prestige to be gained as a great strategist and 'defender' of Ahaggar, but also by reducing the attraction and credibility of Khyar's conciliatory policy.

If I am correct in this surmise then Aitarel must be credited with considerable astuteness, for the action checked any further French encroachment on Ahaggar for nearly twenty years. Furthermore, although a certain 'pro-French' faction still centred around Khyar it held little weight, and Aitarel managed to maintain some semblance of authority over Ahaggar until his death.

There is, on the other hand, the question of how far Aitarel felt he was invoking a 'holy' war. His letter to the Kaimakam of Ghadames,[10] quoted by Schirmer,[11] is particularly interesting in this respect:

> Au nom de Dieu Clément et miséricordieux, écrivait-il, vous nous aviez recommendé de surveiller les routes et de les préserver contre les gens hostiles, c'est ce que nous avons fait. Aujourd'hui ne voilà-t-il pas que les Chrétiens veulent suivre nos routes! Ils sont venus dans l'Ahaggar, mais les gens de cette contrée les ont combattus pour la guerre sainte de la manière la plus

énergique, les ont massacrés et c'est fini. Maintenant, il faut absolument, ô cher ami, que la nouvelle de nos hauts-faits parvienne à Constantinople. On dit que les Chrétiens sont énergiques et batailleurs, donc, ô cher ami, faites parvenir mes paroles à Constantinople et dites en haut lieu que je demande à ce que les musulmans viennent à notre aide pour soutenir la guerre sainte.

This letter, rather than answering the question, makes me even more dubious about Aitarel's motivations. While the Tuareg were certainly intolerant of Christians, or any foreigner or outsider for that matter, they themselves have never been especially devout Moslems, and although there is no reason to doubt the authenticity of the letter, its pious tone is not becoming of a Tuareg and is suggestive of ulterior motivations. My own opinion, which is speculative, is that Islam merely provided Aitarel with a degree of legitimacy and a means to disguise any internal intrigues within Ahaggar. In addition, the letter may well have been designed to gain recognition from important Moslem leaders outside Ahaggar in order to enhance his prestige and status in Ahaggar, as well as to secure foreign support in the case of French reprisals.

If I have speculated on the motives for the Tuareg action, at least the consequences of the massacre are more clear. As far as the French were concerned the shocking outcome of the Flatters expedition put a stop to any further penetration into the central Sahara, at least until the end of the 1890s. In spite of the fact that 400 armed Chaamba from Ouargla were placed immediately at the disposition of the French command, and that Khyar ag Heguir's feelings were known, no reprisal action was carried out against the Tuareg. Such action could have proved acutely embarrassing and difficult for France at the international level, and as M. Belin, the military commander of the Cercle de Laghouat, explained in June 1881, revenge against the Tuareg, in the form of a military operation, would be a hazardous and uncertain business, and the desired results could be achieved just as surely by depriving them of the vital resources which they obtained from Touat. But the realization of this end might have necessitated a prolonged occupation of these oases, an operation which could have dragged on for some time and one which could have hardly been expected to receive much consideration from the government.

French interest in the Tuareg was regenerated in 1887 when the Taitok, on their own initiative, raided the Mouadhi Chaamba, who were French auxiliaries, at Hassi Inifel. Many of the Taitok were taken prisoner and moved by the French to Algiers, where they were detained before being set free. Their capture, however, caused considerable interest and led

Bissuel to undertake a study of the Western Tuareg (Taitok and Kel Ahnet), published in 1888.[12] Also, M. Masqueray, the Director of the 'Faculté des Lettres' at Algiers, became particularly interested in two of the prisoners, Kenan ag Tissi ag Rali and Chekkadh ag Rali, whom he took to Paris in 1889 and introduced to M. Crampel, who was planning to cross Africa from the Congo to the Mediterranean. Crampel decided to take Chekkadh with him as a Tuareg interpreter, but the expedition was massacred in May 1891, a few months after leaving Haut-Oubangui, and Chekkadh was accused of betraying the expedition and instigating the massacre.

The captives were well treated in Algiers and seem to have brought back favourable memories. When Benhazera visited Tacha ag Serada, during his reconnaissance in Ahaggar several years later, he was interested to hear his impressions of his stay in Algiers, and was much amused at seeing him trying to re-enact the reception given by General Poizot, at which the general's niece gave a piano recital to the assembled guests. The piano had obviously made a lasting impression on Tacha for, while humming a tune, he ran his fingers through the sand in imitation of the keyboard.

The real threat to the Kel Ahaggar's independence came in 1899 when the Flamand–Pein expedition pushed southwards to occupy In Salah,[13] followed shortly by the occupation of Tidikelt and the oases of Touat and Guerara. The French occupation of this chain of oases seriously imperilled the Kel Ahaggar, for, as M. Belin had suggested almost twenty years earlier, they were heavily dependent on the oases, with their gardens and palmeries, for many of their food supplies.

The reaction of the Kel Ahaggar to this encroachment was to raid the camps of Arabs under French authority. The Taitok, under their chief Sidi ag Keradji, a veteran warrior, were mainly responsible for these raids. Aitarel, however, was aware of the possibly dangerous consequences of their actions, and tried to restrain them, but with little success, for although Sidi declared his disapproval of such action and expressed his fear of the possible consequences, he maintained that he was being pushed by his people. It seems, however, that Sidi was hoodwinking Aitarel, and that one of the Taitok's motives for the raids may well have been to embarrass Aitarel and implicate their long-standing rivals in French retaliatory action.

Raids on Tidikelt and Touat were not without casualties. In the summer of 1900, the Taitok had raided the Kel Ahem Mellen of the Mouydir and the In R'ar region and had been taught a bloody lesson by Caid Baba, while only a short time later the same Caid heavily counter-raided a group of Ibettenaten and Iforas from the Adrar at the water-hole of Ouallen, about 200 kilometres south of Tidikelt, as they were returning southwards after pillaging the oases of Aoulef and Akabil.

On 10 October 1900, the Kel Rela, who hitherto seemed to have heeded Aitarel's discretion and abstained from these punitive raids, entered into the action by raiding and pillaging eighty camels. Whether Aitarel can be held responsible for this raid is doubtful, for he died in the same month, and his death was to cause far greater turmoil in Ahaggar than any number of incidental camel raids. Aitarel had somehow managed to maintain a degree of centralized authority over Ahaggar in spite of both the Taitok's apparent increase in autonomy during the years since El Hadj Akhmed's death and the opposition faction within the Kel Rela centred around Khyar ag Heguir, but with his death the forces of internal dissent were once again let loose in Ahaggar. The rightful successor was Mohammed ag Ourzig, the son of Aitarel's elder sister (Katouh). Benhazera comments that he was the first in line to succeed as Aitarel no longer had a maternal aunt alive. This statement is particularly confusing as it implies that Mohammed, Ouangadi and El Khoussin could only have succeeded if their mother Tagouzamt was alive (see Fig. 2), but we must conclude that these three were dead at the time of the disputed succession. Mohammed ag Ourzig, however, was old, feeble, and lacking the necessary qualities of leadership, and most of the nobles and all the Kel Ulli preferred Attici, the elder son of Aitarel's younger sister. Whereas Mohammed ag Ourzig did not inspire them with confidence, Attici had a reputation for great courage and energy. He had commanded the Tuareg against the Flatters mission and was vehemently opposed to any peaceful settlement with France.[14]

The most interesting aspect of this dispute is perhaps the reference to the opinion of the Kel Ulli, for this is the first time that we find evidence of their exerting any real influence on the succession. It could perhaps be argued that this was the first time that the rightful successor, on the basis of his descent, was deemed incapable of fulfilling the role, but there is also the more important consideration that the Kel Ulli seem to have acquired much greater military and economic power during the latter part of the nineteenth century. In particular, it seems that they had acquired possession of their own camels as well as more widespread rights over such weapons as the *takouba* (sword), with the result that the Ihaggaren, traditionally a specialized fighting class, no longer held a monopoly over the control of physical force.

Mohammed protested against the choice of Attici and in order to resolve the dispute the fanatical marabout Abidine of the Kunta Arabs, who had come to assist in the 'election', put both hands on his rosary and proclaimed, 'You will be two Sultans with the same title.' He then cut his turban in two and put a half on the head of both Attici and Mohammed ag Ourzig.

The role of Abidine in resolving, or rather inflaming the dispute, is pertinent. He was a dissident of the Kunta and renowned throughout the Sahara for his opposition to the French, and after the capture of Timbuktu had sought refuge in Ahaggar, where he took a wife from amongst the Kel Ahnet. His qualities as a marabout and a warrior enabled him to exert considerable influence on the affairs of Ahaggar, and for over twenty years he operated with fanatical zeal and considerable effectiveness against the French. After naming the two Amenukals, both of whom were known for their anti-French feelings, Abidine campaigned fervently against the French, exhorting the Kel Ahaggar to attack all French or allied caravans passing through their territory, and urging them to break off all ties with Tidikelt, even declaring that the dates were *haram* (forbidden by religion).

The appointment of two Amenukals in Ahaggar merely led to a state of anarchy. In addition to the opposition between the two Amenukals and the consequent breakdown of centralized authority, particularly over the Taitok, who were now acting quite autonomously, the faction that had developed around Khyar ag Heguir was gaining greater adherence, not through Khyar himself, who was now a very old man,[15] but through his nephew Moussa ag Amastane.

Moussa, like El Hadj Akhmed, was a 'foreigner'. His mother, who was *oult ettebel*, had married an Ikerremoien, who, although assimilated into the Kel Rela, were originally from the Southern Tuareg. He had already acquired a great reputation as a warrior for his raids and courageous deeds against the Iwllemmeden and had a considerable influence among neighbouring groups, especially the Iforas in the Adrar, among whom he spent much of his youth. But above all, Moussa had the reputation of being a good and just man, an advocate of peace in the mould of El Hadj Akhmed and his old uncle Khyar, and his emergence as an alternative third force in Ahaggar arose largely from his growing following among the Kel Ulli. They were becoming weary of the tiresome conditions resulting from the embargo on Tidikelt and the dispute between Attici and Mohammed ag Ourzig, both of whom were claiming *tiwse* (annual tribute payments) from them, and they turned increasingly towards Moussa ag Amastane for protection and support.

We can only imagine what the outcome might have been had the Kel Ahaggar been united under a single command, as they were in the Ajjer war. As it was, the factions that divided Ahaggar undoubtedly facilitated the final southward penetration of the French into Ahaggar, and make the final chapter of Kel Ahaggar independence read like a series of 'tribal' or rather 'factional' encounters.

The disunity in Ahaggar during this period was not confined to the Kel Rela drum group. Splinter groups were soon to emerge among the Taitok, the majority of whom, under Sidi ag Keradji, were resolute in their defiance of the French. In October 1900, while the Kel Rela were preoccupied with the death of Aitarel, they had carried out further raids into Tidikelt under the leadership of Amar'l ag Sidi Mohammed ag Mama and El Menir ag Brahim, pillaging camels of the Ulad Ba Hammu and the Zoua of In Salah, which were grazing in the region of In Sokki. This was the same group of Taitok that had suffered at the hands of Caid Baba earlier in the summer and who had in the meantime sought refuge in the Tassili-n-Ajjer. But the following year (June 1901) another group of Taitok, suffering as a result of the break with the oases of Touat, asked the French for pardon, while early the year after Ibedi ag Bassi, chief of the Irechchumen, a small group of mixed origin attached to the Taitok, and Badjhoud ag Makhia, chief of the Kel Ahnet, both wrote to In Salah asking for peace. This defection on the part of some of the Taitok and their dependents left the remainder of the Taitok weakened and isolated in their resistance under the leadership of Aziouel ag Ser'ada and the old chief Sidi ag Keradji.

The Kel Rela, for their part, held no thoughts of submission at this time and in March 1902 a large party, under the command of Baba ag Tamaklast, raided a certain Mohammed ben Msis, from the little oasis of In R'ar, who was an interpreter and guide for the French contingent in In Salah and one of their most important auxiliaries.[16] Mohammed and his sister Fatma were enticed by the Kel Rela into the Oued Telzaghet where they were viciously attacked.

The raid on Mohammed ben Msis had been conceived and engineered by Mohammed ag Ourzig, who had advised Baba to attack the populations of Touat in order to provoke French reprisals against the usurper Attici. As Mohammed ag Ourzig had foreseen, the result of this vicious raid was a state of declared hostility against the Kel Ahaggar. The people of Tidikelt were no longer prepared to suffer the exactions and pillaging of the Kel Ahaggar and they asked Captain Cauvet, the military commander at In Salah, to authorize a punitive expedition. Lieutenant Cottenest, with

100 voluntarily enlisted *meharistes*,[17] left In Salah on 23 March to make a reconnaissance of Ahaggar and inflict a punitive raid on the Kel Ahaggar.[18]

The patrol travelled through the Mouydir and Tefedest mountains to Ideles (23 April), Tazrouk (28 April), Tarhaouhauot (4 May), and on 7 May left Tamanrasset for their return northwards. For a month and a half the Kel Ahaggar had been observing the progress of the expedition. No doubt many of them still remembered the ease with which they had virtually wiped out Flatters's column of ninety-two men, and they finally decided to make their attack at the little cultivation centre of Tit, 40 kilometres north of Tamanrasset. The result of the ensuing battle is well imprinted on the history of Ahaggar. The Kel Ahaggar, consisting mostly of Kel Rela, with many of their Kel Ulli, particularly the Dag Rali, launched a furious assault on the patrol, but although rallied courageously by Moussa ag Amastane, the successive assaults withered before the accurate fire and well-disciplined defence. Over 100 Kel Ahaggar were left dead on the ground, while Cottenest suffered three dead and ten wounded.

The battle shocked Ahaggar. The Kel Ahaggar's notions of their invincibility and their territorial sovereignty had been shattered, and their submission to France can be dated as beginning from that day. The overwhelming defeat left them in a state of depression. Weary from turmoil and fighting, the economic difficulties posed by the occupation of Touat and Tidikelt, and the dissension between the two Amenukals, the Kel Ahaggar turned in their desperation for just and resolute leadership to Moussa ag Amastane, whose desire for peace, military and diplomatic skill, farsightedness and qualities of leadership were already winning the respect of the French.

In the following year, a tour by the Commandant Laperrine, the senior military commander of the Saharan oases, a counter-raid under the command of Guilho-Lohan, and a police visit by Lieutenant Besset to the Ajjer region effectively put an end to any further ideas of continuing the struggle. Although Sidi ag Keradji still remained in refuge with the Kel Ajjer and had actually launched an attack on Lieutenant Besset, Aziouel ag Ser'ada submitted to Laperrine during his tour and, in view of Sidi's stance, was invested by the French with the title of Chief of the Taitok. Finally, in 1904, Moussa ag Amastane, accompanied by many of his followers, rode to In Salah to negotiate peace. He was received with great ceremony and courtesy, and in his negotiations with Captain Metois, the Chef d'Annexe, he guaranteed the cessation of hostilities by the Kel Ahaggar and the security of the trade routes on the condition that France also assured peace to Ahaggar. At In Salah the French authorities invested Moussa with the title of Amenukal. On returning to Ahaggar, however, he did not assert this title, but the Kel Ahaggar, tired of the dissension between Attici and Mohammed ag Ourzig, proclaimed him as Amenukal in his own right.

Sidi ag Keradji, the old Taitok chief, eventually followed in the steps of Moussa ag Amastane and made his way to In Salah, and during the police tour of Ahaggar in the summer of 1905, Captain Dinaux officially invested Moussa ag Amastane in the name of France as Amenukal of Ahaggar, and Sidi ag Keradji as the Amenukal of the Taitok and Kel Ahnet.

The submission of the Kel Ahaggar at last enabled France to link up with her Sudanese territories, and on 18 April 1904 Colonel Laperrine achieved the long-awaited liaison by meeting a Sudanese contingent under Captain Théveniault at the wells of Timaiouine, about 350 miles to the west-south-west of Tamanrasset. The meeting established the frontier between Algeria and French West Africa and another straight line, passing through Timaiouine, was drawn on the map of Africa.[19] There is no record of the Kel Ahaggar ever having been consulted over the location of this frontier, and it deprived them of one of their most valuable pasture areas, the Adrar-n-Iforas, as well as a number of 'tribes' in that area who wanted to remain allied to the Kel Ahaggar rather than the Iwllemmeden Tuareg.[20] Ahaggar's position in the African carve-up was not without loss.

My main concern for the moment is still the question of how far the traditional system of government could be regarded as centralized. It is evident, in spite of our meagre knowledge of Ahaggar society during the nineteenth century, that it is only with considerable qualification that we could refer to the Amenukal as having any real centralized authority and power outside his own drum group for, as we have seen, his control over the Taitok for much of this period was negligible. But the presence of France brought about a profound change in Ahaggar society, not least in the traditional form of government and the position of the Amenukal.

Moussa's submission at In Salah did not bring an end to hostilities, but was rather the first and most important step in the long and turbulent process of pacification. Such inveterate warriors could hardly be expected to lay down their arms immediately, particularly when the battle of Tit had not been avenged. During the next few years there were several incidental attacks against French patrols, in which the Turks, who were still ensconced in surrounding areas, were not without influence. Moussa ag Amastane, however, remained loyal to his word and in 1907, after organizing a raid against Rezkou of the Uraren to avenge the killing of a French *meharíste* and raids on Kel Ahaggar camps, was invested as an officer of the Légion d'Honneur for his services to France.

The policy of France in Ahaggar at this time was to reinforce the authority of the Amenukal, while in Ajjer they strove to demolish the influence of the nobles over their Kel Ulli. This seems to be a clear indication of both the lack of centralized authority in Ahaggar, without which the French could not administer effectively, and their trust and respect for Moussa ag Amastane.

In 1908 the French constructed military forts at Tarhaouhaout (Fort Motylinski), about forty miles south-east of Tamanrasset, and at Ilizi (Fort Polignac) in Ajjer territory. After several more military incidents, especially in Ajjer territory, the details of which are of little importance,[21] French arms brought peace to both Ahaggar and Ajjer by about 1913.

Tranquillity in the French Sahara was very short-lived. Within months of the outbreak of the First World War the fanatical Senussi, pushed by the Turks, were in revolt against the Italian and French 'infidels'. On 23 December 1914 the Italians abandoned their garrison at Ghat just inside the Fezzan border and sought refuge in French territory.[22] With Ghat fallen to the Senussi chief Si Mohammed Lebed (Mohammed el-Abed ben Cherif Mohammed ben Ali es Senussi) and occupied by the dissident Ajjer chiefs, Sultan Ahmoud (of the Imenan), Bubekir ag Allegoui, and I-n-gedezan, the Senussi were poised to attack French Saharan territory.

On 26 February 1916 about 1,000 Senussi, armed with artillery and machine-guns, left Ghat under the command of Sultan Ahmoud and Abdessalem, the Kaimakam of Ghat,[23] to take the French garrison of Djanet. They laid siege to the town and after eighteen days the small garrison of little more than fifty men surrendered. Less than two months later, however (15 May), Djanet was retaken and within another six days the French had reoccupied the little villages of Esseyen, El Barkat and Feouet, and had surrounded the Senussi stronghold of Ghat. But on 30 June, with Ghat under siege, the French column received orders from Paris to cease the campaign and retire.

It can be suggested quite reasonably that it was this extraordinary order from Paris that enabled the Senussi revolt to spread throughout most of the French Sahara. Abdessalem was dismissed by Si Mohammed Labed for allowing this military failure against the French and was replaced as Kaimakam by Bubekir ben Naimi, who set out immediately to avenge this temporary setback. After attacking the French at Tin Iddan he advanced on Djanet, which was evacuated on 23 July.

France's hold on Ahaggar was now gravely endangered. Fort Motylinski was pitifully undermanned and the territory was wide open to the threat from the north-east. France's position in Ahaggar depended on whether the Kel Ahaggar would remain loyal to Moussa ag Amastane and France or go over to the Senussi cause. Senussi from the Fezzan and Ajjer Tuareg rode freely through Ahaggar spreading subversion. France's setbacks on the European front gave them good propaganda; she was not invincible and had already been thrown out of Djanet, and now there was scarcely any defence in Ahaggar.

Although Moussa ag Amastane and many of the older chiefs expressed their loyalty to France the younger men were becoming increasingly impressed by this fanatical Moslem cause. Even Ouksem ag Chikat, whom Charles de Foucauld had taken to Paris only three years earlier, deserted the white 'marabout' and joined the Senussi following. For most of this period Moussa ag Amastane was not in Ahaggar. Senussi dissidents had raided him earlier at Tin Zaouaten (300 miles south-west of Tamanrasset) and taken ten prisoners and 400 camels. After two months he eventually found the rebels and counter-raided them, recapturing all his own camels in addition to those of the raiders. He killed seven men and left the rest to die of thirst! Moussa's hands were effectively tied in the south, where the Senussi leader Kaoucen had succeeded in inciting most of the Tuareg in that region against France.[24]

France's one reassurance came in the summer of 1916. An attack on Fort Motylinski appeared imminent and although it turned out to be a false alarm most of the Kel Ahaggar chiefs expressed their loyalty, while Moussa, already hard pressed 400 miles away in the south, sent eighty mounted warriors to assist in the defence. Throughout 1916 the Senussi threat to Ahaggar increased. After evacuating Djanet the French had suffered further losses in battles at the Oued Ihan, Tabelbalet and Amastane. In late October 300 Senussis captured a supply caravan between Fort Flatters and Fort Polignac, and on 23 December Fort Polignac was evacuated. Ajjer territory was almost completely under Senussi control.

The most treacherous action, however, was the murder of Charles de Foucauld in his bordj at Tamanrasset on 1 December 1916. When peace was finally restored France granted a full amnesty to all the dissidents except the band of thirty-odd men who had been responsible for Foucauld's murder. Captain de la Roche, the commanding officer at Fort Motylinski, had killed several of the band on their way back from Tamanrasset, but when General Laperrine was recalled to the Sahara in the following year he had the names of the murderers circulated to every

French outpost in the Sahara. They were tracked down ruthlessly. Sermi ag Thera, the Tuareg who had fired the fatal shot, was found in 1922 and summarily executed by firing squad, while El Madani, Foucauld's betrayer, who had fled to Libya, was not apprehended until 1944 – twenty-eight years later! In view of his old age and senility he was released.

By 1917 the situation had become critical for France. Although the Senussi revolt was on the wane in the Fezzan, their activity in the French Sahara, combined with locust attacks and drought, brought fears of general uprisings. The entire Ajjer territory was in a state of insurrection. The French had been attacked at Ain el Hadjadj (13 February), Tahebert (17 February) and Temassint (19 February), and convoys were being raided with impunity. Fort Flatters was attacked by Sultan Ahmoud on 9 May, and a convoy was heavily attacked at Hassi Tanezrouft on 12 May. In Ahaggar the situation was becoming equally ominous. In May, the Dag Rali saw their opportunity to avenge the battle of Tit and routed a French column in the Oued Ilaman; while several other incidents, including an attack on a French patrol at In Eker, made France's position in Ahaggar tenuous – so much so that Laperrine, now a general, was recalled from the Somme at the beginning of 1917 to take command of all French Saharan territory.

Laperrine's return to the Sahara gave renewed confidence to the French troops and the turning point came on 2 July when a convoy, reorganized and equipped with modern armaments, heavily repulsed a band of Kel Ajjer at Tadjemout. Hunger was tormenting the Kel Ahaggar and with the French forces rejuvenated and rearmed under Laperrine the dissident Kel Ajjer withdrew from Ahaggar, and Anaba and Souri ag Chikat, two rebellious Kel Rela leaders, asked for pardon. This sudden change in attitude on the part of the Tuareg was further reinforced by Lieutenant Lehuraux's attacks on dissident groups at Tehi-n-Akli, which although insignificant from the overall military point of view had a great effect on the morale of the Tuareg, showing for the first time that the re-equipped French forces were prepared to take the offensive.

In August there was a movement towards submission, and in September Moussa ag Amastane went to In Salah with several Kel Ahaggar chiefs to discuss the terms of pardon, which was granted leniently by the Governor of Algeria to all except Foucauld's assassins.

France's debt to Moussa ag Amastane was considerable. He remained loyal to France when almost all the other Tuareg chiefs, and even some of his close kinsmen, had joined the Senussi uprising, and at In Salah he once again pleaded the case of the Kel Ahaggar in negotiating for their pardon.

During the revolt many of the Isekkemaren and Kel Ulli had acted quite independently and contrary to the commands of Moussa ag Amastane, and nearly all writers have considered this as evidence of the decline in both the Amenukal's authority and the political unity of the drum group.[25] I am inclined to disagree with this conclusion, particularly when we give closer consideration to the circumstances of the uprising. Moussa ag Amastane was away from Ahaggar; the French were suffering setbacks on the European front, and many Kel Ahaggar, of all classes, were subverted by the Senussi activists into doubting both Moussa's loyalty and France's intentions in the Sahara. It was a situation of coercion and distorted information which led to a completely chaotic and capricious pattern of political life. I think, therefore, that it is unjust to cite the events of this disquieting period as evidence of increasing decentralization or any real dissolution of political unity, particularly when we note that the Kel Ulli and Isekkemaren eventually rallied to Moussa ag Amastane when the true facts of the situation were perceived.

The most important and lasting consequence of the uprising was the expulsion of the Taitok from Ahaggar. They had joined Kaoucen in the uprising and sought refuge in Ayr, and when they returned to Ahaggar in June 1918 the French authorities stripped them of their political authority and placed them under Moussa's overall command, not only to punish them for their dissidence but in order to overcome the rivalry between the Kel Rela and Taitok and to reinforce and centralize the authority of the Amenukal.[26] Since then the Kel Rela have held almost exclusive rights as Ihaggaren in Ahaggar, and the authority of the Amenukal, supported and reinforced by the French military administration and no longer disputed by other drum groups, became almost absolute throughout Ahaggar.

The Taitok, stripped of their *ettebel*, progressively abandoned their position in Ahaggar in favour of the south-west. But animosity towards the Kel Rela still continued and in 1935–6, when a few Taitok tents were pitched close to a Kel Rela encampment at the wells of Aloua, a fight broke out which resulted in their chief Mohammed ag Mohammed being gaoled in Tamanrasset. Once again the Taitok felt they had been treated unjustly and they moved more and more towards Niger. By 1938 there were only about thirty Taitok in Ahaggar and in 1945 they became attached to the Niger administration. Their Kel Ulli have remained attached to the Algerian administration, and only a small group of Taitok, who descended from Amr'i ag Mohammed, now live in Ahaggar in the vicinity of Abalessa. According to the 1949 census they comprised nine men, ten women, and fourteen children with ten slaves.[27]

Peace was not restored finally to the French Saharan territories for about three more years, during which time Moussa was actively engaged in assisting the French forces. In the beginning of 1918 he twice raided Kaoucen in Ayr, at Talarak (February) and at Agangan (March), while in October and November he turned his attention towards the Ajjer, assisting contingents of the French Saharan Company from Tidikelt in raiding the camps of dissidents between Djanet and Admer,[28] and in the Anahaf massif in the east of Ahaggar; on 28 October they entered Djanet, but without installing themselves permanently.

At the beginning of 1919 Kaoucen was put to death by Turkish partisans, and in March General Laperrine went to Agades to express his satisfaction at the outcome of the operations against Kaoucen's followers (the Kel Ayr). At the same time the Kel Ahaggar were carrying out raids on the Kel Ajjer. Fort Polignac was reoccupied in February 1920, and in July, following ministerial authorization,[29] Djanet was finally reoccupied with a permanent French garrison. The French installed Moussa as the ruler of Djanet with the sovereign rights formerly held by the Sultan Ahmoud, along with the ownership of all the gardens that were owned by Bubekir ag Allegoui. On 27 July, as the new ruler of Djanet, Moussa led the Kel Ahaggar alongside the French to crush most of the remaining Ajjer dissidents at the Col d'Assakao about thirty miles into the mountains north of Djanet, a site now famous for the cave paintings that have since been discovered there.

At the time of his death on 27 December 1920, Moussa ag Amastane's authority, supported by the French military presence, was unprecedented. Ahaggar was united under his command; he was the ruler of Djanet, and he controlled much of northern Niger. It was during his reign, and primarily as a result of his relationship with France, that the Kel Ahaggar acquired enormous economic resources in the form of the several thousand camels captured by the French from the Kel Ayr and given to Moussa ag Amastane's tribe (Kel Rela) in recognition for his resistance to Kaoucen.

A further important change associated with these events was the Kel Ahaggar's shift in 'socio-economic' orientation away from the Adrar in the south-west to the plains of Tamesna in northern Niger. Overnight, as it were, the political and economic future of the Kel Rela had been assured, but the enormous increase in the size of their camel herds posed other problems. Ahaggar could not carry that number of livestock and the traditional camel grazing areas around Tin Zaouaten and the Adrar-n-Iforas were no longer accessible in view of the new frontier restrictions and the independence of the Iforas. It was at this time that the Kel Ahaggar more or less 'annexed' Tamesna, which, although in Niger, was hardly ever occupied by Niger tribes and formed a sort of no-man's-land between the Northern and Southern Tuareg. General Laperrine condoned this move and may well have seen it as being of strategic value, for Gast mentions that Laperrine left them a number of rifles to prevent any reprisal action by the Kel Ayr.[30] Since that time the Kel Ahaggar have always kept the bulk of their camel herds in the plains of Tamesna, and it is interesting to note that most of the important wells in the region were dug by the Kel Ahaggar – the wells of I-n-Abangerit being the work of the Irregenaten.[31]

# SIX
# NOMADISM AND SEDENTARISM

When the French were at last able to set about the pacification of Ahaggar, after the battle of Tit in 1902, they tended to see Ahaggar society as a sort of feudal hierarchy, with the various classes categorized as either 'white Tuareg' or 'black Tuareg'. By about 1950 'white' and 'black' Tuareg found themselves being reclassified, largely through the influence of certain ethnologists and other outside observers, as 'Tuareg' and 'non-Tuareg'! The distinction between 'white' and 'black' Tuareg arose from an extremely superficial knowledge of the society and was based on the highly dubious criterion of skin colour. This was largely a consequence of a racist notion, which, conscious or not, was in keeping with the ideology of the time.[1] Their reclassification as 'Tuareg' and 'non-Tuareg' was merely a terminological exercise which, if anything, served to validate the status quo maintained by France's traditionalist policy (see Chs. 9, 10).

The so-called 'white' Tuareg consisted of the Ihaggaren (the suzerains or nobles), the Imrad or Kel Ulli (the 'plebeian vassals') and the Isekkemaren. 'Black' Tuareg consisted of the slaves (Iklan, sing. Akli) and the contract cultivators (Izeggaren, Arab Harratin) who began to settle in Ahaggar after the middle of the nineteenth century. Ineslemen, religious men, were classified as 'white', while the Ineden, the blacksmiths, appear for the most part to have been fitted uncomfortably somewhere in between, or regarded as a completely separate 'caste' without receiving much further attention.

Having already discussed the main features of the Ihaggaren, Kel Ulli and Isekkemaren, let us look briefly at these other groups whom we have not yet introduced; namely, the religious men, the blacksmiths, the slaves and the cultivators.

### 'Ineslemen' (sing. 'Aneslem') – 'Marabouts' or Religious Men

Ineslemen or marabouts form the religious class that became established among the various Tuareg groups relatively recently following the advent of Sunni Islam. In Ahaggar, however, they comprise only a few geographically scattered families compared with most southern groups, where they comprise whole descent groups under the leadership of their own chiefs. Their political position and status varies between Tuareg groups: in Ayr, certain Ineslemen *tawsatin* have the same status as the vassals, while others, such as the Iforas in Ajjer, have similar status to the Ihaggaren, except that they have no vassals.[2] In Ahaggar, perhaps because of their paucity of numbers, they can be afforded, for the most part, much the same status as the Iforas of Ajjer.

Ineslemen officiated over certain ritual ceremonies, such as marriages and naming ceremonies, and also held a certain judicial status as arbiters, mediators and advisers in civil disputes and the interpretation of Koranic law. The position of Aneslem could be achieved after the necessary Koranic training and education, but today the term has a broader connotation and is often used to designate any religious person, regardless of whether or not he is a Moslem, such as the Catholic 'Petits Frères de Foucauld'.

The term *ineslemen* should not be confused with *echcherifen* (sing. *echcherif*),[3] for although the two terms are often used almost synonymously the latter means 'descendants of the Prophet' – a status which was often claimed by Ihaggaren families. The pretension to, and utilization of, religious status for secular ends can perhaps be seen in both the 'rise' and 'fall' of the Kel Rela. We have already suggested that the Kel Rela's claimed descent from Tin Hinan might be attributable to their need for enhanced status in establishing themselves as the dominant *tawsit* in Ahaggar. During this century, particularly during the years following French pacification when raiding and warfare were eliminated, and the *temazlayt* relationship disintegrated as the Kel Ulli became more politically and economically independent of the Ihaggaren, the Kel Rela saw not only their nomadic existence but their elevated social status becoming threatened. The tendency of certain Kel Rela families to falsify their genealogies and claim *echcherifen* descent around this time seems to have been a means of acquiring alternative status.

### 'Ineden' (Sing. 'Ened') – Blacksmiths, Artisans

Ineden form an endogamous caste that is found in all Tuareg groups, although among the Kel Ahaggar they are relatively few in number compared with Southern Tuareg groups. Blanguernon, writing in 1955, states that in Ahaggar they numbered only seventeen men, twenty women and forty children, with about ten slaves.[4] Their origin, like that of most groups in Tuareg society, is obscure and according to most traditions they are of Jewish origin.[5]

The Ened in Ahaggar is a glorified general-handyman, and the term 'Kel Ahensowa', which is their most common form of designation, is probably best translated in this sense, for they were in turn armourer, blacksmith, jeweller, wood worker and engraver, and at times healer, herbalist, poet, musician, singer, and general consultant on most matters concerning local traditions and customs, particularly with regard to festive and ceremonial activities. In short, they were essential to the Kel Ahaggar. But while they were admired for their skill and knowledge, they were also looked down upon because of their uncertain origin and skin colour, and resented because of the demands they made on the Kel Ahaggar. These demands stemmed from their alleged mystical power, known amongst the Tuareg of Ayr as *ettama*.[6] The belief in *ettama* is certainly not so widely held among the Kel Ahaggar, but fear of the Ineden's alleged mystical power nevertheless made them reluctant to refuse their claims to 'gifts'.

Ineden families lived either in the cultivation centres or among the Kel Ahaggar, wherever business was best. During the last few years, however, the position of the Ineden in Ahaggar has changed considerably. The development of tourism in Tamanrasset has provided a far more lucrative niche than among the impoverished nomads. While there was one remaining forge among the Dag Rali in Atakor in 1968 I do not believe that any Ineden now live a nomadic existence in Ahaggar. The development of Tamanrasset as a tourist and commercial centre has opened up a new market for them. The growth of a small Ineden community centred around five forges in Tamanrasset, specializing in the manufacture of 'traditional' jewellery and other bric-à-brac made to specification for the tourist market (with occasional excursions into the car repair business), has become a considerable tourist attraction and is now even featured on Algerian travel brochures! But, at the same time, the development of Tamanrasset has also reduced the dependency of both the Kel Ahaggar and the cultivators on the services of the Ineden.

### 'Iklan' (Sing. 'Akli') – Slaves

The social revolution that has taken place in Ahaggar during the last decade has centred, at least from the Algerian point of view, largely on the 'emancipation' of slaves, and the 'liberation' of the Harratin from the impoverishment of the *métayage* system (see below), so that it is consequently not surprising that the whole question of slavery has become a particularly sensitive issue which, so far as most sectors of the population are concerned, is discussed with some reluctance or swept under the carpet altogether. Quite innocent questions have resulted in more than one passing traveller having to leave the region.

Let us turn from the complexities of the contemporary scene for a moment and look briefly at the position of slaves in traditional society. The etymological meaning of *iklan* may derive from a *k-l* root meaning 'to be black',[7] and refers to their skin colour, for they are Negroes, originally brought to Ahaggar by raiding expeditions in the Sudanese regions. According to the various estimates and census figures of the late 1940s (see Appendix I), they numbered about 1,700 compared with a Kel Ahaggar population of about 4,300. Although they comprised about a quarter of the total nomadic population in Ahaggar, this ratio was not reflected uniformly among the various Kel Ahaggar *tawsatin* as nearly half of them were owned by the Kel Rela and Dag Rali, who were both outnumbered by their slaves (see Appendix I).

Slaves belonged to their masters. They were their personal property and could be regarded as part of their personal wealth in the same way as livestock in that technically they could be bartered or used as an exchange commodity. They constituted a viable labour force at the disposal of their masters. But although he was an essential component of the economic system, a slave had no means of gaining any control over the processes of production, for the means of acquiring and transmitting wealth, the fruits of his labour, were denied him by his juro-political status, by which he held no rights of inheritance or ownership. The slave could hold certain usufruct rights over livestock, given to him by his master, but these merely provided him with the means of ensuring or contributing to his own subsistence without in any way prejudicing his master's political authority over him; for the slave could never acquire rights of ownership to these assets in either the jural or economic sense, as these rights were vested exclusively within the corporate body of the *tawsit*.

Although their juro-political status defined them as an economic resource and an object of inheritance, slaves lived in a very close and affective relationship with their masters and might be described more aptly as permanent domestics. Slaves were integrated into Kel Ahaggar society on the basis of fictive kinship ties in such a way that they were the fictive children of their masters – an aspect of 'slavery' that was rarely appreciated by the Algerian authorities in their policy of emancipation. Kel Ahaggar of both sexes were slave owners and were addressed as father (*abba*) or mother (*anna*) by their respective slaves. This system was extended in such a way that a slave addressed all kinsmen of his or her owner in the same way as if he were a real child. For example, all the owner's brothers and sisters who would normally be addressed as classificatory parents by the real children were also addressed as *abba* or *anna* by the owner's slaves. Similarly, a slave addressed his owner's real children as brothers or sisters. This fictive kinship relationship was most clearly illustrated in the case of slave marriages, at which the owner of a slave paid the bride-wealth to the owner of the slave-girl being married. This obligation of bride-wealth payment applied to both male and female slave-owners, so that a Kel Ahaggar woman was responsible for making or receiving bride-wealth payments associated with the marriages of her individual slaves. Upon marriage, the slave's wife (*taklit*) became the fictive daughter-in-law of the slave's owner, and a form of avoidance similar to that among the Kel Ahaggar, but probably not so strict, was maintained. This domestic affiliation of slaves is further illustrated by the observation made by Nicolaisen that the Kel Ahaggar's custom of giving a pair of sandals to the spouse's father's sister's son, or other cross-cousin, on marriage, was, in the case of slave marriages, given by the slave to the real son of the slave-girl's owner's sister.[8] The slave thus belonged to a family, and through the intermediary of the family to the *tawsit*: a slave belonging to a Kel Rela would call himself Kel Rela and adopt the same behaviour towards a slave of a vassal *tawsit* as would his master towards a member of that *tawsit*.

The treatment of slaves seems to have been particularly good. Although they could technically be sold or exchanged as a form of payment, this seems to have been extremely rare, at least in European times, and normally they were inherited within the 'family', although Nicolaisen records that a slave-girl customarily formed part of the bride-wealth payment – at least until a few years before his research during the 1950s.[9] The relationship between slave and owner appears to have contained a considerable degree of affection, for not only was corporal punishment extremely rare, but intermarriage was relatively common. Nicolaisen records witnessing only two instances of corporal punishment and both in a very mild form.[10] This relatively good treatment could to some extent be attributed to the right of the slave to change masters. If a slave wanted to change masters he could do so by cutting the ear of a camel belonging to the man whose slave he wished to be. The meaning of this symbolic action was that a slave-owner was responsible for his slave's actions and was obliged to give the slave in recompense for the damaged camel. A man's treatment of his slaves influenced the esteem in which he was held and in such an instance the new owner would gain considerable prestige while the former owner would be the subject of ridicule. In Ahaggar society, where status and prestige are all-important, such a sanction provided the slave with the means of redress in the event of his ill-treatment.

It might seem from this description of slavery and the position of slaves in traditional society that marriages between Kel Ahaggar and their slaves would have had disruptive implications, but in fact such marriages were more common than marriages between Ihaggaren and Kel Ulli.[11] Let us look at the implications of such marriages, bearing in mind that, according to the colonial classification, marriages between Ihaggaren and Kel Ulli were between 'Tuareg' and 'Tuareg' while those between Kel Ahaggar and their slaves were between 'Tuareg' and 'non-Tuareg', or 'white' and 'black' Tuareg. A man could legally marry his slave, even though she was a fictive daughter, without any loss of status. Furthermore, since she was effectively excluded from the political sphere, there was no threat to the political structure. The children of such a marriage were called *iburelliten* (mulattoes) but their social status is not clear. Bourgeot states that in Ahaggar they were classified as 'free men', but with a status intermediate between vassals and their dependents – that is, their slaves and the Izeggaren (Harattin).[12] I do not believe, however, that there was any fixed rule governing their status and position, which within certain limits seems to have been determined more by their personal qualities and achieved characteristics. Nicolaisen states that in Ayr the children of such marriages would not be considered as mulattoes but had the right to be considered as true Tuareg, although in the case of disagreements and disputes they were likely to be referred to by one of the various terms for mulattoes.[13] There is evidence to suggest that in the case of such marriages a Tuareg man would seek the recognition of his wife and her children by the payment of a high bride-wealth, and Nicolaisen records a case of a Kel Ahaggar (he does not mention whether he was Ihaggaren or Imrad, although the latter is implied) marrying a mulatto girl and paying a bride-wealth of seven camels, customary for a noble Tuareg, although the payment according to traditional rules should not have exceeded one camel.[14] A further aspect of such marriages which safeguarded the political structure was that as descent group membership and succession were reckoned matrilineally, the offspring were consequently denied access to the *ettebel* of their father's *tawsit*. It was possibly for this reason, and the fact that slaves did not have the means to raise the necessary bride-wealth, that marriages between slaves and Tuareg women were unknown.

Although the extensive changes in the traditional form of the class structure during the last few years make it difficult to clarify this issue, it does seem that the position and status of the mulatto was largely determined by personal qualities, for as Nicolaisen remarks: if a man is wise, rich and generous, or if he is a marabout, all Tuareg will be ready to associate with him on equal terms even though he be predominantly negroid.[15]

One of the most interesting marriages, or series of marriages, between Tuareg and slave-girls focus on the rivalries between certain Kel Rela for the love of Dassine, a Kel Rela, whose beauty and intelligence were such that men would come from all over the country to court her. She was a close friend of Charles de Foucauld, and not only renowned as the 'belle' of Ahaggar, but a woman of considerable influence in the affairs of the country. Her first marriage was to Bouhen ag Khebbi ag Adebir, the brother of Amayas. Both Aflan and Moussa ag Amastane, the now almost legendary Amenukal (1905–20), continued to court her, and she soon left Bouhen without bearing him any children to marry Aflan. Moussa, anguished by this rejection, refused to touch another Tuareg woman and took two slave-girls as wives. Bouhen also took two slave-girls (Raeraou and Rahmadu) as wives after Dassine had left him.

Bouhen's descendants now extend over three generations. From the ten children produced by Raeraou and Rahmadu I have been able to trace eighty-five living descendants, living mostly in the Tazrouk–Ideles–Hirafok areas. In spite of their mulatto origin, many of them claim to be Kel Rela. Within their specific social sets some of them have certainly achieved a slightly more elevated social status, but, it would seem, as a result of their personal qualities rather than their alleged noble descent, for amongst the true Kel Rela they are held in derision and usually referred to quite uncompromisingly as 'Noirs'!

Slavery, as I have described it here in its traditional form, had undergone significant changes even before Algerian independence. Particularly during the later years of French occupation, the economic constraints imposed on the Kel Ahaggar made it increasingly difficult for them to obtain sufficient food products to support their slaves. The strategy adopted to overcome this problem was simply to 'free' slaves and transfer them to the gardens in the cultivation centres, where they joined the

Izeggaren (Harratin) in the sedentary agricultural community. This was not merely a question of sending slaves to work in the gardens; rather they were freed from their position as slaves and became reclassified as Izeggaren, who, as will be discussed below, were dependent clients of the Kel Ahaggar, but to whom the Kel Ahaggar had relatively few obligations. Although this process became fairly widespread during the last decade or so before independence, it seems to have occurred sporadically in earlier times, and the term *iderfan*, which derives from the verb *derfu* (to be freed), is widely known, though not often used to designate freed slaves.[16] Thus, by 'freeing' a slave, the owner was relieved of the burdensome obligation of supporting him while the continued production of his gardens was assured. Furthermore, the manumission of a slave by no means diminished either the owner's effective authority over him or his control over the processes of production, for as we shall see the Kel Ahaggar's authority and rights of ownership were asserted through other ties and in multifarious forms.

## 'Izeggaren' (Sing. 'Azeggar'; Arab. 'Harratin', Sing. 'Hartani') – Cultivators

The word *izeggaren*, which derives from the verb *ihwar* (to be red), refers to the dark colour of their skin, and is used to designate the dark-skinned Harratin cultivators, who came into Ahaggar from the oases of Touat and Tidikelt in increasing numbers after the mid-nineteenth century, as well as the freed slaves mentioned above. It is also used commonly, but incorrectly, to designate the 'white skinned' Ahl Azzi (Merabtines) from Touat and Tidikelt, many of whom also came to Ahaggar as cultivators on behalf of the Kel Ahaggar around this time.[17]

The Harratin did not begin to settle in Ahaggar until after 1861, when the Amenukal, El Hadj Akhmed, invited cultivators from Touat and Tidikelt to come to Ahaggar to develop and work gardens on behalf of the Kel Ahaggar. Before that date there was no cultivation in Ahaggar, although some diffident cultivation had been attempted near Ideles about twenty years earlier (*c.* 1840).

On arriving in Ahaggar the Harratin settled around the water-points in the major valleys to cultivate the more fertile land for the Kel Ahaggar. By the end of the century they numbered only a few hundred, but with the attraction of the cultivation centres (*arrems*), the climate, and the relative stability ensuing from French pacification, they immigrated to Ahaggar in increasing numbers during this century and have come to outnumber the Kel Ahaggar by nearly two to one. The position of the Hartani in Ahaggar was that of a dependent client. He worked the land on a contract basis by which he was entitled to one-fifth of the harvest. The details and various modifications of this contract system, known as *khamast* (from the Arabic word *khamsa*, meaning five) will be discussed later (Ch. 9); but, while technically a 'free' man, the condition of the Hartani, or *khames* as he was called, could be described in degrees of poverty – at least until the last few years of French occupation when the accelerated development and exploration of the Sahara provided him with the opportunity to join the emergent labour force. Although the *khamast* system entitled him to one-fifth of the produce his net return was usually far less than this as a result of the improvisions and demands made upon him by the Kel Ahaggar landowner.

In traditional society the Harratin were regarded as the lowest status group, not only because of their skin colour and origin, but primarily because they were despised and held in contempt by the Kel Ahaggar for their menial work. There was no intermarriage between Kel Ahaggar and Harratin, and contact between them was limited almost exclusively to the economic sphere. They comprised a separate community of dependent clientele—the sedentarists—alongside the Kel Ahaggar, but subjected to the laws of Ahaggar and the supreme authority of the Amenukal. The Kel Ahaggar's contempt for the Harratin was reciprocated by resentment which, by the time of Algerian independence, was becoming vocalized on a broad front.

In the broadest analysis these various groups can be categorized as two main classes – free men and dependents.

The term *elelli* (pl. *ilellan*) refers to a man who is free by birth or emancipation (from slavery).[18] We can thus refer to all men except slaves as *ilellan*, but in a more specific sense we understand a 'free man' to be any individual who participates, or who has the right to participate, in the society's political life, and who has some measure of control over the acquisition and utilization of the means of production. In this sense the class of 'free men' comprised the Ihaggaren, Kel Ulli, Isekkemaren, as well as the Ineslemen and Ineden; while the Iklan and Izeggaren formed the dependent class.

This structural analysis or schema of Ahaggar society is a considerable refinement on the earlier 'white'/'black', 'Tuareg'/'non-Tuareg' classifications, but is still essentially a further imposition of our own concepts and categories. It is an analytical construct of the anthropologist which, albeit meaningful to our subjects, is not necessarily identical with their own conceptions of their society. It is apposite that while the term *ilellan* denominates the class of 'free men', there is no specific term in *Tamahak*[19] that denominates the class of 'dependents'. We see that the terminology tends to speak in terms of political class and status rather than economic criteria, so that Iklan and Izeggaren are classified indigenously as separate social groups on the basis of their politico-jural status and profession respectively, rather than as a class of 'dependents', for the conceptualization of such a class rests on economic criteria – namely, the position of the Iklan and Izeggaren in the process of production and the overall relations of production, which are extraneous to the indigenous system of classification.

This is not to imply that the Kel Ahaggar perceived their society as being 'structured' merely in terms of ranked 'political' statuses. On the contrary, it seems that their system of classification was based implicitly on 'life-styles' relating to specific 'economic formations'.

In looking at Ahaggar society since the earliest time we see, not only the immigration of different social and ethnic groups during particular periods, but also an associated modification in the various modes and relations of production. In prehistoric times we assume the existence of a Berber-speaking goat-breeding and hunting community – the Isebeten, who were later conquered and submitted to the dominance of a camel-breeding Berber-speaking people. Sometime, presumably after the immigration of this camel-breeding nobility, slaves were brought back to Ahaggar from raiding expeditions in the Sudanese regions. Not until relatively recently, however, did the cultivators settle in Ahaggar, so that Ahaggar society, prior to the middle of the last century, consisted only of the Ihaggaren, Kel Ulli, Isekkemaren, and their slaves, along with a few Ineden and Ineslemen families.

At the time of the French arrival at the beginning of this century the cultivators were still few in number and it is perhaps natural that these first outside observers, confronted by the nomadic Tuareg and their Negro slaves, should classify the society into 'white' and 'black' Tuareg. After all, they all spoke the same language, wore similar dress, lived the same nomadic way of life, and lived together in the same camps as 'masters' and 'slaves'.

During this century the cultivators have not only increased greatly in number, but the pluralist nature of Ahaggar society has been augmented by the immigration of other smaller non-Tamahak-speaking groups: the Arabic Chaamba who arrived initially as French auxiliaries and later acquired certain land rights; maraboutic (*cheurfa*) religious families who followed the French 'push' south and attached themselves in greater numbers to various Tuareg groups; and the merchants who came into the region after the establishment of Tamanrasset as an administrative and commercial centre. These merchants were predominantly Mozabites from the five cities centred around Ghardaia in the Oued Mzab in the northern Algerian Sahara.

How did the Kel Ahaggar perceive these immigrating groups? Broadly speaking, and perhaps not surprisingly, it seems to have been in terms of a 'we'/'they' distinction. The 'we' were the traditional or pre-cultivating population of Ahaggar – that is the constituent groups of Ihaggaren, Kel Ulli, Isekkemaren, Iklan and the few Ineden and Ineslemen, who referred to themselves collectively within this ensemble as 'Imuhag'. The 'they' comprised the later in-migrating groups of Izeggaren (cultivators) and the other predominantly Arabic-speaking minorities. This rather heterogeneous 'they' was characterized by two features: Tamahak was not their mother tongue, and they settled for the most part in the growing cultivation centres. They came to be referred to collectively as 'Kel Arrem', meaning literally 'the people of the gardens', or in other words sedentarists as opposed to nomads.

This distinction tends to suggest an opposition between life-styles – namely between nomadism and sedentarism. If this is so, then we might expect the total population of Ahaggar, prior to the arrival of the first cultivators in the middle of the last century, to have referred to themselves collectively as Imuhag, perhaps synonymously with Kel Ahaggar or Kel Tagelmoust (people of the veil). However, such a supposition overlooks the possibility of any changes in the meaning or meanings of Imuhag.

Among the Tuareg and other Berber-speaking groups there is a general phonetic shift between *h* (Ahaggar), *z* (Morocco and Algeria), *ch* (Adrar and Sudan regions), and *j* (Ayr), so that it is legitimate to see the terms *imuhag* (Ahaggar), *amazig* (Morocco/Algeria), *amajeg* (Ayr), and *amacheg* (Adrar and Sudan) as being homologous and deriving ultimately from the Berber root *MZG*. There is a general consensus among those linguists who have studied the various Tuareg languages[20] that *imuhag* is the noun derived from the verb *aheg*, meaning 'to raid' or 'plunder'. The most pertinent etymological analysis of *imuhag* is that presented by Clauzel,[21] who points out that this interpretation, based as it is on the general tendency among Berber languages of prefixing the verb stem with *m* to attain the noun (e.g. *imuhag* = *m* + *aheg*), provides a tempting but not necessarily definitive linguistic explanation. Clauzel raises two questions. He admits that while Tuareg are able to tell a questioning European, through a few linguistic riddles and puns, that their name means 'raiders', he finds it difficult to conceive why a people would designate themselves in such pejorative terms. Such a term might be applied to one's enemies or rivals, and one could easily understand Arabs referring to Tuareg in such a way – but surely not the Tuareg themselves? In addition, among the Kel Adrar, the verb *aheg* has the identical phonetic form as in Ahaggar, although the noun *imuhag* changes phonetically to *amacheg* in Adrar. If *amacheg* really does derive from the verb *aheg*, why, he asks, should there be a change in the noun and not the verb from which it derives? Clauzel's reticence on the first point is not warranted and can be safely discarded as an ethnocentric value judgement – for among the Tuareg, raiding was a highly prestigious, indeed, one might suggest, an honourable pastime!

Unfortunately we have a minimal amount of information on the usage and meaning of *imuhag* before the time of Duveyrier (1864), but on the basis of this etymology, and by analysing the usage of the term among the Kel Ahaggar and other Tuareg groups, we can make certain suggestions on the polysemic nature of the term and its possible changes in meaning over time.

In Ahaggar, the term *imuhag* is used in a general sense to designate anyone whose language is Tamahak, or in other words the inner 'we' which comprised the totality of traditional, or, more specifically, pre-cultivating society, but not bilingual persons such as Izeggaren and other immigrant groups whose mother language was not Tamahak. Kel Ahaggar (Imuhag) themselves state that any person who speaks Tamahak is an Imuhag.[22]

This is not surprising, since among the Berber languages a particular language or dialect is usually designated by the feminine form of the name of the people who speak it – so that, for example, we see that the Imuhag of Ahaggar call their language Tamahak; the Imajaren of Ayr call their language Tamajek; the Arab language is referred to as Tarabt and so on. This historical and morphological association between the name of the language and the people is seen even more clearly in the Adrar and Ṣudan where Tuareg groups frequently designate themselves as Kel Tamachek, meaning literally 'the people who speak the language Tamachek'. It could be suggested that the indigenous goat-breeding population adopted the language or dialect of the conquering Ihaggaren. Suggestive evidence for this is provided by the inscriptions on early rock paintings in a script similar to Tifinagh, which appears to be a Berber language but is unknown to the present population, and the tendency for a subjected people to adopt the language of the dominators. But although the term *imuhag* is used in Ahaggar to designate all those Tuareg, whoever they may be, who speak Tamahak, this same general meaning is not found among all Tuareg groups. In Adrar and towards the Niger Bend, for example, the word *amacheg*, which is homologous to *imuhag* in Ahaggar, is not used like the latter in the general sense of 'all Tuareg, whoever they are', but in the more restricted meaning of 'a noble Tuareg of a *tawsit* whose warrior qualities and predominance have been recognized and undisputed for a long time'.[23] In Ayr, the word *amajeg* is equivalent in its broader meaning to *imuhag*, as in Ahaggar, but in a more restricted meaning is equivalent to *amacheg*, as in the Adrar and Sudan. Thus, in Ayr, we must determine from the context whether the term is used to designate any Tuareg or a noble Tuareg.

Does this polysemic aspect exist in Ahaggar? K. G. Prasse, writing as recently as 1959,[24] elaborates on the etymology of *imuhag* and suggests that by inference it applies to the nobles, or, to be more specific – the Ihaggaren. But this inference was not made by either Foucauld or Benhazera, although Foucauld does say that the word Tuareg has two distinct meanings for the Arabs of Tidikelt; namely, 'nobles' and 'Tuareg of all classes'. Neither is Prasse's inference substantiated by present customary usage of the term, which seems to have only the broader meaning – in spite of the linguistic efforts of the nobility to satisfy the enquiries of European etymologists!

In certain Tuareg groups, however, such as the Kel Ayr and Kel Adrar, the term does appear to designate the 'nobility' in its restricted meaning, and perhaps this was also the case in Ahaggar in earlier times.

If we accept the original meaning of *imuhag* as deriving from the verb *aheg* (to raid), then the restricted meaning of the word to designate the Ihaggaren, who until fairly recently held exclusive control over the means of physical force, is clear. The extended usage of the term may thus be explained in terms of the extension of this control to the vassals, who, by the beginning of this century, and probably earlier, could be counted as warriors in their own right.

Alternatively we may see the extension of *imuhag* to include the Kel Ulli, the Isekkemaren and their slaves as an ideological expression, not merely of the distinction between the traditional 'pastoral-cum-raiding' economic formation and agriculture, and the subordination of the Kel Arrem to the Imuhag, but of an opposition between life-styles, between nomadism and sedentarism. This opposition was most clearly manifested in the case of freed slaves and the absorption of foreign nomads. Freed slaves who settled in the cultivation centres as Izeggaren were no longer classified as Imuhag but as Kel Arrem. On the other hand, the few who managed to establish themselves in a nomadic-pastoral way of life were still referred to generally as Imuhag. Similarly, a few immigrant Arab nomads, such as the Ahl Azzi (called Kel Rezzi), who married into, and settled with, certain Kel Ahaggar groups, have come to be referred to as Imuhag.

In other Tuareg societies, where either agriculture had been established for a much longer period of time or 'immigrant' groups had been longer settled, this distinction may not have been so pertinent.

# SEVEN
# DESCENT, CLASS AND MARITAL STRATEGIES

One of the first and most lasting impressions gained by Europeans of the Tuareg was of the beauty and elegance of their women and their prominent roles in social life. The impression was perhaps made stronger by the contrast with the Arabic societies to the north: the women of Ahaggar were neither veiled nor secluded. They owned slaves and livestock in their own right; the camp was their domain, and they were largely responsible for most of its affairs – the tendance of goats, the preparation of food, the education of children, and many other aspects of its organization; while even beyond the confines of the domestic environment they were the foci of much of social life.

They were the 'poets' and musicians of society. Battles, raids, the valour of the menfolk, other significant deeds and love stories were composed and recorded in verse and then recited in song to the accompaniment of their *imzads* – the one-string violin. The news of an *ahal*, as these recitals were called, would attract men from far afield, particularly when performed by an accomplished woman. Mounted on their finest riding camels and adorned in their most splendid robes, men would converge from all over Ahaggar. One Kel Rela once told me how he had ridden seventy miles in a day so as not to miss an *ahal* being given by a particularly beautiful woman. For a young man an *ahal* was an occasion of great social significance, where he could court the girl of his fancy and pronounce his worth as a potential husband, while for a woman it was also an opportunity to print her reputation indelibly on Ahaggar. As the evening progressed the intensity and tempo of the *ahal* increased until well into the night and early hours of the morning, with casual flirtations and courting giving way to the intimacies of mild love-making.

Men would go to untold pains to attract the attentions, let alone the hearts, of the 'noble' beauties of Ahaggar, for they were held in high esteem and were not without influence. Such a woman was Dassine, the 'belle' of Ahaggar at the time of the French arrival. Divorced, and then courted by most eligible Ihaggaren, she not only rejected the proposals of Moussa ag Amastane but was a close friend and companion of Charles de Foucauld.

But while such romantic features of Tuareg life perhaps enabled the European to identify more closely and readily with the Tuareg than the Arabic societies to the north, they also tended to emphasize and focus attention on the fundamental significance of women in Tuareg society, which was that group membership and rights of succession to political office were transmitted matrilineally.

Most literature on the Kel Ahaggar consequently describes them, without qualification, as a matrilineal society, while some writers, such as Murdock,[1] have gone so far as to describe Kel Ahaggar society as a 'matriarchy'. Murdock concludes that the ancestral Tuareg, while still resident in Tripolitania, were patrilineal like all other mainland Berbers, and that the matriarchate, as he calls it, was developed as an adjustment to special local conditions after their displacement into the Sahara.[2] The existence of a pre-Islamic patrilineal system in the ancestral tribes can be neither proved nor disproved, but most writers on the Tuareg tend to uphold the view that matrilineal traits are very ancient.[3,4]

In fact, as this chapter shows, the extent to which the Kel Ahaggar can be regarded as matrilineal is questionable, for descent, at the ideational level, and among both classes, is effectively bilineal. But when the focus is directed on the class structure, and the extent to which each class has manipulated the rules of descent, largely through the adoption of different marital strategies, it is seen that the nobility are predominantly matrilineal, while the vassals are fundamentally patrilineal.[5]

The social organization of the Kel Ahaggar centres around the general arrangement of three specific structures; the basic residential (domestic) group (*ariwan*); the descent group (*tawsit*); and at the highest level of inter-class relations, the drum group (*ettebel*).

The structure and organization of the drum group have already been discussed. The *tawsit*, however, has only been defined in very general terms as a preferentially endogamous, territorially compact, matrilineal descent group, while the domestic group has not been defined except within the very vague context of 'camps'. The omission in defining these two fundamental groups in earlier chapters has been deliberate, for their definition is dependent on an understanding of the class structure, and particularly the ways in which the two classes have manipulated the rules of descent in terms of their specific political and economic interests.

## The Ariwan

During the last decade or more, particularly since Algerian independence, nearly all the Kel Rela (nobles) have abandoned a 'camp life' and have settled in the rapidly growing administrative centre of Tamanrasset, and one or two other villages. The *ariwan* is consequently now found only among those Kel Ahaggar, notably the Kel Ulli, who have persisted in their nomadic-pastoral state.

*Ariwan* means literally a small camp of up to about five or six tents. A tent usually comprises one nuclear family. However, slaves seem to have lived in separate tents,[6] so that a camp of five tents may only comprise two or three such families. In fact, the word for a tent, *ehen*, not only refers to the actual tent itself, but its material contents (domestic utensils, etc.) as well as the people (and their animals) who usually live in it. In this wider sense *ehen* means 'a wife', and by further extension of meaning 'a marriage', for it is the marriage which establishes the nuclear family and the 'tent' as a basic structural unit. Thus, when one speaks, for example, of Mohammed's tent (*ehen*), one is referring implicitly to his wife, children, domestics (ex-slaves), the livestock belonging to these people, the domestic utensils such as churning bags, millet bags, pestles, mortars, quern stones, and so forth, and all other people, livestock, and things, that usually accompany him. Each such 'tent' (i.e. nuclear family) is thus a self-contained and self-supporting unit, having, as the Kel Ahaggar themselves say, 'its own churning bag and its own millet bag'.

'Tents' camping together (to form an *ariwan*) are usually related through agnatic ties. Residency, as we shall see below, is predominantly patrilocal, and most *ariwan* usually comprise a patriline of about three generations in depth, centring around a structural core of male agnates (often brothers, or male paternal parallel cousins).

The size of the *ariwan* is flexible, being determined primarily by prevailing pastoral conditions. With a deterioration of pasture an *ariwan* of four tents may split into two smaller units (also called *ariwan*) and move some distance apart to eke out pasture, while in times of especially good pasture several such *ariwan* may come together to form a larger camp. In such good conditions large camps (called *amezzar* and not *ariwan*) may consist of ten to twenty tents and comprise the whole *tawsit* section (defined below).[7]

Although well adapted to variations in pastoral conditions in terms of their flexibility, most *ariwan* tend to remain fairly constant in their composition over long periods of time, 'splittings' and 'comings together' being temporary adjustments to exceptional pastoral conditions. For example, I believe that the last time large 'section camps' formed in Ahaggar was in the 1950s. The usual or 'normal' *ariwan* thus tends to consist of two or three agnatically related nuclear families who camp together and co-operate in goat-breeding and other domestic tasks.

## The Tawsit

The term *tawsit* is not translated so easily, for although the *tawsit* has the same ideational form among both classes, and is defined ideationally by both of them as a matrilineal descent group, in practice its actual structure differs quite considerably between the two classes.

Throughout this century there has effectively been only one noble *tawsit* in Ahaggar, namely that of the Kel Rela, which comprises a matrilineal descent group of about 275 individuals, nearly all of whom can trace their descent matrilineally from Kella, the wife of Sidi ag Mohammed el Khir, who lived about nine generations ago.

Kel Ulli *tawsatin* differ from that of the Kel Rela in several respects. Firstly, few vassals can trace their descent, through either line, beyond about four generations. Secondly, and as we shall see below, matrilineality, although emphasized at the ideational level, tends to be 'played down' among the Kel Ulli in terms of their actual social organization. Indeed, the actual structure and social organization of Kel Ulli *tawsatin* is now predominantly patrilineal. Thirdly, the various marital strategies adopted by both classes (to be discussed below) have resulted in a high rate of *tawsit* endogamy among both classes. While about 75 per cent of all Kel Rela marriages are endogamous within the *tawsit*, this figure is even higher among Kel Ulli *tawsatin*. Among the Kel Ulli *tawsit* of the Dag Rali for example, who number about 400, and whom we shall consider in detail presently, the endogamy rate is about 95 per cent. One consequence of this almost total *tawsit* endogamy is that although descent group membership is determined matrilineally, the actual question of *tawsit* membership rarely arises. Thus, in practice, the Dag Rali, and I believe most other Kel Ulli *tawsatin*, can be regarded more as a cognatic descent group. Fourthly, the Kel Ulli *tawsatin*, unlike the Kel Rela, are localized descent groups. While the nobility held rights over the entire territory of their drum group, which in the case of the Kel Rela was extended to cover the entire country of Ahaggar, the Kel Ulli *tawsatin* held corporate rights over specifically defined territories within the overall territory of the drum group. Only in the event of drought conditions and pastoral impoverishment, and with the authorization of the Amenukal (or drum chief), did Kel Ulli move temporarily outside their own *tawsit* territory.

All *tawsatin*, of both classes, are divided into a number of 'sections'. Among the Kel Rela there were nine such 'sections', of which only three were numerically and politically significant. Recruitment was based on matrilineal descent, and the three dominant 'sections' form matrilineages of about eight to nine generations in depth. Kel Ulli 'sections', unlike those of the Kel Rela, form clearly defined local groups. Among the Dag Rali, there are four sections, each numbering about 80–100 individuals.[8] But although they are defined ideationally in the same way as the Kel Rela 'sections', in terms of matrilineal descent, in practice, as we shall see later, the 'section' is merely the higher level structural equivalent of the *ariwan* – a patrilineally organized local residence group.

## Modes of Descent (The Rules)

The frequent description of the Kel Ahaggar as 'matrilineal' only makes sense when we stop trying to classify them in terms of one single principle of descent[9] and look instead at the whole complex of rights and their respective rules of transmission. When we analyse descent in this way, in terms of its components of group membership, succession, inheritance and residency, we are confronted with a more complex system, but are thus enabled to understand how the Kel Ahaggar can be both 'nomadic pastoralists' and 'matrilineal'.[10]

*Tawsit* membership among both classes is based on matrilineal descent. 'It is the stomach', as all Kel Ahaggar say, 'which colours the child.'[11] Succession to political office in both classes is also matrilineal, the right to succeed, as we have already seen, is transmitted adelphically through the line of brothers, thereafter through the line of mother's sisters' sons (in order of genealogical seniority), and, finally, through the line of sisters' sons.

In discussing the transmission of property rights, we must distinguish between land rights and those over livestock (i.e. moveable and immoveable wealth). The rules of inheritance, which are discussed below, determine that livestock among both classes are transmitted for the most part through the patriline. Land rights, however, are held corporately by each *tawsit*. The nobility held sovereign rights over the entire territory of their drum group, but in the case of the subordinate Kel Ulli, tenant rights were transmitted in conjunction with political office, being vested in the chief as the representative of his *tawsit*.[12]

This apparent matrilineal bias is modified when we turn to the rules of residency and inheritance.

The analysis of residency rules presents a difficulty, in that it is not easy to ascertain the exact nature of the traditional residency rules, either among the nobles or the vassals. Over the last few years the Kel Rela's situation has changed dramatically, since nearly all of them have abandoned their 'camp life' and settled in Tamanrasset. The result is that their present residency practices are capricious and individualistic. The Kel Rela's own statements of their former, or 'traditional', residency rules merely add to the confusion – partly because of their high geographical mobility and the fluidity in the composition of their camps as they roamed across Ahaggar from one group of Kel Ulli with whom they had *temazlayt* relations to another, and also because they tend to stress the importance of the matriline and maternal kinsmen.

According to Nicolaisen, who, as far as I am aware, is the only person to have published a fairly detailed account of residency rules, 'residency is based on both patrilineal and matrilineal principles'.[13] He states that: (1) immediately after the marriage the husband joins the wife's family for a year or so; (2) after this initial period the couple moves to the camp of the husband's father; (3) on the death of the husband's father, the couple join the husband's matrilineal (Nicolaisen's term) kin – his mother's brothers; (4) on the death of the husband the wife returns to her family. Such 'rules' may be the case in the event of the husband and wife belonging to different descent groups, but are otherwise the exception rather than the norm. Firstly, during the first year or so after the marriage, while the wife remains with her family until certain dowry and bride-wealth obligations are met, the husband, in practice, usually pays her only occasional visits. Secondly, I have found few cases amongst the vassals of a couple moving to the husband's mother's brothers' camps after the death of the husband's father. The couple normally remains in the camp of the husband's father. Thirdly, the question of whether the wife returns to her family after her husband's death depends on many considerations, and certainly cannot be regarded as a 'rule'.

Nicolaisen's rules are, I believe, based on the analysis of an exceptional situation,[14] and can be regarded more as legitimate options than rules, for although residency rules are extremely flexible, residency among the vassals is now predominantly patrilocal, and I am inclined to believe that this has not been otherwise, certainly since the early part of this century.

If we now turn to the inheritance of 'wealth', which consists mostly of individually held livestock (not land), we see that it is determined among all classes by the principles of Koranic law, which, while recognizing the right of women to inherit, are orientated towards males and patrilineal kinsmen, so that a daughter inherits one share to a son's two, without regard to primogeniture. Such 'diverging devolution' is, as Goody notes, 'in a certain sense agnatic'.[15] This is particularly so among the Kel Ahaggar, not only because male siblings are favoured, but because it seems that the daughter, in practice, does not fare even as well as these rules prescribe. I remain hesitant on this point, however, because the Kel Ahaggar are extremely reluctant to discuss questions relating to the number and ownership of their livestock, for fear of the 'evil eye'.[16]

We thus see that, while land rights are transmitted laterally in conjunction with succession to political office, and are held corporately by the matrilineal descent group, livestock are transmitted, as might be expected, within the family, and the *ariwan*, which as we have seen is a patrilocal unit.[17]

If, as is suggested, the transmission of the bulk of 'wealth' and the means of production, in the form of livestock, through the patriline[18] contributes to the unity of the *ariwan*, the special relationship between a man and his mother's brother, who is unlikely to be resident in the same *ariwan*, presents something of a contradiction, for we see that a fairly substantial amount of livestock may in fact pass out of the patriline to the uterine nephew. This seems to be true, generally speaking, of both classes. However, while many Kel Ulli (vassals) have been able to maintain themselves as pastoralists, most of the nobles have settled in Tamanrasset and now have few interests in any form of animal husbandry, so that the relationship with the mother's brother is now probably of greater significance among the Kel Ulli than the nobles.

Although a man does not inherit from his mother's brother (*anet ma*), he should receive certain symbols of his uncle's 'power', such as his sword, his finest robes and religious amulets. Such items are indeed 'symbols of his power', and not productive wealth. However, the maternal uncle may be a continual source of income to his nephew, not only through the gifts that the uncle may give, but primarily through the nephew's institutionalized right to 'steal' more or less anything he wants from his mother's brother. The use of the word 'steal' is a little misleading, for this is no more than the nephew's right to ask his uncle for virtually anything he needs. The uncle cannot legitimately refuse such requests, for, if he does, the nephew has the right to take whatever it is he needs. In practice this right seems to be rarely abused, being controlled by a fairly strict moral code. Of particular interest, however, is the classificatory extension of *anet ma* to other matrilateral kinsmen, such as the mother's mother's brother, the mother's mother's sister's son, etc.[19] What we are seeing here is the outward extension to other *ariwan* and 'sections' of the nephew's right to replenish or maintain his own productive resources through the activation of his matriline, which tends to be dispersed through other *ariwan*.

This type of relationship between the mother's brother and the sister's son is in fact typical of patrilineal systems.[20] Indeed, as we shall see below in examining the implications of the marital strategies adopted by the two classes, the social organization of the Kel Ulli, amongst whom this relationship is most significant in view of their pastoralism, is predominantly patrilineal.

I shall return to this particular relationship presently in discussing the marital strategies of the two classes. For the moment, it should be mentioned that its significance, especially amongst the Kel Ulli, derives from its function as a redistributive or insurance mechanism. Most nomadic pastoralists derive their livelihood from a miserly environment in which natural hazards such as drought and disease, in addition to the threat of pillagers, can wipe out a substantial portion of a group's productive resources. Among nearly all pastoralists, however, we see the adoption of various strategies to overcome these risks, the most common being social institutions of loaning, sharing, or giving of animals, and the consequent development of a network of credit, or primitive insurance, through which livestock can be dispersed over a broad social and geographical base. The Kel Ahaggar, especially the Kel Ulli, are particularly vulnerable to such risks in view of their rate of *tawsit* and 'section' endogamy, but it is in this situation that the special relationship between the mother's brother and the sister's son operates as just such an insurance mechanism and offers a degree of protection against these risks.

The matriline, in the person of the *anet ma*, and the classificatory extension of this term to other matrilateral kinsmen, cuts across the patriline and provides for a more equitable distribution of wealth between the *ariwan* and the patrilocal 'sections' to which they belong, according to their varying needs.

We thus see that, while the 'power' of a *tawsit*, in terms of its land rights and political rights over subordinate groups, is transmitted through the matriline, the wealth accumulated through the exercise of these rights is not transmitted with them, but is redistributed through, and transmitted within, the patrilocal 'sections'.

The various principles of descent among the Kel Ahaggar, in terms of the rules governing the transmission of this complex of rights, thus tend towards bilineality. It is the recognition of this fact that provides the key to the understanding of the social structure and organization of their society, for in the one line we see the transmission of most of the means of production and the reproduction of the domestic unit, and in the other the transmission of 'power' (in the form of descent group membership and succession to political office) and the reproduction of the class structure.

## Marital Strategies (The Manipulation of the Rules)

The way in which the class structure is reproduced, and the implications and significance of these various rules for the two classes, can be seen in their marital strategies.

Although the *tawsatin* (descent groups) of both classes exhibit a high rate of endogamy, there is no prescriptive rule of endogamy as such.[21] The rules are defined in terms of incest categories, beyond which the pattern and effect of endogamy is merely the result of the various marital strategies adopted. This incest category is very small: the only people a man is forbidden from marrying are his mother, his father's and mother's uterine sisters, and other classificatory mothers (which includes those kinswomen of ascending generations), his uterine sister, his daughter, the daughters of his uterine brothers and sisters,[22] and his mother-in-law, sister-in-law and daughter-in-law. In other words, there is no prohibition on marriage with any type of cousin.

Nearly all literary references to marriage among the Kel Ahaggar state that the preferential marriage is with a cross-cousin, preferably the mother's brother's daughter, and that marriages tend to be endogamous within the descent group (*tawsit*). The Kel Ahaggar themselves also state that the preferred marriage is with a cross-cousin, and ideally with the mother's brother's daughter. But, when we look at the actual marriages contracted, we see that not only are other types of cousin marriage more common amongst both classes than that with the mother's brother's daughter, but that each class seems to show a distinct preference for different types of cousin.

The statistical data presented in Table 1 is a more or less complete survey of marriages contracted over the last three generations by members of one noble descent group, namely that of the Kel Rela, and one Kel Ulli (vassal) descent group, namely that of the Dag Rali.[23] However, as a result of the almost total *tawsit* endogamy, paternal and maternal ascendants are often merged, so that individuals may consequently find themselves related through at least three different ties.[24] The classification of marriages on the basis of these relationships is therefore to some extent arbitrary. As far as possible, however, the marriages were classified according to the relationships stated by the individuals themselves, so that the data tend to reflect the sociological perception of the individuals concerned.

If we look first at the Dag Rali marriages, we see:

1. An extremely high rate of descent group (*tawsit*) endogamy.
2. Marriages are contracted with all types of cousin.
3. There is little significant variation in the number of marriages with actual cousins (categories D1, E1, F1, G1) except that the maternal side is slightly favoured (13·75 per cent to 11·25 per cent).
4. This statistical bias is removed when marriages with descendants are included (categories D2, E2, F2, G2) (16·25 per cent to 17·5 per cent).
5. When classificatory cousins are included, there is a significantly greater number of marriages between parallel cousins (30 per cent) than cross-cousins (21·25 per cent) (categories D & E, F & G), although this difference might be overcome if we consider that several marriages in category H are with classificatory cross-cousins.
6. Among cross-cousin marriages (categories F, G) the maternal side is favoured (13·75 per cent to 7·5 per cent). Among parallel cousin marriages (categories D, E) the paternal side is favoured (22·5 per cent to 7·5 per cent).
7. The most common marriages are with patrilateral parallel cousins (actual and classificatory; category E) (22·5 per cent of 'kin marriages', but 44 per cent of 'cousin marriages').

The marriage pattern among the Kel Rela (nobles) appears to be quite different. Although descent group endogamy is very high (74·5 per cent), it is not as high as among the Dag Rali (vassals) (95 per cent). Neither do we see marriage taking place between all types of cousin. On the contrary, with the exception of a scattering of a few statistically insignificant marriages in categories E, F and G, there appears to be a strong preference for marriage with the matrilateral parallel cousin (actual and classificatory;

Table 1 Marriage ties

| | Categories | *Kel Ulli* (vassals) Dag Rali | | *Ihaggaren* (nobles) Kel Rela | |
|---|---|---|---|---|---|
| | | Percentage | No. | Percentage | No. |
| Marriages in which kinship ties could not be traced beyond parents and immediate collaterals, or 'unknown': mostly in ascending generations | A | 27·7 | (33) | 22·2 | (20) |
| Exogamous to *tawsit* (descent group) | B | 5 | (6) | 25·5 | (23) |
| Kin marriages (endogamous to *tawsit*) | C | 67·2 | (80) | 52·2 | (47) |
| | Totals | 100 | (119) | 100 | (90) |

*Analysis of Kin Marriages (Category C)*

| | | | | | |
|---|---|---|---|---|---|
| Parallel matri-cousin | | | | | |
| Actual (MZD) | D1 | 6·25 | (5) | 14·9 | (7) |
| Descendant (MZDD) | D2 | 1·25 | (1) | 4·3 | (2) |
| Classificatory | D3 | — | — | 12·8 | (6) |
| Parallel patri-cousin | | | | | |
| Actual (FBD) | E1 | 6·25 | (5) | 2·1 | (1) |
| Descendant (FBDD) | E2 | 3·75 | (3) | — | — |
| Classificatory | E3 | 12·5 | (10) | — | — |
| Cross matri-cousin | | | | | |
| Actual (MBD) | F1 | 7·5 | (6) | — | — |
| Descendant (MBDD) | F2 | 1·25 | (1) | 2·1 | (1) |
| Classificatory | F3 | 5 | (4) | 2·1 | (1) |
| Cross patri-cousin | | | | | |
| Actual (FZD) | G1 | 5 | (4) | — | — |
| Descendant (FZDD) | G2 | 2·5 | (2) | 2·1 | (1) |
| Classificatory | G3 | — | — | — | — |
| Distant Kin Ties: beyond second cousin | H | 43·75 | (35) | 55·3 | (26) |
| Others | J | 5 | (4) | 4·3 | (2) |
| | Totals | 100 | (80) | 100 | (47) |

category D) (32 per cent of 'kin marriages', but 78 per cent of 'cousin marriages').

Why are the vast majority of marriages among both classes endogamous within the descent group? And why are nearly all such marriages between cousins of one sort or another? The second question really stems from the first, in that it is virtually impossible to marry anyone within the descent group who is not a cousin of sorts! The system of kinship nomenclature is such that all collaterals in a man's generation, with the exception of his true and half brothers, sisters and parallel cousins, are merged together as *ibubah* ('male', sing. *ababah*) or *tibubah* ('female', sing. *tababaht*), the term given to cross-cousins, whether matrilateral or patrilateral. But, with on-going endogamy, most members of a *tawsit* may be related through matrilateral and patrilateral consanguineous and affinal ties, with the result that almost every member of the *tawsit* of a man's own generation may be categorized as a 'cross-cousin'. Thus, when Kel Ahaggar say that preferential marriage is with the *tababaht*, the term is not necessarily being used for the explicit designation of the mother's brother's daughter, but often classificatorily and implicitly to mean a 'cousin of sorts'; by a further extension of meaning, this may be almost synonymous with saying that preferential marriage is with a member of the *tawsit* (descent group).

Such considerations do not explain the predominance of descent group endogamy, nor the apparent difference in preferred types of cousin marriage between the two classes. *Tawsit* endogamy, as I have stressed, is not the rule dictating 'cousin marriage', but rather the overall result of marital strategies favouring such marriages.

### *The Nobles' (Kel Rela's) Strategies*

The marital strategy of the Kel Rela was determined by three overriding political considerations, namely: to maintain their dominant position within the class structure; to overcome or reduce the threat posed by the two other drum groups to their dominant position in Ahaggar; and, at the more individual level, to secure access to political rights and status for their descendants within the Kel Rela *tawsit* itself.

Their position in the class structure was maintained by 'class endogamy'. During the last few years, as traditional political rights have come to assume lesser importance, one or two Kel Rela have married Kel Ulli (vassal) women. But in earlier times there is very little evidence of such marriages taking place, and marriages of noble women with men of subordinate classes are virtually unknown.

As we have seen, the stability of the Ahaggar federation (*tegehe*) was threatened throughout traditional times by both the periodic challenges to the Kel Rela's supremacy by the Taitok and Tegehe-Mellet and the possibility of the inherent struggle for political status and power between the more important Kel Rela 'families' erupting into open conflict. Most of the Kel Rela's exogamous marriages were in the form of alliances with the Taitok and Tegehe-Mellet, and, as in the case of Sidi ag Mohammed el Khir marrying his two sons, Younes and Ag Mama, to Taitok women, were often specifically designed acts of reconciliation or appeasement after periods of hostility between the drum groups, which effectively extended the Kel Rela's influence even further afield.

Internal rivalries amongst the Kel Rela centred almost exclusively on access to political rights, particularly those over the Kel Ulli (vassals). Most of this power, in the form of rights to dues of political allegiance (*tiwse*), land-rents (*ehere-n-amadal*), and so forth, from the subordinate classes, was centralized in the position of the Amenukal.

Within the Kel Rela *tawsit*, however, as with most other *tawsatin* of all classes, the right to succeed to political office (in the Kel Rela's case that of the Amenukal), was restricted to certain matrilineal 'sections' (matrilineages), which were referred to as *agg ettebel.*

The Kel Rela *tawsit* consisted of nine such matrilineal sections, four of which were not *agg ettebel*, because either they had lost their rights to the *ettebel* in earlier times through marital misalliance or they had been incorporated into the Kel Rela without being granted access to the *ettebel.* These four are now numerically insignificant and are not included in the statistical data presented in Table 1. Of the five which were *agg ettebel*, two are of little significance, thus leaving only three politically dominant *agg ettebel* matrilineages. There is also evidence to suggest that *temazlayt* rights, in spite of the contractual nature of the relationship, were accumulated and 'transmitted' within these dominant *agg ettebel* matrilineages.

Rivalries between and within these internal divisions seem to have reached critical dimensions on more than one occasion, as we have seen in the case of the 'election' of two Amenukals, Mohammed ag Ourzig and Attici ag Amellal, in 1900, and in the difficulties involved in the succession of El Hadj Akhmed.[25]

For the nobles, descent was an issue of primary concern, for the ability of Kel Rela families to reckon and manipulate their genealogical descent in the inherent struggle and competition for power was a major factor in determining their fortunes. To be *agg ettebel* was consequently of crucial importance, and marriage with the matrilateral parallel cousin seems to have been preferred (32 per cent of kin marriages and 78 per cent of cousin marriages) as a specific strategy for retaining and limiting access to this power, and for securing these matrilineal sections as minimal corporate lineages, in which the various political rights over subordinate groups and the economic benefits accumulated through the exercise of these rights would be retained.[26]

Bilineality among the Kel Rela was consequently not underscored, for the importance and significance of descent lay with the matriline, through which these political rights, power and status were transmitted, rather than with the patriline, which hardly necessitated the reckoning of genealogical descent, since inheritance effectively involved little more than 'being one's father's son'.

But, before making any comparison with the Dag Rali, it must be realized that the acquisition of 'wealth' among the nobles, in terms of subsistence products, was quite different from that among the Kel Ulli, in that they relied predominantly on their Kel Ulli for these products. In other words, the nobles' economic base, at the subsistence level, was secured primarily through their formal political rights within the drum group, and, at the more individual level, through the *temazlayt* relationship, which, as I have suggested, may not have been as 'individual' as the 'contract' would suggest, in that *temazlayt* rights seem to have been largely retained and transmitted within the dominant matrilineal sections.

The nobles' real 'wealth' lay in their camels. But the camel, compared with the goat, is not a major subsistence resource, especially in Ahaggar, which is not well suited ecologically to the maintenance of large camel-herds. These tended to be pastured (in the care of their slaves) for the most part in the Adrar-n-Iforas (Mali), and since French pacification in the pastures of Tamesna in northern Niger. The camel could be allocated primarily to the political rather than the economic sphere, for it provided the nobles with the means, in conjunction with their rights to carry specialized arms, of maintaining physical control and domination over Ahaggar and, of course, their Kel Ulli. The importance of the camel must be seen primarily within the context of this political control, and it was for this reason that they successfully withheld the rights of camel-ownership from their Kel Ulli for so long.

Political rights were transmitted matrilineally, and the camel, as I have indicated, belonged to the political sphere. It therefore seems reasonable to suggest that camels, amongst the nobility, may have been transmitted in the same line as these political rights. It is not easy to substantiate this suggestion, for not only are all Kel Ahaggar reluctant to talk about their animals (for fear of the 'evil eye'), but most nobles (Kel Rela) are now settled in Tamanrasset and possess relatively few camels. However, the question, on which we can do little more than speculate, focuses primarily on when Koranic inheritance rules were introduced to Ahaggar, and whether they were adopted uniformly by all classes alike.

Although Islamic influences reached the central Sahara around the eleventh century, the Kel Ahaggar have always been relatively lax, and only 'lukewarm' Moslems.[27] Not until this century, following French pacification, did Islam gain a firm foothold in the region (see Ch. 9). Prior to that time, the adoption of Islamic practices in Ahaggar seems to have been characterized by superficiality, particularly amongst the nobility, whose adoption of Islam was probably more a matter of political expediency than religious conviction. The vassals certainly seem to have adhered to Koranic inheritance rules throughout this century. However, there are several early literary sources which indicate that a man inherited from his mother's brother.[28] Few of these references mention class differences, while most of them are ambiguous in that they do not make clear whether they are actually referring to inheritance of property or succession to political office. It is consequently difficult to know whether traditional inheritance rules were in fact matrilineal; whether these sources are really talking about 'succession'; or whether they are a reflection of certain practices amongst the nobility, among whom it seems to have been common practice for a man to transmit his camels, along with his specialized weapons, to his sister's son. Although this practice may have been in accordance with 'traditional' inheritance rules, I am inclined to believe that it was a means of circumventing Koranic inheritance rules, which posed a threat to the political and physical strength of the matrilineage by providing the means whereby camels (the physical basis of political control) could have passed into other matrilineages.

This practice, in conjunction with that of marriage with the matrilateral parallel cousin, ensured the retention of these assets within the matrilineage. We can thus see that the patriline among the nobility, even at the level of inheritance, was relatively unimportant, both structurally and ideologically.

### *The Kel Ulli's (Dag Rali's) Strategies*

In the case of the Dag Rali, and other Kel Ulli descent groups (*tawsatin*), the reduction of the imbalance between the matriline and patriline, in terms of their relevance, as well as the diminished relevance of descent in general as an organizational principle, results primarily from their different political rights and means of acquisition of wealth, in comparison with those of the Kel Rela.

The Kel Ulli's political subordination, expressed through their various tributary payments, provided the nobility with much of their subsistence products. The nobles' desire to gain access to these rights and secure the transmission of their benefits within the same matrilineal section was not paralleled amongst the Kel Ulli, who held no such rights over subordinate groups. On the contrary, the political rights of the Kel Ulli headmen (chiefs) offered few economic benefits, and were to a large extent the inverse of those of the Amenukal or drum chiefs, the headmen of Kell Ulli *tawsatin* being primarily responsible for the collection and payment of the various dues owed to the drum chiefs.

Thus, while most of the nobles' subsistence products were derived directly from their political rights, those of the Kel Ulli were derived predominantly from their internal resources and activities of goat-breeding, and, since the end of the last century, caravan trading (see below). While the primary consideration of the nobles was the maximization of their political rights and power through access to the *agg ettebel* matrilineages, that of the Kel Ulli was the maximization of their pastoral resources – goats and, in more recent times, camels.

In turning to their marital strategies, and particularly the extent to which these reflect their economic interests, we are faced with a major difficulty, namely that the Kel Ulli's economic resources and interests changed dramatically around the turn of the century, and especially after pacification (about 1920). As we have seen, the Kel Ulli had already gained possession of their own camels by the end of the last century. But the camel became a different 'thing' for the Kel Ulli than for the nobles. This difference will be examined in detail in subsequent chapters (Chs. 9 and 10). In short, it relates to the Kel Ulli's development of a substantial caravan trade, carrying locally mined salt southwards to Niger and exchanging it for millet. The first such caravan was undertaken in 1896 by the two Kel Ulli descent groups of the Dag Rali and Aguh-en-tehle. The nobles seem to have taken no part in this new trade, and by the 1920s, when these caravans became organized on an annual basis, Kel Ulli caravans of up to 3,000–4,000 camels[29] were leaving Ahaggar each year and returning some four or five months later with several hundred tons of millet. For the Kel Ulli, the value and significance of the camel was in terms of this highly remunerative caravan trade.

This major change in the Kel Ulli's economic orientation must have necessitated certain changes in their social organization. As goat-herders, the *ariwan*, and even the individual family ('tent'), could function as a more or less independent and viable economic unit. The introduction of the camel and the development of large-scale caravan trading required a greater amount of economic co-operation, in terms of labour resources, than could be mustered within the *ariwan*.

This co-operation is seen in the relations between the *ariwan* and the *tawsit* section. Among the Dag Rali there were four such sections, namely the Kel Tamanrasset, Kel Terhenanet, Kel Hirafok and Kel Tinhart, each of which held corporate land rights over its own sub-areas within the overall territory of the *tawsit*. It is now difficult to define these sections in anything except a territorial sense, as patrilineally organized local groups. In earlier times their structural organization seems to have been similar to that of the Kel Rela (noble) sections, with membership based on matrilineal descent. Among the Dag Rali, however, there is now a tendency to equate membership with residency, which is predominantly patrilocal. Thus, although the section is defined ideationally in terms of matrilineal membership, it is effectively nothing more than the higher level structural equivalent of the *ariwan*, a larger patrilineally organized group co-operating in camel-breeding and caravan trading.

How can we explain the vassals' (Dag Rali's) social system, especially their marriage system, favouring as it does marriage with the patrilateral parallel cousin (at least statistically), and the tendency to equate section membership with patrilocality?

The explanation, I believe, can be found at two related levels. On the one hand, the economic requirements and conditions of pastoralism, particularly those generated by the possession of camels and the development of caravan trading, outweigh purely political interests in the form of access to the *agg ettebel* matrilineages and chieftaincy. On the other hand, I believe it is a misconception, in spite of the structural significance of the patriline, to assume a corresponding diminution in the relevance of the matriline, for, as I shall suggest, it may be that this increasing (?) structural significance of the patriline is in fact permitted, and indeed facilitated, by the greater ideological strength and relevance of the matriline!

The almost total *tawsit* (descent group) endogamy (95 per cent) of the Dag Rali may be explained by their desire to maintain and restrict their wealth within the *tawsit*. Without going into causes and effects, it is interesting to note that the Dag Rali *tawsit* not only has the highest endogamy rate of any *tawsit* in Ahaggar, but is also the most favoured in terms of pasture resources, and is the wealthiest Kel Ulli *tawsit* in terms of livestock holdings. In purely ecological and economic terms, exchange marriages with other *tawsatin* would have procured them no benefits, but would have provided other *tawsatin* with access to their resources.

Endogamy is also practised at the level of the *tawsit* section: a little more than 50 per cent of Dag Rali marriages are endogamous within the section.

This 'lower level' of endogamy can be largely explained in terms of economic considerations. When goats were the Kel Ulli's main resource, the *ariwan* could operate as an economically viable and independent unit. This, however, was no longer the case with the introduction of the camel, and particularly caravan trading, for these new economic activities demanded greater labour resources, and consequently a wider field of economic co-operation, than could be mustered within the *ariwan* itself. This wider field was the section, which we could perhaps refer to as the 'camel unit' as distinct from the 'goat unit', the *ariwan*.[30]

I have very little data on either marriage or residency practices before the beginning of this century, but suggest that with the acquisition of the camel both patrilocality (if matrilocality was in fact more pronounced in earlier times) and marriage with the father's brother's daughter (actual and classificatory) became favoured as means of restricting the circulation of camels, and encysting the section as a more economically corporate unit.

Although the Dag Rali's apparent shift in structural emphasis towards patrilineality may perhaps be explained in terms of these economic changes, it merely highlights the contradiction between their cultural and social systems. There is more to be explained than 'cultural lag', albeit possibly over a short period of time! Indeed, by ignoring what the people themselves are saying at the ideational level, we are in danger of not seeing how their social system really works.

In terms of the residency pattern, a man tends to find his maternal kin, especially his mother's brothers, dispersed farther afield. Exchange marriages between sections, which number a little less than 50 per cent of all marriages, are thus predominantly with maternal kin. Exchange marriages take place between all four sections, and it is interesting to note that the Kel Tamanrasset and Kel Terhenanet sections (who together form the Dag Rali proper) speak of the Kel Tinhart and Kel Hirafok sections (who are together known as the Imesseliten) as 'children of our mother's brother'.

When the people themselves state that the preferred marriage is with the mother's brother's daughter, we must ask what is so significant about this type of marriage, and section exchange marriages in general, in relation to section endogamy and the statistically dominant marriage with the patrilateral parallel cousin (actual and classificatory).

The significance of the marriage with the matrilateral cross-cousin is to be seen in terms of its long-term benefits.[31]

The cultural system of the Kel Ahaggar is permeated by its strong matrilineal emphasis, as reflected in the rules of group membership, succession to political office, land rights, and so forth, and particularly in a man's general relationship with his matriline, especially through the classificatory extension of the term *anet ma* (mother's brother), which 'can always be counted on to render assistance'.

A man does not speak of his agnatic kin with the same sense of ideological and moral commitment.[32] But, on the other hand, it is a man's male agnatic kin with whom he tends to reside and with whom he must co-operate, particularly in camel-breeding and caravan trading activities. This co-operation is essentially 'short-term' and is not based on any strong ideological commitment. The fact that the structure of the section tends to centre around a group of male agnates is merely an expression of the necessary co-operation between them. Indeed, it may be suggested that the high frequency of marriages with the patrilateral parallel cousin (actual and classificatory) reflects the necessity of having to continually reactivate relationships that are characterized by a relatively low moral content in contrast to those with the matriline.

The activation of these kin ties, which are the most necessary in terms of economic co-operation but which have the least moral commitment, is essentially a short-term strategy, and provides for no long-term security. In fact, this strategy, by encysting these ties within the section, and so limiting their outward extension, is at the expense of the section's long-term security against such risks as drought, disease, etc.

This long-term security is provided, as we have seen, by the matriline, in the form of a man's 'mother's brothers', who are usually found scattered further afield in other sections. These relationships have a stronger moral content, and can always be depended upon for meeting future and unknown needs.

And so, while exogamous marriages with the matrilateral cross-cousin ensures a man, or rather his descendants, future security, his short and middle-term interests, in terms of necessary economic co-operation, are vested in the patrilineally defined local group (the section). While these short-term interests are maintained and reinforced by endogamous marriage with the patrilateral parallel cousin (actual and classificatory), it is the system of exchange marriages, particularly between matrilateral cross-cousins, which provides the sections with their long-term security.

# EIGHT THE SYMBOLIC MEANING OF THE VEIL

If we turn our attention for the moment from inter-class relations and look instead at the relationships within the domestic groups (*ariwan*) themselves, we see, as in all endogamic societies, that the relationships contain the quite antithetical values of incorporation and alliance. As a result of endogamy social units look inwards and cannot easily differentiate affinal relationships from those of common descent and kin group membership because mates are taken predominantly from the latter section.[1] The major links of consanguinity and affinality thus tend to be embedded in the same group, with the result that potential role conflict and ambivalence in role definition and differentiation are pronounced.

However, the tendency towards the realization of such conflict and ambivalence is to some extent mitigated by the generally short genealogies, the system of kinship nomenclature, and the restricted use of kin terms in address.

Genealogies, except amongst the nobility, are rarely remembered beyond three or four generations, with the result that demonstrable kin ties with more distant kin are difficult to establish. Related to this 'genealogical amnesia'[2] is the general usage of Hawaiian kinship terminology for all but immediate collaterals, so that those more distant kin, who must be acknowledged and recognized as such, but whose exact kin positioning cannot be readily established, are lumped together under the umbrella of Hawaiian terminology into one amorphous category of cross-cousins.

In a social system fraught with ambivalence and potential role conflict the general state of genealogical amnesia and the usage of Hawaiian terminology provide the individual with little comfort when confronted with the hazards and pitfalls of social interaction. Restriction in the usage of kin terms as terms of address certainly does much to mitigate against ambivalence and role conflict.[3] But, even so, such restraint does not enable the clear demarcation and segregation of roles that is essential if social interaction is to be anything but a precarious and unpredictable business.

It would thus seem that the individual Tuareg's lot is not an enviable one, enmeshed as he is in a social system fraught with such ambivalence and unpredictability. His situation, however, is not that intolerable, for some measure of relief is afforded by the one feature of the Tuareg which has made them an object of almost universal curiosity – namely the veil.

The veil (*tagelmoust*) is a dominant symbol of Tuareg entity, as expressed in their self-designation as Kel Tagelmoust, meaning literally 'the people of the veil', and the Arabic counterpart of El Molathemine or Ahl el Litham (wearers of the veil).[4] It is worn by all adult men in all Tuareg groups, and although there are discreet differences in the style of the veil among the various Tuareg groups, *tawsatin* and classes,[5] its universal importance is reflected in the abundance of terms relating to its many features and attributes.

The traditional veil (*tagelmoust* or *alechcho*) is a piece of Sudanese indigo-dyed cotton, 1·50m. to 4·0m. long and 0·25m. to 0·50m. wide and made of individual strips of cotton sewn together.[6] The cloth is wrapped around the head to form a low turban (*amaoual-oua-n-afella*); one fold is brought across the face to form the veil (*amaoual-oua-n-aris*), so that the top of the veil usually rests on the bridge of the nose, and the bottom (*agedellehouf*) falls across the face to the upper part of the chest. The turban covers the forehead so that when the veil is at its highest there is only a narrow slit around the eyes. At its lowest the veil may fall below the mouth, thus exposing the entire face. The position of the veil varies between these two extremes.

The term *tagelmoust* or *alechcho* is reserved for this Sudanese indigo-dyed cloth made of individual strips, and is not used for the white or black manufactured muslin veil known as *echchach*. Another type of veil is the *khent*, which is a manufactured indigo-coloured cloth, intermediate in both cost and quality between the *alechcho* and the *echchach*. Today, the *tagelmoust* is worn almost exclusively on ceremonial and festive occasions, and then predominantly by the Ihaggaren. The *khent* may be worn on all occasions as well as for everyday use, but the most common type of veil now worn by all Tuareg, particularly for general use, is the *echchach*. This type of veil is white, black or dark blue, and not indigo in colour, and made of manufactured muslin, which is both cheap and readily accessible in the shops of Tamanrasset.[7, 8]

All men wear the veil from puberty for the remainder of their lives, and an adolescent boy's (*elmengoudi*) first wearing of the veil is a family ceremonial occasion marking his initiation or 'passage' from adolescence to adulthood.[9] For the rest of his life he will rarely be unveiled, either when travelling alone or even when sleeping. Women, however, do not wear a veil but a headcloth (*ekerhei*), which is also taken at puberty. This headcloth is quite different from the man's veil, being black, much shorter, and not wrapped around the head but partially draped over it without concealing the face.

The veiling (*anagad*) of Tuareg men is without doubt an ancient custom for reference to the veil is found in the writings of several early Arabic authors such as El Bekri (1028–94) and Ibn Batutah, whose journeys in the fourteenth century certainly took him into Tuareg country. Nevertheless, in spite of numerous hypotheses, many of which have a romantic appeal, the origin of the veil remains obscure and conjectural. But it is the function of the veil that has perplexed those who have had contact with the Tuareg, with the result that the literature is full of numerous unsatisfactory arguments and explanations, all attempting to solve the riddle of this mysterious custom.

Duveyrier, the first to write comprehensively about the Tuareg, saw the veil in terms of its hygienic functions; it protected the eyes from the sun and sand, and the mouth, nostrils and ears from dehydration.[10] But if this is so why do men remain veiled when in camps or asleep, and why do women go unveiled?

Among the more romantic explanations is the suggestion, made especially by Arabs, that the veil serves to mask Tuareg raiders from their enemies, but this explanation is equally unsatisfactory, as recognition is afforded by numerous other features apart from the face. In this vein one might also mention the malevolent remarks made by certain Arabs that Tuareg veil their faces to hide their ugliness![11]

Most explanations, however, have touched upon the mouth in one way or another. Foucauld states that it is shameful to be unveiled and thus expose the mouth,[12] while Gautier, observing that evil spirits were believed to enter through the mouth, recognized some sort of taboo surrounding the mouth and considered that there was consequently a good psychological necessity for veiling it.[13] This opinion is shared not only by Abd el Djalil,[14] but also by Lhote, who considers that there is undoubtedly some taboo surrounding the mouth, that is associated with the veil. Although emphasizing that it is shameful to expose the mouth before women, he also points out that these associations are accentuated among the nobility who, being conscious of their elevated social status, observe the taboo concerning the mouth to such a degree that the veil is never discarded before women, parents or other respected persons. Lhote thus sees the taboo as pertaining not only to women but to all respected persons such as senior kinsmen, chiefs, marabouts, etc. He has little doubt that the veil and its origin are associated with a taboo surrounding the mouth, but admits that the inapplicability of veiling to women remains unexplained.[15]

Bourgeot's conclusion expresses the same dilemma. He considers that the veil has a utilitarian function, affording protection from the sun to the head and preventing dehydration of the nasal passages and throat. He also mentions that the Tuareg are prone to headaches, and that they respond to this affliction by raising the veil to its highest, thus giving the impression of relieving the pain and stopping its penetration. In this behaviour he sees an association with Gautier's remarks, but adds that such functional explanations, even if correct, still do not explain why women and children go unveiled.[16]

An unprecedented conclusion is made by Nicolaisen, who rejects as insufficient both hygienic and magico-religious explanations, notably that the veil may afford protection against persons having an 'evil-eye' or 'evil-mouth' (*tehot*); he sees the main function of the veil as a social one. This is manifested in the covering of the mouth, nose and brow in the presence of foreigners (especially women) and parents-in-law (especially mothers-in-law). But unlike other authors he considers that the men's veil and the women's headcloth are similar in form and shape, and serve the same social function – a fact which he sees proven by their adoption of the veil and headcloth respectively at initiation in Ahaggar or at marriage in Ayr.[17]

This review of the more prominent functional explanations of the Tuareg veil, while indicating the probability of some taboo connected with the mouth, and some fairly indeterminate aspects of social status and behaviour, underlines the inadequate state of analysis of the symbolic meaning and function of the veil.

The veil is a dominant symbol among the Tuareg and as such it is necessary to consider its multivocality in various systems of ideas and beliefs, and the levels of meaning in each system that invest it with an affective as well as a cognitive function. Above all, this involves an analysis of the symbolic significance of the veil in terms of communication in the social interaction process, and its associations with certain magico-religious beliefs.

The tribal variations in the style of the veil have been recognized by several authors.[18] Lhote, on the other hand, considers that the way in which the veil is worn, particularly with regard to the arrangement of the folds and the amount of face exposed, may also be interpreted in terms of dominant traits in the individual's character (either permanent or temporary). He consequently sees the position of the veil more in terms of individual psychological characteristics than in terms of the social situation. For example, he considers that a veil which is always worn in the same way and always in the correct position indicates a steady and serious character, while the full exposure of the forehead, with the turban at its highest, is a general indication of a jovial character, etc.![19]

This sort of 'psychological' interpretation in terms of the identification of individual character traits is not valid. On the contrary, the position and style of the veil is more a reflection or communication of an individual's expected role behaviour in a particular social situation. In other words, the 'self', 'character' or 'personality', or whatever Lhote means precisely by 'un trait dominant du caractère de l'individu', is to some extent concealed, for as Murphy recognized the wearing of the veil by the Tuareg symbolically introduces a form of distance between their selves and their social others: 'the veil provides neither isolation nor anonymity, but bestows facelessness and the idiom of privacy upon the wearer, and allows him to stand somewhat aloof from the perils of social interaction, while remaining a part of it.'[20] Murphy is adopting much of the 'interactionist' approach of Goffman, who states that the individual's sense of worth and significance is threatened by his vulnerability and penetrability.[21]

Among the Tuareg, men will frequently make slight readjustments, or merely the gesture of readjustment, to the position of their veils. These may occur while participating in conversation, as a person enters or leaves the group, at the approach of a particular person (perhaps unknown), or even as the subject or tone of the conversation changes. It is only through the concept of 'social distance'[22] and with an understanding of Tuareg kinship that we can understand the fundamental significance of this dynamic aspect of the veil.

The display of social distance, as Radcliffe-Brown pointed out, may be pronounced in ambivalent or ambiguous relationships.[23] In such situations, where the outcome of the interaction is uncertain or unpredictable, because of some indeterminacy or involvement of contrary interests, the expression of distance or reserve in one form or another promotes a degree of autonomy and flexibility of action.[24]

This is just the situation that we have seen among the Tuareg. Their predominant endogamy results in members of the kin-group being able to trace their relationships in multifarious and often contradictory ways: the bonds of incorporation and solidarity within the social group are charged also with the antithesis of affinality and alliance.[25] Relationships are thus ambivalent and social interaction may consequently be a precarious affair. Although restraint in the use of kin terms and well-defined kinship behaviour partially mediates this ambivalence and potential role conflict, it is in the ritual behaviour attached to the veil that we see the clear demarcation and segregation of roles.

The position of the veil signifies the degree of respect or deference that is expected of a particular social position. Between two actors, the one to whom respect is owed will usually wear his veil lower, so that, generally speaking, the lower the veil the greater the role status. The veil will, therefore, be worn relatively high in the company of such persons as parents-in-law, senior kinsmen and persons addressed as *amrar* (such as sectional or *tawsit* chiefs, old men, etc.). The veil thus symbolizes the relative status and degree of respect that is expected of an individual in various role performances. Under certain circumstances, however, this pattern may be inverted, so that the highest status is symbolized by the veil at its highest, and vice-versa. Situations in which this may arise are, for example, when a person of high status, like the Amenukal or an important chief, wishes to underline or emphasize his role performance, or when an Ihaggaren wishes to stress his higher class status before members of subordinate or 'inferior' classes.

The veil is thus a symbolic manifestation of role status, but in actuality the situation is complicated, particularly at the level of kinship roles, by the ambivalence of so many relationships. But it is in these ambivalent situations, where a degree of social distance is essential, that the veil functions to symbolically remove a portion of ego's identity from the interaction situation, and allows him to act in the presence of such conflicting interests and uncertainty.

Murphy distinguished between two aspects of distance: firstly the external dialogue maintaining the interaction situation and, secondly, the internal dialogue of ego maintaining ego.[26] The first aspect, by cutting down the range of stimuli and creating a diffuseness of his behavioural stance, enables ego to 'play it cool', while the second aspect, by symbolically removing part of his own identity from the interaction situation, is protecting the vulnerability of the self against penetration.

Three interrelated functions of the veil are thus discernible: firstly, it signifies the relative status and degree of respect between role players; secondly, it acts as a mask by reducing the range of stimuli; and, thirdly, it affords protection to the self-image by symbolic withdrawal of part of the actor's identity. The second and third functions are different categories of distance: the external dialogue is a manifestation of 'reserve' and the internal dialogue one of 'privacy'; these, although analytically distinct, are fused in the interaction process.

'That the Tuareg withholds himself while communicating, and communicates through removal, is not a contradiction in terms, but a quality of interaction.'[27] What do the situational attitudes of the veil communicate? Firstly, there is the possibility of role conflict. During the process of interaction the actor may take on a different role, to which a different degree of respect and behaviour is expected. This may be signified unambiguously by a readjustment of the position of his veil vis-à-vis his social others. Secondly, the veil, apart from partially concealing the behavioural stance of an actor, is itself communicating the intent and disposition of the actor. The veil reduces the range of facial stimuli, but does not conceal the identity of the individual. By revealing only the immediate area around the eyes, all labial expression is concealed. Labial gestures, in contrast to ocular gestures, contain a greater element of unconscious or uncontrolled expression. Thus the veil not only protects the self-image by concealing most 'unconscious' gestures, but allows a universally perceptible form of communication which, by expressing or communicating such information as social position, status, respect, familiarity, etc., communicates in what way and through what channels certain information, such as feelings and emotions, may be expressed. In other words, ego is taking his cues not from alter's facial gestures but primarily from his veil, and vice-versa. The veil thus becomes an object of orientational significance in the interaction process. It symbolizes social values, not only by expressing what type of behaviour is expected between actors, but also by symbolizing what behavioural stance an actor is likely to adopt in a situation. As the interaction progresses, so each actor's behavioural stance will change, and be manifested in the changing attitudes of the veil (and/or other expressive gestures). Ego can thus largely evaluate the response to his own strategy by reference to the veils of others, which give him a measure by which he can formulate his expectations and evaluations of further alternative courses of action.[28]

The social values that are symbolized by the veil in the interaction process are only part of the spectrum of referents attached to the veil. They do not explain why the veil is worn by men only, or why it is worn when alone or when sleeping. It is necessary, therefore, to look at the alternative beliefs and meanings associated with the veil.

It is not so much the actual movement or change in the position of the veil that symbolizes social values, but rather its movement in relation to the mouth. Thus, by understanding the implications of meanings and beliefs surrounding the mouth, we can perhaps perceive the whole range of meanings invested in the veil.

Tuareg say that it is shameful to expose the mouth. They have a saying that the veil and trousers are brothers: the relationship between the two garments being that they both cover external orifices – the trousers the genital region and anus, and the veil the mouth. These orifices are considered as zones of pollution, and it is, therefore, extremely disrespectful and shameful to expose them before others. Nevertheless, the mouth is exposed occasionally, in the case of persons of very high status who may allow the veil to fall below the mouth, and also in the case of persons of lowest status. Only in the case of a 'Hadj'[29] can the veil be divested entirely, but in this case it is not his secular status but his sacredness that exempts him from shame.

What are the beliefs that invest the veil with its sacred meaning? Among the Tuareg many internal illnesses are attributed to the Kel Asouf,[30] and the belief that the veil protects against their entry into the body is still commonly held. A similar notion relates to the belief in *tehot*, the 'evil-eye' or 'evil-mouth'. *Tehot* is the fear of laudatory words which express desire or envy: it makes a strong impression on the daily life of the Kel Ahaggar (and other Tuareg groups). Not only is great prudence shown in praises that are addressed to the animals, family or possessions of others, but one is equally inclined to be modest about one's own actions, for the force of *tehot* is believed to harm men and even kill animals. Islamic amulets are worn as protection against *tehot* and *ettama*,[31] but it is suggested by some Tuareg that the veil also protects against *tehot*. This is supported by Westermarck's writings on ritual and belief in Morocco;[32] but the Tuareg, although admitting that the Kel Asouf can enter the body and that the veil may afford protection against them, are reluctant to commit themselves on the association between *tehot* and the veil.

This association between the veil and the Kel Asouf helps to explain why men remained veiled when alone in deserted places (Kel Tenere – 'people of the empty places'), and when asleep (Kel Asouf and Kel Had, 'people of the night', are especially active during darkness). The reasons why women are unveiled may be partially explained by their impurity and status in Islam, but more so, one suggests, because the veil is attached more to the ritual of social relations than to the belief in the Kel Asouf. A woman is not a public figure in the same way as a man, and takes no roles in the political arena. Similarly, it is surely because a boy has little or no social or political status that he does not wear the veil, rather than because the position of adulthood entails a greater susceptibility to attack from the Kel Asouf. On the contrary, it is recognized that babies and young children are most susceptible to the effects of the Kel Asouf.

Although the veil is associated with the beliefs in the Kel Asouf, this does not invest it with sacredness, for it is the intrinsic properties of the veil that are alleged to afford protection rather than any sacred symbolism – its parts are not equal to the whole. The sacredness of the veil, as Murphy recognized, is found in the ritual of social relations, and in the sentiments of shame and pollution that are associated with the mouth. Even the most powerful chiefs wear the veil, while the 'Hadj' may divest himself of it, since his dignity and esteem endues him with status that alleviates him from all sense of shame and respect before others. The status of the chief is secular, while that of the 'Hadj' is sacred, and the symbolism of the veil in social relations belongs to the sacred.[33]

The veil is also imbued with affective qualities. At any ritual, ceremonial, or public gathering, and particularly when a man is courting, great care is taken in the perfection of his dress, especially the veil, the display of his *takouba* and the qualities of his camel. On such occasions the veil serves to preserve the aloofness, dignity and self-image of the actor, as well as communicating an assessment of his worth and standing. We thus see that the veil is associated with those other symbols which pronounce a man's worth and prestige, notably his *takouba* and riding camel, all of which give emotional, sensual and aesthetic gratification.

Above all, the *tagelmoust* symbolizes 'being a Tuareg'. When asked why he wears a veil, a Tuareg usually replies to the effect that it is 'because he is a Tuareg'. One thus sees Tuareg identifying with the veil as a symbol of their entity and consequent distinction from other peoples. The veil is considered to be peculiarly Tuareg, and as such expresses a certain general attitude of aloofness and inherent superiority over all other people. This attitude is similar to that held, amongst others, by the Masai, who consider other peoples, African or not, not merely different and outside their social system, but essentially inferior. This attitude has always been noticeable in the Tuareg's relationships with 'non-Tuareg', and was particularly well illustrated in the years immediately following Algerian independence (1962). Throughout this period, as we shall see later, especially prior to about 1968, there was a marked degree of conflict and antagonism, not only between the Kel Ahaggar and the Algerian authorities but also between the Kel Ahaggar and other groups such as the Harratin, as a result of the Algerian development policies and the consequent transformation of the social, political and economic systems. During this brief period, the veil was clearly seen as a symbol of both ethnic identity and of political values, and was manifested quite blatantly as such in the main street of Tamanrasset, particularly in the vicinity of the Algerian administrative offices.

Since Algerian independence, however, Ahaggar society has changed, and continues to change, so rapidly that it is difficult to draw definitive conclusions except that the present abandonment of the veil by certain Kel Ahaggar supports the general conclusions of this analysis. Certain Kel Ahaggar, while outside the 'Tuareg' social milieu, now tend to discard the veil. These Kel Ahaggar, though still relatively few in number, are those who have entered new roles in the developing and modernizing structure of Tamanrasset and its environs, in such positions as secretaries, mechanics, work foremen, labourers, etc. Likewise, children who have been at the boarding-school in Tamanrasset for several years now go completely bareheaded, in spite of having reached puberty.

These changes may be considered as a sign that the beliefs surrounding the veil and the ritualization of Tuareg social relations are breaking down. Certainly, the change in Tuareg dress during this century, with the adoption of new textiles and garments, has been considerable, but such a conclusion is premature. In fact what we are seeing is a twofold process:

Firstly, certain traditional beliefs, like those associated with the Kel Asouf, are being dissipated through changing cognitive processes associated with increased (and more orthodox) islamization and modernization.

Secondly, Kel Ahaggar are beginning to leave their social milieu more readily, to work in Tamanrasset, at the mines of Laouni, etc. But when these Kel Ahaggar return to their camps they revert to their traditional dress, especially the veil. Bourgeot deduces from this pattern of behaviour, 'que ce tabou de la bouche n'est plus un tabou essentiellement social mais un tabou de milieu ambiant qui tend à disparaître au contact d'un groupe socialement plus évolué'.[34] On the contrary, the taboo is still essentially social, and concerns the ritual of Tuareg social relations. On returning to the camp a man is once again involved in the ambiguous and ambivalent kinship relationships that characterize Tuareg society. In these conditions, no matter whether he be returning to the camp or to a house in Tamanrasset, and no matter what his degree of emancipation or integration into the external society of Tamanrasset or elsewhere, the veil affords him a degree of protection from the conflicting interests of essentially ambivalent roles.

# NINE
# THE COLONIAL PRESENCE

France, according to most French commentators and schoolbook histories, brought peace, stability and material prosperity to Ahaggar. Unlike the Pax Britannica there seem to have been few, if any, references to 'good government', although that is not to say that France did not govern well!

Such claims, particularly that of stability, albeit vague and a contradiction in terms, are more a reflection of France's attitude towards the Kel Ahaggar, and of her *laissez-faire*-cum-traditionalist policy, than the result of her presence.

The French military administration always respected the Kel Ahaggar's traditional organization and customs, and the idea of a Tuareg reserve, in which the traditional form of society would, as far as possible, be protected and allowed to regulate its own internal affairs, was never far removed from the directives of policy. Within this overriding policy framework the changes in the governmental system ensuing from pacification, notably the increased and reinforced authority of the Amenukal, and the greater political unification and centralization of the *tegehe* resulting from the Taitok's expulsion, seem to have been considered by the French not so much as a 'change' but merely a reinforcement and extension of the traditional ideology and principles of social and political organization. This point of view certainly seems to have owed much to the colonial classification of Tuareg society, with its notions of feudalism and consequent designation of the various classes as nobles, vassals, serfs and slaves—terms which were inculcated rigidly (a glance through the literature bears testimony) and not amenable to change!

The notion of 'stability' thus has some validity in so far as French policy sought to establish and maintain a status quo. By recognizing the social stratification of the society, reinforcing the authority of the Amenukal, and supporting the traditional rights of the Imuhag, or 'white' (!) Tuareg, in respect to the other 'inferior' classes, Ahaggar society, at least on the surface or in its outward appearance, may have shown much of its traditional form. But to think that the revolutionary changes that have taken place in Ahaggar since Algerian independence have been experienced by a society that had changed little during the preceding sixty years is a gross misconception. The accusation that the Algerian government has been directly responsible for 'the destruction of the Tuaregs' traditional way of life'[1] not only masks the realities of the colonial presence but denies the many significant changes that took place in Ahaggar as a direct consequence of pacification.

Even by the 1920s the face of Ahaggar was beginning to show a quite different complexion. Caravans to Niger, which traded salt for millet, and which were unknown before 1896, had become a regular annual event. Both the area of land under cultivation and the number of Harratin cultivators had increased; while the ethnic composition of the population had become far more plural as a result of the immigration of Arab nomads, various Islamic missionaries and teachers, and Mozabite shopkeepers, not to mention the European element.

However, the most interesting consequence of pacification and colonial rule, and perhaps the most significant, concerned not only the changing roles of the Ihaggaren, but the whole basis of Ihaggaren–Kel Ulli relations.

As we have already seen the overall relationship between the Ihaggaren and Kel Ulli had undergone significant changes even before the French arrival in Ahaggar. By the turn of the century the Kel Ulli had already acquired their own camels and rights over specialized arms, and were, as several French commentaries noted, equally capable warriors in their own right. These changes, which not only made them more economically independent of the Ihaggaren but provided the means for the exercise of their political rights, had been generated internally by forces that were inherent within the traditional class structure itself and owed little to the presence of France.

Nevertheless, this transformation in noble–vassal relations was accelerated considerably by the French encroachment and subsequent pacification of Ahaggar. On the political front the Kel Ulli's seizure of the political initiative, in which they gave their support to Moussa ag Amastane, can be seen as a result of the emergence of political factions among the Kel Rela, following the Flatters massacre, and the eventual eruption of anarchy after Aitarel's death.[2]

However, of far greater significance, and with more direct consequences in this respect, was the occupation of the oases of Tidikelt and Touat, and finally, with pacification, the cessation of warfare and raiding.

As M. Belin had suggested after the Flatters débâcle, the military occupation of the chain of oases to the north of Ahaggar would present the Kel Ahaggar with insuperable difficulties. It was, as M. Belin foresaw, their 'Achilles' heel', and the eventual occupation of Touat and Tidikelt at the end of the century not only deprived the Kel Ahaggar of access to these vital markets but also posed a serious impediment to their raiding exploits outside Ahaggar, which enabled them to overcome, or at least reduce, the consequences of drought and famine.[3] Even by 1896 it seems that the need to establish new markets outside Ahaggar had been felt, for in that year we see members of the Dag Rali and Aguh-en-tehle undertaking for the first time, on their own initiative and independently of the Ihaggaren, a caravan to Damergou in Niger to barter the salt they had mined in the plain of Amadror for millet.

Amadror is a flat barren waste, encircled by the mountains of Ahaggar. From the Djebel Telertheba, which stands like a great fortress on the south side of the *piste* about midway between Tamanrasset and Djanet, the expanse of gravel stretches for nearly 100 miles to the north before ending, quite suddenly, at the base of the Tassili escarpment. To the west it is bounded by the small massif of Tourha, and to the east by those of Toukmatine and Ounane. The whole plain tilts imperceptibly northwards to the little erg of Tihodaine with its almost pure white dunes[4] wedged up against the base of the scarp. The gravel surface is littered with various neolithic artefacts, testifying to its extensive occupation only a few thousand years ago when the plain supported a savanna-like vegetation and the Erg Tihodaine was an inland drainage basin.[5]

Most of the vehicles crossing to or from Djanet rarely stop in this area, for the terrain is flat and very arid. But there is much in Ahaggar that escapes the eye: about ten miles before the Djebel Telertheba there is a little hill called Tin Koukour,[6] just to the south side of the *piste*, covered with neolithic burial sites. This hill is the landmark for caravans returning laden from the salt deposits at Tisemt[7] in the terrace of the Oued Amadror. In the early morning or evening, when the shadows are long, the well-worn tracks of these caravans can be seen quite easily, beaten smooth into the loose gravel surface as they run parallel almost due north across the plain from Tin Koukour. One wonders how many camels and thousands of tons of salt have passed along these tracks, now sunken into the desert surface like disused tram-lines.

Although the evidence is confusing it seems that these salt deposits were not exploited and, perhaps surprisingly, not even widely known much before this date.[8] Why these Kel Ulli suddenly decided to carry salt about 800 or more miles from Amadror to Damergou in search of millet is not altogether clear. The period from 1886–1900 seems to have been one of relatively good pasture, except for an attack of locusts in 1893, and drought in 1897 and 1900.[9] It must be supposed, therefore, that the need to establish new markets was created more by the deprivations resulting from the French encroachment than by pastoral conditions within Ahaggar.

Further evidence for this need to establish new markets is seen quite clearly in 1903 when Kel Ahaggar (mostly Isekkemaren) sought dates as far afield as the Fezzan as a result of the French occupation of Touat and Tidikelt; though it was not so much the physical presence of the French that halted caravans to Touat and Tidikelt but rather the influence of the fanatical marabout Abidine, who forbade the eating of dates from these oases on religious grounds.[10] Further attempts to establish new markets were made again in 1908 when Kel Ahaggar undertook an expedition to Gao on the River Niger to obtain rice, and again in 1912 when they went to Anderamboukane to obtain millet. The idea of buying rice from Gao was suggested to the Kel Ahaggar by Colonel Laperrine. He considered that rice was cheaper than millet, but did not reckon on the difficulties caused by the Kel Ahaggar's general dislike of the Iwllemmeden Tuareg, who controlled the rice-producing areas in the Niger Bend.[11]

It was not until 1923 that salt caravans returned to Damergou. From 1926 onwards they became an annual event, but it is surprising, when the results of the first caravan had been so encouraging, that there was such a long delay before they became organized on a regular basis. It was certainly not due to decreased need. On the contrary, the curtailment of raiding and intermittent drought during the period of pacification had emphasized the precariousness of subsistence within Ahaggar.[12] Rather, it seems to have been due to the political upheavals, for Captain Florimond referred to 'troubles in Damergou' in 1908 which stopped caravans coming from Ahaggar.[13]

By the 1920s the Kel Ulli had attained an unprecedented level of economic self-sufficiency. Their subsistence base was assured through their goat herds, their slaves, a steady increase in garden produce as Harratin came progressively into the region and more land was put under cultivation; possession of their own camels; and above all their regular and abundant supplies of millet.

The Ihaggaren, for their part, did not find themselves in such an enviable position. Admittedly the Kel Rela, following the Taitok expulsion, gained sole rights as Ihaggaren over Ahaggar, and the camels given to Moussa ag

Amastane by the French as reward for his loyalty during the Senussi uprising provided them with some assurance for their future wealth,[14] but such compensations hardly offset the disturbing transformation in their relationship with the Kel Ulli.

The balance, or exchange basis, of the *temazlayt* relationship was already changing during the latter part of the nineteenth century as Kel Ulli acquired more of their own camels and became more capable warriors. As they became more economically independent so the *temazlayt* and *tamekchit* relationships became progressively more irksome to them, and even by the beginning of this century their attitude towards the Ihaggaren was tending towards resentment, and their demands were refused with greater regularity and assurance. Benhazera witnessed what seems to have been a typical example of this state of affairs. He wrote, 'I saw an Iouarouaren camp (Kel Ulli of Taitok drum group), who were camped near to tents of the Taitok nobles, break camp in order to pitch camp again further away. They had arrived back from Tidikelt with dates and other products, and the noble women constantly came to the Kel Ulli camp to ask for things. Eventually, their chief, In Chikadh, gave the order to leave, saying that it was in order to put a stop to the nobles' pestering.'[15]

Under these conditions, the *temazlayt* and *tamekchit* relationships, which had been the primary mechanisms through which the Ihaggaren had appropriated surplus, in the form of subsistence goods, from their Kel Ulli, no longer found justification and progressively disintegrated.

No longer the protectors of Ahaggar, great warriors, and the controllers of caravans passing through the region,[16] the Kel Rela found themselves initially with little to do except parade arrogantly around Ahaggar. I must not give the impression that their life became one of ease and contentment. That was certainly not the case, and I think that Gast's comment that the nomadic society 'hardened' during this period and lived on the memories of the past[17] was particularly applicable to the Kel Rela, who probably saw the French presence, at least initially, as a threat to their pre-eminent status in Ahaggar. On the one hand the diminution and eventual cessation of raiding denied them much of the prestige acquired as warriors, while on the other hand their modified relationship with their Kel Ulli jeopardized the former security of their subsistence base.

The response of the Kel Rela to this invidious situation was to find some measure of alternative status and prestige through the manipulation of the opportunities offered by the increased centralization of government in the position of the Amenukal and his greatly increased and sanctioned authority.

The Amenukal provided the link between Ahaggar and the French authorities,[18] although in practice the process of 'governing through' the Amenukal was more a process of negotiation, in which the interests of the Kel Ahaggar, particularly those of the Kel Rela, tended to be the dominant factor, so much so that many crucial questions such as land ownership and the position of slaves were never resolved or fully clarified until after Algerian independence.[19] Moreover, within Ahaggar itself the authority of the Amenukal became almost absolute. Supported and reinforced in his position of 'supreme chief' by the French, and no longer impeded by other drum chiefs, his authority became extended to cover almost all matters within Ahaggar as his spheres of competence became almost limitless.

Any individual who considered that he had been legally or morally wronged through maladministration or injustice had the right to appeal to the Amenukal. He was the supreme judicial authority over all affairs, ranging from disputed land rights and the imposition of indemnities to a whole host of domestic and familial matters such as marital disputes, residence problems, the division of inheritance, and so forth.[20] But in addition, the Amenukal's reinforced authority allowed him to intervene with respect to the moral rights and treatment of any individual, especially slaves and Harratin, according to his own judgement. This right or 'threat' of any individual to appeal to the Amenukal to intervene on his behalf acted as a reinforcement mechanism to the moral order.

It was this elevated and reinforced position of the Amenukal that provided the Kel Rela with their opportunity. During the years following pacification several of them, disgruntled by their increasingly tenuous relations with the Kel Ulli and attracted by the privileges and prestige to be found in the Amenukal's 'court', found it economically and politically expedient to attach themselves more permanently to his camp near Abalessa.

The extent to which the Kel Rela effectively formed a 'political élite' is questionable. In view of the lack of documentary records and because statements given by the Kel Rela themselves tend towards an exaggerated sense of their own importance, it is difficult to assess how much influence they exerted within the Amenukal's 'court' or 'council'. But in so far as the Kel Ulli had acquired greater influence during the preceding generation or so, particularly at the level of the *djemaa* and in such affairs as 'electing' the Amenukal, the effective political élite appears to have become more open and representative.

Nevertheless, proximity, both geographically and genealogically, to the centre of administrative authority in the position of the Amenukal provided the Kel Rela with the means of enhancing their waning prestige as nobles. By associating with and taking upon themselves the halo of authority that emanated from the Amenukal, particularly by forming his entourage when visiting the French authorities in Tamanrasset, they gravitated nearer to the centre of government, forming something of a self-styled and self-interested bureaucratic élite – in which their primary concern was for the maintenance of their status as nobles and the administration of their associated traditional rights and privileges; or, to put it a little more blatantly and realistically – 'tax-collecting'! The various levies on gardens, forms of *ehere-n-amadal* and *tiwse*, and certain religious taxes, although mostly payable to the Amenukal himself, were of direct benefit to the Kel Rela and became increasingly valuable to them as the *temazlayt* relationship progressively disintegrated. In this respect it is particularly interesting to note that several Kel Rela seem to have adopted the title of *echcherifen* ('descendants of the Prophet') during this period as part of the overall strategy to maintain their social pre-eminence, and perhaps even more specifically to provide greater legitimacy for their 'tax-collecting' activities and their accompanying demands for 'hospitality'!

## The Expansion of Cultivation

In the same way that the salt caravans to Damergou are often regarded as part of the Kel Ahaggar's 'traditional way of life', so there is a similar tendency to think of Harratin cultivators as an integral part of precolonial society. Cultivation was certainly undertaken in Ahaggar prior to the French encroachment and arrival, but its origins were still relatively recent and its practice was very limited in extent.

Cultivation had been long-established among the Kel Ajjer, but the Kel Ahaggar, being violent and intolerant fighters, could not endure the presence of cultivators in their territory. Since they were scornful of all manual work, it had taken a wise and farsighted Amenukal, namely El Hadj Akhmed, to realize the economic necessity for cultivation within Ahaggar. Some diffident gardening had been attempted by their slaves in the vicinity of Ideles around 1840, but they proved to be unsatisfactory cultivators, and at about 1861 El Hadj Akhmed attempted to extend the gardens at Ideles and to create a new cultivation centre at Tazrouk. In this task he was short-handed and under his protection cultivators consisting of 'white' Ahl Azzi and 'black' Harratin from Djanet, Tidikelt and Touat were invited to come into the region to cultivate the land for the Kel Ahaggar.

Harratin cultivators had thus been settled in Ahaggar from about the 1860s onwards. Nevertheless, at the time of the French arrival they probably numbered few more than 500, for in 1909, only a few years after the submission of the Kel Ahaggar, the sedentary population numbered only 697,[21] while at the same time (1909), Chudeau estimated that only 188 hectares of land were under cultivation.[22] We must therefore conclude that the contribution of cultivation within Ahaggar to the subsistence of the Kel Ahaggar prior to this century was only slight. And yet, by the end of the French period (1962), in the space of only about sixty years, the sedentary population, consisting mostly of Harratin, had increased ninefold, at an average growth rate of about 15 per cent per annum, to equal and perhaps slightly exceed the population of Kel Ahaggar.[23]

This remarkable growth rate was more or less mirrored in the increase in the area of land brought under cultivation. Although statistical material on such significant developments was not readily forthcoming during the French period, Jean Malaurie, in 1949, estimated that 460 hectares out of an estimated 1,420 hectares of cultivable land were being exploited.[24] Much of this land not actually under cultivation at the time of his survey was probably fallow, for Nemo, in 1962–3, estimated that the cultivated area, including fallow, fluctuated between 1,000 and 1,500 hectares.[25]

It is difficult, in view of the absence of any documentary records, to locate the specific factors which led to this rapid growth rate of the sedentary population after the first few years of this century. Ahaggar, with its more equitable climate than the regions to the north, and its opportunities for developing new land in the relatively fertile and well-watered areas of the major valleys, was certainly an attraction. But primarily it seems to have been the security offered by the French presence and the accompanying relative 'opening up' of the region that provided the inducement to settle increasingly in Ahaggar.

Furthermore, it seems that this immigration was actively encouraged by the Kel Ahaggar themselves, particularly the Kel Rela, whose subsistence base was no longer assured through their relations with the Kel Ulli. Although the Harratin were regarded contemptuously their increasing settlement in the region provided the Kel Ahaggar not only with more agricultural produce but, in the case of the Kel Rela, with an additional increase in revenue from their share of garden taxes paid to the Amenukal.

When we consider the scale of this immigration it is perhaps surprising that the history of the Harratin settlement in Ahaggar received virtually no documentary attention during the French period. In the absence of any evidence to the contrary, it seems to have been regarded favourably by the French, at least initially, since it was 'advantageous' to the Kel Ahaggar, extending and diversifying their subsistence base, besides contributing to the realization of the region's productive potential. But like a cancer, the spread and growth of which may pass unnoticed until its critical eruption, the initial growth of the Harratin population seems to have passed almost unnoticed, or as worthy of only minimal attention in so far as its accommodation posed no immediate threat to the 'traditional' socio-political order.

Prior to the development of cultivation, pastoralism in this vast and sparsely populated region required few complex rules on land rights, but was accommodated through the application of a few accepted principles orientated towards the needs of the most valuable resource, livestock.

As we have seen, these traditional rules or principles of land rights were extremely simple, flexible, and designed merely to accommodate the overall interests of stock-breeding.

Cultivation could obviously not be accommodated easily within such simple and loosely defined land rights, and with its introduction they were necessarily subjected to greater definition and diversification in order to reorganize and establish control over this new resource – cultivable land.

Throughout pre-colonial and colonial times, until Algerian independence, the rights that anyone could acquire to cultivable land were limited by two overriding principles: that no one, not even the Amenukal, could sell land; and that no one could hold rights to land without the authorization of the Amenukal and the consequent payment of a land-rent. Within these bounds rights to cultivated land were defined quite clearly.[26]

All cultivation in Ahaggar is undertaken with some form of irrigation. The rights to cultivable land were thus determined by the form of irrigation, so that rights of 'ownership' extended not over a strictly defined area but rather the area or zone which was irrigable by a *foggara*[27] (underground aqueduct) or well.[28] Rights to the possession of land were accordingly held by the 'owner' of the *foggara* or well.[29]

In Tidikelt and Touat *foggaras* may run for tens of miles under the desert surface, but in Ahaggar the mountainous terrain is such that aqueducts are rarely more than a few metres below the surface and few extend for more than a mile or two, as they lead water from the water-bearing strata in the sandy river bed to the cultivated areas.[30] The construction and maintenance of these subterranean aqueducts was a dangerous and labour-demanding task. The occasional heavy rains in Ahaggar can turn the dry river beds into raging torrents that can completely destroy the *foggara* systems. Even if they survived the floods, the continual danger of subsidence made their lives relatively short-lived. Today, more and more *foggaras* are falling into disuse as wells and motor-pumps take over the irrigation of the gardens. Only a few are still in use and most major valleys, especially in the vicinity of the cultivation centres, are pitted with lines of old access vents leading down into the now dry and sand-clogged aqueducts. On the surface, the mounds of excavated sand, thrown up through the vents like enormous ant-hills, and stretching away up the middle or sides of the dry river beds, bear testimony to the former Herculean labours of slaves and Harratin cultivators. Many are the animals and even humans who have stumbled unwittingly into these derelict shafts.

As more Harratin came into Ahaggar little cultivation centres gradually sprang up throughout the region, firstly at Ideles and Tazrouk, and then at such places as Hirafok, In Amguel, Abalessa and Tamanrasset. Most of these centres were located around the foothills of Atakor where the valleys opened out and the alluvial deposits of the lower (neolithic) terrace provided small areas of fertile land, and where the wide sandy valleys enabled the construction of *foggaras*.

A small number of 'non-Tuareg', notably religious men and certain Arab nomads who had settled in Ahaggar, particularly during this century, obtained rights from the Amenukal, albeit precarious and theoretically revokable, to excavate and 'own' *foggaras* or wells. But the Harratin who came to Ahaggar held no such rights. Only the Kel Ahaggar held rights to the possession of cultivable land, for only they could assure the security of the small agricultural settlements that began to develop, and they made contracts with the Harratin to cultivate the land on their behalf. The nature of this contract was such that the Harratin received one-fifth of the harvest for his labours, while the owner of the land retained four-fifths in respect of the costs incurred in the development and maintenance of the cultivated land and the irrigation system.[31] The terms of this traditional contract were that the owner provided the cultivator with the land and paid the cost of clearing and improving it, giving him a hoe, the seed, a *foggara* to supply water to the land, and one-fifth of the harvest. These five conditions of the contract were each equal to one-fifth of the harvest,[32] and for that reason the owner retained four-fifths for himself.[33] Because of its five parts, or conditions, the contract was known as the *khamast* system, from the Arabic word *khamsa* meaning 'five', and the cultivator, with his piteous one-fifth, was known as a *khames*.

Nevertheless, as Gast has pointed out, the *khames* could add to his income if he was farsighted and worked hard:[34]

1. Ahaggar. Mount Ilaman in middle distance.

2. Ahaggar. The author on summit of Mount Tahat, the highest point in Algeria.

3. Kel Ahaggar, adorned in finest robes, prepare to parade their camels.

4. Dag Rali camp.

5. Kel Ahaggar with riding and pack camels at Assekrem.

6. Kel Ahaggar parading in the evening at the beginning of an *ahal* following a marriage.

7. Dag Rali camp in the evening before a heavy thunderstorm.

8. Dag Rali tent – dawn after all-night torrential rain. Note blankets etc. being dried, and old man in white robes lying on ground in front of tent suffering from rheumatism. The small ridge of earth encircling tent was built during the night to keep rainwater out.

9. Kel Ahaggar waiting for tea to be made. The tent, which has no awning, is being erected after having been moved to this location only two days before.

10. Fire providing warmth in colder winter nights.

11. Kel Ahaggar, labouring on the construction of a tourist rest-house at Assekrem, make tea.

12. A nomadic blacksmith at work.

13. Kel Ahaggar gather around a nomadic blacksmith ('Ened') and watch him work.

14. Kel Ahaggar woman preparing millet porridge.

15. The evening meal of *cous cous* being prepared.

16

17

18.

16. and 17. An evening meal of millet porridge cooking on fire while men make tea. Note different position of veils.

18. Reunion of those involved in the Otoul affair after their release from detention in 1968. The plastic cover over the one camel saddle is to protect it from the drizzle.

19. A Hartani working his own *tanout* irrigation system independently at Amsel.

20. Men sitting outside tent in cold morning air. Young boys pounding millet.

21. Gardens at Tazrouk being prepared for sowing.

22. The 'pilot' agricultural co-operative at Amsel.

23

23. Old slave woman, who has chosen to remain in the camp of her former master, tending goat herd.

24. Goat herd being taken out at dawn to eke out pasture.

24

1. The owner paid seven kilograms of wheat for each new well dug to improve the *foggara* system.

2. Barley and wheat sown in small lines alongside the irrigation channel could be harvested by the cultivator.

3. The grain scattered on the ground after the harvest was collected by the cultivator's family.

4. After threshing, the grain mixed in the dust belonged to the cultivator, providing that it was not deeper than his ankle.

5. All the straw belonged to the cultivator.

6. All vegetables that could be harvested outside the gardens watered directly by the irrigation channel belonged to the cultivator.

Although a 'free' man, a Hartani's freedom, in practical terms, entitled him to little more than the right to leave Ahaggar should he so wish. He was a dependent client of the Kel Ahaggar, subject to the laws of Ahaggar and the authority of the Amenukal, and without means of gaining any control over the means of agricultural production. He could acquire no rights of 'ownership'[35] in that ownership rights over the cultivation centres, or *arrem* as they were called in Tamahak, were held by the tenant in whose territory they were located; while the nature of the *khamast* itself effectively denied him any control over his own labour. Neither was he able to acquire any form of 'capital asset', such as livestock, very easily, for his one-fifth merely enabled his family to survive, often in a state of severe malnutrition. Moreover, in spite of the slight additions that he could make to his income if he was farsighted and hard-working, the one-fifth was a gross rather than a net income, as the garden-owner and various other 'passers-by' (*amagaren*), notably marabouts and other Tuareg, would frequently impose themselves on the cultivator for long periods, especially around harvest time, and demand hospitality.

Through the more precise definition and reorientation of the traditional system of land rights to accommodate the introduction of cultivation, with only slight modifications in the last few years of French occupation, the Kel Ahaggar, or Imuhag, were able to exercise complete control over the means of agricultural production. They held exclusive rights over the land and water and the immigration of Harratin effectively provided them with the labour to exploit this new resource. But although cultivation was introduced to Ahaggar several years before the French arrival, the increased immigration of Harratin resulting from pacification and the security of the French presence caused something of a population explosion in terms of the rapid growth of a dependent and impoverished community alongside the nomadic Imuhag – namely the Kel Arrem, or 'sedentarists', whose entrenched position of subordination to the Imuhag came to replace the internal division of 'nobles–vassals' as the dominant and critical line of cleavage in Ahaggar society during the latter years of colonial administration.[36]

## Islamization and Arabization

The penetration of Islam into Ahaggar has been sporadic; the actual settlement of religious groups and families in the region did not become widespread until the early part of this century. Although Islamic missionaries probably arrived among the Northern Tuareg in the first few centuries of Islam, and it is likely that they established the Imenan as a theocratic dynasty, the Tuareg, particularly the Kel Ahaggar, have always been regarded by the Moslems to the north as 'not very devout', or only 'lukewarm' Moslems. Benhazera himself commented that 'Les Touareg, pris dans leur ensemble, sont très peu religieux',[37] while Gast also mentions that Ahaggar, at the time of the French arrival, was 'encore peu musulman'.[38] It is therefore interesting that Lyon reported having seen a group of about 150 Tuareg passing through Murzuk on their way to Mecca in May 1819,[39] but he does not mention where they had come from and it is almost certain that they were Southern Tuareg, among whom entire Ineslemen lineages had been settled for some time.

During the nineteenth century it seems that the Tidjani order counted a considerable following among the Kel Ahaggar, especially the Isekkemaren, although around the turn of the century and particularly during the Senussi uprising it was the Senussi order which came to count the largest following. Nevertheless, the number of *cheurfa*[40] and maraboutic families settled in Ahaggar prior to the latter part of the nineteenth century was relatively few compared with the Southern Tuareg (e.g. Iforas of Adrar), for it was not until towards the end of the century that *cheurfa* and marabouts came into Ahaggar and settled in any significant number.

Ineslemen held considerable status and influence among the Kel Ahaggar. Intermarriages with the Kel Ahaggar were regarded favourably, and their settlement in the region was facilitated by the Amenukal authorizing them to cut *foggaras* and hold land rights in the same capacity as Kel Ahaggar, though theoretically these rights were more precarious in that they were always revokable. However, this movement of *cheurfa* and marabouts into Tuareg country, especially around the end of the century, was motivated as much, if not more, by political ends than by missionary zeal. For the newly arrived colonizers of North Africa, 'maraboutism', particularly in its most fanatical anti-French form, was a dangerous political force.[41]

But as in the case of the increased immigration of Harratin cultivators after the beginning of this century, so it was the French conquest and pacification of the Kel Ahaggar that exposed Ahaggar to the wider reaches and influence of Islam in the form of *cheurfa* and marabouts who, with the opening up of the region and the security provided by the French presence, came in considerable numbers to stake their claim in these hitherto relatively unexploited and lucrative pastures.

Religious persons, Ineslemen, were held in high esteem and shared a comparable status to the Ihaggaren, except, of course, that they had no Kel Ulli. They officiated at such functions as marriages, funerals, naming ceremonies and so forth, and acted very much as legal counsellors, advising on almost all issues, intervening in and resolving disputes, teaching the Koran, administering cures and, perhaps above all else, emitting *baraka*.

The Kel Ahaggar's beliefs in God[42] and the related concept of *baraka* were basically the same as those found elsewhere in North Africa. God was eternal, all-powerful and good, but also a punisher and a condemner. His 'home' was in the sky, but his spiritual presence was everywhere; he saw and heard everything. *Baraka* was closely tied to the conception of God. It was a kind of mystical force or grace; a benediction or holiness deriving from God, and possessed by, or found in, both certain persons and things.[43]

Nobody possessed more *baraka* than the Prophet, and it is therefore found in all his descendants (*cheurfa*), as well as in the marabouts (Arabic *wali*). On their death their *baraka* increases since they become nearer to God, and their tombs, from which *baraka* emanates, may thus become shrines.

The importance of *baraka* to the Kel Ahaggar can perhaps be best understood in their conception of the character of innate human behaviour, which was seen as a somewhat one-sided struggle between God and Satan, or Iblis. Iblis (Echchitan) was considered as the evil tempter and the adversary of God, and like God was found everywhere, in and around all men, including marabouts. But, at the same time, Iblis was an essential part of man, and without Iblis it is difficult to conceive of *baraka*. While everything that grows and lives is good and contains *baraka*, for nothing is born without the will of God, the procreative desire for sexual intercourse is generated by Iblis.[44] For the Kel Ahaggar, this essential association between Iblis and *baraka* was recognized in the conflict between good and evil that is inherent in every human. But in this innate struggle good tended to prevail, for God was stronger than his adversary, and for the faithful *baraka* was always able to overcome the spirit and presence of Iblis.

The status and esteem in which marabouts and *cheurfa* were held can thus be understood, for it was they who radiated the *baraka* which enabled good to prevail. *Baraka*, however, was not confined to such esoteric matters as the nature of good and evil and the innate character of human nature. It also pervaded the more down to earth and mundane activities of daily life.

Success, which might perhaps be seen in terms of survival, was largely dependent on man's ability to overcome and utilize his natural environment, intimate knowledge of which was therefore essential, not only for stockbreeding, but for hunting, collecting and medicinal purposes. If one walks through Ahaggar it is almost impossible to believe that there are over 600 different plant species in the region,[45] of which over sixty have some nutritional value.[46] The several types of wild grain and other plants that can provide some sort of nutritional or medicinal value from their fruits, seeds, stems or roots are known by most Tuareg; but like the many species of wild animals and reptiles, many of which are also eaten, they are not perceived readily by our unaccustomed eyes.[47]

Environmental or ecological factors thus played a significant part in their social organization, determining not only the size of camps but their duration of stay and movement, and to a large extent the expenditure of labour in the exploitation of alternative resources. The whole annual cycle of activities was virtually controlled by man's exploitation of the meagre natural resources at his disposal. More than one year of successive drought could lead to the decimation of the herds, possible famine, and even the loss of human lives. It is therefore not very surprising to find that the Kel Ahaggar's relationship with nature was pervaded by religious and superstitious beliefs to the extent that almost all actions assumed transcendental values.

Disasters, such as drought or illness, were not considered entirely in the fatalistic terms of the inevitable, but rather as an 'act of God' in retribution for man's own actions. The most common cause for such punishment was the destruction of *baraka*, which was found in many things and maintained by a series of taboos. To break one of these taboos was to invoke the punishment of God. As *baraka* was found in all that was living[48] and good – in short, all that was pure – so the taboos which applied to its maintenance were related to the impure. The distinction between pure and impure found expression in much symbolic action and pervaded almost every sphere of activity, providing a means of classification for nearly all action and a regulation of the moral code.

*Baraka* was found in such things as good pasture, date palms, milk and so forth, but was destroyed by contact with impurity. Menstruating women, for example, were consequently not permitted to drink the milk of animals with young, nor water from skin bags that had just been made. Similarly, both the earth and fire were considered impure and destructive of *baraka*. Milk should therefore not be spilled on the earth, and even the water used to wash a milk bowl was usually thrown over a nearby rock or plant.[49] In the same way, date stones were not thrown into the fire, and Nicolaisen mentions that this taboo was applicable to many living organisms, including the rather detestable leach-fly (*Ixodes ricinus*), which sucks the blood of camels.[50]

Responsibility for the overall maintenance of *baraka* throughout the land was partly encumbent on the office of Amenukal, who visited the Cherif of Issellisken (near Abalessa) annually to pray for the fertility of the camels and rain for the pastures.[51] At the more individual level *baraka* was derived mainly from living marabouts and *cheurfa*, and their tombs.[52]

It is the relationship between these religious personages and the Kel Ahaggar in which we are most interested, and for this reason I have briefly outlined the belief in *baraka*. But before looking at the more 'this worldly' aspect of their relationship, I may be permitted, in connection with these beliefs and man's relation to both the natural and supernatural, to stray a little and introduce another 'population' whose presence was a continual source of bewilderment to the Tuareg.

### '*Things That Go Bump in the Night*'

The Islamic conception of Iblis recalls the belief in *djenoun* (demons).[53] Among the Kel Ahaggar (and other Tuareg) Iblis is always referred to in the singular and is of a different nature to the demons, who are known as Kel Asouf, the 'people who live all alone' or 'people who talk to no one'; or alternatively as Kel Had, the 'people of the night', Kel Tenere, the 'people of the desert' (empty places), or Kel Amadal, the 'people of the earth'. Unlike Iblis, which is conceptualized not in terms of human characteristics, but rather as a 'state of mind', or 'force' that influences the state of mind and hence actions,[54] the Kel Asouf have distinctly human qualities. They live and die like humans, marry and reproduce like humans, but are always disfigured in some way or another with such features as a tail, eyes in the back of the head, more or less than five fingers on each hand, and so forth.

The Kel Asouf are essentially mischievous and wicked, and many of the daily mishaps of life are attributed to their doing. Even though many of these traditional beliefs are now held with a degree of scepticism, there are still those who maintain that most internal illnesses are caused by the Kel Asouf entering the body, and who believe that they can even kill both humans and animals. In the same way that a series of taboos maintains *baraka*, so a considerable amount of behaviour is motivated by beliefs in the Kel Asouf. The places where they are found, such as in fire, trees, caves, holes in the ground, bloody areas (where an animal has been killed), dirty places, empty places (e.g. Tenere) and water-holes, tend to be avoided, or at least treated with a little circumspection. Many superstitions surround the belief in the Kel Asouf and those places which are known to be their specific domain, such as the Garet el Djenoun, the craggy mountain at the northern end of the Tefedest massif, and Amdelis and Timdilisene, about 150 kilometres down the Oued Tamanrasset,[55] will not be visited readily. Certain barbary sheep and gazelles with a nick in their ear, or the end of an ear missing, are believed to belong to the Kel Asouf, and will not be killed for fear of illness befalling the hunter.

Protection against the Kel Asouf and the treatment of internal illnesses alleged to have been caused by them are afforded by many herbs. Kel Asouf are particularly active during the hours of darkness, and in the evening the aroma of *teheregele*,[56] which is believed to drive the Kel Asouf away, can be tasted in the tea or scented in the air as a few sprigs are placed on the embers. This herb does not grow in the Sudanese regions and it is quite common to see several sacks piled outside the customs office in Tamanrasset, waiting to be transported south. The veil, as we have already mentioned, is also believed to offer some protection against the Kel Asouf, and it is for this reason that great care is taken to ensure that it is well above the mouth and nostrils while travelling in deserted areas, and during the night. In this context it is interesting to note that men are more susceptible to Kel Asouf than women; a belief which almost certainly relates to their impurity, and leads us to assume that there may be an association between the Kel Asouf and the concepts of *baraka* and Iblis, although Tuareg have always assured me that the Kel Asouf are quite distinct from these two concepts.

Discussions with Tuareg about the Kel Asouf have provided many amusing incidents, for although such beliefs are being subjected to a certain reappraisal in the light of more orthodox Islamic influences and the forces of modernization, they have not been entirely discarded, and tend to be discussed in the same hesitant manner as a child stating quite affirmatively that it does not believe in ghosts!

My first major confrontation with the Kel Asouf perhaps shows something of the seriousness with which they can be taken. I was visiting the camp of a rather disgruntled old Dag Rali, whom I shall refer to as El Khoussin, and with whom I had planned to stay for a few weeks. At the time his camp was about twenty miles from Assekrem, and on setting off from Assekrem at dawn I decided to pass by a small gorge in which there was a particularly welcoming *guelta*. The water-hole was about halfway to the camp and would have enabled me to travel without having to carry water as well as providing me with the opportunity of a much-needed bath. I entered the gorge at about midday only to see goats grazing contentedly and the water-hole already occupied by El Khoussin's daughter-in-law, an attractive young woman of about twenty who, while watching the goats and her baby, was bathing completely naked. It was something of a crisis. Not only was I much in need of a bath, but I had drunk no water since leaving Assekrem at dawn. After sitting for an hour or two above the pool it was evident that its vacation would not be imminent, and for fear of causing considerable embarrassment and jeopardizing extremely valuable relations with her camp, I set off, to arrive in El Khoussin's camp more thirsty and dirty than ever.

About half a mile from his camp was another rock water-hole, but each time I mentioned going to it to wash I was met with considerable resistance from El Khoussin. His opposition had nothing to do with my fouling the pool as drinking water was taken from small wells dug into the sandy *oued* floor. Indeed the water was already well fouled by the goats who drank there. For four days I raised the subject of bathing in the pool at opportune moments only to meet with El Khoussin's insistence that it was extremely dangerous and that I might even die. How could this be? Only a few days earlier I had seen his own daughter-in-law bathing naked in a similar pool, and I, a full-grown man and reasonable swimmer, was hardly likely to drown in a pool only three or four feet deep!

Eventually, when I sensed that El Khoussin's son was sympathetic to my request, I set off determinedly to the rock pool. The old man, faced by this divided loyalty and the laughter of the women, picked up his stick and threatened to walk to Tamanrasset to tell the Algerian authorities that he would be in no way responsible for my death, or any other misfortune that might befall me while staying in his camp. It was not until later, when I had become more aware of such beliefs in the Kel Asouf, that I learnt that El Khoussin's concern for my safety derived from his own fear of the Kel Asouf in the water-hole.

Such widespread and pervasive beliefs, especially that of *baraka*, and the naïve admiration afforded to marabouts by the Kel Ahaggar, made Ahaggar a particularly attractive region for 'religious exploitation'. The institutions of *amagarou* and *tabauhak* provided the marabouts and *cheurfa* with an extremely lucrative livelihood. *Amagar* means literally 'someone who presents himself or calls to receive hospitality (food)' – whether he receives it or not.[57] An *amagar* was not an invited guest, but literally anyone, regardless of their class, origin or nationality, who came with the hope or expectancy of receiving hospitality (*amagarou*), and applied equally to the Kel Ahaggar, who claimed hospitality from their cultivators at harvest time, and to complete foreign strangers such as myself, who might find themselves by accident or design in a Tuareg camp.[58] *Tabauhak* is literally a type of slipper,[59] but refers to collecting, or, more appropriately, 'passing round the hat'!

The *cheurfa* and marabouts who came and settled in Ahaggar were *amagaren*, moving from one camp to another, relying on hospitality and alms – *tabauhak*. The admiration and esteem afforded them by the Kel Ahaggar gave them easy access to the camps. They descended on their 'congregation' to give *baraka*, and sometimes religious amulets to ward off various spirits, in exchange for hospitality, which was expected automatically – but always at a price. *Baraka* was given in exchange for a few 'gifts', such as one or two goats, which usually had to be given in any case before the *amagar* would leave the camp.

The *cheurfa* and marabouts were glorious parasites, relying on the fear and esteem of the Kel Ahaggar for this religious culture. Their audacity was remarkable. Benhazera tells a story about Beketa ag Ibrahim, the marabout who with Abidine had forbidden the eating of dates from the French occupied Tidikelt oases: when entering a Kel Ulli camp to ask for dates he was reminded by the Kel Ulli that they came from Tidikelt and were consequently forbidden by religion. Faced with this challenge Beketa replied that 'all that is now finished' – and duly accepted the dates![60] Gast even records having witnessed these 'collectors' accept animals (goats and camels) and immediately resell them on the spot in the same camp to meet their preference for bank-notes![61] When we consider the haughty pride of the Kel Ahaggar and their violent reaction to injustice, the patience and humility shown to these religious personages was remarkable.[62]

Even more parasitical and feared than the marabouts were the *tolba*,[63] who made and sold protective amulets and religious inscriptions at a considerable price. The *taleb* was especially feared for his mystical power (*ettama*), and the Kel Ahaggar were at his unscrupulous mercy. It is said by both Kel Ahaggar and Harratin, who suffered equally if not more, that at harvest time and the return of the caravans the *cheurfa* and *tolba* would descend on them like crows.

Religious personages also performed the role of 'tax-collector'. In addition to the *tiwse* and *ehere-n-amadal* payments there was a further religious tax known as *zakat*, which has become more or less institutionalized in Ahaggar over the last century. *Zakat* was of two kinds: a sort of income tax levied on animals, harvest, monetary income and so forth; and a form of gift tax, *zakat al fit'r*, or *achour* as it is usually known in Ahaggar, given at the end of the fast. In 1964 *zakat al fit'r* became fixed at two dinars per head, thanks to the intervention of the government authorities.

These taxes are prescribed by Islamic doctrine, but in Ahaggar were not collected from all groups alike, due to the lack of public administration and the fact that most persons claimed to have less than their taxable minimum, which among the nomadic population was obviously not easy to refute. In Ahaggar the rates were clearly defined:[64]

The owner of five camels must give one goat.

The owner of ten camels must give two goats.

The owner of twenty-five camels must give one camel.

The owner of forty goats must give one goat.

The owner of five charges of wheat (at the rate of about 150 kg. per charge, consisting of two sacks) must give one sack (seventy-five kg., i.e. 10 per cent) if the wheat comes from a garden irrigated by a *foggara*, and fifteen measures if the grain is irrigated by a draught animal (e.g. *tanout* system); one measure = 2·5 kg.

Wheat grown by irrigation from a counter-weighted pole and bucket (*aroudid*, Arabic *khottara*) is not taxed whatever its quantity, in recognition of the expenditure of physical effort required by this system of irrigation.

Five charges of raisins are taxed like wheat at the rate of one sack, although anything less than five charges is untaxed.

*Zakat* was paid much more readily by the 'non-Tuareg' section of Ahaggar society, particularly the cultivator, and the pious shopkeepers of Tamanrasset whose relationship to God is conveniently close at certain times of the year! As far as the nomadic Kel Ahaggar were concerned, *zakat* and *tabauhak* were one and the same thing, and just part of the overall exactions made on them by *cheurfa* and *tolba* in the name of 'Islam'.

This form of exploitation of the rural populations by religious men was not peculiar to Ahaggar society. What is perhaps surprising is that so few religious men seem to have managed to stake a claim in Ahaggar prior to the end of the last century, compared with neighbouring regions, for the collection of 'food' by religious men was, as Desparmet described so well, a generalized institution throughout the Maghreb:

> Les marabouts et les cheurfa ont le droit de réclamer l'achour aux laics, mais les cheurfa peuvent exiger du laic le tiers de la récolte. Il est des marabouts qui n'ont pas honte de venir en toute saison chez le cultivateur; ainsi, au printemps, ils lui réclament du beurre frais et, en été, des agneaux. Quant à ceux qui ont quelque retenue, ils ne viennent qu'à la moisson. Après les marabouts, c'est le tour des t'olba des Zâouias de venir, en la personne de leurs 'valets' et du moqaddem. Eux aussi apportent des sacs. Ils s'installent chez le paysan en attendant la fin des battages. Ils mangent, ils boivent, ils passent la nuit sur l'aire et surveillent jalousement chez le grain. Les khames se moquent du t'aleb, font des chansons sur lui et disent:
>
> 'A l'heure où le vent sifflait et où le froid nous glaçait, toi, tu étais à la mosquée, bien et chaud; maintenant, j'en jure par Dieu, tu n'emporteras ni criblure ni grain.' Mais bien qu'ils rient des t'olba, ils leur donnent leur part au nom du Qoran vénéré. On dit: 'S'il n'y avait pas d'eau ou de savants, ce bas monde serait plongé dans les ténèbres.' On dit encore: 'Les t'olba sont les yeux des bovins', par 'bovins' on entend les laics.[65]

During the more recent years, particularly since Algerian independence, the general relationship between the Kel Ahaggar and this maraboutic class has changed considerably. With the rapid increase in the size and relative wealth of the sedentary population since independence, the marabouts are taking firmer roots in the villages and directing their attentions more to the sedentary community in preference to the impoverished nomadic camps which were formerly their main source of provision. Furthermore, with all affairs now regulated more closely by the Algerian authorities, the marabouts' spheres of influence and authority are becoming more confined to strictly religious and familial matters. Legal matters and disputes are no longer their prerogative as they may now be taken before the official *cadi* (magistrate), or the various official delegates of the Commune of Tamanrasset.

As a result of these modifications and constraints, and the Kel Ahaggar's re-evaluation of many of their traditional superstitions and beliefs in the overall process of modernization and change, the Kel Ahaggar are now less fearful of this maraboutic class and less plagued by their exactions.

The Harratin and maraboutic populations that began to arrive in Ahaggar in increasing numbers after the end of the last century were distinctly 'Arabic' in character in so far as their mother tongue, and various other cultural features, were Arabic. Their immigration thus had a strong 'arabizing' influence on the region, particularly in the religious and linguistic spheres.[66] But ethnicity in Ahaggar, as in the Maghreb as a whole, is a dangerously misleading and hazy concept, especially when we try and define Arab–Berber, or in this case Arab–Tuareg, distinctions, beyond certain immediate cultural characteristics.

In its more specific and restricted usage the term 'Arab' refers primarily to a linguistic classification, but as used more frequently by the Kel Ahaggar in its wider ethnic context is merely a convenient and often derogatory classification for all 'foreigners' (assuming obviously that they are Moslem) from the north. So loose and generalized is the meaning of the term that the Algerian authorities, and the government as a whole, are often referred to quite simply as 'the Arabs', regardless of their individual ethnic origins. A Kabyle administrator in Tamanrasset thus tends to find himself re-classified as 'Arab' in the local context – regardless of the fact that he is a Berber!

Although this generalized usage of the term is partly a reflection of the Kel Ahaggar's general attitude towards the 'Arabs', and the north in general, in that they are not attributed clearer ethnic definition, its generally derogatory and often hostile content is more a reflection of their ambivalent perspective of the distinctly 'non-Tuareg' world to the north. On the one hand the impinging Arab tribes such as the Kunta and Ulad ba Hammu, as well as most of the other Arab tribes of Tidikelt and neighbouring areas, were regarded as relatively easy prey for raiders, and hence in some way 'inferior'. On the other hand, the Arabic populations to the north, particularly the powerful Chaamba tribe, with whom there had always been long-standing enmity, were perceived as potential adversaries and threats to their sovereignty.

The connotation of 'Arab' thus goes beyond what we might regard as a purely ethnic distinction in that its implicit reference is towards the 'external' and not the 'internal': its viewpoint looks outwards and not inwards. The massif of Ahaggar was an impregnable refuge from which the Kel Ahaggar could venture forth in attack and into which they could withdraw in defence. The various Tassili escarpments were their cordons of sanctuary behind which they could remain inviolate. The potentially threatening and hostile world to the north was held beyond these defences. That which passed in, such as Harratin cultivators, religious persons and certain Arab nomads, was what was needed or could be accommodated without posing any threat to their political and territorial sovereignty. By entering into Ahaggar these elements no longer belonged to the 'outside', but in a sense were transformed into a part of the 'interior'. France was not from this 'outside' world, but beyond it, and her presence, regardless of whatever else, ensured the maintenance of this sovereignty. Not until Algerian independence did the 'exterior' – 'the Arabs' – violate the defences and sovereignty of Ahaggar.

We can thus understand why 'Arabism', in spite of the accelerated immigration of Arabic elements into the region after the turn of the century, was relatively insignificant as a criterion of classification, for it was not only accommodated but subsumed and assimilated within the broader distinction that was emerging between the pastoral (-cum-raiding) and agricultural economic formations, and through the Kel Ahaggar's control of land rights, the maintenance of their territorial sovereignty, the subordination of the latter. Indeed, the 'ethnic' dimension of this distinction was blurred, for if the sedentary community was exclusively 'Arabic',[67] the nomadic community was by no means exclusively 'Tuareg'. In fact the extent to which foreign, or rather 'Arab' nomads, were accommodated and became assimilated into the nomadic community of Ahaggar is perhaps surprising.

The two major infusions of Arab nomads have been the Ahl Azzi and Chaamba. Although most Ahl Azzi were *khames*, it appears that several of them acquired precarious land rights on the basis of their maraboutic claims similar to those acquired by the marabouts and *cheurfa*.[68] But in addition to these cultivators several Ahl Azzi pastoralists were also allowed to settle in the region. Through three or four generations of intermarriage with the Kel Ahaggar, notably the Dag Rali (especially the Kel Tinhart section), with whom many of them live, they have become totally assimilated into the Kel Ahaggar nomadic community (Imuhag) and should be classed, as Nicolaisen suggests, 'rather with the Tuareg than with Arabs'.[69] When I first began to work among the Dag Rali I was constantly perplexed by the Kel Rezzi (as these Ahl Azzi are known), thinking that they were perhaps another section of the Dag Rali. My confusion was made no easier by the Kel Rezzi and Dag Rali themselves assuring me that they were 'Kel Rezzi like the Dag Rali'! But as my knowledge of Tamahak improved, so the situation became clear to me and their genealogies gradually found their way back to In Salah!

The settlement and assimilation of Chaamba is even more surprising in view of their long-standing enmity with the Kel Ahaggar. The French *mehariste* corps consisted predominantly of Chaamba, and as ancient enemies of the Tuareg and equally competent cameleers and warriors they provided the French with an admirable means of beating the Tuareg at their own game. Many of them brought their families with them, and on retiring from the corps were given authorization by the Amenukal, to whom they paid the customary land-rent, to settle in the region. In the same way as the Kel Rezzi, their assimilation and overall relationship with the Kel Ahaggar has been facilitated through numerous intermarriages, and several of them, in spite of the move towards sedentarization in recent years, are still living in their nomadic camps.

The number of Kel Rezzi and Chaamba who settled in Ahaggar was small and consequently posed no threat to the domination of the Kel Ahaggar, particularly since as foreigners their land rights were theoretically revokable. But primarily it seems that this assimilation of 'Arab' nomads was facilitated by the fact that Arab–Tuareg ethnicity, in its more general context, was a dimension of the 'external' domain, while in its more specific context it was relatively insignificant to and subsumed within the emerging and overriding distinction between 'nomad' and 'sedentarist'.[70]

# TEN
# RESISTANCE TO CHANGE AND THE PRESERVATION OF THE STATUS QUO

Pacification, as we have seen, was a turbulent process that brought many changes to Ahaggar. But the following generation, from the 1920s until the 1950s, might well be described as relatively stable and quiescent so far as the dominant forces in Ahaggar were conservative. France's 'traditionalist' policy was determined largely by political expediency on the wider international front, and in more active terms could be described fittingly as 'muddling through' rather than *laissez-faire* in the more deliberate sense; while the Kel Ahaggar for their part activated against any sort of change, particularly in the realms of land reform and political representation.

Such a summary assessment in itself does not bode well. No mention is made of the growing sedentary community as a dominant force, but then it was the subordination or 'silence' of this emerging majority that gave Ahaggar its apparent stability.

When we consider the vast area and scant population of Ahaggar it is perhaps a little ironic that the question of land ownership should have presented a crucial problem. The traditional concept of 'ownership' obviously conflicted with French civil law, but in spite of endless debate and the pressure of vested interests the question of the legal basis of land ownership and appropriation was never completely resolved throughout the French period, and it was left for the Algerians to clarify the issue, which they did in no uncertain manner.

The initial difficulty was that the recognition of the Amenukal's immutable ownership of all land in Ahaggar meant that citizens of French statute law or Moslem law were subjected to an unwritten custom. Such an unsatisfactory situation could not persist, and shortly after the establishment of Tamanrasset as the administrative centre the French reached some sort of agreement with the Amenukal in which he delegated to the French administration his authority regarding the division of land, except that which was already under cultivation. Through this agreement the French were able to establish a 'Public Domain' under their administration, but as far as the official records go the agreement does not appear to have had any written or signed legal validity, and as time went by the whole basis and validity of the agreement became shrouded in contention. Although the Amenukal had apparently given his assurance that he would not intervene in the administration of this land, it was not at all clear whether he had in fact relinquished his right of ownership over it. Bay ag Akhemouk, after his election as Amenukal in 1951, contested the agreement by stating that the Amenukal did not even have the right to dispose of any land! Although rights over cultivated land were defined quite clearly (they remained under the Amenukal's jurisdiction according to traditional custom), the ambiguous situation created by the agreement was never resolved. The Public Domain remained a questionable entity with neither the administration nor the army able to assume rights of ownership over any land, with the overall result that by 1959 no lands had in fact been registered officially as part of the Domain.[1]

The details of all the negotiations and dealings within this confused state of affairs cannot be ascertained easily owing to the almost total lack of official records. Nevertheless, Jean Nemo does state that around 1930–35 the 'Annexe' claimed that several areas of land belonged to the French. The precise form of these claims is not known, although it does seem that they had been claimed by payment, and had even been resold, even though the only trace of such sales that Nemo could find were a few hastily executed deeds.[2]

As in all such tiresome situations the means of circumvention are soon discovered, and in 1936 a devious procedure was developed that was to become an established means for those persons who wanted to become outright property owners.[3] Not surprisingly the first case involved a certain high-ranking official, who found and developed what was undoubtedly an ingenious loophole in the agreement made between the Amenukal and the French authorities. The legal difficulties of this procedure would probably have been extremely long and arduous – but such are the ways of aspirant property owners! The high-ranking official managed to get a village chief to sign a document stating that certain land was vacant and without an owner. The land was then taken over in the same way as the Public Domain and resold to the private individual. After this first test case, the procedure seems to have been adopted quite frequently, but it had no legal validity and would have been easily annulled in court, since no land in Ahaggar was 'vacant and without an owner'; neither did the signatory have any authority whatsoever to authorize the 'sale'. Again, there are records of several lands being bought from the Amenukal (Bay ag Akhemouk) between 1950 and 1960, but there was still the same ambiguity as to which party retained ownership, for as Bay had himself stated after his election, the Amenukal, according to traditional custom, had no right to sell land.

Throughout the French period the absence of any legal or statutory texts meant that the legal status of land was determined effectively by Tuareg custom, and the inevitable conflicts with French law were settled on a case basis with little or no legal foundation. The whole system was totally unsatisfactory, for not only did it give rise to the purchasing of land from owners who had no authorization to sell, and the cession to an individual from the Public Domain on the illegal fabrication of 'vacant land without ownership'; but, more significantly, it became a serious impediment to any form of development scheme and capital investment, particularly in the agricultural sector.

As the French became increasingly aware of the Harratin's living standards and the need for some sort of agricultural improvement, the whole question of the traditional *métayage* system began to be raised. France's conservative policy, directed largely to the preservation of the Kel Ahaggar's interests, certainly made any agricultural or land reform scheme politically dangerous. But, apart from any such political consequences, the rational implementation of agricultural development through such means as new collectives, co-operatives and credit facilities, as envisaged through the Secteurs d'Amélioration Rurale (S.A.R.), required a precise legal definition of land rights that would finally resolve the problem of land ownership and accession to property, and so secure the rights and heritage of cultivators settled on such new schemes.

The solution to this ill-defined state of affairs, and the only way that any such schemes could be realized, was through a reform of the land tenure and *métayage* systems, which would inevitably have required a considerable modification and redefinition of the traditional system of land ownership. The general features of such a reform, which seem to have been agreed upon, at least in principle, by the French authorities, and which could have been effected through incorporation into the Saharan Land Act, or even by a particular application of this Act, which was being prepared in 1961, were as follows:—

1. The owner would be the Tuareg 'Collectivity', consisting of the Kel Ahaggar tribes of Ihaggaren, Kel Ulli and Isekkemaren, both masters and slaves, but excluding foreign nomads and free cultivators (Arabs and Harratin). The Collectivity would be represented by the Amenukal, who, in his relations with all those who were not part of the Collectivity, would be the representative of the Collectivity, and not the eminent owner of the land.

2. The owner, thus defined, must be given greater power over the disposition of his land, so that, within certain limits, it would become a more negotiable asset. In order to meet demands for this land, the owner must be able to cede the recognized legal ownership of it.

3. There must be an order of priority of beneficiaries in the accession to land rights, and for each category of beneficiary (e.g. administration, military, local communes, civil corporations and companies, etc.) there must be clearly defined conditions of cession.

4. Finally, as the Amenukal would be the representative of the Collectivity, and not the eminent owner of the land, sales must benefit the Collectivity accordingly. Under the supervision of the Administration, funds could be invested in a Société Agricole de Prévoyance (S.A.P.) of stockbreeders, or used as credit to assist those Tuareg wanting to sedentarize and, especially, to begin cultivation.[4]

Needless to say, Algerian independence put an end to any further discussion of the Saharan Land Act, which never reached the legislative stage. The ideas may have been good, at least in as much as they would have given France rather more free rein, and may have relieved the embarrassment posed by the poverty-stricken Harratin. But as far as the Harratin were concerned the conflict between Tuareg custom and French statutory law in no way touched upon the *khamast* system, which remained undisputedly under the jurisdiction of the Amenukal, with little modification until the last few years of French occupation, and it was left for the Algerian government to effect a far more wide-reaching and revolutionary reform.

It is not surprising that the Algerian government, with its concern for 'slavery' and social equality, regarded the position of the Harratin *métayage* worker in Ahaggar as scandalous. In the context of the Algerian socialism of the 1960s the economic and political situation of the *métayage* worker certainly provided the platform for radical reform, although a more apt and dispassionate assessment of the Harratin's condition is found in

Augustin Bernard's comment on the Saharan peoples that 'il y a des degrés dans leur pauvreté, il n'y a pas de véritable richesse'.[5]

Even when detailed quantitative data enables us to derive various indices of standards of living based on income, dietary content, or whatever else, it is still not easy to explain or define exactly what we mean by 'poverty' except in the most relative terms. This is especially true of Ahaggar, where the collection of quantitative data during this period was limited to a few crude and largely unsystematic calculations. Nevertheless, it is worth spending a moment in discussing these figures, for they at least enable us to draw a reasonably well-qualified picture of the position of the *khames* and the contribution of the *khamast* system to the Kel Ahaggar economy.

An attempt to derive some sort of quantitative comparison between the standards of living of the Harratin and Kel Ahaggar was made by Jean Malaurie in 1953.[6] On the basis of the statistics presented in a report of the Chef d'Annexe in 1948, he calculated that the income of a Tuareg during the 1940s was equivalent to about 50,000 (old) francs (approximately £50–60) per annum, and that of a Hartani about 10,000 francs (£10–12).[7] Although these figures are only approximate monetary equivalencies, the ratio of five to one between the incomes of the two groups gives some indication of the relative standards of living of the nomadic and sedentary communities. The most important factor, however, in making any such comparison is that the subsistence base of the Kel Ahaggar was not only substantially more viable but provided for a more varied diet.

The diet of the Harratin consisted predominantly of cereals and oil. According to Captain Cauvet,[8] the total amount of grain (wheat, millet and barley) available to the Harratin population was 280 tonnes per annum, thus allowing about 300 grams daily for each individual.[9] This figure strikes me as hopelessly inaccurate and may have referred to the total harvest, or estimated total harvest, based on theoretical optimum yields and without consideration for the dues of the *khamast*; for Galan's research showed that the harvest of 1950, which was a bad but not catastrophic year, yielded 121 tonnes of wheat, five tonnes of millet and barley and four tonnes of tomatoes. This would have allowed about ten kilos of wheat for each individual in Ahaggar, both nomad and Harratin, on the basis of an equal distribution throughout the entire population.[10]

When we consider that the Hartani's feeble income had to provide for his clothes, as well as the tea, sugar and oil, etc., with which he supplemented his diet, it is not surprising that many observers at that time regarded his state as one of abject poverty and malnutrition. In fact, Malaurie's own conclusion was that seven people in every 100 living in the cultivation centres in 1940 lived in abject poverty.[11] Whereas the Harratin subsistence was limited almost totally to the one-fifth or less derived from their gardens and their very limited purchasing power, the nomadic subsistence base was substantially more varied and viable. In addition to the produce derived from their gardens, pastoralism provided both meat and milk products, while the caravans to Tidikelt provided them with dates[12] and those to Niger with millet.

When the first caravans journeyed south to Damergou one load of salt was exchanged for between fifteen and twenty loads of millet. This extremely favourable rate of exchange continued throughout the 1920s and 1930s, but from about 1940 onwards the changing demand for salt in Niger, resulting from alternative sources and mechanized transport, led to a progressive deterioration in the terms of trade:—[13]

| | | |
|---|---|---|
| 1945–50 | 6–10 | loads of millet for 1 load of salt |
| 1955 | 5 | ,, ,, ,, ,, ,, ,, ,, ,, |
| 1956 | 3–4 | ,, ,, ,, ,, ,, ,, ,, ,, |
| 1957 | 2·5 | ,, ,, ,, ,, ,, ,, ,, ,, |
| 1958 | ? | ,, ,, ,, ,, ,, ,, ,, ,, |
| 1959 | 1·5–2 | ,, ,, ,, ,, ,, ,, ,, ,, |
| 1960 | 1·2–1·5 | ,, ,, ,, ,, ,, ,, ,, ,, |
| 1961 | 1 | ,, ,, ,, ,, ,, ,, ,, ,, |

The annual caravans to Niger were the central event in the Kel Ahaggar's calendar, leaving Ahaggar in November–December and returning some five to six months later at the end of spring. Estimates of how many camels these caravans comprised vary considerably. Malaurie put the number at about 2,500[14] while Rognon put it as high as 3,000–4,000.[15] But in view of the fact that the Kel Ahaggar possessed in the order of 10,000–12,000 camels,[16] of which over 75 per cent were pastured semi-permanently in Tamesna,[17] I think that the number of camels was probably nearer 2,000, although it obviously fluctuated considerably from year to year, and caravans numbering 4,000 or more camels may have been undertaken.

Salt, mined at Amadror, was carried in the form of solid bars, each weighing about fifty to sixty kilos. With two of these bars packed onto either side of a camel its load was in the order of 200–40 kilos, but as only one in three or four camels on the caravan carried salt, we can conservatively estimate the total amount of salt transported south to Niger by a caravan of 2,500 camels as somewhere between 125 and 200 tonnes (metric).

It is clear from these rates of exchange that the Kel Ahaggar could exchange their salt for more millet than they could carry back to Ahaggar. Much of it was in fact resold in the Sudan for such important artefacts as: camel saddles; numerous wooden utensils, particularly pestles and mortars; earthenware pots; indigo cotton; and many other essential commodities that were unobtainable in Ahaggar. Furthermore, much of this surplus millet was resold for butter and cheese, which is perhaps surprising in view of their own pastoral resources in Ahaggar, but, as we shall see later, these resources were often insufficient, particularly in dry years. On their return from Damergou, many of these products were often resold or exchanged either in the cultivation centres of Ahaggar or in the oases of Tidikelt to the north. The northbound caravans to Tidikelt traded mainly their surplus goats, camels and dried meat for dates. However, in years of good pasture some of the butter and cheese brought back from the Sudan might also have been traded northwards, while those with sufficient supplies of millet might even have sold some of the wheat grown in their gardens in Ahaggar.[18, 19]

There are few men in Ahaggar today who can remember the time before there were caravans to Niger, and by 1962 they were certainly regarded as part of their traditional way of life. A boy's first caravan was part of his initiation into manhood. It was a magnificent journey, requiring endurance, discipline, skill, and courage, for there was always the risk of dangers like that which befell Ihemod ag Ikemma of the Dag Rali. As Essebet, his old widowed wife of nearly eighty, recounts it: 'He left here [Ahaggar] with the camels and took Moussa [his son], who was then very young. One morning when they had reached Tamesna, somewhere near In Abangerit, he went off to look for the camels. He told Moussa and Howedi [the son of a slave now living at Ideles] to stay with the baggage until he returned. He went off – and walked, and walked, and walked a long way looking for the camels until he was tired and had still found nothing. He slept until the next day, and I don't think he could find water. By the evening of the next day he had still not returned. He died there – at a well called Tamer, not far from In Abangerit. I can't remember when it was now – I heard about it when Moussa returned here.'[20]

From Ahaggar the caravans trekked south for about a month to Tamesna and the wells of In Abangerit. There, they rested for a month or so while the weaker animals from Ahaggar were turned loose to graze and were exchanged with fresh camels from Tamesna for the continuation of the journey southwards to Tawa and the other markets of Damergou. Many times, when I was learning Tamahak or just chatting with Kel Ahaggar, I would ask them to tell me about the caravans to Niger, and especially the return journey to Ahaggar. Some of the recordings of these conversations sound almost like music, with the excitement building up as the familiar camp sites on the way back north are counted off like days in a month.

Six nights from In Abangerit to In Guezzam (about 210 kilometres), off-loading each night to camp 'at Tin Massao, then the Oued Kazourmet, then on to In Seberaka, then Ikadeimellen [the white stone], Taberok, and In Guezzam. And then up to Ahaggar [about 410 kilometres to Tamanrasset] – first to Eradarr, In Teluk – two days at Tagellai, then to In Attei – Tiouar Tin Zaouaten – Iref In Zedalazen – Tessali – Tigrine – Ain Faig – Tin Adar – Agalella – and then Tamanrasset'.[21] Just to the south of Tamanrasset they would stop and off-load, and one or two of the men would ride directly up to the camps to bring the news of their return. Another three or four nights from Tamanrasset, skirting around the steep mountains through Arechchum along the western foothills of Atakor to avoid constant loading and off-loading on the steep mountain tracks, and finally returning to the camps in March or April. It was a time of plenty and happiness. Their return coincided with the first harvest, and after the hard winter months there was the knowledge of abundance and an increase in the velocity of social life.

The caravans were thus not solely a means of trade. They constituted something of a 'hidden asset' to the pastoral economy by providing the means of transhumance, whereby the weaker camels of Ahaggar were taken south and replaced by animals which had already spent a season or more in the rich pastures of Tamesna.

A further asset or resource of the Kel Ahaggar, which makes it even more difficult to derive a quantitative comparison between the nomadic and Harratin economies, was the Iklan, whose labour provided the nomadic economy with much of its viability. In addition to their many other tasks, it was the Iklan who were sent to Amadror in summer to extract the salt, and who provided much of the labour required in tending the caravans on their long return journey to Damergou.

Nevertheless, some measure of the value of the sedentary community to the Kel Ahaggar is given by the amount of grain made available to the Kel Ahaggar through the *khamast* system. Malaurie calculated that in 1946 375 tonnes of salt were exchanged for 720 tonnes of millet, which was augmented by a further 179 tonnes of grain from the Harratin-cultivated gardens.[22] Such a contribution, about 20 per cent of their total grain consumption, or perhaps even 25 per cent if we include the exactions of hospitality, was certainly not enormous. But the value of the *khamast* was not so much in terms of its absolute quantity of grain, but rather the security it provided against the declining rate of exchange between salt and millet and the vicissitudes of pastoral resources.

Whatever we may infer from these extremely inadequate statistics, there is no doubt that the Kel Ahaggar would not have accepted readily any reform of the *khamast*, which in any case was never very likely since the French, who tended to favour the Kel Ahaggar, also considered that the abolition or reform of the *khamast* would have led to the ruination of their 'traditional' nomadic existence.

The French were not unaware of the poverty and dietary insufficiencies in Ahaggar, especially among the Harratin, for Galan's research, published in 1951, estimated that between twenty and 100 people died each year either directly or indirectly from famine.[23] They did give some medical assistance and distributed free grain, which to some extent alleviated the risk of famine in drought years, but this intervention did little more than scratch the surface of the problem.

The obvious question that must be asked is that if the state of poverty among the cultivators was so wretched, why did they continue to settle in the region and not leave? With no documentary records giving any details of the Harratin's settlement in the region this question cannot be answered easily. They were attracted to the region by the possibility of developing new lands, by the climate, and by the security from raiding offered by the French presence; but on arrival, their lack of capital and the land tenure system forced them to accept the 'help' of the nomad and so enter the *khamast* system. The increasing exploitation of the *khames* by the nomad, and other *amagaren*, undoubtedly reduced his psychological incentive and resources; this, in conjunction with his lack of capital resources, physical enfeeblement, and possible ignorance, led to a state of resigned malaise, ensnaring him within the 'culture of poverty'.

It is of course only reasonable to ask how far the French contributed to this wretched state of affairs, and whether they could in any way have alleviated it. Their initial policy towards the Kel Ahaggar of preserving and in fact reinforcing the traditional political system denied the increasing number of Harratin any form of political representation, while the maintenance of the Kel Ahaggar's 'traditional rights', notably the land tenure system, denied them any control over the means of production. The French merely protected the domination of the 'nomadic-pastoral' community of the Kel Ahaggar, and so reinforced the division between Imuhag and Kel Arrem.

With respect to France's traditionalist policy, it might be argued that the *khamast* system was not really very 'traditional' in Ahaggar, since it was introduced only in the mid-nineteenth century, and, perhaps ironically, only became widespread as a result of the security offered by French pacification. In the same vein it might also be argued that the *khamast* system was not really justified in terms of the traditional system of land ownership, which was already recognized through the payment of a garden levy, similar to the *ehere-n-amadal.* This land-rent was only ten kilos of grain per garden, divided equally between the garden owner and the *khames*, and although of considerable value to the maintenance of the Amenukal's court, it was relatively insignificant, compared to the *khamast* system, in aggravating the Harratin's condition.

It thus seems that there were plausible means of reforming the *khamast* without defying tradition, but such a reform was obviously unacceptable to the Kel Ahaggar, and consequently undesirable to the French authorities, who were only too well aware that provocation of the Tuareg might have dangerous consequences in the form of anti-French agitation, not only elsewhere in the Sahara but throughout the whole of Algeria. There was also the possibility that the Kel Ahaggar might even have left Ahaggar altogether and emigrated to the more attractive Sudanese regions.

The only solutions that the French could entertain were those that in no way caused further deprivation to the Kel Ahaggar. But even within this overriding constraint there were several possible schemes, along the lines of co-operative development projects on virgin land, the installation of motor pumps, and improved cultivation techniques. Such schemes, with financial assistance from the government on the principles of the Secteurs d'Amélioration Rurale (S.A.R.) being developed elsewhere in Algeria, and through negotiations with the Amenukal with regard to the question of land ownership and the gradual modification of the *khamast*, could not only have ameliorated the condition of the Harratin but also have brought considerable benefit to the Kel Ahaggar. But again, as Malaurie himself commented, 'it is surprising, in a region that has been protected by a great colonial power for over forty years, that no sustained effort has been made in this direction'.[24]

The picture that I have painted of France in Ahaggar is perhaps unkind, especially when we look at the problems of the region in their wider perspective. Such development schemes would have been very costly and could not have been justified easily, particularly when the needs of

Ahaggar were considered in relation to those of the overpopulated lands and cities in the north of Algeria. Of course it can be argued that the problems of northern Algeria were of France's own making, but that is another and a far more complex story, which is not our present concern. Nevertheless, if we look at Algeria in its entirety, the problems of Ahaggar were dwarfed and were almost insignificant, alongside those of other regions; this to some extent accounted for, and perhaps excused, the inadequate resources placed at the disposition of the local administrations of the Saharan regions (Térritoires du Sud).

When we consider the overall physical conditions of the region, the difficulties of transport and communications, the shortage of funds at the disposal of the local Saharan authorities, and the political consequences that would almost certainly have been incurred in other regions through any provocation of the Kel Ahaggar, our criticism of the administration of the Annexe should be moderated. The local administration was well aware of the shortcomings and needs of the region and had in fact envisaged and planned various less expensive development schemes, such as the construction of small barrages to augment the volume of the water-table and assist irrigation, and the development of a large palm-grove at Silet.[25] This latter scheme was not only well conceived but would have been extremely beneficial to the region. The idea was quite straightforward. Palms were not abundant in Ahaggar, and the substantial demand for dates was met largely by importation from the oases of Touat and Tidikelt. The Kel Ahaggar had never established any extensive palm-groves, and most of the palms in Ahaggar, such as those at Silet, had been planted by foreigners.[26] Furthermore, the quality of the dates grown in Ahaggar was poor. The climate was not favourable, and since the palms were owned by the Kel Ahaggar the Harratin gave little care to their tendance. The proposed development of the palm-grove at Silet, where the climate was more suitable, would thus have made the region self-sufficient in this essential commodity.

The failure of the scheme is generally regarded as being due to the irregular labour and the shortage of both qualified personnel and supplies. But this was not entirely the fault of the administration. On the contrary, the French went to great lengths to persuade the Amenukal to sell the palm-grove to a private development company, and the Amenukal's rejection of the offered price of 100,000 francs gives an interesting insight into the forces operating within Ahaggar at that time. Although the palms at Silet were owned by the Amenukal, usufruct rights were held by the Kel Tamanrasset and Kel Terhenanet sections of the Dag Rali, the

Ikechchemaden, and the Kel Tahalra and Kel Silet sections of the Iklan-Tawsit, all of whom paid an annual tax to the Amenukal. In the case of the Dag Rali this tax consisted of one bunch of dates for every palm bearing more than two bunches, while for the Iklan-Tawsit it consisted of a collective payment comprising four bags of dates, twenty goats, two goat-hair ropes and five water-bags.[27]

Even if the Amenukal had wished to sell the palms, he did not have the right to do so, unless perhaps the Kel Ulli, who held the rights of possession, were also in favour of such a sale. But the Kel Ulli were resistant to any form of development and not willing to yield their rights over the palms, and the Amenukal, fearing the difficult consequences that would be encountered with the Kel Ulli, consequently rejected the French offer of 100,000 francs with a counter-demand for a million francs![28]

The question with which we are most concerned, however, is the nature of this resistance to change on the part of the Kel Ahaggar. How did they perceive such development schemes as the Silet palmerie, or proposed reform of the *khamast*? What values and attitudes were embodied in this resistance, and among which classes or groups were they most prevalent?

As far as the Ihaggaren were concerned their overriding interest was in the maintenance of their pre-eminent social status, and although initially embittered and deprived by the impediments to their former way of life, they had begun, at least by the 1940s, to reconcile themselves to the 'inevitable'. Their greater contact with the French authorities made them more pragmatic and provided them with wider experience and certain 'esoteric' knowledge that made them more aware than the Kel Ulli and other groups of the general aims of the French administration and the overall situation confronting Ahaggar.

Thus, although the Ihaggaren resisted any form of change that threatened their traditional rights and privileges, the new opportunities presented through their association with the French were gradually accepted and exploited, especially in the 1950s, as a means of maintaining their elevated social position.

The Kel Ulli, on the other hand, as we have already seen, emerged from the period of pacification with greater political influence and representation, and economic autonomy, and must have experienced a certain feeling of achievement and self-confidence which, in the case of the Dag Rali, certainly received a considerable boost from their almost complete annihilation of a French column in the Oued Ilaman (1917). In a sense the Kel Ulli had come to emulate the nobles in everything except status. They too were 'warriors', albeit redundant; they had a sufficient number of their own camels; their subsistence base was relatively secure; their gardens had increased in number; and they had developed a substantial caravan trade to Niger more or less on their own initiative and with their own resources. I think we can conclude somewhat speculatively, but with good reason, that by the 1920s the traditional aspirations of the Kel Ulli had been fulfilled. In the modern idiom they had 'arrived', and were what might be called the *nouveau riche*, although their richness was only relative to Ahaggar!

As far as they were concerned, any further modification of the 'traditional' system was a threat to their newly acquired and relatively fortunate position, and change, in the agency of the French administration and Tamanrasset, was perceived in a traditional rather than a modernizing context.

# ELEVEN
# THE DEVELOPMENT OF THE SAHARA: WAGE LABOUR AND THE SEEDS OF DISCONTENT

The status quo could not last. Even by 1950 the relationship between the Harratin cultivators and the Kel Ahaggar garden owners was tending towards open hostility. Not only did the owner demand his four-fifths, but, not trusting his cultivators, he would camp close by the gardens at harvest time (April – barley) and often remain there for several weeks until the wheat harvest in June, dependent on his 'host's' hospitality. This form of exploitation not only reduced the cultivators' one-fifth, but was merely one aspect of the Kel Ahaggar's overall abuse of the *khamast* contract.

An indication of the internal pressures in Ahaggar and the subsequent modification of the *khamast* is seen in Nicolaisen's comments when he wrote:[1]

> The *khamast* . . . which is widely found in North Africa . . . disappeared in Ahaggar some years ago. It is said that it was abolished by the Amenukal because it frequently gave rise to disputes between Tuareg garden owners and their cultivators. It is now replaced by two other systems, the *tilt* system allowing one third of the crops to the cultivator, and the *aril* system according to which crops are divided equally between the owner and the cultivator. The last system is that almost exclusively used in Ahaggar nowadays.

The issue was not this simple. During the 1950s the *khamast* underwent considerable modifications, but it was not abolished by the Amenukal, neither had it 'disappeared' by 1962, for at that time there were still several Kel Ahaggar enjoying the benefits of their four-fifths.

The modification of the *khamast* during the last ten years or so of

French occupation was not simply the outcome of hostility between the Tuareg and their cultivators. It was far more complex, multi-faceted, and merely one dimension in the overall process of change that took place in the region during the decade.

Nicolaisen's reference to the role of the Amenukal in abolishing the *khamast* in fact concerns the proclamation made by Bay ag Akhemouk, after his election as Amenukal in 1951, that anyone developing virgin land should give only one-fifth to the owner of the land. He stated quite explicitly that anyone could develop virgin land by cutting a *foggara* or well on the condition that he paid the customary land-tax. A few years earlier, as Khalifa to the previous Amenukal, Meslar ag Amayas, he had already stated that a garden owner who did not pay his obligatory contribution of the *khamast* for more than one year had the right to only one-fifth of the harvest.

Bay's proclamation was not a new regulation, but merely the reiteration or reinforcement of the original basis of the contract. The *khamast*, as we have already seen, consisted of five clauses, or parts, and the owner, by meeting four of them, was consequently entitled to four-fifths of the harvest. All Bay was in fact saying was that if the owner absolved himself of his obligations he forfeited his right to all but the one-fifth due to him as owner of the land. Bay's motivation for making this proclamation is not altogether clear. It certainly seems to have met with the approval and encouragement of the French, but the extent to which they exerted influence on him is questionable. He was undoubtedly aware that increased disputation between the Kel Ahaggar garden owners and the cultivators, which resulted primarily from the abuse of the *khamast*, could lead to a state of declared hostility and even physical conflict, the consequences of which would ultimately have only been disadvantageous to the Kel Ahaggar. He was also almost certainly aware of the impending 'development' of Ahaggar, the wage-earning opportunities of which might attract the cultivators away from the land *en masse*, unless perhaps some sort of conciliation or appeasement was offered them.

If his proclamation was thus made with a degree of wisdom and foresight, it was also made quite pointedly towards the Dag Rali, notably at Hirafok. There, the Dag Rali had taken to camping alongside the cultivators at the time of the barley harvest in April and staying until after the wheat harvest in June, thus living for several weeks at the expense of the cultivator before moving off with their four-fifths. This form of exploitation had become common practice among garden owners throughout the region, but at Hirafok, many of the cultivators who worked the Dag Rali gardens were Bay's own Iklan! Not only was their practice an abuse of the system, but in a sense a direct challenge to Bay's authority. His proclamation was thus made in defence of the rights of the cultivators, especially those at Hirafok, and served as a warning to the Dag Rali and other exponents of these malpractices.

It is perhaps surprising that the 'independence' offered to the cultivators was accepted in only a very few instances, but in the cases that did arise the owner of the land claimed nothing at all.[2] Ideles was one centre where advantage was taken of this new opportunity. Several cultivators soon began to desert the main cultivation centre and establish new gardens on virgin land in some of the smaller *oueds*, such as the O. Istene and O. Saouak, adjoining the main valley, where they worked collectively in sinking wells and installing motor-pumps with the credit assistance of the Secteurs d'Amélioration Rurale (S.A.R.).

Why did not more cultivators accept this new opportunity of relative, or even total, independence? Firstly, we must consider the possibility of the slow dissemination of information through Ahaggar, which in this instance was probably impeded or retarded even further by the Kel Ahaggar themselves. Secondly, this change in the agricultural system must be considered in relation to other new opportunities that arose during the 1950s, particularly wage-earning, which attracted a considerable number of cultivators away from the land. Finally, it must also be realized that the development of virgin land required a certain amount of capital resources. This was especially true in the case of *foggaras*, which required a vast amount of labour in both their construction and maintenance. Wells, on the other hand, could be sunk relatively easily, and involved a payment of only ten measures (five kilos) of wheat to the land owner. But perhaps what was more important than material resources was the necessary self-confidence and psychological state of the *khames*. To those Harratin living outside Tamanrasset, Ahaggar was still the absolute domain of the Tuareg, and in spite of assurances from the French administration, they had no effective recourse against the intimidation of the Kel Ahaggar. Their political and legal rights did not extend far beyond the right of appeal to the Amenukal, and when we consider the physical distances involved, the resources necessary to undertake such an appeal, and the almost certain risk of further reprisals or intimidation, it is not surprising that their fragile rights were scarcely utilized. The Harratin in the outlying villages did not see the new alternatives and opportunities offered them reflected in their immediate social environment. Only in Tamanrasset and other centres such as Ideles, where they were in closer contact with the French and more aware of the changes taking place in Ahaggar, did the proclamation offer them any real alternative.

This psychological aspect is important, and perhaps difficult to understand, but even after Algerian independence, when the Harratin were given full political representation, ownership of the land, and the protection of their rights as Algerian citizens, it was not until about 1968 that they felt sufficiently confident to stand up to the Tuareg and retaliate against their provocations and so finally put an end to their demands and intimidations.

Modification of the *khamast* did not occur overnight, but was a gradual process throughout the 1950s, resulting primarily from the growing shortage of *métayage* cultivators, caused not so much by the Amenukal's proclamation but rather the Harratin's acceptance of wage-earning opportunities.

Prior to about 1950 there had been little outward change in the appearance of Ahaggar. Tamanrasset was little more than a dusty and isolated administrative outpost in the central Sahara. Thereafter, however, significant changes began to take place, the reasons or motivations for which were as much political as economic and to be fully understood require an appreciation of France's post-war policy, particularly with regard to her colonial territories.

The period 1945–56 was one of systematic development of the Sahara. Three factors made its exploration possible:

1. The law of 20 April 1946 ordaining a systematic exploration of all the regions of the 'Union Française' with the view to utilizing fully all the resources in the 'Franc Zone'.

2. The enactment of 30 October 1945, which gave birth to the Bureau de Recherches des Petroles (B.R.P.); this in effect was to be the directing organization for all petroleum research in France, North Africa, the Sahara and Black Africa.

3. The technical developments of the Second World War, which in itself had prevented any such systematic exploration between 1939 and 1945.

During the six years 1950–56 numerous organizations and institutions were created with specific Saharan interests. For example, the Secteurs d'Amélioration Rurale initiated various projects involving the development of water resources, the creation of new agricultural schemes for sedentarizing nomads, and so forth. Not all of these ambitious projects were fulfilled, but the process of modernization in the Sahara was under way, and the enormous injection of activity came to fruition in 1956 with the discovery of important oil-fields at Edjeleh (In Amenas and Hassi Messaoud.

Since 1902 the French Algerian Sahara had been organized into the four Territoires du Sud and administered by the Governor-General of Algeria in the name of France. About 1950 it was realized that for both economic and political reasons the unitary character of the French Sahara must be safeguarded. However, the existing administrative structure of the French Algerian Sahara, whereby the region was divided into the four Territoires du Sud, not only militated against this end but was not well suited to the further exploration and development of the region as a whole. France wanted to reaffirm her presence in the Sahara and create a new entity endowed with its own special budget and means. Eventually, after several years of debate, the law creating the Organisation Commune des Régions Sahariennes (O.C.R.S.) was published on 10 January 1957.

The initial manifestation of these developments in Ahaggar was the establishment of a base by the Bureau de Recherches Géologiques et Minières (B.R.G.M.) in 1954 to undertake prospective research throughout the region. The establishment of Tamanrasset as an administrative centre had already given rise to a new class in Ahaggar – the 'labourers', who comprised a small force of builders, masons, cooks, and so on. Most of them were either second or third generation cultivators who had begun to specialize in certain trades, or cultivators who left their gardens for intermittent periods. But they were too few in number to satisfy the labour demands of the B.R.G.M. in the immediate construction of new *pistes*, airstrips, public buildings and other installations.

With the exception of this small nucleus, local labour was unskilled and of poor quality, and could hardly meet the demands of the new companies[3] in the development of this initial infrastructure. Its recruitment also posed delicate political problems. In view of the difficulties that would be created by the importation of more skilled labour, the employment agencies and the administration agreed that recruitment would be confined, as far as possible, to the local population of Ahaggar. Far more serious, however, was the need to avert the possible mass exodus of Harratin from the cultivation centres, which would have given rise to untold political, social and economic difficulties among the Kel Ahaggar.

The labour force that was eventually recruited in 1954 contained no nomads. It comprised about 500 Harratin,[4] 'les noirs', drawn mostly from Tamanrasset – they were the only ones 'used to the pick and shovel' – and paid about 4·15 NF per day, after the deductions for food, insurance, and so forth. Thus, while the annual income of a cultivator was about the equivalent of 100 NF, which could perhaps be doubled by the inclusion of a few goats and chickens,[5] a labourer could earn in the order of 900 NF merely by working for the six winter months. It is consequently not surprising that there was an immediate flow of cultivators away from the gardens and the onset of a malaise in the agricultural population as a whole.

The difficulty posed by the increasing shortage of *métayage* workers was partially offset by the Kel Ahaggar 'freeing' their slaves, and transferring them to the gardens, where they joined the Izeggaren (Harratin) in the sedentary agricultural community. This move not only relieved the owner of the burdensome obligation of having to support his slave, but was a means of transferring labour that to some extent assured the continued productivity of the gardens. It seems, however, that this practice was sporadic, and would probably have provided only temporary relief to the problem, for the only real alternative for the garden owners, apart from working the land themselves, which was quite out of the question, was to modify the *khamast* in favour of the cultivator, so as to make the *métayage* system a more attractive proposition. The actual processes of this modification are vague, but by independence (1962) most gardens were worked on the basis of the *aril* system.

The main difference between the *aril* and the *khamast* systems was that the *aril* (which means 'half') entailed an equal division of the harvest between the cultivator and the garden owner, as well as an equal division in the provision of seed-corn. This system, although still profitable to the garden owner, was obviously far more attractive to the cultivator than the traditional *khamast*.

Nicolaisen's reference to the *tilt* system is interesting as there is little or no reference to it in other documentary records, and I myself found little evidence of it having been practised extensively or continuously. Nicolaisen's visits to Ahaggar took place in the early 1950s,[6] shortly after Bay's proclamation, and it seems quite likely that the *tilt* system to which he refers was a transitional phase between the *khamast* and *aril* systems. This would certainly seem to be a logical process of transition when we consider the economic implications of the three systems. Fortunately for us, Nicolaisen was able to draw up a comparative balance-sheet for the three systems (see Table 2), as well as noting that:

The profit of the cultivator in all three systems is somewhat bigger than indicated. The hoe is given by the Tuareg garden owner, who must also make certain payments for irrigation work and the making of new garden beds. The garden owner's profit is consequently somewhat lower than indicated, but it should be mentioned that payments made by a garden owner are hardly ever made in wheat or barley, but mainly in millet and dates which are less valuable, particularly so because the pastoral Tuareg acquire millet and dates at very low prices during their caravan expeditions. Therefore, the profit made by a Tuareg garden owner cannot so easily be given in kilogrammes of agricultural food products.[7]

One should also add to Nicolaisen's conclusion that the cultivator, in spite of Bay's warning, still lost a considerable amount of his income to *amagaren*.

It is quite apparent from Nicolaisen's research that the *aril* system was more profitable to the cultivator than the *tilt* system, which was in turn more profitable than the *khamast*, and that all three systems were profitable to the garden owner in inverse proportion to the cultivator. Unfortunately Nicolaisen does not mention the specific centres or areas in Ahaggar where he observed the different systems being practised. If, as I have suggested, the *tilt* was a transitional phase in the overall modification, we would expect to have found the *aril* system being introduced sooner in those centres where the cultivators had closer access to the opportunities offered by modernization, notably Tamanrasset and some of the larger outlying centres such as Ideles and In Amguel. This seems to have been the general case, for the *khamast* certainly appears to have persisted longer in the more remote centres where there were few alternative opportunities for the cultivator.

Manual work, particularly the use of the 'pick and shovel', whether for irrigation and gardening or road-building, was regarded contemptuously by the Kel Ahaggar as a gross degradation of status. They took virtually no part in this initial phase of development. A few of them acted as guides, but this was not a new development and was justified within the context of the traditional value system. A small handful of Kel Rela, whom we shall discuss presently, were employed as general personnel overseers and foremen, but apart from these few exceptions the attitude of the Kel Ahaggar to these developments was one of general aversion. The developments and changes taking place in Ahaggar were still only in the middle distance, being localized for the most part in Tamanrasset, which had always been the symbol of the 'foreign' and potentially hostile outside world. They thus remained as non-participating onlookers, disgruntled by the whole state of affairs; talking about the Harratin 'revolution', contemptuously smiling on it, blaming it, and trying to ignore it. In the relative isolation

Table 2 Contracts between Tuareg and agriculturalists (after Nicolaisen, 1963, p. 199) Calculations are based on a garden with an annual yield of 700 kg. of wheat and barley.

| | Cultivator | | Tuareg Garden Owner | |
|---|---|---|---|---|
| | Receipts | Expenditure | Receipts | Expenditure |
| *The Khamast System* | | | | |
| The *khamast* division | 140 kg. | | 560 kg. | |
| Land-rent | | 5 kg. | | 5 kg. |
| Yield of one garden bed to blacksmith | | 5 kg. | | 5 kg. |
| Seed-corn | | | | 50 kg. |
| Food given to the cultivator | 150 kg. | | | 150 kg. |
| | 290 kg. | 10 kg. | 560 kg. | 210 kg. |
| Net profit | 280 kg. | | 350 kg. | |
| *The Tilt System* | | | | |
| The *tilt* division | 233 kg. | | 466 kg. | |
| Land-rent | | 5 kg. | | 5 kg. |
| Yield of one garden bed to blacksmith | | 5 kg. | | 5 kg. |
| Seed-corn | | 25 kg. | | 25 kg. |
| Food given to the cultivator | 150 kg. | | | 150 kg. |
| | 383 kg. | 35 kg. | 466 kg. | 185 kg. |
| Net profit | 348 kg. | | 281 kg. | |
| *The Aril System* | | | | |
| The *aril* division | 350 kg. | | 350 kg. | |
| Land-rent | | 5 kg. | | 5 kg. |
| Yield of one garden bed to blacksmith | | 5 kg. | | 5 kg. |
| Seed-corn | | 25 kg. | | 25 kg. |
| Food given to the cultivator | 75 kg. | | | 75 kg. |
| | 425 kg. | 35 kg. | 350 kg. | 110 kg. |
| Net profit | 390 kg. | | 240 kg. | |

of their camps, their contact with this revolution was largely limited to the inconvenience and relative deprivation caused by the flow of cultivators away from the gardens. Even the Iklan showed little interest in the new opportunities available to them in the wage-earning sector of Tamanrasset, and most remained with their masters.

But in spite of this 'ostrich-type' behaviour, the developments taking place in Tamanrasset were viewed with consternation. A school, attended exclusively by children from the sedentary community in Tamanrasset, had been opened by M. Claude Blanguernon in 1947. Harratin soon learned that schooling and a working knowledge of the French language were the passports to employment, regular salaries and promotion within the labour force. As the sedentary wage-earning community became more affluent, so more of their children were able to attend school as there were less demands on their labour for domestic tasks. By 1949–50, eighty-eight pupils were attending school, and by the mid-1950s French was commonplace in Tamanrasset.[8]

Social action among this modernizing or 'evolving' section of the Harratin population, no longer tied to the *khamast* and presented with new alternatives, became more elective; change tended to assume an ideological perspective and become institutionalized; and the beginnings or emergent signs of structural differentiation and institutional specialization could be recognized. From Blanguernon's description of this rapid transformation we can see that the progressive secularization of this section of the Harratin community was manifested on both the psychological and normative levels.[9] He described how the initial attitudes and behaviour of those that entered this new social and economic environment were the expression of suddenly acquired 'freedom' and status, and how the year 1954–5 witnessed young Harratin buying splendid robes and headdresses in imitation of their former masters and then quickly discarding these symbols of affluence for those of the European – shoes, shirts and blue-jeans.[10] Among this developing and emerging community there was a rejection of the past, the creation of new roles, and the adoption of new values orientated towards change and their upward social mobility.

Even though this modernizing community was still very small in proportion to the total Harratin population of Ahaggar and was localized in Tamanrasset, there was an outwash that sent ripples throughout the region. Some Kel Ahaggar, particularly the youth and those who visited Tamanrasset more frequently, were becoming not only intrigued by the possibilities of regular wages but jealous and affronted by the Harratin showing off their new-found affluence. Harratin, even in the more remote areas, were also becoming aware of the gradual transformation of the traditional order, and the emergence of a modernizing élite in Tamanrasset.

The first conscious political expression of this awareness occurred at the local council elections announced by the O.C.R.S. at the end of 1958. The elections warrant little comment. They represented the transformation to a civil administration and as far as the local populations of Ahaggar were concerned were nothing more than a farcical gesture towards wider political representation, in the mode of the already notorious 'élections à l'algérienne'. Candidates for both local *mairies*[11] were appointed by the Amenukal, who was himself represented in the duly elected council by his Khalifa, Marli ag Amayas. Nevertheless, for several months preceding the council elections there was an element of opposition and conscious awakening among the Harratin population, which, albeit slight, signified that the seeds of resentment towards the traditional form of political representation were germinating.

The feelings and attitudes of the Kel Ahaggar towards these developments were epitomized by their attitude towards schooling. Shortly after M. Blanguernon opened his school in Tamanrasset, the French felt that such opportunities should not be denied the nomadic population, and in 1949 they established three nomadic schools.[12]

The principle of these schools was quite simple. As the nomads were obviously reluctant and unable to send their children to Tamanrasset, a French teacher would attach himself to a particular group and give classes to the children in their own camps. The teacher himself was virtually a nomad, subservient to the demands of a pastoral way of life, and holding classes in the evenings when the children were free from domestic tasks.

The attitude of the Kel Ahaggar on hearing about the proposed establishment of these schools was expressed quite clearly by the Khalifa Bay ag Akhemouk in a letter to the Amenukal Meslar ag Amayas:

> Salut! Ta lettre m'est parvenue. Quant à ta prétention d'envoyer quelqu'un pour enseigner à nos enfants – en français – ne t'imagine pas que nous l'admettrons. Nos enfants ne sont ni des chameaux ni des moutons dont on ne peut disposer . . . Persuade-toi bien de ceci; c'est que mon enfant, je ne le donnerai qu'après ma mort . . . Tu nous demandes bien notre avis pour le bezra (l'impôt): à plus forte raison aurais-tu dû nous tenir informé de cette mesure qui concerne nos enfants qui nous sont plus précieux que nos coeurs. (1949 Tamanrasset)[13]

It is not surprising, with the Amenukal himself disapproving of such schools, that attendance was minimal. In 1949 only eighteen children attended, while throughout their duration until Algerian independence the total attendance in any one year never exceeded thirty-five,[14] while it seems that the Dag Rali school was actually closed through lack of attendance.[15] If anything, these schools provided a little amusement and a distraction from the routinization of camp life. A few children acquired a smattering of French, but the real educational benefit was to the teachers. The young men who volunteered for these posts (Gast, Barrère, Bobo and Roche) soon developed a sympathetic understanding of the Tuareg. They learned Tamahak and have since published valuable papers on certain aspects of their way of life. Gast and Barrère in particular have become part of Ahaggar, as much as the Frères at Assekrem,[16] who are known affectionately by almost all Kel Ahaggar.

The development of Ahaggar during the 1950s was marked by two distinct phases. The first, as we have already seen, witnessed the introduction of the primary processes of economic development and social modernization among a relatively small population in Tamanrasset, and incorporated, to a lesser degree, a proportion of the Harratin population in some of the larger outlying villages, particularly Ideles, Tazrouk and In Amguel where schools had been opened in 1956, 1957 and 1958–9 respectively.

The second phase, which saw the extension of these primary processes of development and modernization into the peripheral and outlying areas, and the nomadic population as a whole, was not directly related to the first, neither growing out of it in some sort of logical extension and transformation nor even emanating from Tamanrasset itself. It was introduced by the establishment in 1959 of the French atomic research base at In Eker – a development which was not only enormous in its scale, but, as we shall see, one which was to have extraordinary implications and consequences for the Kel Ahaggar in years to come.

About ten miles north of In Amguel and about 100 miles north of Tamanrasset, the base was an enormous complex of scientific and military installations surrounding the towering granite mountain under which France exploded her first atomic device. My first impression of the base left a striking memory. Just after independence there was little trans-Saharan transport and I had been fortunate in finding accommodation for about four days on the journey south from Ghardaia amidst a host of pipes and other hardware on the platform of a large transporter, bound I assumed for Tamanrasset. Lodged comfortably between the pipes, I watched the arid wastes of Tademait and Tidikelt slowly rolling by. On the fourth day, after climbing through the Arak gorges, we stopped for an evening meal somewhere on the plateau of Ahaggar. It was already much cooler than on previous days, and as we set off once more into the night I was distinctly cold. I sat huddled on the top of the platform watching the headlights picking out the track, and the silhouettes of the mountains that loomed up on all sides. I have now forgotten most of the details of that first journey, but remember suddenly becoming aware of a strange light high above the horizon in front of us. It was uncanny and most eerie, and at first I thought it was perhaps a freak effect caused by the rising moon, but it never moved, and stayed fixed in front of us like a spaceship, with an almost incandescent glow arcing upwards into the night sky. At that time I was quite unaware that In Eker existed, and for that matter had very little knowledge at all of my whereabouts, except that we were in the Hoggar and a place called Tamanrasset was a hundred or more miles on the map further south. I sat and watched this weird illumination as we rumbled on through Ahaggar. Then, when the light seemed almost above us, I saw the barbed wire, the signposts, and around a bend in the track the barrier gates and the gendarmes. I never discovered the source of the light but gathered it emanated from one of the vents on top of the mountain under which the atomic device had only recently been exploded. I slept that night on the truck, and in the morning was taken by the gendarmes to the south entrance of the base. We took a back road for what seemed more than twenty miles, seeing nothing but miles of perimeter fence and barbed wire, with occasional glimpses of bunker excavations, storage tanks, aerials and other installations that indicated that In Eker was obviously a place of extreme importance.

On later occasions I frequently found some excuse to pass through the base and avail myself of the opportunity to restock with cigarettes and quench my thirst with beer. On this first occasion, however, I was ushered from the base and told that there was a village about ten miles down the road to which I could walk quite easily and from where I would find transport to Tamanrasset. The land outside was, and still is, a peculiar tint of green, from having served over the years as the main disposal ground for many thousands of green beer bottles and much of the other industrial effluence of the base. At In Amguel there was no transport, nor any likelihood of transport, and not for the last time I walked for three days to Tamanrasset. It was a strange introduction to Ahaggar, and the walk to Tamanrasset gave me my first real contact with a Tuareg.

The C.E.A.'s (Commissariat a l'Énergie Atomique) decision to create an atomic research base at In Eker turned the hitherto desolate and rock-strewn waste into a hive of intense activity. The construction of an airstrip, the erection of prefabricated buildings, tunnelling and excavation, the piping of water from the Oued In Amguel, the paving of roads, the building of perimeter fences and many other tasks required a large force of unskilled labourers. Most of the available Harratin went there, but they were not enough, and for the first time the Kel Ahaggar descended from their camps to sign on as manual labourers.

The precarious nature of the nomadic labour and the lack of detailed records makes it difficult to ascertain the exact size of the In Eker labour force. Even so, it is worth spending a moment looking at what figures do exist, as they provide an interesting picture. Blanguernon, quoting the figures of the unpublished report of M. de Geyer d'Orth, Main d'oeuvre au Hoggar, which summarized the details of the labour force handled by the Centre d'Action Sociale, states that in 1961 the agency had recruited 1,181 labourers from Ahaggar, of whom over half were employed by the C.E.A. This number included 448 nomads, most of whom worked at In Eker and In Amguel. In addition, a further ninety-nine nomads, forty-nine of whom were from Tamesna, were refused employment as they did not want to work in Tamanrasset.[17] Gast, also quoting from M. de Geyer d'Orth's report, states that between January and October 1961 the agency registered 681 nomads, 250 old cultivators (Harratin) from the cultivation centres, and 302 villagers from Tamanrasset; in addition to which there were 144 nomads in the *méhariste* corps. Gast also mentions that this labour force, recruited from the local population of Ahaggar, was insufficient and that 936 workers from other Saharan regions, notably Niger and Mali,[18] were also employed in the region.[19]

The apparent discrepancies between these figures is not serious,[20] and both confirm that the labour force received a total sum of 2,700,000 NF in wages in 1961.[21]

We can thus conclude that:

1. After 1959 there were two main centres, or labour forces, in Ahaggar: Tamanrasset and In Eker.

2. The total labour force in 1961 exceeded 2,000, of which about 900 came from other regions and about 1,200–1,300 from Ahaggar.

3. Over half the labour recruited in Ahaggar worked at In Eker.

4. About half of the In Eker labour force was nomadic Kel Ahaggar.

5. Very few Kel Ahaggar worked at Tamanrasset.

6. The average monthly wage for labourers was about 280 NF.

Most of the In Eker labour did not come from Tamanrasset but the cultivation centres of In Amguel, Hirafok, Ideles and Tazrouk, and the nomadic camps of the Dag Rali, a few other Kel Ulli *tawsatin*, and the surrounding Isekkemaren groups. After their almost total rejection of the opportunities afforded by the initial processes of development, what induced the nomadic Kel Ahaggar to descend upon In Eker and enrol in the labour force? Whether the number of nomads was in fact 448 or 681 in 1961 is of little consequence. What is significant is that the number comprised not only Kel Ulli and Isekkemaren but also Ihaggaren (Kel Rela). Although no detailed studies were made at the time, I think that we can identify four main factors that led to this change in attitude among the Kel Ulli, particularly the Dag Rali, and in a varying degree among all the other nomadic groups.

Perhaps the most important issue as far as the nomads were concerned was that In Eker was not Tamanrasset! Tamanrasset was the centre of administration and commerce.[22] It was associated with the 'foreign' and potentially hostile outside world, and as the symbol of change was consequently antithetical to Kel Ahaggar values. It was also the centre of the evolving Harratin community, which posed a threat to the maintenance of the traditional social order. In Eker, on the other hand, prior to the development of the base was nothing but a ruined bordj, while the 300 or so square kilometres[23] of barren desert which it encompassed was regarded as part of their territory. It was thus more acceptable to them in that, unlike Tamanrasset, they did not feel so much that they were entering the 'outside world'.

There was also the economic need caused by the continuously decreasing rate of exchange between salt and millet, which by this time was less than two to one in favour of salt, and the modification of the *khamast*, which was reducing the income from the gardens. This need for money was further stimulated by their jealousy and resentment of the increasing affluence of the Harratin, who spared no trouble in tauntingly showing off their latest purchases. It is also probable that the Tuareg from Niger and Mali who had immigrated to Ahaggar during this period were influential in changing the Kel Ahaggar's attitude to wage-earning.

The Ihaggaren (Kel Rela), as we shall see presently, held a very different position in the labour force to the Isekkemaren and Kel Ulli, who were engaged solely as manual labourers. As a labour force they were of very little worth. They had no aptitude for work, were difficult to organize and command, and formed a most unstable force, returning to their camps on their first wage payment and not returning to the base until it was expended. The quality and stability of their labour improved a little as the C.E.A. offered instruction and training in such trades as masonry, carpentry and so forth, but most of them were totally uninterested in the work itself and frequently left on some such pretext as having to see their families or supervise the garden harvests. In their defence, however, it should be said that the Kel Ulli never really regarded this employment as 'work', a word for which there is no equivalent meaning in Tamahak,[24] or in terms of any future that would present an alternative to their nomadic pastoral existence. It was regarded purely as a temporary and alternative means of income, almost with the same attitude as booty from raids, which would subsidize, or rather offset, the deprivations imposed on the 'nomadic economy' by the declining rate of exchange on caravans and the modification of the *khamast*.

The opportunity and attraction of wages at In Eker was to some extent reconciled with traditional norms, notably by the Dag Rali, who adopted the practice of engaging their Iklan in the labour force and then collecting their pay![25]

Nevertheless, the precarious nature of the nomadic labour force reached some degree of stability as the irregularity in signing on and off gradually developed into a shift pattern whereby the workers would return home at the end of the month and be replaced by another shift. This meant that there was usually at least one male from each encampment at the base, and consequently a more regular monetary income to the camps.

The Kel Rela's position in this labour force was uniquely specialized. It is hardly surprising that their abiding preoccupation with their status and prestige made them quite useless as manual labourers, and, as the French were only too well aware, it was quite out of the question for a Kel Rela even to be considered in such terms. They were thus engaged almost solely in the direction of personnel as labour overseers and general foremen – positions that were admirably suited to their aristocratic nature.

I do not know the exact number of Kel Rela employed at this time. It was not more than a few dozen, but their motivations for entering employment and the means by which they came to occupy these élitist or managerial positions were complex and cannot be understood merely in terms of such general forces as economic need and fear of the Harratin 'revolution', which were common in varying degree to all Kel Ahaggar.

Let us reflect and elaborate for a moment on the remarks made earlier about their resistance to change, bearing in mind particularly their concern for the maintenance of their elevated social status and their contact with the French.

After overcoming, or at least resigning themselves to, the deprivations caused by pacification, the Kel Rela, to use Lhote's phrase, 'drew closer' to the French. Through the reinforced and sanctioned authority of the Amenukal they found a degree of alternative status in the Amenukal's court and, as we have already said, formed something of a self-styled and self-interested political élite. I have already questioned the extent to which they could be regarded as a political élite in view of the greater representation of the Kel Ulli, and suggested that their effective political power may actually have declined. This is, however, a questionable point, particularly when we consider the political influence they derived from their association with the French.

Through this association, which developed considerably from the 1940s onwards, they were able to exert influence not only on the French administration but in a more diffuse manner over the rest of Ahaggar society. It was extremely difficult for the French administration, although superordinate to the Kel Ahaggar, to undertake any action, particularly of a reformist nature, which was in any way opposed by the Kel Rela, for fear of provoking anti-French feelings and backlashes in both Ahaggar and other areas. This is not to say that France was answerable to the Kel Rela, but merely that their contact with the administration, and France's fairly undefined 'traditionalist' policy, provided them with the forum and means to exert their self-interest. At the individual level there may even have been an identification on the part of the French with the noble Tuareg. Their relationship with the Tuareg was certainly sympathetic, and the parallel that has often been drawn between the aristocratic French officer with his baton and the noble Tuareg with his camel whip and veil worn high was perhaps not entirely without meaning. In these respects their élitism was not as imaginary as I have perhaps insinuated, or even as some Kel Ulli might have liked to think.

Their contact with the French made them more aware of the general attitudes and policies of the French. They began to acquire a working knowledge of the French language, experience of the administration, an appreciation of shops and commerce, and of the many other modernizing influences in Tamanrasset. This greater experience and knowledge contributed in some measure to their status, for through their access to, and experience and knowledge of, the overall processes of government and administration, they were able to inform and advise other Kel Ahaggar.

This relationship with the French enabled them to retain certain qualities of their traditional roles of 'communicators', acting to a limited extent as go-betweens and informers between the French and the rest of Ahaggar society. It was through the elaboration of this diffuse and 'unstructured' role that the Kel Rela were largely able to maintain much of their pre-eminent social status in the face of the transformation taking place in Ahaggar.

The conservatism of the Kel Rela did not embody a totally negative attitude towards development, but was rather directed specifically to the protection of their own privileged position, and the sight of Harratin displaying their sudden affluence in the high street of Tamanrasset held ominous threats. A few younger Kel Rela, witnessing this alarming situation, intrigued by the possibilities of wage-earning and finding it increasingly difficult to maintain themselves in a nomadic way of life, realized that the only way of maintaining their noble and élitist status was by exploiting the forces that threatened to overthrow the traditional social order. And so, although no Kel Ahaggar were enlisted in the initial labour force recruited at Tamanrasset, about four or five younger Kel Rela left their camps and settled in Tamanrasset, where they found employment in such 'prestigious' positions as official guides or interpreters to organizations like the gendarmerie and the new development agencies, for example, the B.R.G.M. and C.G.G.

By 1966 the number of nomads living in and around Tamanrasset had risen to about 100. Most of them were Kel Rela, and although the move towards sedentarization and entry into the wage-earning sector had begun with the trickle of four or five Kel Rela into Tamanrasset about ten years earlier, it was the creation of the atomic base that accelerated this transformation and provided them with the opportunity to exert some control over the modernizing forces that threatened the traditional social and political order.

The means were facilitated by the magnitude of the development at In Eker, and the composition and quality of the labour force. The management and supervision of this large unskilled labour force posed considerable difficulties. What sort of personnel held sufficient authority and status to command both the nomadic and Harratin contingents? Who could handle all their various personal problems regarding wages, signing on and off, and so forth? And how was the language problem to be overcome? In Eker was obviously ideally suited to the Kel Rela, for only they had the qualities to handle such problems. They were not only usually sufficiently bilingual, or even trilingual in Tamahak, French and Arabic, to act as interpreters between the French and the various elements in the labour force, but their noble status and experience of the French administration made them eminently qualified to fill such positions as personnel supervisors and general overseers.

Through their exploitation of these supervisory or white collar positions, as liaison officers between the manual labour force and the French – effectively only an extension and elaboration of their roles as 'communicators' – the Kel Rela established themselves in a seemingly paradoxical position. In a sense they bridged the traditional and modernizing value systems, whose opposition was becoming more clearly defined during these last few years before Algerian independence. On the one hand we see the survival and perpetuation of the traditional social and political order, epitomized in the maintenance of the traditional form of political representation and the authority of the Amenukal, and on the other hand the modernizing structures emergent in the development of Ahaggar.

While this opposition more or less followed and accentuated the division between the Imuhag and Kel Arrem, or nomad and sedentarist, their respective élites were fused in the personification of the Kel Rela. France's traditionalist policy, as evinced in the municipal elections, ensured the Kel Rela's position in the political élite, while their position in the modernizing élite was achieved, admittedly as a response to the threat posed by the modernizing system itself, through their ingenious manipulation of their roles as 'communicators'.

In these positions the Kel Rela were probably better informed of what was going on in Ahaggar than even the French. Their network extended to almost every corner of Ahaggar and beyond. When I first arrived in Tamanrasset I had little idea of where and how to start my investigations. I knew almost nothing about the Tuareg, spoke no Tamahak, and my knowledge of Ahaggar was confined to a map. A few tentative enquiries resulted in an introduction to Moussa ag Mohammed,[26] a Kel Rela, whom I had been told had an excellent knowledge of French, and who was prepared to spend the early hours of each morning teaching me Tamahak. His knowledge of Ahaggar and its peoples was remarkable. He had come to Tamanrasset in the mid-1950s as a young man in his twenties and had been employed as both chief guide to the gendarmerie and as an overseer of about 300 men at In Eker. Moussa is still probably the finest guide in Ahaggar and there can be few spots within a 500-mile radius of Tamanrasset that he does not know. But his detailed knowledge of the individuals in Ahaggar was equally astonishing, particularly for a man of his age. Much of his vast store of information had been acquired through his position at In Eker, and on many occasions when I was consulting him on some question to do with genealogies, marriages, or other social matters, he would often point out that the person in question had in fact been married before, had wanted to marry someone else, had been jilted, had been the centre of a scandal, or similar additional snippets of valuable information that had either been forgotten, deemed irrelevant, or purposely concealed by the individual concerned.

It is ironic that the one 'scandal' that he managed to keep concealed from me centred around himself. Like most Kel Rela he was vain, aloof and proud, and although he would sometimes laugh at himself he was an artful impression manager. He had been widowed only two or three years before I first met him; his wife died in tragic circumstances, and although he often spoke intimately about his personal and family relationships he rarely discussed his deceased wife. They had been married for a little more than ten years and had three children, and Moussa had always given the impression that it had been his first and only marriage. About three years after I had first met Moussa, I was discussing some casual matter with M. Cistère, a Frenchman with an intimate knowledge of Ahaggar, when he asked me if I had known Umeyda, Moussa's wife. I told him that his wife was called Aisa and that she had died before I first came to Ahaggar. Cistère chuckled and proceeded to recount the story of Moussa's other marriage.

Umeyda was Moussa's father's sister's daughter and had wanted very much to marry Mohammed ag Bubekir, a Kel Rela, who, unfortunately for the poor girl, was already married to a Kel Rela woman who eventually left him, presumably in jealousy or anger, but without a divorce. Mohammed, however, was still not interested in Umeyda, and instead married an Aguh-en-tehle girl, thus having two wives at the same time. Moussa at this time was a young man in his twenties, and married Umeyda, but immediately the wedding ceremony was completed she walked out on him without even consummating the marriage, and eventually returned to Djanet. It was after this terrible humiliation that Moussa married Aisa. The scandal, according to Cistère, who was there at the time, caused quite a stir through Ahaggar and a considerable loss of face to all concerned, especially Moussa, who, knowing that I was interested in such affairs, had quite naturally kept the whole matter well hidden. Nevertheless, a little while later, on the pretext of checking some genealogical material with him, I asked him if he knew Umeyda. He merely shrugged his shoulders, and with no change of expression said that she lived in Djanet, and that he had never really known her very well, which I suppose was the most truthful summary of their brief relationship.

Enough has been said for us to refute the claim that Algeria has been responsible for destroying the traditional way of life of the Kel Ahaggar. As I have already said, the roots or initial processes of many of the more dramatic changes that have taken place since independence can be traced to these last few years of French occupation. This is particularly true of the sedentarization of nomads, which has perhaps been the most obvious and dramatic change in their way of life, and in some respects the saddest. By 1968, I do not think that any Kel Rela in Ahaggar could be described as nomadic; neither do I think that there were more than a handful living 'under canvas'.[27] Of 259 Kel Rela, there were at least 104 living in or around Tamanrasset in 1968, and at least fifty-nine in other cultivation centres. Their move to 'town' was well under way before Algerian independence, and had been motivated, as we have just discussed, partly by the difficulty of maintaining themselves in a nomadic existence, and partly as a means of adjustment to the forces which threatened their élitism.

The most significant aspect of this initial move towards a sedentary existence during the 1950s is that it was not confined solely to the Kel Rela. Among several of the Isekkemaren and poorer Kel Ulli *tawsatin* there was already a noticeable shift to a more sedentary way of life. Not all Kel Ahaggar were extensive garden owners, slave owners, or rich in goats. The limited areas of fertile alluvial terrace were found predominantly around the periphery of Atakor where the main *oueds* issued from the central mountains, so that most of the more important cultivation centres were in either Dag Rali or Aguh-en-tehle territory. Similarly, the distribution of slaves was most unequal. The Dag Rali, with 426 slaves,[28] had a slave ratio of 1·1 : 1, which was surpassed only by the Kel Rela with a ratio of 1·17 : 1,[29] compared with a ratio of about 0·25 : 1 among most other Kel Ulli and Isekkemaren.[30]

Some of the Kel Ulli, especially to the east of Atakor, and certain Isekkemaren groups were finding it increasingly difficult to maintain themselves in their traditional nomadic way of life. The Ait Lowayen, for example, in the vicinity of Tin Tarabine and Azrou to the east of Atakor, had few gardens, relatively few slaves, and were geographically distant from Tamanrasset and other developing centres. By the late 1950s a few of them began to settle and establish, in a semi-sedentary way, their own gardens in the *oueds* of Tin Tarabine and Azrou, temporarily abandoning them when pasture was replenished. A similar process took place among some of the Isekkemaren to the north of Atakor in the regions of Tefedest, Tourha and Tazulet, where there was progressive sedentarization in such centres as Ideles and Tazrouk. These Isekkemaren quickly adopted the values and attitudes of the developing sedentary community and found work in the general construction of buildings (schools, infirmaries, etc.), and began to develop their own gardens alongside the former *khames*.

We can thus see that the initial move towards sedentarization was manifest at both ends of Kel Ahaggar society – among the Kel Rela, and among some of the poorer Isekkemaren and Kel Ulli. Both groups were finding it increasingly difficult to maintain themselves in a nomadic existence, but while the strategy of the nobles was designed to maintain their élitist position within the traditional form of social stratification, the transition among the poorer nomads was dictated primarily by economic necessity and was characterized by a greater willingness to comply and identify with the sedentary community.

Among most of the Kel Ulli, however, particularly the Dag Rali, there was greater resistance to these changes. The Dag Rali, richer in goats, better endowed with Harratin-cultivated gardens, and with more Iklan than any other *tawsit*, had a greater degree of economic viability and were able to maintain themselves more in accordance with traditional patterns. Wage-earning was accepted, not so much in a modernizing context but as a supplement to the declining revenue of the traditional economy.

On the psychological level, attitudes and behaviour among all sectors of the population manifested a certain degree of confusion and 'disorientation'. From pacification until the early 1950s the status quo within Ahaggar had been preserved with only relatively slight modifications in the social, economic and political systems. During these last few years of French occupation, however, the economic development that touched Ahaggar was not paralleled in the social and political systems. The French administration implemented change within the economic framework, but actively encouraged conservatism in the social and political spheres, with the result that by 1962 Ahaggar society was being polarized into two totally opposed and conflicting value systems – that of the Harratin, orientated towards modernization and change, and that of the Kel Ahaggar, resistant to it. Increasing affluence did not facilitate social mobility nor remove the stigma of being a Hartani, while education, the prerequisite for modernization and the panacea for all ills, did not lead to an extension of political participation. It merely added to the confusion by affording the means of affluence without fulfilling the need for respect and human dignity.

By 1962, discontent was becoming vocal. Cultivators were beginning to express their desire to own the land they cultivated, and Iklan to resent their bondage; even among the Kel Ahaggar a few younger Ihaggaren were beginning to reject traditional political and familial authority in preference to the less inhibiting structures of the outside world.

It is not surprising, therefore, that many of the French who left Tamanrasset at that time, in spite of any possible ill feelings and prejudice towards an independent Algeria, found it difficult to foretell the future of Ahaggar.

# TWELVE
# ALGERIAN INDEPENDENCE

Ahaggar was little affected by the Algerian Revolution or 'War of Independence'. The bitter atrocities, the reprisals, the death and devastation that tore Algeria apart from the outbreak of the war in November 1954 until the declaration of independence in July 1962 were of little concern to most of the Saharan peoples. Most of them, particularly the Tuareg, were predominantly pro-French, and the news of the war was not met with much approval. Neither did the Harratin have much awareness of the imminent political changes that would favour them.

Throughout the war, nationalist operations were confined to northern Algeria, and even when the Conseil National de la Révolution Algérienne (C.N.R.A.) announced, on 23 October 1957, that military operations, previously limited to territories north of the Sahara, would be extended 'to all national territory', there was little effect on the Sahara. The few incidents that did take place in Saharan territory consisted of two oil tankers being blown up on the road to Edjeleh, an attack on a party of French prospectors escorted by legionaries near Timimoun, and the destruction of the power station at Laghouat. Not only was there an astonishing lack of information and interest regarding the Sahara, but its terrain, compared with the mountains of Kabylia and the Aures, was most unsuitable for concealed military or guerrilla activities. In addition, a degree of influence was undoubtedly exerted by the Libyan government, which, although sympathetic to the revolutionary cause, did not want the disruption of oil operations close to its borders. The main reason, however, for excluding military operations from the Sahara, particularly in the latter stages of the war, was probably the nationalists' consideration that they would one day possess the Saharan oil installations and that their destruction would only endanger the country's economic future.

At independence Algeria comprised two regions – the north and the south. One might almost say two countries, for there was nothing very Algerian about the Sahara, with its almost complete social, political and economic dissociation from the north. In almost all respects the Sahara was an alien region to most Algerians, who had little feeling for its arid wastes or sympathy and understanding for its meagre population. Its development and exploitation had been entirely French, while at the sociological level it confronted Algeria with the problem of integrating and assimilating a growing population of diverse ethnic groups which made up only 7·8 per cent of the total Algerian population, but extended over 87 per cent of the national territory. It is not really surprising, therefore, that the initial Algerian government's interests in the Sahara were limited almost solely to the calculation of oil royalties. When President Ben Bella toured the Saharan towns in 1963 he made no reference to any plans for the development or integration of the region into the national framework, other than those which concerned the oil industry.

The Sahara was a curious anomaly in independent Algeria, for its lucrative oil resources were partially offset by the increasing problem of its underdevelopment and separatist identity. In many respects this problem had been made more acute by the declaration of independence, for the immediate impact on the Saharan population of independence and the withdrawal of many French concerns was a sudden deprivation and loss of salaries.[1]

The social revolution that has taken place in Ahaggar during the last decade or so may perhaps be seen as just another small 'tribal' society being wrenched from its traditional enclave and painfully undergoing the transition into the twentieth century. Such a view is of course not only grossly generalized but, as we have already seen, is not an altogether true account of what has happened to the Tuareg in Ahaggar. Nevertheless, it is a reasonably fair reflection of how many sympathetic Westerners view the process of transition and upheaval taking place among most 'primitive' societies. Many of us, when witnessing these transitions, tend to 'take sides', for it is an emotive experience in which our sympathies tend to rest with the primitive. Several tourists I have met in Ahaggar have spoken to me in such terms, expressing sadness at the state of the Tuareg nomad and occasionally going so far as to condemn the Algerian authorities for 'depriving' the Tuareg or imposing another brand of colonialism on them.

In 1971 I returned to Ahaggar after eighteen months' absence, and on driving up to Assekrem was completely shattered at seeing a hideous monstrosity of a tourist 'resthouse' being built at the top of the col. After knowing for so long the solitude and beauty of Assekrem I was naturally upset at seeing what the local tourist office in Tamanrasset had undoubtedly conceived as its *pièce de résistance.* I had time to spare and a European tourist who had also driven up from Tamanrasset invited me to share his lunch with him. We had talked about the Tuareg and Ahaggar for some time when he asked me if I did not find it sad watching Tuareg carrying building materials back and forth in a regimented labour gang. I must admit that I did not give the question much consideration and replied that it was an inevitable outcome of development and modernization, and that we should not let ourselves become emotional over what were 'facts of life'. It was a stupid and flippant answer that was not warranted by his kindness and hospitality. Neither was it a true reflection of my feelings. His forthright rebuke for what he considered to be such callousness was deserved, and although I did not agree with the accusations he levelled at anthropologists and other social scientists for the way in which they 'used' such unfortunate peoples in their preoccupation with 'objective analysis' and search for 'explanations', it made me think of Khabte, Beh, Hosseyni and the many other Tuareg who had given me their hospitality and friendship so unreservedly, and I wondered if I did ever know what they really felt and thought.

It is sad to see the progressive abandonment of the nomadic camps and the necessary adaptation to a new way of life. Nevertheless, it is true that the sight of Tuareg labouring menially at Assekrem on that brief visit did not sadden me. It was, after all, merely one dimension of the overall process of modernization and change that had been going on in Ahaggar since before Algerian independence, and a sight that had become familiar to me. If anything, my companion's rebuke made me realize how I no longer saw Ahaggar so much in terms of individual Tuareg, but rather in terms of the overall processes and patterns of change. Whereas the presence of the labour gang merely provided me with further confirmation of these patterns, and an opportunity to reacquaint myself with some of its members, it was an emotive experience for my companion, who had come to Ahaggar to see the 'noble warlord of the Sahara'.

My seemingly callous attitude probably owed much to my new-found sympathy with the Algerian authorities. The greatest difficulty in my working in Ahaggar had come not from the Tuareg but from the Algerian authorities in Tamanrasset, for it was to them, rather than to the Tuareg, that I was repeatedly having to explain my activities and interest in the region. I had shared with the Tuareg a common fear of the administration in Tamanrasset! Now, I was for the first time officially a 'tourist' and no longer had to live with the constant fear and anxiety of having notes and records confiscated or being served with an expulsion order. A consequence of this new 'status' was that I was able to talk more openly and freely with members of the administration without the same risk of punitive action, and was able to learn much more of their 'side of the story' in Ahaggar.

The difficulties encountered by the initial Algerian administration in Ahaggar were a reflection of the general situation throughout the country, but compounded, particularly at the individual level, by the peculiar conditions of Ahaggar.

During the Revolution little thought had been given to the future socio-economic policy of an independent Algeria except that it would be socialist, but even three years after independence the real nature of Algerian socialism was still not clear.[2] The basis of Algerian socialism[3] was the principle of 'auto-gestion' (self-management), which was inaugurated largely by the peasants themselves, who took over the management and exploitation of the lands left vacant by the *colons*.[4] All land that was vacant or which had been expropriated from the French became the property of the state, but was managed by the former workers of the land. The general administration and management of these lands was carried out through a hierarchy of assemblies and committees, culminating at the highest level in the Comité de Gestion (Management Committee). Representation at all levels of this administrative hierarchy was by popular election,[5] but while 'Populaire' and 'Démocratique', this form of organization was initially more of an ideology, directed to the satisfaction of the 'dehumanized' peasants, than a rational implementation of economic development policy. It was what Michel Goué, writing in *Le Monde*, called 'empirical socialism',[6] which was a fairly neutral and even charitable interpretation of events compared with the more vehement and sceptic critics of Algeria: Kamal Jawad, writing in *Jeune Afrique* later in the same year, concluded that Algeria was already socialistic simply because private property was no longer safe![7]

During the first three years of independence, production figures in the agricultural sector could be interpreted optimistically, but like many other aspects of the Algerian economy they masked the fact that 'auto-gestion' was only operative on the more fertile land of the former *colons*, which comprised only a fifth of the country's cultivated land and a similarly small proportion of the country's peasants, most of whom remained outside this privileged sphere on privately owned but poor land.[8] In the industrial sector the precipitate instigation of 'auto-gestion' affected production even more seriously.

The economic problems that accumulated in Algeria during the first three years of independence, prior to Boumedienne's *coup d'état*, cannot be blamed entirely on the principle of 'auto-gestion', in spite of its ideological rather than economic base, but rather on insufficient management and guidance, resulting from the shortage of trained technical and administrative cadres[9] and the failure to consolidate the ideology of the Revolution at the level of individual responsibility.

In addition to these more general national problems, the administration that took over in Tamanrasset in 1962 was confronted with its own singular problems. The young men who filled the various posts in the administrative services, gendarmerie, police, military and so forth came from the north, about 2,000 kilometres away, and were foreigners to the region. They were a long way from their homes and the security of their families. Few of them had ever been into the Sahara, and Ahaggar, with its unfamiliar language, customs and physical environment, was desolate, hard and alien. Most of them wanted nothing more than to see the end of their posting. Even today, there are still many Algerians in the north who are totally unaware of the nature, or even the existence, of Ahaggar and the Tuareg.

The young men who went to fill the administrative and other posts left vacant by the French in other parts of Algeria, even if far from home and confronted by what they may have perceived as distinct cultural and ethnic differences, as for example between predominantly Berber or Arab regions, at least found themselves in relatively friendly surroundings. They were the new heroes, the 'liberators', and bound to the local population through their shared experience of the Revolution. In Ahaggar, however, there were no heroes' welcomes, but rather the resentment and disdain that is more usually offered to an occupying or conquering people. The Algerians who went to Tamanrasset were of course neither of these, but as far as most Tuareg were concerned the precise definition of their presence was largely irrelevant, for even if the consequences of Algerian socialism in Ahaggar could not be foreseen, their experience of Algerian nationalism was sufficient to breed resentment: in 1961 the Armée de Libération Nationale (A.L.N.) had intervened in Mali to assist President Keita's forces in curbing the dissident nomadic Tuareg.[10]

While the Tuareg tended to classify all Algerians derogatorily as 'Arabs', regardless of their ethnic origin, the same was more or less true of the Algerians, who had little sympathy or understanding for the Tuareg nomad. The Tuareg, after all, had played no part in the Revolution; they had made no sacrifices or contributions to Algeria. Indeed, their loyalty had probably been more towards the French than the nationalists, while their traditional society, with its various forms of 'slavery', was quite antithetical to the principles of the Revolution and Algerian socialism.

The undesirability of the region to northern Algerians is still a major impediment to the development of any permanent local administrative and technical cadres, and consequently to the development of the region as a whole. But in these formative years the many difficulties facing the Algerian administration in Tamanrasset were aggravated by the continued French presence at In Eker and their unfamiliarity and lack of detailed knowledge of the region, which limited the extent of their effective authority and control.

Algerian policy in Ahaggar has fallen into three periods, coinciding with the terms of office of the three Sub-Prefects who have administered the region since independence. In the most general terms, and more especially since about 1966, this policy has been to assimilate the Tuareg and the other population groups in Ahaggar into the Algerian system[11] and integrate this isolated region, in conjunction with the Sahara as a whole, into a unified national state in which the Sahara would no longer be an underdeveloped area exploited by the north.

It is questionable, however, whether the enactment of Algerian policy, or even its ultimate aim, during the initial three years of Algerian administration, could be considered assimilationist or overly concerned with any form of development; for not until the formulation of the Ouargla Plan in 1966 was there any concerted development programme for the Saharan regions.

On the one hand the Algerians could not feel that they had established effective control over the region in view of the continued French presence and their unfamiliarity with the country and its peoples; while on the other hand the socialist and egalitarian principles and values of the Revolution were totally incompatible with those of traditional Tuareg society. Their initial policy thus tended to be a willy-nilly implementation of Ben Bella's 'have-not' socialism, and designed primarily to liberate the 'enslaved' Iklan and Harratin populations from Tuareg domination.

The Tuareg institution most abhorrent to the Algerians was that of slavery; it was totally incompatable with the principles of a government that was 'Démocratique et Populaire'. Gendarmes scoured the camps coercively encouraging the Iklan to leave their masters and to take their few belongings to Tamanrasset and freedom. The number of Iklan who left the camps during this period is not known, but it must have been several hundred, for of an Iklan population of between 1,000 and 1,500 only a few were left in the camps. A few, the more fortunate ones, found work and settled predominantly among the Harratin in the El Hofra quarter of Tamanrasset; but for many, there was no work, neither could they establish themselves independently as nomadic pastoralists, for they did not possess the necessary resources of livestock, tents and other essentials, or the money with which to buy them. They began to huddle in squalor around the outskirts of Tamanrasset, particularly in the Imechouen quarter, in what Gast described as a *bidonville*,[12] dependent on their wits and public charity.

The presence of armed gendarmes leading their slaves away from the camps increased the Kel Ahaggar's fear and resentment of the Algerian authorities. Iklan were not merely an economic resource but an integral part of Kel Ahaggar society, and their removal was perceived by most Kel Ahaggar as a calculated act of aggression, which more than anything else hardened their hostility towards the government.

During the latter years of French occupation the Kel Ahaggar had become increasingly dependent on their gardens. As the terms of trade on the salt caravans depreciated progressively, so the revenues from the gardens offered relatively greater security against the vicissitudes of a purely pastoral economy. But with independence the Harratin found themselves freed from their obligations to the Kel Ahaggar – for in Algeria, is not the land free? Their hostility towards the Kel Ahaggar became more open as they refused increasingly to pay their garden dues, although the degree of refusal varied according to how far they could depend on the support of the administration. In practice, governmental authority in the more remote centres was minimal, so that to a large extent the cultivators found that their dependence on government support was determined by the distance and accessibility of their gardens from Tamanrasset.

With some cultivators a degree of collaboration took place, in that the Kel Ahaggar would perhaps pay for the motor pump for irrigation, or the cost of the irrigation channels, and then come to an agreement with the cultivator over the cost of these capital investments in relation to a share in the garden produce. Others, wanting to free themselves completely from the Tuareg, began to cultivate virgin land without any form of obligation or payment to the Kel Ahaggar. At Ideles, for example, in 1964, several tons of wheat were transported from the village by truck after being harvested and sold by the Harratin without any interference from the Kel Ahaggar.[13] The Harratin were beginning to feel confident in their independence; they were beginning to stand up to the Tuareg, but even so, by 1965, many of them, still fearful of Tuareg intimidation and with little or no effective protection from the administration, were still giving half their harvest to the Tuareg garden-owner.

## Minority Status

The local council elections, announced by the O.C.R.S. at the end of 1958 to mark the transition from a military to a civil administration, were nothing more than a gesture towards 'democratization' and the extension of political representation to the Harratin community, for the appointment of candidates by the Amenukal still denied effective political power to all but the Kel Ahaggar. With independence the Algerian administration instigated a complete change in the political system. Full political representation was granted to all 'Algerian citizens', with the result that when the first commune elections were eventually held in 1965–6, the Kel Ahaggar, who by that time had become outnumbered by the rapidly growing sedentary community, were assured of political minority status.

One of the most intriguing questions about independent Algeria is why the Tuareg, with all their grievances and resentment of the Algerian administration, did not resort to militant action. The fact that there has been no uprising in Ahaggar tends to render the question superfluous and direct our attention instead to the process of their assimilation. Nevertheless, if a Tuareg uprising now appears to be out of the question, its possibility did not seem so unlikely in the years immediately following the Algerian takeover in Ahaggar.

Before ever visiting Ahaggar I had heard many rumours of trouble and discontent among the Tuareg – stories of how the Algerians had taken away their slaves and their gardens, and how they would surely revolt. For the most part these stories seem to have been circulated by disgruntled *pied-noirs* and other anti-Algerian elements, and to have been fuelled by the grossly exaggerated and distorted information that percolated northwards across the Sahara. It was these stories that attracted me to Ahaggar and when I first crossed the Sahara it was with the anticipation of an imminent Tuareg uprising!

The Algerian authorities were fully aware of the rumours and stories of Tuareg unrest and were consequently suspicious of foreigners, especially Frenchmen, who visited the region. The extent to which the Algerians perceived a conflict situation in Ahaggar and how far the Tuareg ever considered resorting to militancy cannot be assessed easily. Not only is discussion of the subject regarded as 'subversive' and a 'danger to national security', but most of the Algerians who held office in Ahaggar in these early years have since been transferred to other regions, while most Kel Ahaggar, for their part, now deny that they were ever opposed to the Algerian authorities! Several Europeans whom I met in Tamanrasset told me that they had heard Tuareg discussing an uprising. With the exception of the mysterious developments surrounding Chaabani's unsuccessful coup in 1964, which I shall discuss presently, I do not think that the Kel Ahaggar have ever expressed their resentment of the administration in such terms, neither can I believe that they would have taken a passing foreigner into their confidence. The origin of most of these stories rests with police informers who, in the guise of Tuareg, are only too willing to discuss the oppressive policies and actions of the Algerian authorities! Many passing Europeans, after discussing the merits of slavery with such 'aggrieved Tuareg' at the hotel bar in Tamanrasset, have been expelled from the region or discreetly hurried on their way. In 1968 a young Frenchman, allegedly 'freelancing' a story of the 'Tuareg Revolution' for a leading Paris journal, came to me one evening to tell me that he now had evidence of a planned uprising, and that a Tuareg was going to take him into the mountains on the next day to show him the secret arms caches! His informant was a policeman, and on the next day he was instead flown to Hassi Messaoud to explain himself to the regional authorities in Ouargla.

Although rumours of an impending Tuareg uprising were rife there were several factors which mitigated against such an eventuality. Predominant among these were the recent experiences of the uprising in Mali, which was crushed by President Keita's forces with disastrous consequences for the Tuareg, many of whom fled to Ahaggar to seek refuge and settle among the Kel Ahaggar.

A further important factor mitigating against an uprising was the lack of cohesive leadership amongst the Kel Ahaggar. I am not saying that the Tuareg did not unite in armed resistance against the Algerian government because no charismatic leader such as El Hadj Akhmed or Moussa ag Amastane emerged at the time, but rather that there was considerable confusion and lack of surety regarding the identification and recognition of leadership and their means of political representation.

Prior to independence the Kel Ahaggar had been linked to the French administration through the Amenukal. In 1963, however, the Amenukal was 'elected' as a Vice-President of the National Assembly and paid a salary as a deputy in the new Republic. In this honorary position, which as far as I am aware he has never exercised, the Amenukal lost his official status as 'traditional chief'. His authority no longer found sanction in the administration at Tamanrasset, while his recruitment into the Algerian political hierarchy, albeit in an honorary capacity, compromised his position, which for many Kel Ahaggar became one of ambiguity. Although several of them continued to pay him *tiwse* in spite of its official abolition at the end of the French period, many of the nomadic Kel Ahaggar began to look towards Hadj Moussa, the half-brother of the Amenukal Bay, as their political leader.

Local government representation from independence until the commune elections in 1965–6 was through a Special Delegation or Council, the government-appointed President of which was Hadj Moussa. The shift in political support from the Amenukal to Hadj Moussa could thus be seen as merely the Kel Ahaggar's logical response to their perception of the change in local government organization. To some extent this was true; Hadj Moussa was their appointed representative in Tamanrasset and the official channel through which their representations could be made to the Algerian authorities. Several Tuareg, not fully informed of the changes taking place and thus perhaps not readily perceiving the Amenukal's position, even felt that they could no longer look to the Amenukal for support as their traditional leader as he had been 'weak' and not ready to stand up for them.

Nevertheless, the rise of Hadj Moussa as a popular leader, his appointment to the presidency of the Special Council, and his eventual removal as a threat to both the Amenukal and the Algerian government raise questions to which we will probably never have the final answers. What was the basis of his political following? Was he a political usurper, motivated by frustrated ambition and jealousy of his half-brother? What was his involvement, if any, in the abortive coup against Ben Bella, and the skirmish between Kel Ahaggar and ex-slaves at Otoul in 1964? Or, was he a politically naïve and largely passive instrument in an ingenious government strategy of 'divide and rule'?

I have met few people, either members of the government, Frenchmen or Tuareg, who have not been reluctant to give information or voice their opinion on these intriguing and politically volatile questions. They are, by their very nature, controversial, and I can do little to clarify them other than present certain facts, some speculative suggestions, and my own tentative opinions.

Hadj Moussa held considerable status and influence among the Kel Ahaggar. Not only was he a Hadj but, as the son of Akhemouk ag Ihemma, the Amenukal from 1920 to 1941, he had been born close to the centre of power; while his extensive network of consanguinous and affinal kinship ties[14] related him in varying degrees not only to most Kel Rela, but also to members of the Taitok, and more indirectly to the Irregenaten,[15] the Chaamba, and the Aguh-en-tehle.

With the economic development that began to take place in Ahaggar during the 1950s Hadj Moussa was one of the first Kel Rela to settle in Tamanrasset. Through his status, extensive connections and experience, he was well equipped to fulfil the role of 'middleman' or 'broker' between many of the nomadic Kel Ahaggar and the administrative and commercial sectors of Tamanrasset. He was relatively affluent and generous, and not only gave personal assistance to many nomads but often acted as counsel or adviser on their behalf. Hadj Moussa was not unique in this role, for, as we shall see later, most of the Kel Rela in Tamanrasset acted in varying capacities as brokers or agents for the nomadic Kel Ahaggar, but it seems that Moussa in particular had acquired a considerable degree of popularity and respect from certain sections of the nomadic community and by independence had established himself as something of a 'patron' or 'big man' in Tamanrasset.

Moussa's activities in Tamanrasset during this period certainly provided him with a potential political following amongst the nomads, for not only was he popular but, as in the case of all brokers, there is the question of indebtedness, which may be activated in terms of political support.

There is some reason to suppose that Moussa, motivated by frustrated ambition and jealousy of Bay, was actively aspiring towards political leadership even before independence. Although always close to the centre of traditional power, Moussa, because of his descent, was not in line of succession: he was not *agg ettebel* and could thus never become Amenukal. At the death of his father, Akhemouk, the succession was contested by three candidates: Meslar ag Amayas; Louki, the son of Moussa ag Amastane's sister; and Bay ag Akhemouk, Hadj Moussa's half-brother through Akhemouk's first marriage. Louki was immediately rejected because of his feeble character, and the succession passed to Meslar, but not until after Bay's claim, which, in spite of his youth and the contravention of the traditional principles of matrilineal success, had been supported by a considerable number of younger Ihaggaren, an important group of Kel Ulli, and the influential Arab marabouts who wanted to see him succeed his father. However, at the death of Meslar in 1950, there were no brothers, sons of maternal aunts or sons of sisters, and the *ettebel* reverted to Bay as a more distant matrilineal cousin.

Throughout most of his life Moussa had thus seen his half-brother contesting and eventually succeeding to the centre of power. Certain Frenchmen, who knew Ahaggar before independence, have told me of Hadj Moussa's jealousy of Bay, and the leaders of the abortive coup against Ben Bella in 1964 certainly seem to have been aware of it. Nevertheless, although I believe that Moussa has always been jealous of Bay, I do not think that he ever saw himself seriously as a popular political leader or a potential usurper prior to independence. In fact, I am extremely doubtful whether at any time he ever entertained serious thoughts of usurping his half-brother. I say this for several reasons. Firstly, I have never received any definite confirmation from Hadj Moussa or persons closely related to him to make me believe otherwise. Secondly, Moussa was undoubtedly aware that the traditional political system, which was reinforced and sanctioned by the French, would always have prohibited his succession as Amenukal. Furthermore, to have been able to predict the situation that was to provide him with a legitimate basis for power, as President of the Council, and so consciously to use his position in Tamanrasset prior to independence in anticipation of that end, would have required a remarkable degree of foresight and political sophistication – neither of which Moussa possessed.

The fourth reason relates to the events surrounding the abortive coup of 1964 and the related Otoul affair.

In the summer of 1964 there was a renewed wave of opposition against Ben Bella, which intensified during the last weeks of June and early July, and culminated in the attempted coup of Colonel Chaabani, the commander of the well-armed garrison at Biskra.

Biskra was Chaabani's home town, and during the Revolution he had risen at a young age to become commander of Wilaya VI,[16] which covered the Saharan region and centred on such towns as Bou-Saada, Laghouat, Djelfa and Biskra.[17] He was a local hero and his perception of his position in Algeria was undoubtedly coloured by the intense local support that he received from the population in the Biskra district. Chaabani's coup seems to have been precipitated by Boumedienne's disclosure of his fraudulent misappropriation of army funds. The story, which I heard some years later from Algerians serving in Biskra at the time, was that Chaabani was claiming funds and equipment for troops far in excess of the number actually garrisoned in the town. According to the files, Chaabani had recruited several thousand 'fictitious' troops. I do not know how Boumedienne's suspicions were raised, but it appears that he gave fifteen days' notification of his intention, as commander of the army, to inspect the Biskra garrison. Somehow Chaabani succeeded in parading a sufficient number of men for the inspection, but the guise failed and the fraud was exposed. The uprising was crushed without much ado within a week. Ben Bella made a few utterances to the press about oil royalties in an attempt to implicate French interests, and Chaabani was summarily executed on 3 September.

The summer of 1964 was the time of my first visit to Algeria, and one of the many rumours circulating about Tuareg unrest was that they had already risen up in arms and attacked their ex-slaves at the little village of Otoul, twenty kilometres north of Tamanrasset.

The five Kel Ahaggar involved in the Otoul skirmish were served with varying detention sentences, and it was not until 1968, four years after the incident, that I was finally able to meet them and establish a little more clearly in my own mind not only the details of the skirmish but the general circumstances that surrounded it.

There is sufficient evidence to believe that Chaabani intended his coup to synchronize with a planned uprising among the Kel Ahaggar. He was well aware of the Tuareg grievances and their resentment of the Algerian authorities and was undoubtedly relying on Hadj Moussa's jealousy of Bay. Although it seems that Moussa was to have been installed as Amenukal, I am doubtful whether Chaabani ever made any direct overtures to Hadj Moussa himself. I have always considered Moussa to be relatively naïve politically, and doubt whether he would have understood the implications of any such advances.

Whatever plans Chaabani and Hadj Moussa's supporters made for an uprising, they were ill-conceived and executed in the clumsiest manner. Word was passed among the Kel Ahaggar to ride on Tamanrasset, but the nomads, not knowing the authenticity and origin of the messages, ignored them. Amidst the intrigues and general lack of information, certain Kel Ahaggar, on their return from the Niger caravans, were thus led to believe (so they maintained!) that they could reclaim their former slaves. Five Kel Ahaggar, under the impression that the government had modified its views on slavery during their absence in Niger, set off to the little cultivation centre being developed by some of their ex-slaves in the Oued Otoul. Four of the five, Khabte ag Abahag, and his cousin Sidi Mohammed of the Kel Tamanrasset section of the Dag Rali, and El Mouden ag Amanrassa and his brother Ehenu of the Isanden section of the Aguh-en-tehle, were all closely related to each other. Ehenu was married to Sidi Mohammed's sister and all four men could sometimes be found in the same camp. The fifth, Mellou, claimed that he was a Kel Rela from Tazrouk and related to Marli ag Amayas. I have met him only once, just after his return from prison, and believe that he is in fact one of the 100 or so descendants of Bouhen ag Khebbi ag Adebir, an illustrious Kel Rela who three generations ago took two slaves as concubines!

The five men duly set off to Otoul to reclaim their slaves. Some commentators have regarded the incident which followed as a militant expression of the Kel Ahaggar's resentment and opposition to the government. This opinion, which was the basis of so many of the rumours concerning a Tuareg uprising, has little relationship with what I believe to have been their immediate interests and perception of the situation. They had certainly been misled by the conflicting stories being rumoured in Ahaggar, but I cannot accept that they rode to Otoul in complete innocence and with the altruistic intention of carrying out a government proclamation – namely that slaves could be reclaimed! With the exception of Mellou, whose prison record indicates that he was a black market racketeer of some excellence, the other four men subsequently became well known to me. They were, in the nicest sense of the word, 'rogues' – and I can think of few less likely candidates to be trusted to 'keep the peace'!

They were in high spirits after returning from the caravan. For six months or thereabouts they had been enacting their 'traditional way of life'. During the years immediately following independence the caravans seem to have attained a symbolic meaning within the transient revivalist movement that was perceptible among the nomads at this time. The caravans provided an escape from the repression of the Algerian authorities and the confusion and uncertainty of Ahaggar, and their return to Ahaggar may well have provoked a degree of belligerence and intolerance towards the changes instigated by government action. The rumour about the reclamation of slaves was, I believe, seized upon in this context – and the journey to Otoul seems to have been made as much with the intention of provoking the slaves as of securing their return. They must, I am sure, have doubted the rumour, in the same way that most Kel Ahaggar doubted the authenticity and origin of the messages to ride on Tamanrasset. For why had not other Kel Ahaggar reclaimed their slaves, and why did Fendu, a close kinsman of Ehenu and El Mouden, refuse to co-operate? Fendu's reluctance to join them must have engendered some doubt as to the legality of their proposed action. Fendu, for his wisdom, was shot in the foot by Ehenu and seems to have been the most serious casualty of the whole affair!

The details of the skirmish at Otoul are not clear. From what I have been able to gather, a vociferous slanging match led to a brief skirmish, during which two Tuareg and two slaves were injured. The slaves sought refuge behind an outcrop of boulders and most of the ensuing action was verbal, with both parties hurling abuse. It was not, as some exaggerated accounts have claimed, a bloody battle.[18] Fortunately, a passing vehicle heard the commotion and informed the police in Tamanrasset.[19]

If I have spoken of Otoul in a slightly light-hearted vein, it is because as I came to know the characters involved and the background situation, so the comedy of the situation revealed itself. It was not, as many commentators have considered, a manifestation of Tuareg militancy against the Algerian authorities or part of a general uprising, although it may have stemmed indirectly from Chaabani's ill-fated coup. The action of the Algerian authorities indicates that they considered the incident to be relatively insignificant. There were no reprisals, apart from the detention sentences passed on the five Tuareg, and Hadj Moussa continued as President of the Special Council until the commune elections. I do not know the official wording of the sentences passed on the Tuareg but imagine that it would have read to the effect of 'disturbance of the peace, and assault with intent to inflict grievous bodily harm'!

In the final analysis of Moussa's position we must ask why he was appointed as President of the Council, and why he stood as a candidate in the commune election. My own opinion, which I put forward as an extremely tentative suggestion, is that Moussa was a 'pawn' of the Algerian government.

Moussa's appointment must be seen in relation to Algeria's immediate aim in Ahaggar of introducing the socialist principles of the Revolution without precipitating a Tuareg uprising. These principles centred on the abolition of slavery, the freeing of the land, and the extension of political representation to all population groups – or, more exactly, to all 'Algerian citizens'. In short, Tuareg domination in Ahaggar was to be eliminated. The Amenukal was seen by the Algerians not only as a symbol of Tuareg domination but also as the likely focus of the inevitable opposition that their actions would generate. His 'election' as a Vice-President of the Republic thus seems to have been designed to diminish his effective political power and authority, and, by compromising his position, to reduce the chances of his becoming a symbolic or active focus of opposition.

In this respect, the appointment of Moussa seems to have been an extremely ingenious move, and although it is perhaps difficult to credit the Algerian authorities at that time with such detailed insight of Tuareg society, I believe his appointment was designed to ease the removal of the Amenukal from the centre of the stage. Hadj Moussa was not *agg ettebel* nor a Khalifa, and would thus not have been identified as an extension of the traditional political system centred on the Amenukal. Furthermore, the Algerians must have been aware of his jealousy of Bay; once they had provided him with a legitimate basis of power it would probably have taken little further encouragement for him to utilize it in fulfilling his frustrated ambition and presenting himself as an alternative political leader to his half-brother.

If the appointment of Hadj Moussa was intended to cause some sort of division amongst the Kel Rela, it did not result in the formation of clearly opposed followings or factions but rather a discrete separation of power, between political representation and certain administrative responsibilities on the one hand, and traditionally sanctioned authority, in the form of the Amenukal, on the other.

The fact that *tiwse* was still paid to the Amenukal in the years immediately after independence indicates that most Kel Ahaggar still recognized and desired his traditional authority, in spite of his somewhat ambiguous position in the new political structure. Moussa's position, however, was not sanctioned by any such traditional authority but rather by the whim of the Algerians, who provided him with legitimacy, and the popular support of the nomads, which depended largely on his success as an 'opposition spokesman'.

Moussa's position, so delicately balanced between these two opposed forces, was perhaps inevitably and necessarily transient. Compliance with the government would have jeopardized his popular following among the nomads, while successful opposition would obviously have led to his removal by one means or another. The extent to which Moussa did pose a threat to the government is questionable. Chaabani's coup poses several intriguing questions, but there is little evidence of Moussa's personal involvement, and the government, for its part, was well aware that Moussa had little traditional authority among the nomads, that he was politically unsophisticated, and that he could be removed from office or discredited with relative ease. His opposition, within certain limits, could be tolerated, for as long as the Kel Ahaggar looked to Moussa as the 'champion of the nomads', as one French observer described him, there was less likelihood of opposition centring around the potentially more volatile and cohesive position of the Amenukal.

Moussa's defeat in the commune elections draws attention not so much to why he was defeated but to why he stood for election in the first place. An electoral victory would have secured his ultimate goal, perhaps at the expense of unleashing the hostility of the Harratin community,[20] but the likelihood of gaining such a victory was remote. Defeat, in the face of the Harratin's numerical superiority and their bitter resentment of Hadj Moussa, was almost a foregone conclusion. Such a defeat, as the nomads' candidate, would not only have confirmed the political domination of the Harratin community, but the inevitable discredit and disillusionment in his failure would almost certainly have led to a waning in his popular support among the nomads, and to his effective removal as a serious threat to the government.

The most logical course of action for Moussa to have taken, by which he could have saved face among the nomads, would have been to withhold his candidacy on some such pretext as the unfair representation afforded by the ballot and the threat to nomadic interests. By withdrawing and remaining aloof from the whole business he could probably have retained much of his support, a degree of credibility, and a less compromised position from which to develop a future strategy.

Such a course of action was clearly not in the government's interest. By abstaining he could not have been discredited so easily, nor would he have entirely jeopardized his chances of any future oppositionary action.

I do not know how Moussa himself saw his position at the time, or what promises, encouragement and guarantees were given to him by the government. It is possible that his perception of the situation may have been blinded by ambition and his immediate supporters so that he was not fully aware of the Harratin's hostility towards him and their numerical superiority. My own opinion, however, is that the Algerian authorities played an active role in encouraging him to stand, for it is difficult to believe how he could have otherwise been unaware of the opposition directed against him. To some extent he may have been a victim of his own personal ambitions, but more, I believe, a victim of his own naïvety, through which he was manipulated with relative ease.

After his defeat, which effectively removed him from the wider political arena, he was transferred to the Bureau Politique, from which he has since retired.

# THIRTEEN
# DROUGHT AND ECONOMIC DEPRESSION IN AHAGGAR

The Kel Ahaggar's progressive abandonment over the last decade or more of a predominantly pastoral and nomadic existence, or, as it is more commonly referred to, 'the destruction of the Tuareg way of life', cannot be ascribed solely to the enactment of Algeria's socialist policies in Ahaggar. On the contrary, the plight of the Kel Ahaggar during this period has arisen as much from an act of God as an Act of state – in the form of drought, or, to be more specific, a combination of factors centring around the cumulative effect of several years of inadequate rainfall and overgrazing.

The misfortune for the Kel Ahaggar has been in the coincidence of these two forces. Their complex interaction in determining the processes of change in Ahaggar has been such that it is impossible to attribute either with the *coup de grâce*. On the one hand we can ponder on the possible fate of an Algerian administration in Tamanrasset had it been confronted by the Kel Ahaggar with abundant pastures and productive herds to ensure the resources and confidence of their resistance. On the other hand, as will become evident later, it is not too much to suggest that Algerian policies have enabled the Kel Ahaggar to retain some semblance of nomadism, or at least to avoid the ultimate disaster of drought.

Rainfall in Ahaggar varies considerably in its annual amount, seasonal and geographical distribution, and intensity. At Tamanrasset (1,400 m), annual rainfall amounts have varied between 159·0 mm (1933) and 5·3 mm (1949, 1961). Similarly, in the central mountains of Atakor, where the annual mean average is about three times higher than at Tamanrasset, readings at Assekrem[1] range from 40 mm to 257 mm. To talk in terms of mean average rainfall, which at Tamanrasset is 51·0 mm per annum, consequently obscures the significance and relevance of these considerable fluctuations in the amount of rain from one year to the next.

Nor is there any certainty as to what time of the year rain may come. Although the monthly precipitation records at Tamanrasset[2] indicate three main periods of rainfall – August–September, May, and a lesser peak between November and January – it is unusual for rain to fall in any significant quantity in more than one of these periods in the same year, and the concern of the Kel Ahaggar is whether rain will come at all.

Although there may be several successive days of intermittent drizzle, much of the summer rainfall, if it comes, is in the form of torrential thunderstorms during which several centimetres of rain may fall in a matter of an hour or two. In such storms runoff is intense. The land surface becomes a network of little rivulets, and the dry sandy beds of the *oueds* are transformed into raging torrents within a few hours. Such floods rarely last for more than a few days, and only in exceptional conditions, when rainfall has continued over several days, do the *oueds* flow for any length of time. But in spite of these heavy downpours, the net effective rainfall in Ahaggar is considerably reduced, for much of the water, once channelled into the main *oueds*, is lost to the Kel Ahaggar and dissipated over the far-off plains.

The danger of such floods to both humans and livestock is very real, and camps are rarely pitched on the valley floors, especially in summer when these storms are most likely. But it is these same rains, towards the end of summer, that are most appreciated by the nomads, as they ensure fresh winter pasture and so reduce the risk of hunger and possible famine during the hardest months.

Under these conditions drought is a purely relative phenomenon. One or even two years of low or negligible rainfall may cause hardship, but cannot really be considered as a drought. Only after several successive years of insufficient rain, when pasture has been unable to regenerate and herds have become skeletal, can we start talking in terms of drought.

One of the most peculiar features of this climate, which emerges not only from the rainfall recordings but also from the recollections of the people themselves, is that such drought periods have occurred in an almost cyclical pattern. The decade prior to 1934 seems to have been reasonably good. From 1934 to 1949 there was only one year in which rainfall was significantly higher than the mean average; while during the following nine years only two were below average. 1959 saw the first of further successive drought years, and by 1964 there had been six consecutive years in which rainfall had been below average, with both 1961 and 1964 recording only 5 mm. The Kel Ahaggar were thus confronted not only by an independent Algerian government, but also by the worst drought conditions since the 1930s.

Such drought periods are of course nothing new to the Kel Ahaggar. They are part of their experience, and like nomadic pastoralists the world over they have developed certain means of 'insurance' against them. The maximization of herd sizes, migration into other regions, diversification of livestock holdings, and such social institutions as bride-wealth payments, corporate holdings, sharing, and so forth, which function in various degrees to maximize the circulation or dispersion of livestock, all provide some measure of insurance against loss.

The problem of drought, however, is not so much that it is unusual or unexpected, but that each drought period tends to find the nomadic pastoralist confronted by new constraints and by situations that inhibit his traditional responses. This is particularly true today when frontiers may prohibit migration, and where the extension of cultivation or the introduction of new crops may have upset the ecological balance or denied access to formerly 'marginal' areas. Similarly, the opportunities afforded by external markets may have been at the expense of livestock diversification, and the natural balance maintained by the periodic outbreak of epidemics may have been upset by the introduction of vaccines without any commensurate rationalization of other aspects of stock-breeding.

The complex and dynamic interrelationship between factors of this nature has unfortunately been ignored all too often in the analysis of the causes of drought conditions and subsequent 'relief' programmes, let alone in their prevention. This, we have recently seen, with tragic consequences, in the Sahel – a region in which the rainfall is characterized by the same sort of unreliability and periodicity as in Ahaggar, and where the root cause of the problem is as much socio-economic (overgrazing) as climatic (rainfall).

The traditional responses of the Kel Ahaggar to the risk and consequences of drought centred primarily around the diversification of stock-holding – in the form of camels and goats – migration to other regions, and raiding. With poor pasture in Ahaggar, camels could be grazed quite easily in more distant regions – traditionally the Adrar-n-Iforas, and more recently in Tamesna.[3] Goats could not be trekked over such vast distances, but goats, in contrast to camels, are more resilient to the climatic exigencies of Ahaggar, and herds are able to make up their losses within a short time of fresh pasture becoming available. Furthermore, local migrations from one *tawsit* territory to another, under the authorization of the Amenukal, provided a means of rational adaptation to pastoral variations within Ahaggar itself. The most general response to severe drought conditions, however, was to raid outwards from Ahaggar. In the same way that we have seen the Taitok raiding neighbouring groups to recoup their losses at the hands of the Kel Rela, so there seems to have been a similar escalation of raiding to compensate for losses from drought.

During this century, however, the dependency on a purely pastoral (and raiding) subsistence has been lessened by the development of caravan trade to Niger, the extension of cultivation within Ahaggar, and, in more recent years, the opportunities of wage-earning – so that the risk of drought, although by no means averted, has at least become less critical.

The devastation and suffering recently experienced in the Sahel makes it particularly difficult to discuss the conditions prevalent in Ahaggar in the early 1960s with any meaningful perspective. From the end of the summer of 1958 until the summer rains of 1965 only 15 cms of rain fell at Tamanrasset. By 1964, many of the Kel Ahaggar from Tamesna, who had been attracted back to Ahaggar prior to independence by the opportunity of wages, had returned once more to the south. Most of the she-camels and many of the males held in Ahaggar had been moved south to the pastures of Tamesna, and, as in the 1930s, the Kel Ahaggar had become increasingly dependent on alternative resources to alleviate the hardships of pastoral degeneration.

Although rainfall during these years was certainly inadequate, the general opinion of several people who had had intimate knowledge of Ahaggar over a long period was that the number of goats in Ahaggar had come to exceed severely the carrying capacity of the region, with the result that pasture was suffering not only from insufficient rain but also the ravagings of goats. The problem of Ahaggar over the last decade, like that of much of the Sahel, seems to have been primarily one of overgrazing.

When I first visited Ahaggar in 1964 I was not struck by the prevalence of drought conditions. On the contrary, after the journey across the desolate wastes of the Algerian Sahara, Ahaggar seemed relatively well vegetated and watered. It would certainly have been difficult to convince a stranger such as myself of the gravity of the situation. There were, after all, no apparent signs of animals dying, as one might expect in times of drought. My pleasant vision of Ahaggar was further reinforced when, on my first journey through the mountains, I came across a group of nomads in the In Azrou area with a herd of 50–100 camels. There were several calves and I was offered much fresh milk. But of course I had no means of comparison, and was not to know that it was the only time that I was ever to drink camel's milk in Ahaggar. As I visited more nomadic camps on that first journey I was admittedly surprised at the dearth of pastoral products such as milk, cheese, butter fat and so forth, which I had expected to find in abundance.

The collection of statistical material about herd sizes, milk yields and other related aspects of goat-breeding is obviously essential for the analysis of the effect and severity of drought conditions. The collection of this sort of data, however, is not easy. 'Counting heads', which is not easy when one is confronted by a hundred animals milling their way through the rock-strewn terrain, is particularly misleading in that it conceals such crucial information as ownership of animals, possible division of herds, changes in herd sizes, and so forth.

Although the Kel Ahaggar do not show the same interest in their goats as their camels, they are all known by sight and owned individually; even young children are stock-owners as a result of presents from their parents and other kinsmen at important ceremonies and festivals. One of the most striking features of a nomadic camp is the degree of intimacy and domestication of the goats. On their return to the camp in the evening the question of territorial prerogative is barely defined, and goats are shooed off only after they succeed in muzzling into a cooking pot or the grain sacks in the back of the tent.

On several occasions, sleeping on the ground outside or even inside a tent, I have woken to the warmth of a goat sharing my blanket. On one such occasion a heavy thunderstorm began in the late afternoon and did not abate until the early hours of the morning. In spite of our attempts to build dams and diversion channels around the tent, almost everything, including the blankets, was soon awash, and as it grew darker it became more difficult to ward off the goats, who were determined to share the relative protection of the tent. Khabte lay huddled under a pile of sodden blankets in the centre of the tent, doped with aspirin to keep the cold and wet (or Kel Asouf!) out of his head, and oblivious to the nightmarish proceedings, save for his periodic coughs and groans which told us of his discomfort. On either side of him his wife and I clung on to our valuables as goats piled themselves on top of us, almost suffocating us with their steaming mass of wet hair, and with their urine contributing even more to the already soaked and stinking interior. It was a long sleepless night, but the goats had at least provided some warmth and none of us was willing to move out into the cold damp morning air.

As the Kel Ahaggar have such a personalized relationship with their animals, the collection of this crucial statistical material would seem to be a relatively straightforward matter. But this is not the case at all, for not only is it extremely impolite to discuss such matters and improper even to show interest in their animals, but the people themselves are most reluctant to talk about them. While the condition of the pasture may be discussed in infinite detail, no reference will be made to the number of animals, and rarely even to their condition, except perhaps in the general context of their emaciation and the dearth of milk. The reason for this rather surprising reluctance to discuss their most valuable and important asset (this includes camels) is their fear of the 'evil eye' (*tehot*). The expression of admiration, praise, or any sort of covetous remark, for one's own or another's possessions, may invoke the 'evil eye', which can cause illness and even death to both humans and animals.

It is thus virtually impossible to give any reliable and meaningful figures on herd sizes, for as Gast has emphasized[4] there is nothing among the Tuareg that is more difficult to calculate; while Nicolaisen,[5] who has probably studied pastoral practices among the Tuareg more than anyone else, warns that statistics concerning the ownership of livestock must always be regarded with much suspicion, as it is extremely difficult to obtain data.

Although every household, or 'tent', is self-supporting in that 'it has its own churning-bag and its own millet bag', as the Tuareg put it,[6] the extended family or *ariwan*, which usually comprises between two and seven such tents, co-operates in goat-herding and certain other tasks. But, as we have already mentioned, the *ariwan* is merely the lower-level structural equivalent of the *tawsit* section, and when pasture is exceptionally good the whole section, comprising several *ariwan*, or 'goat-camps' as they may be called, will come together to form a single camp of anything up to twenty tents. I have never seen such section camps in Ahaggar as a result of the poor pastoral conditions over the last decade or more, but Nicolaisen observed them in the 1950s[7] and noted that there was generally a distance of 50 to 100 yards between each constituent goat-camp to prevent their goat herds from mixing.

This occasional concentration and subsequent dispersal of the constituent units of the *tawsit* section is merely one expression of the general fluidity of their social organization. Camps cannot be regarded as constant in terms of their composition, even over relatively short periods of time. On the one hand we see the *ariwan*, like the *tawsit* section, splitting into even smaller units of just one or two households and then reuniting as pastoral conditions dictate; while at the individual level there is a considerable degree of fluidity as a result of the continual comings and goings of individuals and households as members go off in search of work, on caravans, to visit other camps or villages, or for some other such reason. It is quite apparent, therefore, that attempts to 'count' herd sizes may give a totally false impression of the average number of goats per household and so forth, for the composition of a camp may be doubled or halved at any one moment without there necessarily being any change in the size of the herd. This, in itself, is not in any way surprising or unexpected; nor would it present any sort of problem if the Kel Ahaggar themselves were not reluctant to discuss the details of their herds.

A look at three quite typical camps among the Kel Tinhart (Kel Rezzi), Kel Tamanrasset and Kel Hirafok sections of the Dag Rali will illustrate this sort of situation, and the difficulties involved in collecting any meaningful statistical data, a little more clearly.

On my second visit to Ahaggar (1965) I was travelling through Atakor with my camel (which I later managed to drown in a flooded *oued*!) and had stopped at the very beautiful series of *gueltas* at Afilale, to be met by a young Tuareg man hobbling with a badly infected big toe. He had been bitten by a horned viper and the wound had become infected; after giving him a little first aid I encouraged him to make the journey to the hospital in Tamanrasset. This he did, and I met him there a week or two later. He spoke good French and Arabic, and on my return to Ahaggar in 1968 he was willing to help me as an interpreter, and took me up to his camp, a little to the south-west of Assekrem, which at that time consisted of eight tents and about thirty people. As he spent much of his time working in Tamanrasset, it was not until the winter of 1969 that I decided to make another visit to his camp. I left him in Tamanrasset in the company of a group of tourists who had contracted him as a guide on their search for rock paintings in the Tefedest. He planned to leave them at the village of In Amguel, from where he would make his own way up to his camp, which was then pitched in one of the most beautiful parts of Atakor, in the Oued Ilaman just to the north-east of the peak. Having arranged a rendezvous with him for early December I duly set off on foot from Tamanrasset and reached the *oued* four days later. Five tents, perched on the high terrace of the *oued* and sheltered by massive granite boulders, looked down the open valley beneath them. Dogs barked and a child cried, but otherwise there was no apparent sign of life. The goats were obviously out grazing and the tents stood forlorn and seemingly deserted beneath the towering rocks. It was not for some minutes after the dogs

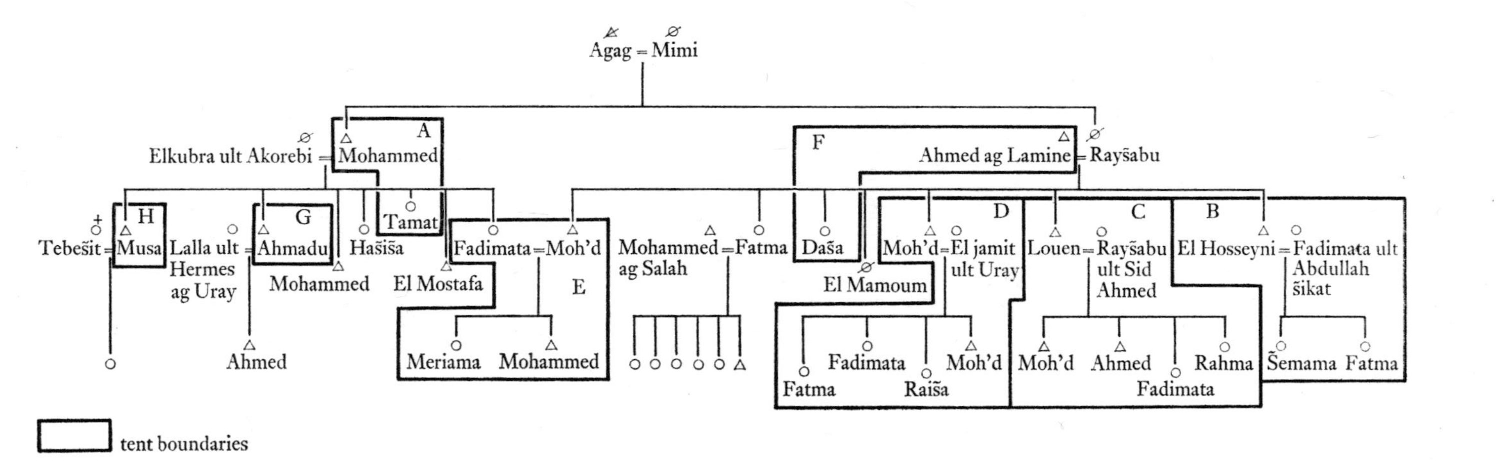


Figure 4 The 'normal' or full complement of a Dag Rali camp.

had sounded the alarm that a woman peered from the protective awnings of a tent. Neither my informant (Hosseyni) nor any other men were there. It was an acutely embarrassing situation, for the camp consisted of only five women and eleven children, and it was clearly impossible for me to stay. No one had seen or heard of Hosseyni for several weeks, but after my explanations were gradually understood and Hosseyni's promised supplies of sugar, tea and tobacco were delivered, I stayed with them until nightfall, inquiring the whereabouts and news of the other members of the camp.

The 'normal' or full complement of the camp, which conformed fairly closely to that of my visit one and a half years earlier, is shown in Fig. 4. The whereabouts of all those whom one might have expected to find in the camp were:

*Tent A* The whereabouts of Mohammed ag Agag could not be verified at the time. He was 'resident' in the camp, but at the time of my visit was apparently away visiting a neighbouring camp.

*Tent B* Hosseyni, after arriving at In Amguel, had tried to buy grain with the money earned from his tourist trip, and after making arrangements for its transportation (with donkeys) to the camp had been fortunate enough to meet another group of tourists who were willing to contract his services as a guide. It was a good month for him and he did not return to the camp for another two to three weeks. His daughter Semama was living with her mother's father.

*Tent C* Louen was away working (at the mines at Laouni). His wife and children had remained in the camp.

*Tent D* Mohammed ag Ahmed Lamine was staying temporarily with his father while looking for work in Tamanrasset.

*Tent E* Mohammed was with his brother also looking for work. Ahmed ag Lamine, the old chief of the Kel Rezzi (married into Dag Rali), spent the cold winter months at Mataka, a few miles down the Oued Tamanrasset from the town. His unmarried daughter Dasha accompanied him. In summer he returned to the camp, thus comprising another tent (F).

Ahmadu and Moussa were both away somewhere looking for work. Theoretically, their return to the camp would contribute two further tents (G and H), although in the case of Ahmadu his wife and child were still in his father-in-law's camp while they prepared the tent. Similarly, Moussa's first wife, after divorcing him, had returned to her own family

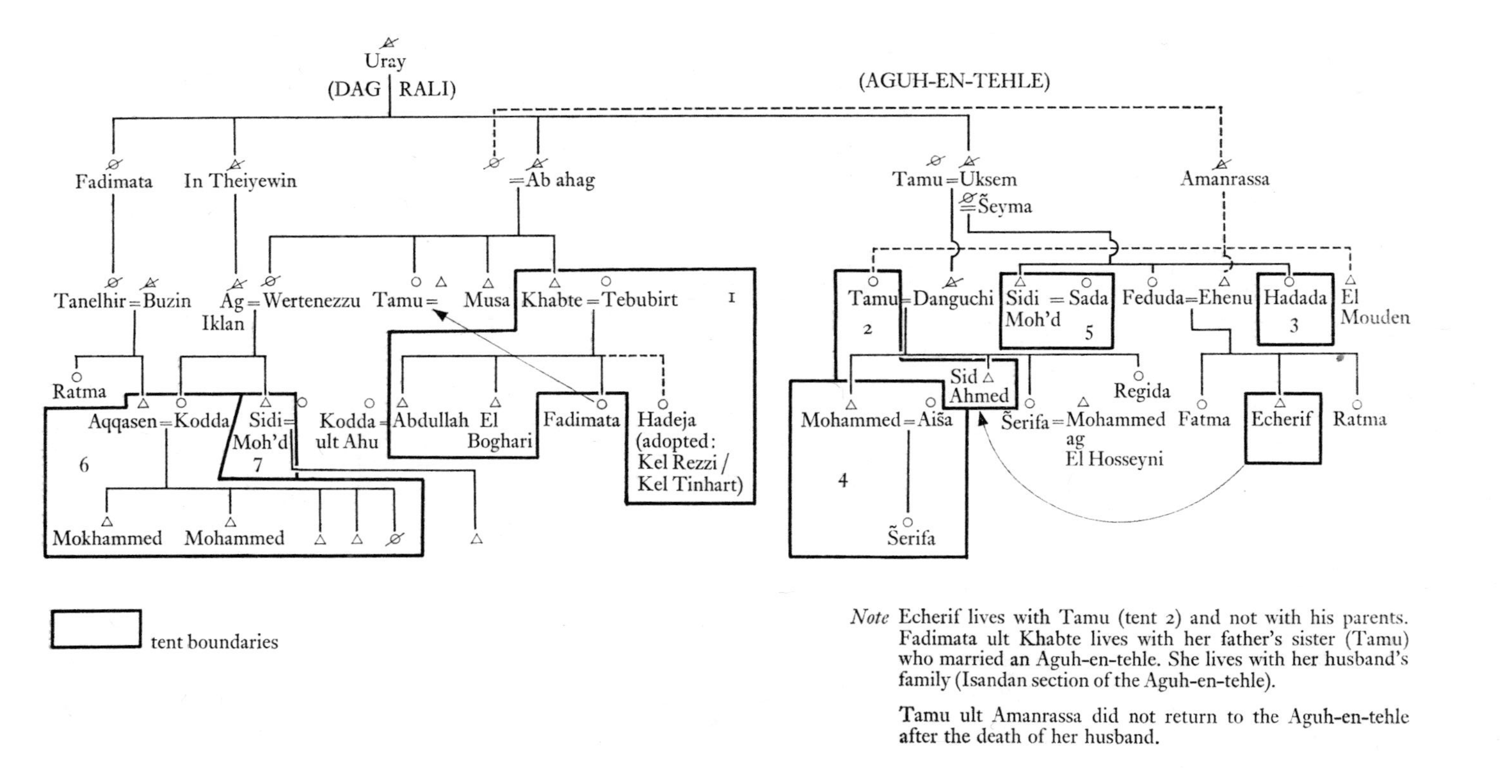


*Note* Echerif lives with Tamu (tent 2) and not with his parents. Fadimata ult Khabte lives with her father's sister (Tamu) who married an Aguh-en-tehle. She lives with her husband's family (Isandan section of the Aguh-en-tehle).

Tamu ult Amanrassa did not return to the Aguh-en-tehle after the death of her husband.

**Figure 5** **The move towards 'semi-sedentarization' in a Dag Rali camp.**

with their daughter, while his second wife was still living with her parents, preparing the tent.

El Mostafa normally lived with his father, but was away at boarding-school in Tamanrasset. His sister, Hasisa, lived with one of her father's cousins (Kel Terhenanet), who was without children.

With the possible exception of Ahmed ag Lamine's seasonal migration to avoid the extreme winter cold in the mountains, I do not think that the absence of these persons resulted in much change in the size of the herd attached to the camp.

The most interesting feature of this camp was that it was fairly typical of the composition of camps during winter in 'traditional' times, when men would often be away on caravans or raiding, with only the women, children and aged left in the camps. In this instance, some years after independence, there were no ex-slaves attached to the camp, and most of the men were away either wage-earning or looking for work.

The second example (Fig. 5) illustrates the move towards 'semi-sedentarization' as Kel Ahaggar were gradually forced to abandon their nomadic existence. In the summer of 1968 households 5 and 6 were living temporarily at Tagmart, a growing Dag Rali centre (mostly Kel Tamanrasset) about twenty kilometres north-north-west of Tamanrasset. During this period Aqqasen made frequent visits to the camp, while Abdullah (tent 1) was away in Tagmart and Tamanrasset for most of the time, preparing for his first caravan trip to Niger. In the winter of 1969–70 all seven tents were pitched in the Oued Amsa, although most of the men were making constant trips to Tamanrasset (via Tagmart) in search of work and other means of monetary remuneration. Twelve months later the entire camp was living 'temporarily' in Tagmart. During the comings and goings to Tagmart, prior to the 'temporary' settlement of the entire camp, I believe that households 5 and 6 left most of, if not all, their goats in the nomadic camp. During the winter of 1969–70, as we shall see later, most of the men spent a considerable amount of time in Tamanrasset, while Abdullah provided them with something of a *coup* by being contracted as a guide-cum-interpreter-cum-camel-hirer for a travel company offering camel treks through Atakor.

By the 1970s pastoral conditions were impoverished; many nomads, such as this group, were finding it almost impossible to remain in their nomadic camps and the temporary settlement began to take on a more permanent outlook. These camps that did remain in the 'nomadic milieu' were obliged to split into even smaller units and move more frequently in

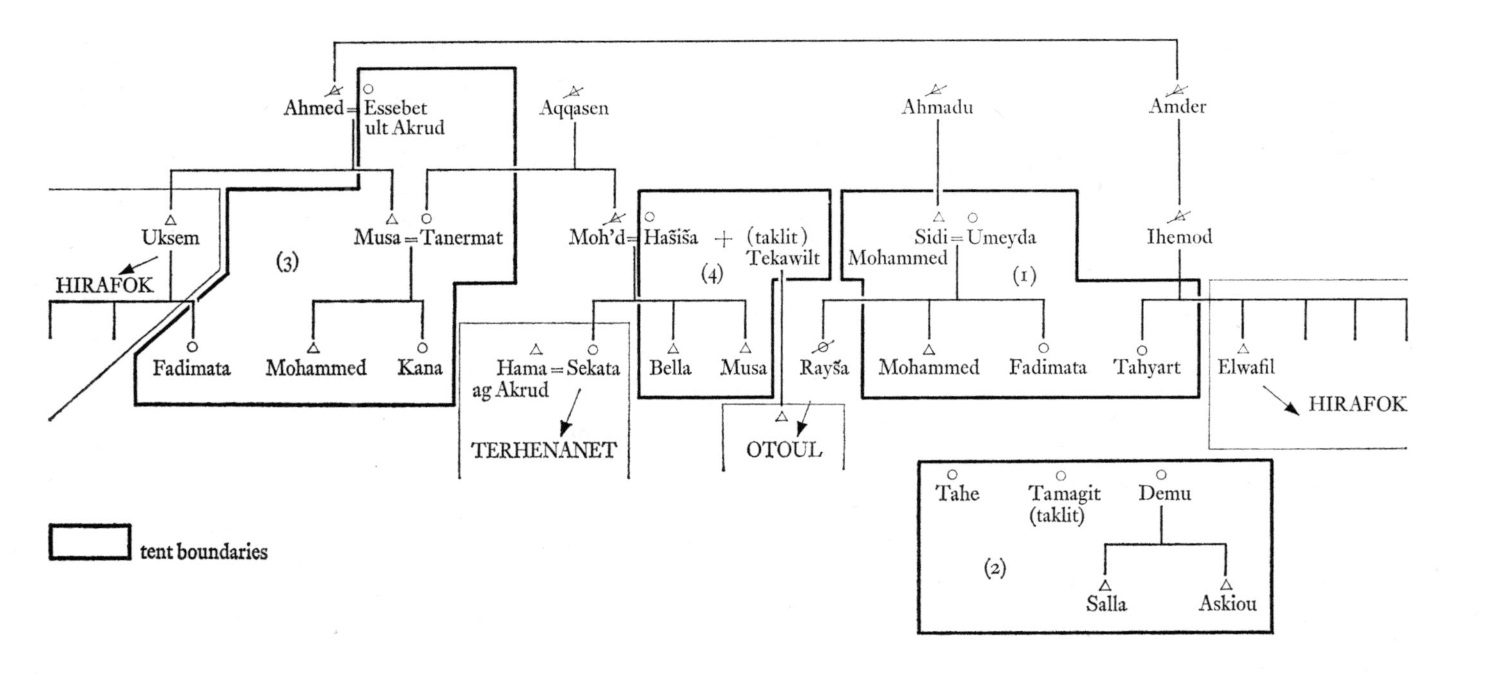


Figure 6 The organization of a Dag Rali camp under pressure, winter 1971–2.

search of pasture, while becoming increasingly dependent on external sources of income, such as tourists, wage-earning, 'exchange' with the cultivation centres, particularly with section members who had established gardens in the cultivation centres, and so forth. Fig. 6 shows the organization of such a camp in the winter of 1971–2 under such extreme pressure.

This camp was not really an 'extended' family but rather two such families with only distant kinship ties, who were co-operating, at least temporarily, in goat herding. In the winter of 1971 I spent six weeks with the camp, during which time it was obliged to split and move in search of pasture. The camp was initially located on the north-west slope of Assekrem, which was a particularly advantageous site, especially in winter months, because of the number of tourists who visited the hermitage and provided a convenient market for the 'traditional' artefacts manufactured by the women of the camp. By the middle of November there was little pasture in the area and insufficient water in the wells dug in the *oued* floors, and the camp was forced to abandon its favourable 'commercial' location and move about eight to ten miles further west to the Oued Terourirt. The move itself involved a temporary division of the camp. Tents 1 and 2 established the new camp site and were not joined by tents 3 and 4 for a little over a week. The reason for this brief separation was partially due to the dearth of pack animals (all the camels in the camp had died and there were only a few donkeys), but primarily because it provided an opportunity for the goat herd to make a circuitous detour and eke out more distant grazing.

By the early 1970s goat herds were skeletal. There was virtually no milk yield at all, and during this particular winter they were suffering even greater losses than usual from the almost daily attacks by jackals. It was the first time that I had seen jackals actually venturing into a guarded herd during daylight and having to be driven off with great difficulty, but they too were suffering from the wretched conditions. On one night we were awakened by great commotion to find at least two jackals in the midst of the camp. Three goats had been killed that week and it was presumably the same culprits. The dogs had drawn their attention and cornered them among the rocks, and somehow, in the pandemonium of shouting and stumbling through the darkness, Sidi's young son had skilfully succeeded in stoning both animals to death. For most of the two following days he proudly skinned his trophies which his mother duly treated and made into bags, which were later sold for ten dinars each to tourists at Assekrem.

The size of this herd numbered between sixty and seventy goats, and one might have assumed quite reasonably that it represented the wealth of the members of the camp. This, however, was not the case. As nomads are settling more and more in the cultivation centres in a 'semi-sedentarized' state, many of their goats are kept in the camps of kinsmen who are still able to maintain themselves in the mountain camps. The net result of this developing relationship is that kinsmen in the villages have access to pastoral resources, while those in the camps have access to agricultural resources.

It is usually difficult, especially as Tuareg are so reluctant to discuss their animals, to ascertain the details of this 'exchange'. In this particular case, the presence of Tahyart in Sidi Mohammed's camp could not be explained through the normal principles of residence. Her family was now resident in Hirafok and she herself merely said that she was staying in the camp for a while. Sidi elaborated a little more by saying that she was helping to look after the goats, but without mentioning whose goats. Similarly, Moussa's brother Uksem stayed in the camp for a week and said that he was merely paying a visit to his brother's family on the way back from Tamanrasset to spend the festival of L'aid with his own family in Hirafok.

The question of ownership of goats in the herd might have been left there. Tahyart's assistance was surprising in view of the adequate labour resources (five ex-slaves), and Uksem's 'social call' was perhaps a little longer than might have been expected. It transpired, however, that Tahyart was responsible for several goats belonging to members of her family in Hirafok, and that Uksem had also left several of his goats in the care of his brother's family. I do not know the exact number of goats belonging to the Hirafok families, but the danger in associating the size of a herd with the wealth of a camp is quite evident. In this case, the members of the camp did not own sixty or seventy goats, and the difference represented reciprocal assets in the form of rights to certain garden produce from their kinsmen now cultivating their own gardens in Hirafok.

It was during my visit to this camp that I heard one of the most piteous stories in Ahaggar, which, although it has nothing to do with our interest in drought and goats, gives a touching insight into the more personal and human aspects of life in the mountain camps. Sidi Mohammed had two children, a son (Mohammed) aged about fourteen and a little girl, Fadimata, who was only a baby. Sometime before my visit to this camp I had heard that he had had another daughter who had died. Sidi was in his mid-fifties and I had a great deal of affection for him, and always felt that his magnificent face, build and gestures were well-suited for an understudy of Anthony Quinn. He was, to use the cliché, one of the 'last of the nomads', despising the sedentary life and not able fully to understand the changes overcoming Ahaggar. He had never made any reference to his deceased daughter, which was not surprising since Tuareg rarely show grief. A death is the 'will of God', and after the three days of mourning it is cast aside.

We were sitting together one day, talking about pasture, when I asked him what happened to Raysa. His head lifted suddenly and he met my eyes with an almost frightening look of surprise and anger: 'Who told you about her?' I said that I had heard somewhere that he had had more children in the past. There was a long silence as he stared at the ground, fiddling with some stones. I expected a rough denial and to see him get up and walk off, but instead his whole face and tone took on the most piteous expression.

'We were camped in a place like this, close to here. My daughter wandered off at about five in the evening – at dusk. She wandered off alone. It was winter and very cold, and she wasn't wearing a shirt – she wasn't wearing anything, and she got lost. After she had wandered off into the rocks we realized she was missing. We searched throughout the night but couldn't find her. In the morning, in the daylight, we soon found her – dead. She had died of exposure. She was about three or four years old. Mohammed, my son, found her body – her brother found her. Ahmed, Demu's brother, and Nati were also there when they found her. It was down in the valley over there – not very far away – in the Oued Tourtourine. It happened about four years ago [1967–8]. After that I decided to have another daughter – Tata was born.'[8] He looked up and was smiling.

The statistical material that we would ideally like to have about goat-breeding and the contribution of goats to the subsistence economy of the Kel Ahaggar should concern the changes in herd sizes, milk yields and so forth, in relation to variations in ecological, economic and social factors. Such a study would obviously not only be very difficult, in view of the foregoing remarks, but would necessarily have to extend fairly intensively over a number of years, as the physiology of goats and goat-breeding practices are such that it is possible, although most unlikely, for a herd to quadruple its size in a year.

The gestation period of a goat is about five months and the same animal is able to give birth twice a year. Since most goats bring forth two kids we can thus see that herd sizes can be increased tremendously under free-mating conditions. If the size of the herd needs to be increased rapidly, as after periods of drought, all the goats may be mated twice in the year, but milk yield decreases and may even stop after mating, so that free-mating, although providing for large herds, does not give the highest milk yields.[9] Free-mating is consequently rare, and one finds that most Tuareg practise extremely efficient methods for regulating goat-breeding in order to maximize milk production.

Effective goat-breeding, as Nicolaisen has shown,[10] is more than anything else a question of appropriate birth control. Although goats may yield milk for up to two years after the birth of kids, they give much more milk when they have kids. The pattern of mating is obviously determined by climatic conditions, which vary considerably from one year to the next. In dry years, and particularly in periods of drought, goats may be too emaciated for mating, in which case the penis of the male goat will be bound. Rainfall during the period 1950–58 was good, with the exception of two dry years in 1954 and 1956. Although 1954–5 was not excessively dry, it is interesting that Nicolaisen observed that no goats were mated in Ahaggar in that year. Similar, or worse, conditions have persisted throughout the 1960s and I have consequently never been able to witness the 'ideal' conditions which allow for regular mating. Under such 'normal' conditions, which Nicolaisen was able to observe, the herd is often divided into two parts so that kids may be born at different seasons. In Ayr, he noted that one part of the herd bore kids during the season of *akasa* (the rainy season – late summer) when annual pasture is rich, and the other part at the end of the winter (a period known as *tafsit* – spring) when other plants germinate. In other words, one part of the herd is rested when the other part is bearing young, with the result that the camps are assured of a more regular supply of milk.

Although climatic variability is greater than in Ayr, the same pattern of mating is usual in Ahaggar, with kids born either in autumn (*amewan*) or spring (*tafsit*).[11] As in Ayr, the best period for bearing young is in the late summer and autumn when the late summer rains have germinated the tender annual plants. These kids will be fully grown in twelve months and thus able to bear young in the spring season eighteen months later, while those born in spring can be mated twelve months later to bear young in the autumn.

Suckling of kids is controlled vigorously, sucking being allowed freely for only a short period after birth. According to Nicolaisen, this period is about two to four weeks if pasture is good, but up to two months if pasture is poor.[12] Numerous techniques are used to prevent and control suckling.[13]

In Ahaggar and Ajjer little stone enclosures (*agror*), which can be found around all camp sites, are used to isolate the kids and prevent them following their mothers when they leave the camp in the morning to graze, as well as to protect them from predators. Similarly, kids are often tied to tent posts, rocks or other anchorages to prevent them suckling when the mother animals are in the camp. Long before the kids are fully weaned they will eat the green annual plants that may be found close to the camp or the fresh shoots of acacias and other herbs carried into the camp by the women. Nicolaisen also mentions that if kids are very numerous they may be taken to separate grazing grounds away from the camp and forced to live exclusively on plant foods. There are, however, several devices to wean those kids which graze with the mother animals. The general principle of most of these devices is to prevent the kids' mouths from sucking. This is done by inserting a small stick transversely in the kid's mouth, rather like a bit, and holding it in place by means of string, or some suitable substitute, attached at either end and tied behind the head. Alternatively, the stick, sharpened at both ends, might be pierced through the cheek, a method which, although simple and crude, is apparently more efficient as the stick will not be displaced so easily.[14, 15]

The primary value of goats to the Kel Ahaggar is for their milk and the various cheese and butter derivatives. When fresh-green annual pasture is available, goats with young kids may yield up to two litres of milk a day, but after the conditions of the last ten or more years this is something which the Kel Ahaggar have long ceased to experience. It should be stressed, however, that even under good conditions such a yield is a rarely attained maximum and that a yield of ten to fifteen litres per day from a herd of twenty goats, with abundant pasture, is considered by Gast to be more realistic.[16] In dry conditions the yield of a herd may be reduced to a few litres a day, while under conditions of severe drought the herds may be virtually 'dry'; but to say, as Nicolaisen does, that goats are valueless for subsistence in drought periods is not entirely correct.[17] He is of course referring to milk, but we must also consider that it is in such drought conditions that the meat value of goats becomes relatively more important.[18]

Most Tuareg, as Nicolaisen has mentioned,[19] state that they are reluctant to kill their goats for meat except at certain religious feasts, for propitiatory sacrifices, in according special hospitality to visitors, or in the case of a sick animal, which may be sacrificed and eaten. But as he points out, Tuareg are generally not so irrational as to allow their goats to linger on through a life span of up to twenty years and die a natural death. As only a few he-goats are needed for mating, most are killed as kids, or castrated and fattened for meat. It is also clearly preferable to substitute the declining yield of an old milk-goat (after about eight to ten years) with that of a younger one. Such animals are either sold for meat (e.g. in Tamanrasset), used as a means of payment (e.g. to blacksmiths), or killed for consumption at feasts.[20]

The selection of goats for killing is thus rationalized in terms of maximizing milk productivity. Nevertheless, although I have not been able to collect detailed statistical data, there is little doubt that the onset of drought leads to an increase in meat consumption, which testifies to the rationale and efficiency of goat-breeding in Ahaggar. The killing of goats in drought periods offers a limited degree of security to the members of the camp by reducing the threat of starvation. Moreover, it cannot be said that such killing is at the expense of reducing milk production, for not only are the herds virtually dry in such periods, but it is clearly wise to kill the weaker animals before they themselves die of hunger. In such conditions the herds are gradually reduced to what might be termed an 'effective core minimum', which is able, with the regeneration of pasture and two matings in the year, to ensure the re-establishment of the herd. As the number of goats becomes less, so there is proportionately more pasture available for the survivors, or, in more realistic terms, the size of the herd tends to keep pace with the rate of degeneration of pasture. There is also the additional consideration that the number of he-goats required to cover the diminishing herd is correspondingly reduced. Thus, while it is true that milk production is almost negligible in such drought periods, the same is not altogether true of the subsistence contribution of goats, for it is in such times that their meat provides some insurance against the most serious eventuality.

I have refrained, for obvious reasons, from quoting any of the several published 'counts of heads', but now that the difficulty of collecting statistical data on goat-breeding, and the suspicion with which most such material should be regarded, have been illustrated, it is of largely quizzical interest to lift the veil of secrecy that I have drawn over these reports during the last few pages.

Estimates of the number of goats in Ahaggar have ranged from 11,000[21] to 50,000–100,000[22] – a good indication of our problem. The official statistics produced by the administration in 1948 gave the average number of goats per household among the Kel Ahaggar as fifteen.[23] This figure seems to have been derived from tax lists, and would probably have been too low.[24] Lhote, with a little more realism, considered that the number of goats per person under ideal conditions was thirty-five to forty. Any increase on this number produced a surplus, beyond the needs and labour resources of the household, which was slaughtered or sold to sedentarists in the oases.[25] I agree with both Nicolaisen and Gast that this estimate is at least theoretically feasible and would probably be attained in ideal conditions among some of the wealthier Kel Ahaggar, especially the Dag Rali, who are extremely rich in goats and among whom many households are said to have possessed 100 to 200 goats when pasture was ideal.[26] This estimate certainly bears little relation to the reality of the present situation, and even in the past would have been quite rare among most *tawsatin*.

From very rough calculations made among Kel Ulli and Isekkemaren *tawsatin* Nicolaisen estimated that households on an average possessed sixty to seventy goats when pasture was not too badly developed.[27] But even this estimate bears little relationship to the current size of herds, which for the last decade have been skeletal. This figure now conforms more closely to the size of herds in the more resilient nomadic camps rather than in individual households. In 1968, Gast considered that a family of two adults and two children possessing forty goats and two camels was rich, and that the minimum number of goats needed for this family's survival was twenty.[28] There are now few families who are not approaching this minimum.

During the early 1960s, pastoral conditions in Ahaggar might be best described as 'dry', in relation to normal years, rather than as 'drought', and from my own experience in 1964–5 I would estimate that the milk-yield in most camps was in the order of two litres per day.[29] The contribution of pastoral resources to subsistence was thus minimal, but although such a quantity of milk is not sufficient for the manufacture of cheese, and produces only a little butter fat, it is sufficient for the camp's survival providing that adequate supplies of millet can be assured. As we have already seen, the rate of exchange between millet and salt in Niger had been declining constantly over the previous two decades. By 1962, however, the terms of trade were becoming even more disadvantageous to the Kel Ahaggar as a result of the progressive monetization of the markets of Damergou. Barter exchange was becoming a thing of the past as Kel Ahaggar found themselves having to sell their salt to 'middlemen', who, not having millet, paid them in money, with which the Kel Ahaggar were then obliged to buy their millet. If we look at the economic feasibility of these caravans during this period in purely monetary terms we see that the yearly increases in the price of millet in Niger were compensated by an almost equivalent price reduction in Tamanrasset:

Price of millet[30]

| | bought in Damergou | bought in Tamanrasset |
|---|---|---|
| 1963–4 | 0·20 dinar per kilo | 0·70–1·00 dinar per kilo. |
| 1964–5 | 0·25–0·50 „ „ „ | 0·70 „ „ „ |
| 1965–6 | 0·50 „ „ „ | 0·60 „ „ „ |
| 1966 | Importation of millet from Niger blocked. | |

The price increases in Damergou seem to have been caused by the increased monetization of the market and increased demand from the south, while the decline in Tamanrasset resulted primarily from the government's attempts to reduce and stabilize the price of staple foods throughout the country, which effectively meant a subsidy on transport costs to Ahaggar.[31]

By 1965–6, therefore, the price difference between Tamanrasset and Damergou was only 0·10 dinar per kilo in favour of the south. If we consider the time and labour expenditure involved in these caravans, it might be argued that it would have been more profitable for the Kel Ahaggar to have bought their millet in Tamanrasset. But the Kel Ahaggar did not reckon the feasibility of their caravans in such terms. On the contrary, the price of millet in Tamanrasset was virtually irrelevant, for the caravans enabled a return, albeit diminishing, without any initial monetary resources.

Neither did the lowering of the price in Tamanrasset present them with any real alternative, for they had little money with which to buy the millet; and Tamanrasset provided them with no more than an incidental and virtually insignificant market for the sale of salt. Also, besides the fact that it was impossible to cost the time and labour involved on the caravans in monetary terms, one could view this expenditure as an investment in other ways; for not only did the absence of the men and animals give some relief to the subsistence of those remaining in the camps, but the caravans were also the means whereby the weaker camels of Ahaggar were transferred to the richer pastures of Tamesna.

The salt caravans, in spite of their diminishing returns, were thus not only critical for the survival of the camps, but, as we have already mentioned, they acquired a certain symbolic value which could not be measured in economic terms.

For us to understand this symbolic value of the caravans, we should pause for a moment to consider the general picture of change in Ahaggar immediately after independence. The Harratin community was characterized by a form of conscious awakening. The unimpeded exploitation of virgin land, although not fully realized in all areas, assured the cultivator's control over the means of production, while the wages that they had been able to earn over the last decade enabled them to free themselves from all debts, to accumulate capital resources and to invest it in new agricultural equipment.[32] Harratin children were going to school regularly and several were beginning to fill important positions in the local administration. Neither were they restricted any longer by the traditional political system: their political representation was assured, and their participation in the political development of the country was manifested in their attentive listening to political radio broadcasts and the payment of regular contributions to the Party. The Harratin of Tamanrasset were rapidly adopting the secular values of a politically independent and modernizing society. After independence, their material benefits began to be reflected in their immediate socio-political environment, and the stigma of being a Hartani was transformed into political consciousness and the development of civic pride and dignity.

The general optimism and institutionalization of change which characterized the Harratin community was not found among the Kel Ahaggar. Their resentment towards the administration, Tamanrasset, and the evolving Harratin community, and their general state of confusion and uncertainty, to which the onset of 'drought' conditions had contributed considerably, became manifested in their adoption of revivalist values, which seem to have been symbolized especially by the veil.

Revivalist movements are usually the expression of attempts by peoples to overcome threatening and previously unexperienced situations by the intensification of, or reversion to, known and well-tested practices. The revivalist values attached to the veil were associated with two other systems of thought. Firstly, it was a referent associated with and thus maintaining other referents in the traditional belief and value system, particularly the caravans, which throughout the memories of most living men had been not only the mainstay of the nomadic economy but, after the cessation of raiding and warfare, the expression of all that was 'Tuareg'. After independence, not only did these become critical to the subsistence of the camps, but, as we have already suggested in discussing the Otoul affair, they provided a means of escaping from the hostile and encapsulating Algerian system.

Secondly, although the veil has always been a symbol of 'Tuaregness' (Kel Tagelmoust) this symbolic expression of ethnic identity began to take on a new form and acquire a new meaning as a symbol of political values and expression vis-à-vis the Algerian authorities. In this new context, however, the veil became more than just a symbol; it became a political 'tool', especially among the Kel Ahaggar resident in or entering Tamanrasset. The frustrating concealment afforded by the veil provided them with the means of exploiting the Sub-Prefect's personal weaknesses and the administration's general lack of information and control over the region. I always remember how one Kel Rela told me laughingly how the Sub-Prefect was 'afraid of him'. His use of the word 'afraid' seems to have referred to the masking provided by the veil. The Sub-Prefect, seated behind his desk, was confronted by a 'nameless' and 'faceless' antagonist – an ordeal which he never seemed to manage with the aplomb expected of his position. Most of these Tuareg were Kel Rela who had used the opportunities afforded by the initial processes of economic development and modernization, during the French period, to maintain their traditional status and privileges, but who now saw their position being once again threatened.

The revivalist movement was transient, difficult to perceive, and, one may suggest, the response to a state of partial anomie resulting from their displacement in the socio-economic and political hierarchy, and a reflection of their uncertainty and confusion in being unable to perceive the consequences of this inevitable change.

One of the most significant changes that took place among the Kel Ahaggar after independence, and which at first glance may seem almost paradoxical in the light of the foregoing remarks, was the distinct change in their attitude towards manual labour.

Throughout most Saharan regions the withdrawal of French interests after independence caused a recession in employment. This was also true of Ahaggar, where most of the French concerns based in Tamanrasset pulled out. But as a condition of the Evian treaty the atomic base at In Eker remained operative and consequently became the main centre of employment throughout Ahaggar. In 1964, an average of 1,100 workers were employed in the base at any one time – a figure which in reality represented a total labour force of 2,000–3,000, as most workers were employed on a monthly shift basis. A minimum of 300,000 dinars (£15,000) was paid out monthly in wages, with most labourers earning about £20–£25 a month. I do not have details of employment figures prior to 1965, as the Algerian authorities kept no records before that year, but the Director of the Labour Exchange in Tamanrasset[33] estimated that Kel Ahaggar comprised 80 per cent of the In Eker work force. His estimate was certainly too high and probably refers to the percentage of the labour force that was not drawn from Tamanrasset, including not only the Kel

Ahaggar but the sedentarists from the villages of Tazrouk, Ideles, Hirafok and In Amguel. Tazrouk, in particular, was almost totally dependent on the wages brought back from In Eker.

The nomads' increased acceptance of wage-earning at In Eker after 1962 was brought about by two factors. Firstly, with the general decline in the nomadic economy, caused by the impoverishment of pasture and emaciation of the herds, the loss of garden revenues, the diminishing return on salt caravans, and the loss of Iklan,[34] manual labour was no longer regarded as undignified, entailing a loss of social status, but as a necessary means of survival. Indeed, the nomadic camps during this period were supported almost entirely by the caravans to Damergou and the wages from In Eker.

Secondly, In Eker was controlled by France and not Algeria, and the degree of acceptance, indeed affection, that was shown towards the base can, I think, be partly understood in terms of revivalist values. In Eker was something that the Kel Ahaggar knew and had experienced, even if only with limited enthusiasm, in the 'past'. In addition to now providing them with the means of survival, I believe that most Kel Ahaggar thought that the base afforded them a certain immunity and independence from the Algerian administration. It also provided them, like the annual caravans to Niger, not only with material security but also with the security of continuity with the past; for although not even ten years old, In Eker represented France and the more favourable years before independence. In a sense In Eker had suddenly been reclassified in the category of the 'traditional'!

If, by 1965, the future of the nomads looked bleak, the region as a whole, particularly in terms of its economic framework, had no cause for optimism. Apart from the impediments posed to the further economic development and modernization of the region by its internal cleavages, Ahaggar was handicapped by its geographical isolation, its lack of commercial stimulus, its traditional and inefficient methods of agricultural production, and its thin scattering of population. The pessimistic outlook was accentuated by the lack of potential for mineral exploitation, and the shortage of employment opportunities, which placed a ceiling on the size of the actively engaged labour force and the amount of money in circulation – factors which became critical, as we shall see presently, with the closure of the atomic base.

Ahaggar was characterized in 1965–6 by a state of economic depression in all sectors. Although the Harratin population was now represented politically and was self-sufficient in its subsistence production, its further development could be envisaged only through the development of new opportunities for employment and a complete reorganization of the agricultural system, including co-operative development of new land, the implementation of new methods, and the installation of credit and marketing facilities. But in the Algeria of Ben Bella such projects were little more than academic pipe-dreams, and observers such as Gast[35] and Blanguernon,[36] who were familiar with the region, considered the future economic stimulus to be in tourism – the dubious cure for impoverishment and underdevelopment!

# FOURTEEN
# THE PRECONDITIONS FOR SOCIALISM: AGRICULTURAL CO-OPERATIVES AND THE 'RUINATION' OF THE NOMADIC ECONOMY

The tanks that stationed themselves outside the Palais d'Été in Algiers in the early hours of 19 June 1965 heralded Boumedienne's successful coup, and with it the restatement of the aims of the Revolution, which under Ben Bella's regime had failed to identify and overcome many of the basic social and economic problems within the country. In the Sahara these problems had become particularly glaring. The region's integration within a national framework had been limited almost solely to the exploitation of its oil resources, with the result that the imbalance between the facilities and standards of living of the north and south had, if anything, become accentuated during the first three years of independence.

In November 1966, the Council of Ministers, under the presidency of Boumedienne, met in Ouargla to draft a 'special programme' for the long-awaited development of the Saharan regions. The emphasis of the plan was on agricultural reform. Land was to be reorganized on the basis of co-operative development schemes with financial credit assistance and technical advice being given by the government; a transport and marketing infrastructure was to be developed; and education and other social benefits and amenities were to be extended on a massive scale to the entire population – including the nomads, who were to be encouraged coercively to sedentarize and send their children to school. As a member of the École Nationale d'Administration (E.N.A.) put it when visiting Ahaggar, 'Le problème du Hoggar se dépasse le Hoggar.'[1] The region was no longer regarded quite so much as an isolated and burdensome appendage of the national state, but rather as part of Algeria, created by the Revolution and the sacrifices of Algerians, and whose problems were also those of Algeria.

The relatively successful implementation of the Ouargla Plan in Ahaggar between 1965 and 1969 owes much to the personal qualities of Aktouf, the Sub-Prefect who was installed in Tamanrasset in 1965. Unlike his predecessor, Aktouf was an extremely capable and fair administrator, and by the time of his departure in 1969 had become both feared and respected by the Kel Ahaggar, in spite of his 'hard-line' attitude towards them. Aktouf was determined to eradicate the traces of slavery and *métayage* labour that still existed in Ahaggar. As far as he was concerned, the Tuareg had played no part in the creation of Algeria; they had given nothing and had nothing to offer, and were politically unimportant. He offered them no compromise: they either accepted his policies or left Algeria!

The initial problems to be overcome by the new administration in Tamanrasset were those of the liberated Iklan squatting around Tamanrasset in their poverty-ridden shanties, together with the need to reorganize the archaic and traditionally orientated agricultural sector on a more viable economic and socio-political base.

Aktouf's administration saw the first step in overcoming these pressing problems in the development of small agricultural co-operative schemes in or close by the main cultivation centres. Their organization was based on the principles of 'auto-gestion'. Once the government had put forward a constitution for a co-operative scheme and encouraged interested persons to join, virgin land was taken over for development and registered in the name of the co-operative. The total amount of land involved was not great. The schemes were small-scale, and of the twenty co-operatives constituted between 1966 and 1969, only three contained more than twenty hectares (see Table 3). The larger co-operatives were divided into separate areas, or perimeters, each irrigated by a diesel pump, with the cost of the pump as well as the initial capital expenditure involved in establishing each perimeter being met by the government. The members of the co-operative then signed an agreement to the constitution; each member had a vote in the election of a management committee, which normally consisted of five men, one of whom was elected President. This committee was responsible for the internal management of the co-operative, seeing to such matters as the allocation of labour and work schedules, the marketing and sale of produce, and so forth, and the President himself was responsible for its financial accountancy and the recording of production details. The government, for its part, gave considerable assistance, ranging from extensive credit facilities to advice on such technical matters as systems of crop rotation, the introduction of new crops, etc., while the maintenance of the diesel pumps was provided by the agricultural department attached to the Sub-Prefecture,[2] although the cost of diesel fuel was met by the co-operative itself.

Although the number of cultivators involved in these schemes appears to be relatively small (see Table 3) – there are only 360 registered members – the total population either directly or indirectly dependent on co-operative production is probably in the order of 2,000, if we consider the wives, children and other dependants of members.[3] For the many cultivators who continued to work their own private gardens in preference to joining a co-operative, the government provided extensive credit facilities for the purchase and installation of motor-pumps.

The main achievement of these co-operatives, at least in the initial stage of their development, was in easing the problem of the liberated Iklan. At Otoul, for example, just twenty kilometres north of Tamanrasset on the main road, the development of a co-operative with fourteen registered members, all of whom were slaves of the Dag Rali, has led to the settlement of about sixty individuals.

However, the success of these schemes is questionable and cannot be assessed easily. They have been subjected to considerable criticism on purely economic grounds and the government itself has been the first to admit that their economic feasibility and efficiency leave much to be desired, but as far as the government was concerned the underlying conception of their development was as much political and social as purely economic.

Their development, economically, has certainly been impeded by serious difficulties, not least of which has been the inadequacy of the marketing and transport system in Ahaggar. Ahaggar has no external markets for agricultural produce, so that the ability of each co-operative to sell its produce depends largely on its access to the local market of Tamanrasset. In some cases the totally inadequate communications and transport system, and the vast distances involved, have precluded co-operative development. At Timiaouine, for example, which at 700 kilometres from Tamanrasset involves something of a trans-Saharan expedition in its own right, the co-operative has had to cease operation.

Aktouf himself was fully aware that this communications and transport problem was a serious impediment not only to the marketing of the co-operative produce but also to the effective administration and further economic development of the region as a whole, and consequently arranged for the installation of two-way radios in some of the larger villages such as Tazrouk, Ideles, and Abalessa in an attempt to alleviate the difficulty. But although radios facilitated the general administration of the region they did little to ease the problem of marketing, for without guaranteed transport facilities agricultural production lacked incentive and tended to

Table 3 Details of cooperatives.

| Name and Location | Area (Hectares) | Date of Agreement | No. of Adherents | No. of Perimeters | No. of Motors | Date of Constitution | Distance from Tamanrasset |
|---|---|---|---|---|---|---|---|
| Amsel | 30 | 22.3.67 | 28 | 3 | 3 | 1966 | 30 km |
| Hadrian (Adriane) | 10 | ,, | 10 | 1 | 1 | ,, | 4 |
| Abalessa | 50 | ,, | 80 | 4 | 4 | ,, | 100 |
| Issellisken (Asliskine) | 8 | 24.7.67 | 4 | 1 | 1 | 1967 | 60 |
| In Amguel | 12 | 23.3.67 | 53 | 2 | 2 | 1966 | 135 |
| Imechouene | 15 | ,, | 18 | 2 | 2 | ,, | 3 |
| In Azrou | 6 | ,, | 4 | 1 | 1 | ,, | 120 |
| Ideles No. 1 | 12 | 24.7.67 | 28 | 2 | 2 | ,, | 225 |
| Iglene | 8 | 22.3.67 | 33 | 1 | 1 | ,, | 96 |
| Otoul | 15 | ,, | 14 | 2 | 2 | ,, | 20 |
| Talat-n-Echiouke | 8 | 24.7.67 | 9 | 1 | 1 | 1967 | 16 |
| Tabharhait | 8 | 22.3.67 | 8 | 1 | 1 | 1966 | 6 |
| Tazrouk No. 1 | 8 | ,, | 15 | 1 | 1 | ,, | 300 |
| Tahifet | 6 | au cours | 12 | 1 | 1 | 1967 | 96 |
| Tazrouk No. 2 | 10 | ,, | 10 | 1 | 1 | ,, | 310 |
| Ideles No. 2 | 6 | ,, | 13 | 1 | 1 | ,, | 225 |
| Hirafok | 8 | ,, | ? | 1 | 1 | 1969 | 195 |
| In Guezzam | 20 | ,, | 9 | 1 | 1 | 1968 | 400 |
| Timiaouine | 10 | ,, | ? | 1 | * | ,, | 700 |
| Arak | 8 | ,, | 12 | 1 | *Foggara* | ,, | 400 |
| | 258 | | 360 | 29 | 27+1 *foggara* | | |

* Ceased operation due to excessive distance from Tamanrasset.

become orientated towards local subsistence needs. In fact, the Tazrouk co-operative, in its particularly isolated position 'at the end of the road', actually went so far as to buy its own truck, which makes the journey to Tamanrasset about once a fortnight, serving Ideles and Hirafok on route. But this is a precarious business and quite inadequate for the needs of the three centres.

Other villages, however, are even less fortunate and are usually obliged to wait for some passing truck whose driver is prepared to negotiate a deal over transport costs. The range of cash crops that can be grown is thus inevitably restricted, and it is not surprising that dried tomatoes, which can be easily stored after harvest to await transportation, are the main cash crop.[4]

In addition to the problems of marketing, production in most co-operatives is characterized by an under-utilization of capital resources, the predominance of traditional techniques and methods, and the consequent inefficiency of labour expenditure. At Ideles, for example, three pumps, serving three separate perimeters, operate for only three hours per day. There is abundant fertile land for the extension of irrigation agriculture, so that with the increased utilization of the pumps and a modification of traditional agricultural methods, productivity could be increased considerably without any further increase in labour expenditure. Increased productivity, however, is not merely a question of the application of basic economic principles. The extension of education, the inducement to change from traditional manual agricultural methods, on which no cost is placed on time or labour, and the establishment of local administrative cadres with more understanding of and interest in the detailed problems of the region itself are prerequisites not only for the increased efficiency and productivity of the co-operative, but for the further economic development of the region as a whole.

The local administration in Tamanrasset must shoulder much of the blame for the present shortcomings and problems in Ahaggar, for the interests of many of its members centre on their own material self-gain and the maintenance of their élitist positions rather than on the needs of the region. A typical example of this attitude was seen in 1968 when the administration in Tamanrasset despatched a truck and a land-rover to collect nomads from their camps and take them to the boarding-school at Ideles. The chief of the village at Ideles, a member of the Bureau Politique, and the Vice-President of the commune (Tamanrasset and Hoggar), made the journey and succeeded in collecting four children! These responsible personnel had had neither the time nor inclination to leave the *piste* and visit the nomadic camps. With such demonstrations of administrative competence and conscientiousness, it is hardly surprising that outlying villages lack the incentive and direction for increased efficiency and productivity.[5]

While the development of most agricultural co-operatives has been subject to such general 'regional' difficulties, each has had its own singular problems. Factors such as the village's proximity to Tamanrasset; its physical situation, in terms of drought susceptibility and the availability of land, etc.; its general economic disposition; its social structure, particularly in terms of its 'ethnic' composition and degree of solidarity and value consensus, and the nature of its ties with neighbouring villages and surrounding nomadic groups; the presence or absence of modernizing agencies, particularly schools; all these are critical to the acceptance and successful implementation of co-operative schemes. The significance of schools relates not only to the acceptance of schooling and level of education among the villagers, but especially to the quality and character of the teacher, whose influence in the village extends far beyond the schoolroom. A full discussion of each co-operative is beyond our immediate concern, but a brief description of a few of them will illustrate these points and show how the development of agricultural co-operatives has not been uniform or entirely without resistance in all cultivation centres.

The co-operatives of Hadrian and Amsel are the most successful in terms of both their economic and socio-political development. Amsel in particular, which is the government 'pilot' scheme, has received close government supervision. New cash crops (e.g. citrus) have been introduced; scientific crop rotation methods have stimulated yields, and the proximity of Tamanrasset provides an easily accessible and guaranteed market. The high degree of solidarity and co-operation amongst the villages has been reinforced by the economic success of the co-operative and the government's close attention. Most important visitors to Tamanrasset are taken on an official tour of Amsel, and the villagers are not only proud of their achievement but aware of their privileged position.[6] One of the most interesting features of this particular co-operative is the relationship that has developed between the villagers and the surrounding nomadic population (Tegehe-n-Efis and Aguh-en-tehle), which as we shall see later is manifest in a degree of economic co-operation and exchange of pastoral and agricultural products and resources.

Ideles and Tazrouk are both long-established centres some distance from Tamanrasset whose populations, like most other cultivation centres, have increased considerably during the last decade or so as a result of the influx of liberated Iklan and the sedentarization of surrounding nomads, particularly Isekkemaren. However, while Ideles is endowed with considerable fertile cultivable land, Tazrouk now suffers from severe overpopulation caused as much by an absolute increase in population, which has doubled in the last thirteen years, as by the reduction in the area of cultivable land as a result of heavy floods washing away much of the lower terrace. Thus, while the future of Ideles as a cultivation centre is assured, that of Tazrouk is largely dependent on how far agricultural production can be intensified.[7]

A particularly interesting feature of both these villages is that they are the only centres outside Tamanrasset in which there are permanently resident Frenchmen: namely, M. Barrère, the director of the school at Ideles, and Frère Abdullah (Louis Pilate), a member of Foucauld's order of the Little Brothers of Jesus, at Tazrouk. Their positions and spheres of influence in the two villages differ markedly. Louis Pilate, as a Frère, cannot become involved in or be responsible for anything that will affect change. But as the elected President of the co-operative he has found himself in something of a personal dilemma, for he is fully aware of the difficulties facing the village and has taken upon himself the task of impressing the seriousness of these problems on the villagers and, by exemplification, the possible means of overcoming them. Indeed, his example of hard work, enthusiasm and innovation of new agricultural methods has done much to maintain the co-operative's solvency.[8] But at the same time this direct participation involves him intimately in local village affairs, and his example has aroused a degree of jealousy and resentment among certain members of the community.

M. Barrère, on the other hand, in spite of the fact that he is married to a Tuareg, has no such vested interests in the economic organization of the village. His role as director of the school is quite unambiguous, and the villagers not only respect him but appreciate the school's scholastic achievements, which are unsurpassed in Ahaggar. In addition, his considerable knowledge and experience of Ahaggar and its peoples, and his relative detachment from the affairs of the village, enable him to be more forthright and impartial in offering any consultation, and aloof from the multiple intrigues and implications of village life.

Both men can only be admired for the dedication and benefits that they have given to the people among whom they have chosen to live, but while the role of one may be considered as potentially disruptive, that of the other contributes considerably to the relative harmony and solidarity of the community.

The most interesting co-operative in terms of the problems of its development is probably that of Hirafok, where there is no sign of any development apart from a pump lying idle in the middle of a few hectares of crudely fenced uncultivated land. The constitution for this village was drawn up in 1969, but its agreement was still awaiting ratification in 1971. The co-operative, or rather its absence, seems to be rarely discussed by the villagers. When I once asked a villager why the pump was not working, he replied without any hesitation, 'C'est les Arabs!' referring to the administration in Tamanrasset.[9] The fault, however, is not entirely the government's, as many of the villagers are inclined to believe, but the result of a combination of factors, all of which are found individually, to a greater or lesser degree, in other centres, but which together have militated against the successful development of an agricultural co-operative in Hirafok. It is hardly the administration's fault that the villagers could not decide upon which side of the *oued* the co-operative should be located – in the same way that the 'government' could hardly be held responsible for the collapse of the well! But the 'government' is merely a scapegoat for problems and difficulties experienced within the village itself.

Although it numbers few more than 300, the population of Hirafok, like that of most villages, is now fairly heterogeneous, consisting of ex-slaves, Harratin, a few sedentarized or semi-sedentarized nomads from surrounding Isekkemaren groups, and the Dag Rali, as well as a family of Kel Rela and a few Ineslemen. With some of the nomads, particularly the Dag Rali, ties between the nomadic and sedentary members of the *tawsit* are strong and impede the necessary transformation from family-kinship-based economic organization to co-operative organization. Even so, the nomadic presence in itself is hardly a significant factor. They comprise only a small percentage of the population, living together at the extreme eastern end of the village furthest away from the co-operative, and although prepared to cultivate their own gardens alongside their former slaves and *khames* they are not particularly interested one way or another in the development of the co-operative.

If, as many villagers believe, the administration in Tamanrasset is partly to blame for the unsatisfactory state of the Hirafok co-operative, many of the members of the administration feel that the villagers have shown undue arrogance in their demands and expectations of the government. This manifestation of ill-feeling and discontent by the villagers results primarily, I believe, from their inherent feeling of insecurity. Hirafok has always been susceptible to drought and the consequent temporary abandonment of gardens. With the development of In Eker the village experienced something of an economic boom. The base was close by and the regular monthly wages reduced their dependency on agriculture. The closure of the base in 1966 deprived the village of its main source of income, and many of the villagers, not understanding the reasons for the closure, felt that the Algerian government was in some way responsible. This was also true of other villages, but in the case of Hirafok their feelings of insecurity and resentment were aggravated by the village's geographical location midway along the *piste* between the main road through In Amguel and the centres of Ideles and Tazrouk. Nearly all traffic to Hirafok is consequently in transit, either on its way to or from Tazrouk and Ideles, or even Djanet and the Ajjer region. When a member of the administration does arrive he is usually in a hurry to get on to Ideles or Tazrouk or to return to Tamanrasset; while as far as the agricultural co-operative is concerned, the truck from Tazrouk is usually already overladen by the time it reaches Hirafok. It is not surprising that the villagers feel that the administration is not interested in their problems.

Not the least hindrance to the development of the Hirafok co-operative has been the unsatisfactory calibre of the schoolteacher. His professional irresponsibility and disgruntled attitude towards both the local administration and the village not only led to an especially low school attendance but also seems to have acted as a catalyst in provoking dissension among the villagers themselves. The Director of Education in Tamanrasset, who eventually dismissed him from service, considered that it was his negative and disruptive influence in the village that was largely responsible, not only for the lack of organization in the development of the co-operative but also for the general ill-feeling of many of the villagers towards the administration in Tamanrasset. With his dismissal, however, no adequate replacement teacher could be found and the school was necessarily closed for the academic year 1970–71 (and again in 1971–2). This, as far as the villagers were concerned, was proof that the administration in Tamanrasset was not interested in them![10]

However, the conclusion that most co-operatives are 'uneconomic' is largely irrelevant in the present context of development and modernization in Ahaggar. The cultivators themselves do not count the cost of their time and labour in monetary terms, while the under-utilization of capital resources and the predominance of archaic agricultural techniques gives some idea of their potential for increased efficiency and productivity. Whether this potential will be realized is a different matter, but in terms of the government's long-term modernization policies the co-operatives are viewed as the primary agents of change. The introduction and commercialization of cash-crops, albeit unimpressively, is leading to a differentiation in the social contexts of production and consumption. The economic unit is no longer primarily the family but the co-operative, in which production is regulated not so much by kinship ties and other familial commitments but by the legal constitution of the co-operative and the control and allocation of labour with regard to an external market.

The real achievement of these co-operatives, at least in these initial years, has been in the political rather than the economic context. The government's active role in their development has not only given affirmation of the Harratin's and ex-slaves' political representation, but has given them a feeling of 'ownership' and 'belonging' within the new state. In conjunction with increased opportunities for education, and political participation in the form of the Party, the co-operatives have become the main mechanism by which secular and nationalist values, or what Aktouf's successor referred to as the 'preconditions for socialism',[11] are taking root among the sedentary population in the outlying areas.

The finalization of the Ouargla Plan was of little immediate relevance to the nomadic population. For them, 1966 was a year of unmitigated disaster. In the autumn an embargo was placed on any further exportation of millet from Niger, and by December the French withdrawal from In Eker was complete. Within a matter of months the two main pillars of the nomadic economy had been destroyed.

The seriousness of the closure of In Eker is reflected in the employment statistics compiled by the Labour Exchange office in Tamanrasset. No records were kept for 1962, 1963, and 1964; those for 1965 and 1966 are complete; those for 1967 are 'lost';[12] while those for 1968 were compiled in an abridged form and are hence of little use for comparison with earlier years. From the details given in Table 4 it can be seen that 1,248 jobs were allocated in 1965, compared with 377 in 1966 and 311 in 1968 – a reduction of about 75 per cent, which can be attributed almost entirely to the closure of the base.

It was not the population of Tamanrasset, which made only a small contribution to the In Eker labour force, but rather the villages of Tazrouk, Ideles, Hirafok and In Amguel, and the surrounding nomadic population, that were most severely affected by the closure. But while the villages at least had their gardens and the proposed agricultural co-operatives, the nomadic Kel Ahaggar were left with their emaciated herds and precious few other means of acquiring a livelihood.

It seems that most nomads were generally unaware of the impending closure of In Eker, and even after 1966 many of them tended to hold a similar attitude as that towards 'drought' conditions – that good rains would come soon! When discussing In Eker with members of the Dag Rali in 1968, almost two years after its closure, I was quite surprised to find that several of them believed, perhaps more in hope, that In Eker would come back.[13] Not surprisingly, few nomads understood the reason for the French departure, which was bound up with the Evian treaty and subsequent negotiations between the French and Algerian governments, and many of them felt that they were the victims of just another act of reprisal by the Algerian government.

The reasons for the embargo on caravan trade have been shrouded in mystery. The Algerians themselves were never very explicit on the matter, and on several occasions made vague comments about the poor harvests in Niger. The real reason, however, seems to have centred around a commercial dispute between the Niger and Algerian governments, which was perhaps inflamed by hostilities between Kel Ahaggar and local Niger tribesmen in Tamesna. It certainly seems to have had little to do with the state of the millet harvests, which were still quite reasonable in 1966. But as far as most of the nomads were concerned the frontier restrictions were seen in the same context as In Eker – as further selective reprisal action by the Algerian authorities!

Although the frontier officially remained closed to caravan trade for three years, until 1969–70, a few caravans left Ahaggar in 1967 without any form of governmental permission and arrived in Damergou only to be turned back by the Niger authorities. Some of these caravans did succeed in obtaining a little millet, but in view of their clandestine nature I was never able to ascertain the exact number of men and camels involved. Several groups of Dag Rali made the journey with a modicum of success, but many of their stories were similar to that of an Ait Lowayen caravan of 150 camels, which was intercepted by the Niger authorities and turned back empty-handed. Similarly, about 200 Kel Ahaggar applied for permits in 1968 but without success, and although a few decided to chance their luck, very little millet was brought back to Ahaggar. Finally, in 1969, when commercial relations between the two countries had been normalized, caravans were allowed to journey south, but only after receiving a 'laissez-passer' from the Sub-Prefect in Tamanrasset, which was granted in accordance with the quota allocations imposed by the Niger government.

The caravan trade with Damergou constituted what Nicolaisen referred to as 'the great stabilizing factor in the economy of the pastoral Tuareg of

Table 4 Details of employment (registered by Labour Exchange, Tamanrasset).

| 1965 | J. | F. | M. | A. | M. | J. | J. | A. | S. | O. | N. | D. | Total |
|---|---|---|---|---|---|---|---|---|---|---|---|---|---|
| 1. | 40 | 208 | 63 | 87 | 132 | 96 | 23 | 72 | 85 | 84 | 71 | 85 | 1046 |
| 2. | 408 | 472 | 252 | 169 | 262 | 220 | 202 | 259 | 175 | 158 | 205 | 210 | 2992 |
| 3. | 3 | 12 | 11 | 10 | 17 | 8 | 7 | 8 | 14 | 31 | 23 | 4 | 148 |
| 4. | 0 | 0 | 2 | 0 | 0 | 0 | 0 | 0 | 2 | 0 | 1 | 0 | 5 |
| 5. | 2 | 75 | 34 | 186 | 84 | 42 | 40 | 20 | 24 | 164 | 118 | 48 | 837 |
| | 32 | 90 | 32 | 60 | 14 | 26 | 40 | 6 | 18 | 28 | 41 | 24 | 411 |
| | (34) | (165) | (66) | (246) | (98) | (68) | (80) | (26) | (42) | (192) | (159) | (72) | (1248) |
| 1966 | | | | | | | | | | | | | |
| 1. | 27 | 112 | 116 | 28 | 64 | 12 | 17 | 1 | 60 | 92 | 34 | 29 | 592 |
| 2. | 242 | 151 | 197 | 229 | 275 | 297 | 192 | 172 | 219 | 361 | 398 | 305 | 3038 |
| 3. | 2 | 7 | 5 | 2 | 12 | 0 | 2 | 1 | 0 | 4 | 13 | 18 | 66 |
| 4. | 0 | 0 | 0 | 0 | 0 | 0 | 0 | 0 | 0 | 0 | 0 | 0 | 0 |
| 5. | 23 | 38 | 30 | 12 | 8 | 0 | 0 | 0 | 0 | 8 | 24 | 42 | 185 |
| | 0 | 32 | 21 | 0 | 36 | 0 | 14 | 11 | 0 | 0 | 60 | 18 | 192 |
| | (23) | (70) | (51) | (12) | (44) | (0) | (14) | (11) | (0) | (8) | (84) | (60) | (377) |
| 1967 | | | | | | | | | | | | | |
| 1968 | | | | | | | | | | | | | |
| ** | 492 | 507 | 429 | 511 | 0? | 492 | 249 | 176 | 211 | 549 | 443 | 151 | 4210 |
| 4. | 0 | 0 | 0 | 1 | 0 | 0 | 0 | 0 | 0 | 1 | 0 | 0 | 2 |
| 5. | 19 | 2 | 24 | 17 | 0 | 0 | 93 | 44 | 0 | 109 | 2 | 1 | 311 |

** Number of requests for labour registered.

1. Number of requests for labour (on first registering for work the individual was given a green card).
2. Number of requests for labour 'non-satisfaits' (i.e. those already in possession of a green card who came back to the exchange only to find that employment opportunities were still not available).
3. Number of offers of work received by exchange (e.g. from SONAREM).
4. Number of offers of work received 'non-satisfaits' (presumably for specialized workers, e.g. metallurgists).
5. Number of work placements { permanent / temporary

Ahaggar'.[14] It was hardly affected by drought in Ahaggar and provided the Kel Ahaggar with the bulk of their food products, and its almost total cessation dealt a stunning blow to the nomadic community.

The closure of In Eker and the embargo on caravan trade were not the only disasters to strike the nomadic society during this period. The arrival of Aktouf as the new Sub-Prefect was soon regarded by the nomads as an equally threatening development.

The government's inability to enforce its authority in many of the more remote parts of the region during the first few years of independence meant that the cultivators in these areas had little or no effective means of resisting the demands and intimidations of the Kel Ahaggar. Thus, in spite of the 'freeing' of the land and the abolition of all forms of *métayage* labour, many of these gardens were still being worked on an *aril* basis. Aktouf was determined to put an end to these practices, but with the nomads' plight for food some sort of showdown was inevitable.

The nature of the confrontation and its final outcome can be seen in the protracted developments that took place in the Abalessa area, which was the focal point of the conflict. At Abalessa there were four *foggara* systems owned or part-owned by the Kel Ahaggar:—

1. owned by Bay, the Amenukal.
2. the Taramast *foggara*: owned on a fifty-fifty basis by the Cherif of Abalessa and the Dag Rali.
3. owned by the Dag Rali.
4. owned by the Kel Rela – ag Meslar family.

Prior to independence the Dag Rali thus held rights over 1½ *foggaras* at Abalessa. At independence the Taramast *foggara* was abandoned, but the other three continued to be worked on an *aril* basis until 1965. With Aktouf's determination to stop this form of exploitation, and his close surveillance over the cultivation centres,[15] the cultivation of the three *foggaras* was temporarily abandoned as the Kel Ahaggar and cultivators entered into what the cultivators referred to as 'negotiations'. The cultivators, with Aktouf's assured support, felt sufficiently self-confident to refuse further cultivation of the *foggara* gardens. As the conflict or 'negotiations' dragged on the *foggaras* remained inoperative, although the Kel Ahaggar, especially the Dag Rali, still descended on the centre at harvest time to claim their dues. In both 1966 and 1967 the cultivators, intimidated by their threats and demands, gave them a certain amount of produce and fed their 'guests' from their own gardens. When the Kel Ahaggar returned in 1968, the cultivators, reassured by Aktouf, refused to give them anything and threatened to send for Aktouf immediately if they persisted with their demands. By this time the Kel Ahaggar had had sufficient experience of the determined ways of Aktouf's administration. Unlike his predecessor he was not to be trifled with, and the threat was enough to deter them from prolonging or renewing their presence in Abalessa.

In 1967–8 the administration agreed that Bay could retain the ownership of his *foggara*, providing the cultivators were paid in money, but although the Harratin agreed to this in principle their resentment of the Tuareg was such that no cultivator was prepared to work for him, even with monetary payment. In 1968–9 the Harratin finally took over the Taramast and ag Meslar *foggaras*, and the Dag Rali *foggara* the following year.

At the small cultivation centre of Tiffert, not far from Abalessa, the Dag Rali owned two more *foggara* systems which continued to be cultivated on an *aril* basis until 1968, when they too were both taken over by the Harratin.

In 1962, prior to independence, the Dag Rali thus held rights of ownership over twelve gardens irrigated by their *foggara* at Abalessa, half of the eighteen gardens irrigated by the Taramast *foggara*, and seven gardens attached to each of the two *foggaras* at Tiffert, giving them a total of thirty-five gardens. Between 1962 and 1965 they retained their rights over all these gardens except those of the Taramast *foggara*, thus giving them a total of twenty-six gardens; but during the period 1965–8 they retained rights over only the fourteen gardens at Tiffert.

The loss of food products to the Dag Rali through the final takeover of their *foggara* gardens cannot be measured easily since the area of a garden under cultivation and the crop yield vary according to the availability of water, the possible disease of crops and the expenditure of labour. The size of a garden may vary between 0·30 and 0·60 hectares, while the wheat yield of a 0·60 hectare garden in optimum conditions may attain a maximum of 1·2 tonnes.

On the basis of these optimum conditions the income of wheat would have declined from 21 tonnes in 1962, to 15·6 tonnes between 1962 and 1965, and 8·4 tonnes between 1965 and 1968, but as optimum conditions never prevailed at any time during this period, a more realistic estimate would probably reduce these figures by about half.[16] Furthermore, the hostility between the Kel Ahaggar and Harratin was manifested in an extremely low labour input on the part of the Harratin, and in this respect it is particularly interesting to note that the Dag Rali *foggara* at Abalessa now irrigates eighteen rather than twelve gardens, which is an indication of the Harratin's enterprise and self-confidence. It is also interesting to note that the hostility of the villagers towards the Kel Ahaggar was reflected in their designation of the Kel Rela as 'Tuareg' and the Dag Rali, who were their main intimidators, merely as 'Dag Rali' as distinct from other Kel Ahaggar.

Abalessa, which was once an integral part of Dag Rali territory and one of their main cultivation centres, is now 'alien' territory to them, and few will venture there willingly for fear of ridicule and resentment.

The total loss of income to the nomadic population resulting from the closure of In Eker, the cessation of caravan trade and the takeover of their gardens cannot be assessed easily in purely quantitative terms. Nevertheless, if we assume that the nomads comprised half the In Eker labour force, we can estimate that the closure of the base resulted in a loss of about 1,800,000 D. (£150,000)[17] per annum in wages. Similarly, the loss of millet can be estimated conservatively at about 150 tonnes per annum, which is sufficient grain, allowing 400 grammes per person per day, to maintain about 1,000 adults for a year.[18] The loss of revenue from the Harratin-cultivated gardens is even more difficult to assess, not only because it was spread over a number of years, but also because annual production varies enormously. However, we can estimate, on the basis of recorded production figures in earlier years,[19] that the overall loss of garden produce (wheat) to the Kel Ahaggar, following the abolition of the *métayage* system between 1962 and 1968, was between 50 and 100 tonnes per annum.

The crucial question facing us is whether these impediments and deprivations affected the Kel Ahaggar uniformly. What alternative courses of action were open to them, and how were they perceived?

It was the Kel Ulli, particularly the richer *tawsatin* such as the Dag Rali, and perhaps to a slightly lesser extent the Aguh-en-tehle, whose more extensive pastoral resources had enabled them to maintain themselves longer in the nomadic environment, that suffered most heavily from these precipitate disasters.

For reasons that we have already mentioned, the Kel Rela and several of the poorer Isekkemaren had been sedentarizing progressively since the mid-1950s. By 1966 most Kel Rela were settled either in or around Tamanrasset or the Amenukal's camp. With their increasing 'urban' interests they were scarcely affected either by pastoral impoverishment or the cessation in caravan trade, which in any case had always been conducted almost exclusively by the Kel Ulli, particularly the Dag Rali and

Aguh-en-tehle.[20] Furthermore, it might even be argued that the closure of In Eker was advantageous to the Kel Rela, for the experience they acquired there in their white-collar positions qualified them to fill similar positions in the general administration at Tamanrasset. Several of the younger Kel Rela who had received some schooling or equivalent training at In Eker took secretarial positions in the Sub-Prefecture, Mairie, and other branches of the local administration, while a small handful who had received some specific training took even more skilled positions: one, for example, became a fully trained radio operator, while another, who had assisted in the infirmary at In Eker, became a highly paid medical orderly with SONAREM[21] after it established bases at Tamanrasset and In Eker in 1969. A few of these younger Kel Rela even entered the army!

The Ouargla Plan was not orientated specifically towards the interests and benefits of the 'deprived' Harratin and ex-slaves, but rather towards the region as a whole. Indeed, as far as the government was concerned the Kel Ahaggar were encouraged as much as the Harratin and ex-slaves to join co-operatives, develop their own gardens, send their children to school, and so on. Many of the Kel Rela living in Tamanrasset availed themselves of these new opportunities, especially the agricultural credit facilities which enabled them to buy their own motor-pumps and develop their own gardens. One such Kel Rela, with whom I spent much time, had developed his own garden about a mile up the Oued Tamanrasset. At midday he could often be found there, resting alone in the shade of a crude shelter he had built himself. It was an incongruous sight: a man who had grown up in the nomadic camps to despise such menial work, and whose father and other senior kinsmen had been great warriors, now content in his small garden plot. He derived a certain aesthetic pleasure from his garden. It was, he said, an ideal place for solitude, away from the noise and commotion of the town.[22]

The Kel Rela's fairly rapid acceptance and utilization of these new opportunities, and their identification with the modernizing 'urban' community of Tamanrasset during this period, owe much to the role of the Amenukal. In spite of his somewhat ambiguous political position and questionable authority over the Kel Ahaggar, he had remained in relatively close contact with the Algerian administration and was well aware of government policy and the inevitable direction of change. Not only had he discouraged the Kel Ahaggar from any form of militant resistance but he had himself tried to set an example by encouraging them to send their children to school, and by patronizing the development of one of the first agricultural co-operatives – that of Issellisken, which is close to his camp, is worked by four Kel Rela, and largely provides for the camp. In spite of many denials, both by members of the administration and several Kel Rela, it appears that the relative immunity of the Kel Rela to the disasters afflicting the nomadic economy derived from the Amenukal's 'low-key' conciliatory policy towards the Algerians. His response to many of their policies, such as the freeing of slaves, land, and so forth, was that although he himself was not totally opposed to them it was particularly difficult for him to comply in view of the many expectations and responsibilities incumbent on him as the 'supreme chief'! The essence of his bargaining position was that as Amenukal he was traditionally and morally responsible for the care and provision of most of his 'family' (the Kel Rela), as well as of many slaves and other dependants! – and unless compensation was provided in one form or another these moral obligations and responsibilities could not be met!

The nomadic population, on the other hand, was faced with the stark reality of suddenly losing most of its traditional means of income. From our more objective standpoint we can see, in the broadest terms, four main alternative courses of action open to them: they could settle in the villages, or Tamanrasset itself, and develop their own gardens; they could seek manual labour in Tamanrasset; they could emigrate altogether from Ahaggar and settle perhaps in Tamesna; or they could more or less sit tight and hope for an improvement in pasture and the reopening of caravan trade, and in the meantime eke out a living from the meagre resources still available to them.

Of these various alternatives, the idea of emigrating to Tamesna seems to have been given little or no serious consideration. It was certainly the most impractical course of action both in view of the risk involved to the already emaciated goats and the uncertainty surrounding the question of frontier controls and restrictions. In any case, it is difficult to conceive of the Kel Ahaggar, especially the Dag Rali, leaving their traditional territory so readily.

Similarly, the idea of seeking work in Tamanrasset was effectively eliminated by the general economic recession and consequent dearth of employment opportunities. The more fortunate found occasional work on labour gangs repairing the *pistes*, and other general maintenance, but such opportunities were scarce.

Among the Dag Rali and Aguh-en-tehle, who were probably most severely affected by these changes, and with whom I was more familiar, there was a general underlying belief that these disasters were of a temporary nature. There was a constant hope that good rains would soon come and that the blockage on caravan trade would be lifted before the next year. This belief was certainly bolstered by the rumours, that were not entirely without foundation, that the Russians or an Algerian organization would soon take over the empty base at In Eker.[23] However, even within this relatively optimistic framework, the only real alternative for the nomadic population, as the means of subsistence in the camps became more precarious than ever, was to develop their own gardens in the cultivation centres.

Throughout the previous decade there had been a gradual trickle of nomads into the village centres – many of the Kel Rela, the poorer Isekkemaren, and here and there a few Kel Ulli, such as the Ait Lowayen in the Azrou district, a few Aguh-en-tehle in Tahifet and Tarhaouhaout, one or two families of Dag Rali at Hirafok and in the Oued Ifrak about ten miles south-east of In Amguel, and others. From about the mid-1960s onwards there has been a marked acceleration in this process, as nomads, unable to maintain themselves in their camps, have developed and cultivated their own gardens.

This process, however, has not been a matter of merely packing up a tent, moving into a village, setting up house and cultivating virgin land. On the contrary, the process of sedentarization has been more gradual and diffuse. Many of the nomads who were in cultivation centres tended to see their situation as a transient one; they were awaiting the regeneration of pasture, when they could temporarily abandon the gardens and move back to the mountain camps. But with the continued impoverishment of pasture their footholds in the cultivation centres have become more permanent. Nevertheless, it is difficult to 'count' the nomadic population of a village, as each family tends to be an appendage of that amorphous entity, the *tawsit* section, scattered in its camps somewhere in the surrounding mountains.

In a sense these nomads are not structurally part of the village. They may live there on a more or less permanent basis and participate extensively in village life, but they remain territorially compact, comprising what might almost be called a 'quarter', with their main ties extending not into the village but outwards to the nomadic camps. As we have already seen in the case of Sidi Mohammed's camp, the residency of kinsmen in Hirafok provides the means of exchange between the agricultural and pastoral sectors. With harvest time, changes in pastoral conditions, various social occasions, and so forth, the nomadic population in a village may be more than doubled or reduced to almost nothing. The establishment of a dwelling in a village provides not so much for the sedentarization of a family but for access to the agricultural products, and leads therefore to a coming and going of personnel between the village and the camps.

Although it is not possible to determine a quantitative relationship, the rate of sedentarization of nomads, as we would expect, seems to correlate quite closely to the economic situation of their camps, or, more specifically, to the difficulty of sustaining themselves through any other means than developing their own gardens. Within this fairly general pattern, however, there were certain significant exceptions, notably the Dag Rali, whose general response, compared to the neighbouring Aguh-en-tehle, was not quite what we might have expected.

Comparisons between the economic situations of any two *tawsatin* must inevitably be largely qualitative and relative. The Dag Rali have always been the wealthiest *tawsit* in Ahaggar in terms of their goats, and with the Kel Rela possessed the greatest number of slaves. Nevertheless, by the 1960s slaves were no longer relevant to their economy, and with the general state of pastoral impoverishment there was probably little difference in the number of livestock held by the Dag Rali and Aguh-en-tehle. Both *tawsatin* lived in similar territories, the mountains of Atakor and surrounding foothills, and experienced similar ecological conditions. Their territories were virtually equidistant from Tamanrasset, and between them they held, or had held, rights over most of the more important cultivation centres. Furthermore, the Dag Rali and Aguh-en-tehle have always been the main caravan traders to Damergou and were both equally affected by the blockage of this trade.

While there were many broad similarities in their economic situations there were also significant differences. More Dag Rali than Aguh-en-tehle had been employed at In Eker, and they consequently suffered a relatively greater loss. On the other hand, the presence of the Frères of Foucauld's order of the Little Brothers of Jesus at Assekrem, in the heart of Dag Rali territory, provided them with certain benefits and opportunities, although by no means sufficient to compensate for the loss of wages from In Eker.

Although both these two *tawsatin*, like most other nomads, lived in the hope that the following year would bring an amelioration in pastoral conditions, the removal of caravan restrictions and the reopening of In Eker, there was a noticeable difference in their general responses to this situation; the Dag Rali showed a greater traditionalist orientation in their determination to maintain their nomadic existence, which was manifested not only in their adverse attitude towards sedentarization and the cultivation of their own gardens, but in their general fear and resentment of the administration and Tamanrasset. Thus, while sedentarization among the

Aguh-en-tehle was seen within the broader framework of their developing economic ties with the Kel Ahaggar resident in Tamanrasset, and the developing agricultural centres such as Amsel, the Dag Rali remained more introvert and insular in their attitude to and relationship with Tamanrasset and the sedentary community in general.

A few Kel Hirafok began to cultivate gardens in Hirafok, while the Oued Ifrak has now become a bustling little community, as several Dag Rali have begun to cultivate gardens along the *oued* margin. Most of the Dag Rali at Ifrak, however, were Kel Tinhart, and their greater predisposition towards cultivation was probably due to the presence and influence of the Kel Rezzi. The Kel Terhenanet and Kel Tamanrasset tended to focus more on the little villages of Terhenanet and Tagmart respectively, but these two villages were distinctly 'Dag Rali' and structurally more akin to section camps, in which tents had given way to huts and a few mud-brick houses. One should also add that the almost negligible amount of cultivation at Tagmart and Terhenanet was undertaken mostly by a few ex-slaves who had chosen to remain with their former masters.[24] The more outward-looking attitude of the Aguh-en-tehle towards sedentarization was certainly not mirrored by the Dag Rali.

The means by which the nomads, particularly the Dag Rali, were able to maintain themselves after 1966 says much for their resilience and ingenuity.

Subsistence among the Dag Rali during this period became dependent on a precarious and often incidental assortment of incomes. The goat herds remained skeletal, although fairly heavy rains in the summer of 1965 had temporarily broken the drought and given hope of an overall improvement in pasture. This, however, was not to be, and although some breeding took place the herds continued to contribute only minimally to their subsistence. In spite of the restrictions on caravans a small but insufficient quantity of millet was brought back by clandestine caravans. Some Harratin-cultivated gardens, such as those at Tiffert, continued to provide them with a small quantity of garden produce until 1968, while their own gardens (e.g. Hirafok and Ifrak) became of increasingly greater relative value.

Nomads were no longer reluctant to seek work, but with the general economic recession in Ahaggar employment opportunities were few and far between. It is ironic that after despising manual work until only a few years previously, the nomads felt that the government now had an obligation to provide them with employment – 'on demand'! Fortunately for the Dag Rali, the administration undertook extensive maintenance and reconstruction work on the 'inner circuit' *piste* in 1966. The Assekrem–

Ilaman section of the road was in particularly poor condition, and about twenty Dag Rali men found employment almost a stone's throw from their camps.

The nomads also received a certain amount of American Aid grain during this period, although I have no record of the extent or basis of its distribution beyond the fact that it was extremely haphazard. In February 1970, however, I was fortunate enough to be in Tamanrasset when the administration was distributing 'aid' grain, on the basis of one quantel (100 kilos) to each family registered at the Mairie. After numerous visits to all the relevant offices in the Mairie to enquire about the basis of grain distribution I was presented with a 'finalized' list accounting for the distribution. The figures made extraordinarily interesting reading. According to the register of families accompanying the list, which I hasten to add was most unreliable, the average size of families among the Kel Rela, Kel Arefsa section of the Aguh-en-tehle and Iklan-Tawsit was 6·9. The Dag Rali, who number about 400, should then have received about sixty quantels. Instead they were given 105 quantels of grain! The Dag Rali, perhaps in their wisdom, were not able to enlighten me over this large discrepancy, and I can only assume that their definition of what constituted a 'family' was flexible enough to enable them to claim about twice as much grain as they were entitled to.

As subsistence among the Dag Rali became increasingly precarious, the presence of the Frères at Assekrem and the purchasing power of the tourists took on a new dimension. Through the influence of the Frères, who encouraged the Dag Rali to manufacture their 'traditional' artefacts, such as sandals and other skin goods, and market them to the tourists visiting Assekrem, the crude barter and begging to which tourists had formerly been subjected became channelled into a well-organized 'cottage industry'. The Frères sold the various artefacts directly to the tourist without taking any commission, so that no 'middleman' or excursions to Tamanrasset were involved. Tourism, through the agency of Assekrem, thus provided the camps with a meagre but vital monetary income.

This rather dismal account of Dag Rali subsistence in 1968 was, as it perhaps sounds, the last gasp of traditional society. If that sounds overly dramatic it is because 1968 marked the turning point, or rather what we might think of as the end of the Dag Rali's resistance to modernization, at least in as much as their resentment of the administration and avoidance of Tamanrasset underwent an almost total *volte-face* within a matter of a year or two. There was certainly a realization that a purely nomadic subsistence as I have described it above was no longer possible. Restrictions on caravans and the impoverishment of the herds continued; Harratin had finally taken over their gardens; and such tenuous 'perks' as free grain, tourists and occasional *piste* reconstruction did little more than provide for a hand-to-mouth existence. And yet, if this realization was the overriding pressure on the Dag Rali, it does not account for the amazing speed of their transformation, nor the fact that we can almost date this transformation to the day, in the autumn of 1968, when army trucks arrived in the Dag Rali centres to 'take their children away to school'.

# FIFTEEN
# THE 'ALGERIANIZATION' OF THE KEL AHAGGAR

Since Boumedienne's coup the emphasis placed on education as the fundamental means of realizing the 'Algerian Revolution' has led to a progressive increase in the allocation of the national budget on education, from one-sixth in 1965 to over one-quarter in 1969.[1]

This massive extension of education has not been a willy-nilly process of 'education for education's sake', but rather a rigidly planned development, or, to use the national jargon, a conscious policy orientated towards 'democratization' and 'Algerianization'. As the government itself stated, 'education is the key to the harmonious cultural and political development of Algeria'.[2] These two concepts, 'democratization' and 'Algerianization', embody the aims and ideology of the Revolution, namely that all children should be given the full opportunity for education and the development of their vocational talents, in conjunction with the concomitant development of the 'consciousness of the entity of Algeria as a unified, independent, cultural and modernizing state'![3]

At the pedagogical level, 'Algerianization' has necessitated a complete reorientation of the curriculum to meet the new needs of the country. A knowledge of the climate and natural vegetation of Normandy was totally irrelevant to the urgent need of filling the vacuum created in the intellectual and technical cadres by the French departure! At the primary level, the curriculum for the entire country was reorientated specifically towards overcoming the low level of literacy, and consolidating Arabic as the national language. At the secondary level, history, civil and moral education were taught in Arabic, although science subjects were necessarily taught in French; while at the higher level of education the emphasis was on technical and economic training (see Appendix III).

The development of such an educational system in the rural and underdeveloped regions was perceived as the basic means of reducing the disparity between 'rural' and 'urban', and 'developed' and 'underdeveloped'. But in many of these regions its instigation was impeded by numerous problems, particularly the general shortage of adequately trained teachers, which in some of the more undesirable parts of the country has temporarily precluded the extension of these facilities. In some areas, where the population is either nomadic or scattered over a wide area, the government has had to contend with the various administrative and social problems arising from the establishment of boarding-schools. In addition, these difficulties have been compounded in certain regions by various degrees and forms of resistance associated with the particular nature of the Arab–Berber cleavage.

Not surprisingly, it has been in the Saharan regions, especially Ahaggar, where these problems became critical, and where their resolution has been more a matter of good luck than good judgement on the part of the central authorities. To whatever extent the Ministry of Education now regards the extension of education in Ahaggar as having been successful, it must be thankful for the persistence of drought conditions and the presence in Tamanrasset of a French expatriate of rare professional ability and courage.

In 1962, at the time of the French departure, there were five primary schools in Ahaggar.[4] By 1965 this number had increased by only three (see Appendix IV). Admittedly there had been a threefold increase in school attendance during this period,[5] but it was essentially sectarian, being restricted almost exclusively to the sedentary population of Tamanrasset and the other larger villages. The nomads, with a few exceptions, gladly remained 'uneducated'. But, with the finalization of the Ouargla Plan, primary education was to be extended to all the remaining village centres as well as to the nomadic population.[6] Between 1965–6 and 1967 a further seven primary schools were built, and secondary education was introduced in Tamanrasset with the opening of the Collège de l'Éducation Agricole (C.E.A.) and a Collège de l'Éducation Générale (C.E.G.) in 1967 (see Appendix IV, and Fig. 7).

However, the difficulties of extending primary schooling to the nomadic population were of a quite different order and far more complex than those of merely having to build and staff schools in the more remote and 'unattractive' villages. Although most of the Kel Ahaggar living in Tamanrasset were sending their children to school in the town, the village schools were not easily accessible to the vast majority of the nomadic population. For the French, this problem had been met by establishing 'écoles nomades'. But the Algerians, for their part, regarded these schools

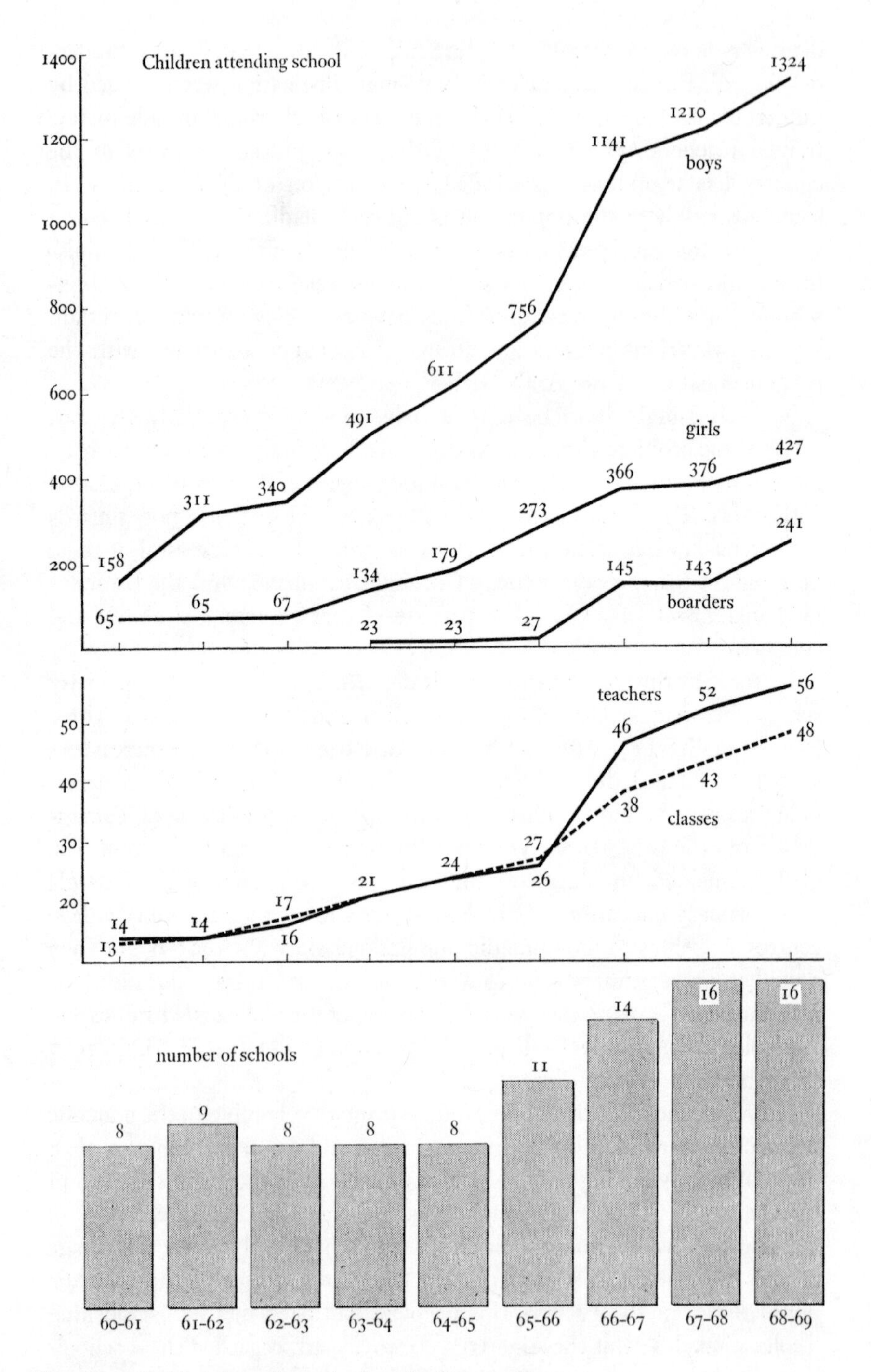


Figure 7 Children attending school, 1960–61 to 1968–9.

as both economically and educationally unfeasible. Above all, they considered that the nomadic population precluded the 'harmonious cultural and political development of the country'. Their education was therefore seen primarily in the context of Algerianization, but not in the form of 'écoles nomades', which had been abolished immediately after independence, for such institutions, by affording the nomads a *raison d'être*, merely retarded their assimilation. Instead, children were to be removed from the nomadic milieu at an early age and brought into boarding-houses adjoining the village schools.

It is consequently not surprising that education was not welcomed by the nomads with open arms. Resentment and fear of the government, particularly the fear that the government was trying to take their children away and draft them into the army, and the fact that children filled an essential role in the economic organization of the camps, lay at the heart of their adverse feelings towards schooling.

The boarding-school system was not orientated specifically towards Ahaggar or the nomadic populations, but had been decided upon at the national level as the only feasible means of extending schooling among the many sparsely scattered rural populations in various parts of the country. Nor for that matter was it even a novel idea in Ahaggar, for in 1963 a group of religious and merchant families in Tamanrasset had opened a private boarding annexe to the 'Koranic' Ibn Khaldoun school to house a small number (twenty-three) of selected fee-paying children drawn from the richer, predominantly Moulay, families in the outlying village centres.[7]

The commitment to the extension of primary education to the nomadic population was made in 1965–6 with the construction of boarding annexes in the villages of Abalessa, Ideles, Amsel, Tahifet, Iglene and Tazrouk.[8] Prior to this time scarcely any nomadic children had attended school, apart from a handful of those who had settled in the larger villages and who therefore could no longer be regarded as nomadic.

The task of overcoming the nomads' general resistance and hostility to schooling, especially the idea of boarding-schools, fell upon the shoulders of Aktouf. His method was direct. If parents were unwilling to send their children to school then they would have to be collected. And so, at the start of the school year in the autumn of 1966 he ordered the despatch of military vehicles from Tamanrasset to collect children from the nomadic camps. The whole operation seems to have been a most haphazard affair and, not surprisingly, the sight of military vehicles coming 'to take their children away' brought back memories of the liberation of the Iklan and merely intensified the nomads' general fear and resentment of the government.

Aktouf's drive resulted in 145 children being collected.[9] But although classified as 'nomads' the majority of these children were not Kel Ahaggar, but either ex-slave and Harratin children from isolated cultivation settlements or the smaller villages where there were no schools, or children from village schools that did not extend beyond the third or fourth grade.[10]

In the following year, 1967–8, the same number of boarders was registered (143), with little or no change in their composition. In spite of Aktouf's determination to impose education on the nomads, the disorganization and general lack of conscience displayed by the local authorities in their collection of children meant that most of the camps further away from the *pistes* were not touched, with the result that the number of nomadic children actually brought into school was relatively small. Furthermore, the general policy of recruiting children at a young age, between six and nine years old, made it fairly easy for the nomads to escape this loosely flung net. Without any detailed registration of births the administrative personnel involved in the collection of children found themselves confronted by a remarkable number of five and ten year olds!

Aktouf himself was fully aware of the small proportion of nomadic children and the difficulties being experienced in their collection, and at the start of the school year in 1968 ordered a more concerted drive through the camps. This time the more accessible camps were scoured with parents being coercively 'encouraged' to send their children to school regardless of age. It was a field-day for Aktouf, with 241 children, including fourteen Dag Rali, being brought into the boarding-houses.

In many ways the arrival in Tamanrasset of fourteen scraggy little Dag Rali boys in the autumn of 1968 was the crucial watershed in Tuareg–Algerian relations. It was, as we have already said, the turning-point in the Dag Rali's resistance to modernization, Algeria and Tamanrasset. But to understand the related consequences of this otherwise seemingly insignificant event we must return to the Dag Rali camps from which these children had come. What were the choices and decisions involved in loading the children into the army trucks, and why, from among all the Dag Rali children, was it just these particular fourteen that were 'taken away' to Tamanrasset?

Following only a few months after the Harratin takeover of their *foggaras* in the Abalessa area, few Dag Rali were now prepared to regard Aktouf's authority lightly, and the coercive presence of administrative personnel in army trucks effectively denied them a choice in whether or not to send their children to school. Nevertheless, if the outcome of the game was predetermined there was still a considerable latitude of choice in the way its intervening stages could be played, and the selection process whereby these fourteen particular children were 'given to the government' highlights the critical pressures being generated within the camps themselves.

By the autumn of 1968 the subsistence base of these Dag Rali camps had become critical. Although there had been rains in the summer[11] the herds were still skeletal; the embargo on caravan trade to Niger had not been lifted; Harratin had taken over their *foggara* gardens; and the opportunities for wage-earning were scant. In addition, the precariousness of the subsistence base was aggravated further by the relative 'overpopulation' of the camps. With few men going away on caravans or leaving the camp to take up employment at In Eker or elsewhere, there was not only a surplus of labour in the camp but a greater number of mouths to be fed during the hard winter months than under normal conditions. Related to this situation was the fact that the traditional activities and education of boys centred around the many aspects of camel husbandry, but with the almost total cessation of the caravan trade and the prevalence of drought conditions, those camps containing several boys were having to maintain an additional, and essentially unproductive, labour force.

The response of the Dag Rali, and most other nomadic groups, to this coercion thus involved two related dimensions. Firstly, boarding-school attendance would at least provide some relief to the camps in that the children concerned would be fed and clothed at government expense. Indeed, the only positive attitude expressed towards schooling at this time was that there would be one less mouth to feed in the camp! Secondly, the actual selection of children seems to have been undertaken primarily on the basis of the expendability of this essentially unproductive labour force in the camps. The selection of boys for school was thus a rational process directed towards the increased economic efficiency of the camp. As we shall see presently, the Dag Rali regarded the 'giving' of children to the government in the same context as paying 'tax'. Within the overall bounds of these criteria for selection, we see that the 'payment', although it came mainly from the two Dag Rali centres of Tagmart and Terhenanet,[12] was spread fairly evenly across the camps; all the boys came from separate camps in which there were at least three boys between the ages of six and twelve, and their individual selection was based on their qualities as herdsmen. The one deemed least knowledgeable and competent in camel husbandry was selected to meet the demands of Aktouf's representatives and taken to the boarding-house in Tamanrasset.

What would have happened if Aktouf had been left to pursue his policy of coercion in Ahaggar is a matter of speculation. Fortunately for the Kel Ahaggar, and Algeria, Aktouf's drive through the camps coincided with the appointment of a new local Director of Education in Tamanrasset – M. Laporte – a man of the highest integrity, intellectual ability, and with many years of intimate experience of education in Algeria. Although he had retained his French citizenship, his 'good work', as he called it, had been achieved in Algeria as a village school teacher in the war-torn mountains of Kabylia, and after independence as an educationalist attached to the Ministry at Algiers. For health reasons he had requested a transfer away from the coast and was duly posted to the Saharan regions, where his previous knowledge and experience of the Chaamba nomads made him particularly well qualified to tackle the far more delicate problems of Ahaggar.

Although Laporte and Aktouf shared the same ultimate goals their perceptions of the nomadic situation and their methods were quite opposed. While Laporte's experience among the Chaamba led him to believe that nomads would only accept what was 'voluntary', Aktouf favoured coercion. Similarly, whereas Aktouf was impressed by high school attendance figures, Laporte realized that the nomadic population's acceptance of the values of a modernizing state could be achieved more readily by example than coercion; for the spectacle of a large number of children being poorly educated, and consequently unable to achieve the necessary qualifications for role fulfilment, would probably bring disillusionment and reinforce the nomads' resistance to modernization. Thus, in spite of the government's desire for impressive statistics, Laporte remained committed to the creation of an educated élite among the nomads, which would, by its example, attract the more recalcitrant elements of the population.

The sight of military vehicles collecting children at the start of the school year horrified Laporte and he immediately stated that all future collections were to be the responsibility of the commune (Mairie) with the use of civilian vehicles. Nevertheless, the damage was done. In rounding up 241 children of all ages and from all quarters of Ahaggar Aktouf had succeeded in increasing 'school attendance', but at the expense of strengthening the general nomadic resistance towards schooling and the administration in Tamanrasset.

The relative success of the boarding-school system in terms both of the assimilation or 'Algerianization' of the nomads and of scholastic results can be attributed largely to Laporte's ability in subverting the stringent policy guides laid down in Algiers, and implementing, with uncompromising integrity and courage, his own personal values and beliefs. His main objective during this formative period was to ease the cultural assimilation of these young nomadic children into a modern and quite alien environment, at the same time establishing the trust and confidence of their parents. In this latter respect it was imperative to overcome the fears and prejudices of the parents about having their children 'taken away'.

At the age of six, and having lived completely within the network of familial relationships in the tranquillity and 'freedom' of the camps, the regimented and prison-like atmosphere of the boarding-house, the lack of familial and other kin ties, and the total absence of females, in conjunction with the unfamiliar and 'shocking' cultural environment, threatened to pose serious social and psychological difficulties and dangers to a child's development. However, during the first year of Laporte's office (1968–9) these problems were alleviated by the use of the boarding-annexes in the larger villages, notably Ideles and Abalessa. These transit boarding-houses, as they were known, had been designed to provide a transitional phase between the nomadic camps and the twentieth century of Tamanrasset, so that the youngest children, between the ages of about six and nine, would spend their first three years of school in a cultural environment that was not wholly dissimilar to that of the camps, before being transferred to the central boarding-house in Tamanrasset. However, transit boarding-houses only eased Laporte's problem, for of the 241 children rounded up by Aktouf, Abalessa and Ideles could accommodate only forty-eight and forty-two respectively, so that the remaining 151 were sent to Tamanrasset.

The creation of a more familial and less regimented atmosphere in the Tamanrasset boarding-house was facilitated, perhaps ironically, by the one problem that educational policy in Algeria was designed to overcome, namely the shortage of qualified personnel in the administrative and technical cadres. Throughout the country the appointment of staff at all levels in the boarding-houses was subject to the approval of the Ministry in Algiers, which, in blissful ignorance of the problems facing a six-year-old nomad, laid down that all *surveillants* in the boarding-houses should have a baccalauréat! The role of the *surveillant* was something between that of a matron and a guardian – to look after the children in the boarding-house and help them adjust to such overwhelming 'problems' as buttons, shoe-laces, water taps, shower closets, beds, and the host of other 'shocks' confronting them in the 'concrete jungle' of the boarding-house and, of course, in Tamanrasset itself. In a bed, the child was sleeping above the ground for the first time in his life and lying awake at night in fear of what was beneath him.[13] How could an Algerian man, with his baccalauréat, deign to lower himself to the odious task of toilet training a dormitory of bed-wetters?

Fortunately, no 'baccalauréats' volunteered for this remote and uncivilized outpost of Algeria, and for the time being Laporte was freed from the difficulties of appointing the 'educated élite' to such menial tasks. This administrative difficulty, combined with Laporte's emphasis of the 'cultural' problems, enabled him to exert pressure on the ministry to allow him to recruit his own staff. Although prohibited from appointing women, whom he felt would have replaced a little of the domestic and more feminine environment of the camps by substituting as 'mother' figures, he hand-picked his own staff of locals who, although quite unqualified to meet the ministry's demands, were familiar with the nomadic environment and adept at comforting the homesick child and introducing him paternally to this strange new world.[14]

While Laporte's 'guardians' eased the transition into the boarding-house they were unable either to provide the necessary female and domestic companionship to which the children were accustomed or to integrate them into the family life of Tamanrasset, for the boarding-school was something of a curiosity in Tamanrasset, an appendage tacked onto the outskirts of the town and in almost every way extraneous to town life itself. If the barriers between townsmen and nomads were to be broken down it was important not only that the townsmen should feel in some way responsible for and interested in these children – that they were in fact part of Tamanrasset – but also that the children themselves should be integrated, or at least introduced into the family life of Tamanrasset. But in view of the nomads' inherent dislike of the merchants and sedentarists of Tamanrasset the likelihood of any such integration being accomplished readily and without 'incidents' seemed remote.

Laporte, however, held less conservative views, and relying on the shopkeepers' boastful religious practices and their consequent reluctance to refuse any public religious commitment, he deviously solicited their co-operation in inviting the children to their homes for the religious festival of L'Aid Es Rir in November. Aktouf could obviously not have given his official consent to this action, for if it had failed and led to any hostile incidents or repercussions from the Kel Ahaggar the government's position would have become even more tenuous. The administration was therefore not consulted, nor even informed, until after the invitations had been given, by which time it was placed in an extremely difficult and embarrassing position, for it could not easily repudiate such a charitable act – especially when undertaken in the name of Allah! The result of the experiment was a great success in that many friendships and fictive familial bonds were established within these 'adopted' homes. Only between fifteen and twenty of the 151 children in the boarding-house declined the invitations, but these were the eldest children, who, like their parents, remained aloof in their attitude towards the population of Tamanrasset.

The experiment of L'Aid was only a first tentative step. No real degree of integration could be achieved if the children felt 'imprisoned' in the boarding-house, nor especially until their parents' prejudices and fears that their children had been 'taken away' were removed. And so, at Christmas, only a few weeks after L'Aid Es Rir, Laporte once again took the initiative. Although the schools were closed for the five-day holiday, this was not long enough to justify the closure of the boarding-house. Nevertheless, Laporte told the boarding children that they were all free to return to their camps, some of which were a considerable distance from Tamanrasset, and that school would recommence on the following Monday morning. Aktouf was neither consulted nor informed of this decision until after it had been effected. In spite of his grave misgivings that any nomadic children would again be seen at the school, and the undoubted state of apprehension in which he spent his Christmas holiday, all the children, without exception, were in school on the Monday morning – a remarkable achievement which was not only a tribute to the respect, trust and affection in which Laporte was held by the children, but an expression of a complete change in attitude by their parents.

Even though the children's return home at Christmas and their general show of enthusiasm towards the school and Tamanrasset dispelled the rumours of what the Algerians had done with their children, their parents' consequent change in attitude towards schooling reflected no positive commitment towards educational values. Instead, their perception of the boarding-school as a 'hotel', in which their children would be clothed and fed at government expense, was merely reinforced! Laporte's goal, however, was not merely to make the boarding-school system more acceptable to the nomads but to increase its 'economic' feasibility and hence justify its continuation and later expansion. In this respect he believed that 90 per cent of the nomadic children coming to school were potentially capable of passing their school certificate examination, but not until there was a reorientation of values in which, to use his own words, 'the boarding house became first of all the head, and secondly the stomach'!

His consequent reorientation policy began at the end of the school year in the spring of 1969, when he issued all the departing children with a card classifying their return for the following year as either 'compulsory', 'voluntary', or 'not at all'. The 'not-at-alls' were, for the most part, the elder children, the 'bad herd boys' whom Aktouf had rounded up at random and who, in view of their age, had no chance of obtaining the school certificate. 'Compulsory' was effectively a 'laissez-passer', which gave the bearer official permission to use any form of government transport or other means to return to school.

In spite of Laporte's considerable achievements in both increasing the acceptability of schooling among the nomads and orientating the whole boarding-school system towards greater educational efficiency rather than impressive attendance figures, his policy was severely threatened at the beginning of the following school year by the government's extraordinary decision to abolish transit boarding schools. With the emphasis of education being on 'Algerianization', why remove the primary means of facilitating the transition from a nomadic to an 'Algerian' culture? Whether the merits of transit boarding-schools, as they were operating in Ahaggar, were given more than the slightest consideration in Algiers is dubious, and however their positive aspects were perceived they were soon swept under the carpet in the name of 'planification' – the stereotyping of the administrative system throughout the country without regard to such crucial factors as cultural and ethnic differences and other regional peculiarities.

A further reason put forward to justify the closure of the transit boarding houses in Ahaggar was the question of their maintenance in terms of supplies. It was considered, quite rightly, that they overloaded the resources of the villages and were consequently having to be supplied from Tamanrasset. But the presence of the transit boarding-houses in the larger villages presented a golden opportunity for developing a transport service, which could have been co-ordinated to serve both the schools and the agricultural co-operatives. There appeared to be no real obstacles to the development of such a scheme. As it was, this justification merely reflected the inability and lack of interest of the administration, at the level of the local commune, to organize a weekly truck service over the 100 kilometres to Abalessa and 225 kilometres to Ideles.

Transit boarding-houses were certainly causing administrative problems in other regions and may have been regarded as unfeasible on various economic and educational grounds, but their abolition in Ahaggar can only be regarded as a particularly short-sighted move.

The new directive regarding boarding-houses stated that each *arrondissement* was to have one central boarding-house with 100 places. This reversal of government policy not only called for a complete reappraisal of the boarding-school system, but threatened to create either acute logistical problems or a particularly embarrassing and potentially dangerous situation by possibly having to refuse admission.

At the start of the school year in 1969 155 old boarders with sixteen newcomers arrived at the boarding-house in Tamanrasset. After one child had died and another left, Laporte was thus faced with the problem of having to accommodate 169 children in 100 (official) places!

The first and most interesting question is what had happened to the eighty-five children from the previous year who had not returned to school. The immediate assumption, particularly in view of the nomads' general resistance and aversion to the administration and Tamanrasset over the preceding years, was that parents had taken advantage of Laporte's emphasis on 'voluntariness' to keep the children in their camps. However, after several months, during which time I was able to visit most of the camps concerned, it appeared that this had not been the case at all, and that very few parents had been reluctant for their children to return to school. Of the eighty-five children concerned, six had graduated to the college at El Golea and seventeen had either found jobs or were too old for school and had in fact been told by Laporte not to return. Of the remaining sixty-two, it seems that the majority had wanted to return to school but after the closure of the transit houses at Abalessa and Ideles had found it virtually impossible to reach Tamanrasset. Twelve Ait Lowayen and five Isekkemaren (Kel Tefedest, Kel Amguid, Kel Tourha) from the remote areas to the north-east of Ideles were unable to make the journey to Tamanrasset, while seven Kel Ahnet children who had previously gone to Abalessa were also unable to reach Tamanrasset. The return of a further nine children from Tin Zaouaten, four from Timiaouine, and seven from Tamesna was also precluded by the difficulty of finding transport to Tamanrasset.[15] Among the Dag Rali, only one child, who was needed in his camp, did not return to school.

The fact that only nineteen children[16] from the previous year could not be accounted for bore testimony to the relative acceptability of schooling and seemed to justify Laporte's rejection of all coercive or compulsory measures.

The alternatives facing Laporte when confronted by these 169 children were either to single out certain ones for rejection, which was inconceivable, or to find some alternative 'temporary' accommodation that would be approved by the Ministry. The only possible solution was to transfer those that could not be squeezed into the boarding-house at Tamanrasset to the new central boarding-house at In Salah, about 700 kilometres to the north, where there were at least seventy vacancies. One possible implication of such a move, however, was that parents, most of whom could not be notified, on hearing of the transfer, might go and collect their children and take them away from school altogether. Laporte, realizing this possibility, and the effect it might have on the nomads' future attitude towards schooling and the administration, resolved reluctantly that the eldest children with least aptitude for education, and least chance of obtaining the school certificate in view of their age, and all known 'trouble-makers', would be transferred, so that their possible loss would have less serious consequences on the future development of education in Ahaggar. Thirty-eight children, including three Dag Rali, were finally selected for transfer to In Salah, and 131 were left in Tamanrasset.[17]

It is, of course, difficult to discuss the extension and further development of education in Ahaggar without relating it to the other very significant changes taking place alongside it and in association with it. This is particularly true of the nomadic community, whose incursion into Tamanrasset during the last few years, particularly since 1968–9, has not only been closely related to changes in, and their experiences of, the educational system, but has inevitably placed the boarding system in a different perspective.

Furthermore, it is a particularly misleading and dangerous generalization to refer to the 'nomadic community' as a whole, for notwithstanding the somewhat liberal misuse of the term 'nomad' in referring to those Kel Ahaggar not resident in Tamanrasset or the other village centres, the responses of certain *tawsatin* to the overall processes of modernization taking place during this period have differed markedly.

We should, therefore, pause for a moment, not only to consider the other related changes taking place among the nomadic society, but more especially to elicit and define the more pertinent questions more clearly.

The changes taking place within the nomadic society at this time struck me quite forcibly in the autumn and winter of 1969. When I had left Ahaggar in the latter part of 1968 there were few Dag Rali in Tamanrasset. They were tending to concentrate around Tagmart and Terhenanet, making occasional sorties into the town, but rarely staying for more than a few days at a time, while the atmosphere in their camps was one of depression and despondency. A year or so later, when I returned to Tamanrasset, there appeared to be Dag Rali everywhere. In the shops, in the hotel, in fact almost everywhere I went in the town I was confronted with the embarrassment of being greeted by Dag Rali in whose camps I had stayed, but whose veiled faces, so seemingly out of place in Tamanrasset, could often not be readily provided with names. In the hotel, where I would occasionally eat breakfast to enjoy the luxury of coffee and marmalade – and, perhaps more important, the peace and quiet of its cool interior – I found myself suddenly confronted one morning by El Khoussin. Only a year before he would never have come into the hotel, or, if his courage was running high, which it was wont to do if he had made a 'kill' of a few dinars on the tourist market, he would hover around on the pavement in front of the hotel and await an opportune moment to pass a garbled message to one of the waiters. On this occasion he walked straight into the hallowed precincts of the dining-room, sat himself at my table and announced that he had not yet had breakfast!

The greatest shock, however, was on walking down to the house on the northern edge of the town which the commune had placed at the Dag Rali's disposal. In the previous year it was normally inhabited by a few Dag Rali making a brief visit to town. On this occasion, not only were twelve men staying there but in the open space that lay more or less between their house and the Labour Exchange office about 200 men were sitting or sprawling on the ground in the shade of the overhanging tamarisk trees. It looked like a refugee camp, with occasional comings and goings and a modest decline in numbers around midday, but otherwise there was an air of permanency and insistency in their 'squatting'. Only a small proportion of these men were Dag Rali, but what was so surprising was that although the Exchange was able to offer only minimal employment opportunities, most of them were persistent, even demanding, in their 'right' to work.

This sudden transformation amongst the Dag Rali depressed me in as much as I could not understand it. It was not what I had expected and I consequently began to wonder if perhaps my knowledge and awareness of their situation over the previous years had been misguided – or, what was it that had happened during my absence that had led to this almost total *volte-face*?

It was indeed the things that had happened during the intervening year or so, or rather their experience of these things, that had led to this quite radical change in their cognition. During this relatively short time their perception, evaluation and conceptualization of both their own situation and the 'Algerian' order had undergone a considerable transformation.

However, in focusing our interest on the Dag Rali, we must bear in mind that they represented the most traditionally orientated element of Kel Ahaggar society, so that their actions cannot be regarded as typical of the nomadic Kel Ahaggar except at a fairly general level, for, as we have already seen in the comparison between the responses of the Dag Rali and Aguh-en-tehle during the preceding years, any assumption that the nomadic Kel Ahaggar shared a common 'stock of knowledge' is a dangerous one. On the contrary, and for reasons which we shall examine in the next chapter, the various *tawsatin*'s definitions of social reality and their concomitant actions were by no means uniform.

It is all too easy to see this rapid transformation in the nomadic community, especially in the case of the more traditionally orientated Dag Rali, as determined primarily by their economic situation. Indeed, one can ponder endlessly over the hypothetical question of what the situation might have been if consistently good rains during this period had provided them with a viable pastoral subsistence base. But to suggest that we can understand the nature of this transformation simply in terms of economic determination merely highlights the fundamental question: why was it so rapid? If we are to locate the cause, in the singular, in the purely economic domain, then we might expect to find there some element of critical significance. But when we examine this domain it is difficult to suggest that the changes within it during the relatively brief period between 1968 and 1969–70 were other than a matter of degree. Certainly, there is the consideration, suggested earlier, that many Dag Rali were realizing by the end of 1968 that a purely nomadic existence, as described in the previous chapter, was no longer possible. But, on the other hand, by 1969 the horizon was beginning to show a glimmer of brightness, since the embargo on caravan trade was lifted in the autumn, and the well-founded rumours of the 'return of In Eker' and the consequent likelihood of employment opportunities took a more concrete form with the establishment of a base by SONAREM (Société Nationale de Recherches et d'Exploitations Minières). These developments, however, although significant, were not critical in determining this transformation. Furthermore, if we focused our attention purely on the economic, we would have to explain how the 'economic', which was subordinate to the values and attitudes embodied by the resistance to 'Algeria' and modernization, suddenly emerged to become the determining factor in the Dag Rali's transformation!

If any one factor could have been singled out as dominant in this process of transformation, it could have been understood more readily. As it was, the confused state in which I found myself on my return to Tamanrasset in the summer of 1969 was the result of 'plurideterminatiοn', in that the almost total *volte-face* that I found amongst the Dag Rali was the result of a multiplicity of closely interrelated causes or factors. Nevertheless, the various 'incidents' and experiences that led to this remarkable change in their perception, evaluation and conceptualization not only of their own situation but of the nature of the Algerian order can be unravelled and categorized, somewhat arbitrarily for the purposes of analysis, into three interrelated areas or sets of factors.

Firstly, and not in order of significance, was the notion that as they had 'given' their children, the government was now indebted to them. Several Dag Rali actually used the term *tiwse* to explain and legitimize the sending of their children to Tamanrasset, while a few of those who spoke French, when asked to explain the meaning of the term in this context, translated it as *impôt* (tax) or qualified it with *comme* (like tax!). Whether they perceived this payment in terms of some form of 'redistributive' tax system is not clear. Rather, it seems that they felt that by having met Aktouf's demands and 'given' their children, they, in turn, now had a right to make demands on the government.

It is difficult to consider this notion outside the context of the various other factors involved, which we shall discuss presently, but it certainly seems to have been an important factor in their general 'psychological transformation', as seen in the extraordinary increase in confidence manifested in their attitude and approach to Tamanrasset, and displayed in such actions as El Khoussin's entry into the hotel and their 'demand' for employment at the Labour Exchange.

Emerging more or less synchronously with this conceptualization of their 'new relationship' with the government, and closely related to it, was a general re-evaluation of the Algerian order, based on their growing experience of the government's lack of discrimination against the 'nomad', and the Kel Ahaggar in general, and their increasing awareness and realization that it could be counted on to 'keep its word'.

The actual process of re-evaluation was not, of course, a common concurrence, but rather the ongoing synthesis of differential levels of shared and individual knowledge and experience of both general and particular incidents and situations. The process was also characterized, at the cognitive level, by the 'feedback' tendency to re-evaluate past experiences and perceptions in the light of the new, with the result that the former acquired new meanings and levels of significance; so that for example, by about 1970 some Kel Ahaggar denied quite emphatically that they had ever been in any way 'opposed' or 'resistant' to the government!

It is difficult to relate all the various incidents and situations involved in this process, for as there were probably many which were unknown to me, I have perhaps placed undue emphasis on incidents that were relatively insignificant in the overall context but which I was more closely involved with and able to 'follow up'. Nevertheless, there can be little doubt that the one incident of overwhelming importance in this respect was the return of the children from school at Christmas. Their arrival back in the camps, all alive and well, dispelled the many underlying fears and prejudices of what the government had done with them. It was 'living proof' of Aktouf's word – that the children would be well cared for and returned unharmed. Moreover, the children's general enthusiasm and 'favourable' reports of both the school and Tamanrasset, albeit perhaps coloured by the novelty and excitement of their experience, made their parents more predisposed both to return their children and to go and see with their own eyes.

I was not in Ahaggar during the first half of 1969 and consequently have no detailed records of Dag Rali visits to Tamanrasset during those months, but by the time of my return around midsummer their sorties into town were becoming commonplace. What they 'saw' in Tamanrasset tended to reinforce their initial tentative reappraisal of the government. Those who had believed that the embargo on caravan trade, the closure of In Eker, and at times even the lack of rains could be attributed to selective reprisal action by the Algerian authorities found an almost total lack of prejudice and discrimination against them. It is true that the nomads, as Algerian citizens, had always been possessed of the same rights, in the purely legislative sense, as other population groups, but there was also a noticeable change in the attitude of the 'Algerians' towards the nomadic population around this time. Whereas ridicule and intolerance of the nomad had not been uncommon, there was now a noticeable effort to accommodate the 'customs' and 'habits' of the nomads in their transformation, and a general desire among most government officials to avoid or minimize any possible conflict and antagonism.

This more tolerant and understanding attitude towards the nomads seems to have been closely related to the Algerians' growing confidence in their control over the region, and was impressed upon me most forcibly through an incident that gave a most revealing insight into the position of the government official in Tamanrasset at this time – in this case the officer commanding the gendarmerie.

It was mid-morning, and I was sitting in my hut when a gendarme knocked and told me that the officer commanding the gendarmerie wanted to see me immediately. A heavy sinking feeling went through my stomach as I realized that there were few other reasons for being summoned other than to be notified of my expulsion. I lived daily in the fear of this eventuality, and as I walked slowly down the main street towards the gendarmerie I wondered how many more months or years it would be before I would be allowed to set foot in Ahaggar again. The last time I had been summoned, it had been by the police. On that occasion I was bedridden with a painful infection in my feet and legs. It was in the evening and raining, and the 'messenger' had escorted me on a quite unnecessary detour around the town merely to increase my physical discomfort. The Chief of Police, a permanently unshaven and uncouth individual, delivered a long prepared speech about 'national security', which he had obviously been rehearsing for some time, confiscated all my written notes, and ordered me to travel to Algiers!

I entered the gendarmerie. It always took a few seconds for one's eyes to become accustomed to the dark interior, and at first I did not see the commandant waiting for me in the corridor. After all, it was I who had been summoned and should be standing. He smiled, shook my hand, showed me into his office, called for two cups of coffee, and closed the door behind us. My fears were quite unwarranted. He told me straight away that he had a very 'delicate' problem and was wondering, in view of my knowledge of the Tuareg, whether I could help him.

He had with him a Dag Rali man, waiting in a back room, who was suspected of theft. The Dag Rali had been involved in an argument in one of the shops, apparently over the payment or cost of some item, and on producing a wallet containing several hundred dinars had been accused, in the course of the fracas, of having stolen the wallet. By chance, a gendarme had heard the commotion and the accusations against the Dag Rali and had brought him into the gendarmerie. The accusation seemed to have been made in the heated exchanges of the argument and was more an expression of the shop assistant's prejudices against the nomads. To provoke the Dag Rali he had claimed that a nomad could not have earned that amount of money, and it must therefore have been stolen!

The wallet, which lay on the commandant's desk, contained nothing except a wad of bank-notes and an old battered passport-size photograph. The Dag Rali, so the commandant told me, had claimed that he had been given the money by some tourists who had bought a lot of 'souvenirs' from his camp and that it was his picture, with his name written on the back of it, taken some years ago at In Eker. The commandant realized that there was no way of checking the man's story about the tourists, which he felt was probably true, and also agreed that the photograph appeared to have been inside the wallet for a long time, and in all probability was the picture and name of the owner of the wallet. As far as the commandant was concerned, it was therefore merely a matter of confirming the man's identity with the name on the photograph. This, however, presented the problem, for not only was the man in the photograph veiled, but the suspect had no other means of proving his identity, except to call in some other Kel Ahaggar to identify him, which the commandant was reluctant to do in view of the possible 'scandal'. If, on the other hand, the commandant could establish the particulars of the man whose name was on the photograph through some other means, he could then question the suspect accordingly.

He asked me whether I could help him in this matter, and having collected my notebooks, I was soon able to locate the genealogical particulars of the man whose name was inscribed on the picture, and provide the commandant with a list of the man's more immediate kinsmen, their camp locations, and various other particulars which I felt might help confirm the suspect's identity and establish what seemed to me to be his innocence. The commandant, armed with this information, then left me to go and talk to the suspect. The man's identity was confirmed, and later in the day I was able to find him in the town and ask him about his experience in the gendarmerie.

He told me how some tourists had visited his camp and had bought a lot of old skin bags and various other leather goods, and that he had come into Tamanrasset with the proceeds to buy some provisions. I did not understand how the argument in the shop had begun, but gathered that he had doubted or not understood the price of some blankets, and that in the ensuing argument some people in the shop had ragged him about living in a tent and had even accused him of having stolen the money. He had, however, been most impressed by the gendarmes, for, as he told me, they had given him tea while he waited for the 'chief', and was particularly impressed by the 'chief', who showed so much interest in his family and their camps, and was most surprised that an 'Algerian' should have known so much and shown so much interest in his people and their problems!

A similar incident, but one with more far reaching consequences in view of the rapid dissemination of the news, took place one morning in

November. The embargo on caravan trade had been lifted in the autumn subject to the individuals leaving Ahaggar being given a 'laissez-passer' from the Sub-Prefecture in accordance with the quota restrictions laid down by Niger, and receiving customs clearance through Tamanrasset. This presented no difficulty for most *tawsatin*, since their caravans would in any event pass through or relatively close to Tamanrasset. However, for the Ait Lowayen, living some 200 to 300 kilometres to the east of Tamanrasset, these administrative requirements posed insuperable difficulties. Normally, they would travel in a south-south-westerly direction down the Tin Tarabine valley and cross the frontier into Niger in the region of the wells at In Azoua. Checking through Tamanrasset would thus necessitate journeying through two sides of a triangle and adding about 200 to 300 kilometres of rough mountainous country to their journey. Under normal pastoral conditions such a detour would merely have been an inconvenience. With the prevailing drought conditions, which were especially severe in the Ait Lowayen territory, it was quite impossible for the desperately weak camels to cover this additional distance. As it was, the Ait Lowayen were anticipating the loss of several camels on the journey. They were thus faced with the choice of ignoring administrative regulations, which they regarded lightly, and by-passing Tamanrasset, or making the detour at grave risk to their camels.

On 2 October an Ait Lowayen caravan, deciding to ignore the demands of Tamanrasset, left directly for Tamesna. Five days later, on 7 October, news of this caravan somehow reached the customs office in Tamanrasset.

On the morning of the seventh I had decided, by chance, to pay a visit to Beh ag Ahmed, a Kel Rela living in Tamanrasset, who had given me much assistance over the years. His house was on the south side of the *oued*, a little beyond the customs office. It was early morning and I was walking quickly, for although the sun was getting higher there was still a cold nip in the air. On approaching the customs office I was surprised to see Beh walking towards me at an even more energetic pace. He barely stopped to greet me, telling me that he was 'needed' urgently in the customs office, and that in the meantime I should wait in his house. Such undignified haste by a Kel Rela, and his reference to being 'needed', indicated that a crisis was in the air. I ambled back to the customs office on the pretext of changing money, only to be assured that there was no money available and that I should return tomorrow. But the sound of raised voices in the inner office confirmed my suspicions. Beh's return, three hours later, bore the hallmark of victory.

The customs, on learning about the unauthorized Ait Lowayen caravan, had called for Beh, in his capacity as an influential Kel Rela and former chief guide to the French gendarmerie, to advise on its route and location so that it could be intercepted and recalled to Tamanrasset. Beh had argued the Ait Lowayen case, showing how it was impossible for caravans originating at Serouenout, Tin Zaouaten or other distant parts to check through Tamanrasset, especially with pasture in its present condition, and that in the Ait Lowayen case their camels would never have the strength to recover in the pastures of Tamesna if they had to make the extra journey through Tamanrasset. In any case, it was quite unnecessary, so Beh had argued, for the caravans to obtain customs clearance, for, as the customs should have known, the caravans were not involved in contraband but merely the exchange of salt and millet, and nothing more! Beh won his appeal, and officialdom turned a blind eye to the Ait Lowayen caravans. By the next day it appeared that most Kel Ahaggar in Tamanrasset had heard of the incident and how the government was beginning to understand their problems!

One of the greatest revelations for many of these nomads coming into Tamanrasset, and for the Kel Ahaggar in general, was their introduction to, and familiarization with, the activities of local government agencies. Contrary to their widely held expectations of discrimination, the general 'policy planifaction' and bureaucratic nature of government administration tended to reduce the applicant to an 'Algerian citizen' with an identity card, giving particulars of his name, place and date of birth, marital status, and number of dependants, but no reference to 'ethnicity' or 'mode of existence'. Furthermore, most of the staff employed in such agencies as the Labour Exchange, agricultural department of the Sub-Prefecture and so forth were from the north and usually had insufficient experience of or interest in the region to know whether an applicant was a Dag Rali or a Harratin cultivator, or whether he came from a camp somewhere in the mountains, Tamanrasset, or some remote and isolated cultivation centre.

At the Labour Exchange, for example, employment was allocated on a 'pointing system', which cut across all local ethnic and geographical cleavages. On requesting labour, an individual presented his identity card for registration and was then issued with a 'green card', noting the same information as marked on his identity card. If labour opportunities were available, they were allocated, except in the case of specifically skilled labour, on the basis of equal distribution in relation to social needs, so that priority was given to married men with children, regardless of whether they were nomadic Kel Ahaggar or ex-slaves living in Tamanrasset. If, for example, twelve jobs were available, six would be given to married men with children, three or four would be given to married men without children or bachelors, and a maximum of only 25 per cent to workers resident in other regions. A married Dag Rali with children, living on the northern slopes of Assekrem, thus had better prospects of being given unskilled employment through the Exchange than an unmarried ex-slave living in Tamanrasset.

Nevertheless, although this system of labour recruitment was designed to allocate jobs fairly, it held certain obvious disadvantages for most nomads, particularly those who made only brief and infrequent visits to town, for within these broad principles of fair allocation there was also the additional principle of the 'early bird catching the worm'. It was necessary for those wanting work, especially with the shortage of employment opportunities, to present their green cards at regular monthly intervals, as well as to keep in touch with the 'grapevine', to learn when future labour demands might arise. Furthermore, several of these nomads, particularly the elder ones with relatively little or no experience of Tamanrasset and the bureaucratic ways of the Algerian system, and remembering only the casual signing on and off process at In Eker, did not at first understand the complexities of the 'green card' and 'pointing' system of the Labour Exchange.

An example of this lack of understanding was the case of El Khoussin. Admittedly he was old, verging on senility, and a high labour risk, but even by 1971, when I was last with him, he had still not grasped the importance of the 'green card'! His insistence, in the autumn of 1969, when SONAREM opened its base in Ahaggar, that 'it was just like In Eker again' caused me no end of inconvenience.

At the time of my 'ordeal' with El Khoussin there was the possibility of moderate winter pastures in certain parts of Atakor. 80·4 mm of rain had been recorded in Tamanrasset between late August and November and I was anxious to see if it had had any significant effect on the organization and movement of certain camps. One such camp was El Khoussin's, which had only recently moved higher into the Taessa area in search of winter pasture. The other areas I wanted to visit were to the north of Ilaman (Kel Tinhart), the Assekrem area, Hirafok and the Tazulet region. As I would be travelling on foot for about 400 kilometres it meant careful planning, for if the object of the tour was to be achieved speed in travel and prearranged rendezvous were essential.

El Khoussin was in Tamanrasset at this time, and as his overtures to the Labour Exchange had proved fruitless he was keen that I should travel up to his camp and work with him. I had always given him fifty dinars for every week I stayed in his camp, in addition to fairly substantial supplies of tea, sugar, grain and tobacco. He seemed delighted by the prospect and I gave him fifty dinars in advance to buy whatever supplies he needed. We arranged to meet on the following morning, when we would leave Tamanrasset. An hour or two later he returned, saying that he needed fifty kilos of wheat! I jogged his memory about the fifty dinars he had just received, and we once again arranged to meet in the morning. But in the morning there was no sign of El Khoussin, and at midday I went to the Dag Rali house to make enquiries, only to learn that he was having 'problems' with a camel and was somewhere in the Oued Sersouf! By evening he had still not returned, but had apparently been seen several kilometres up the *oued*. On the next day I made an early start to search for him. When we at last met he was by no means apologetic. On the contrary, he told me straight away that he didn't want to go up to the camp with me as he was off to work for SONAREM at the mines at Laouni[18] and was now rich, and consequently had no need for the fifty dinars, which he dug out of his wallet and handed to me! Knowing that SONAREM had not yet been recruiting labour, and that the likelihood of El Khoussin being given employment was remote, I gave him ten dinars to see him through the next few days. At the Labour Exchange the director told me that he was anticipating demands from SONAREM in the near future, and as I suspected there was no record of El Khoussin having registered or ever being given employment. He had seen a cloud and followed it, like In Eker, and in a few days it would have disappeared from the horizon.

It was imperative that I visited El Khoussin's camp, but I decided in the meantime to avoid further loss of time by visiting the Kel Tinhart camps north of Ilaman and then returning directly to Tamanrasset – even if this necessitated doubling my tracks over nearly 200 kilometres – hoping that by this time his illusion would have passed and we could recommence our journey up to Taessa. I returned to Tamanrasset five days later, footsore and weary, only to find that El Khoussin was no longer there. The Labour Exchange knew nothing about him, and the general opinion of other Dag Rali in town was that he had returned to his camp. There was little option but to make the journey to Taessa alone. And so, after sleeping through the day, while it was warm, I set off to retrace my steps through the night, climbing onto the central plateau of Atakor around dawn. By nightfall I had found no sign of his camp, and stopped in a small valley to light a fire and scoop a hollow in the sand in which to shelter for the night. It was too cold to sleep much, the moisture of my breath condensing in my moustache, but with the light of dawn the welcoming red granites of Taessa loomed above me and gave me the energy to rekindle the ashes of my fire. When its warmth had been replaced by that of the sun I moved off and had barely topped the next rise when I saw the five little yellow dots of El Khoussin's camp sheltered under a spur of Taessa. Tanelhir, El Khoussin's wife, recognized me at a distance and came a long way from the camp to greet me, her beautiful face showing the lines of a young woman rather than her fifty years. El Khoussin was not in the camp, and had not been seen since his departure for Tamanrasset about three weeks before! I could only guess that he had gone to Tagmart before coming back to the camp, perhaps to regain his confidence or 'recuperate' before launching another raid on Tamanrasset so as not to return home empty-handed! I told Tanelhir that I was heading towards Tin Haren and would be at Assekrem in about five days' time.

It was dark when I eventually reached the col below Assekrem and I was grateful to find shelter for the night in one of the stone rest-huts built there for passing tourists and other travellers. I was awakened by the sound of knocking and the door grating open, to see El Khoussin standing in the entrance with his wizened old face creased in a broad grin. He had indeed gone to Tagmart where, amidst the security and comfort of other Dag Rali, he had decided, so he told me, that he was too old to work for organizations like SONAREM! He blamed his misfortune in Tamanrasset not on the Algerian authorities, the Labour Exchange, who had 'given' him work, but, as he explained to me, on the Algerians from the north, SONAREM, who did not understand him! But now he was on another raid. On returning to his camp, Tanelhir had told him of my plans and he had cut across country to Assekrem to ask me to return and work with him in his camp – at fifty dinars per week! I gave him fifty dinars and set off for Hirafok, telling him that I would be back in Tamanrasset within a month and would then come and work with him again!

It is true that El Khoussin did not understand the 'green card' system, but what was significant was that he did not put the blame on the Algerian authorities in Tamanrasset, but rather on 'outsiders', namely SONAREM.

Similarly, among the younger men who understood the system and who were yet unable to obtain work, the fault did not lie with the 'government' or in any form of discrimination against them, but in the overall economic recession in Ahaggar, and to some extent in themselves, for they saw that the majority of offers made for employment were not for temporary unskilled labour, but skilled labour – the criterion for which was 'education'.

The realization that the crucial factor in securing employment was achieved and not ascriptive began to place the educational system in a new perspective. Schooling began to be re-evaluated more positively in the strictly educational sense, and acquired a more futuristic orientation. Several nomads, even single men who did not yet have children of their own, when asked during this period about their attitudes and feelings towards the boarding school, said that they would like their children to go to it so that they would be able to get work when they needed it. However, although these statements were made within a futuristic context, they did not embody the assumption or implication that these children would leave or abandon 'camp life'. Such an eventuality was inconceivable within their perceptions of a future state. This noticeable change in attitude towards Tamanrasset, and particularly to the boarding-school, during this relatively short period was evidenced most clearly by the sight of children being 'dropped off' at school in October as their fathers, or other senior kinsmen, headed on southwards to Niger with the caravans. The school year fitted in well to the nomads' year, with southbound caravans checking through Tamanrasset at the beginning of the new term, and returning in the spring in time to collect the children for the summer holidays.

The third main factor leading to this transformation, particularly during the latter part of 1969, was an awareness of new opportunities, or at least a relaxation in some of the impediments that had been confronting them.

For three years there had been an embargo on caravans to Niger, and the opportunities for wage-earning had been minimal since the closure of In Eker. Now, in the autumn of 1969, the Sub-Prefect gave notice of the lifting of the caravan embargo, while the recruitment of 450 personnel by SONAREM during the first two weeks of November more than doubled the size of the engaged labour force. These two factors, in particular, generated a degree of optimism among the nomads and lifted a little the veil of depression that had been lying over the camps for so long.

The nomads' reaction and response to these events, in terms of their changing perception and re-evaluation of both their own situation and the Algerian order, was interesting. The lifting of the caravan embargo tended to reinforce their more positive evaluation of the government, and since permits had to be obtained from the Sub-Prefecture in Tamanrasset, it led to a further incursion of nomads into the town. The importance of these caravans to the nomadic economy cannot be assessed easily. Between 170 and 200 permits were issued, and although about 1,000 camels were involved, I do not think that a great amount of salt was transported south. The official figures of both the Sub-Prefecture and customs were denied me, although I doubt whether either had recorded this information. The relatively short notice of the lifting of the embargo gave little opportunity for salt to be brought from Amadror, but this was not a serious matter, as moderate quantities of salt had been stockpiled around the camps. The critical factor was the wretched condition of the camels, most of which were too weak to carry any heavy load, and most Kel Ahaggar seemed more concerned about moving the camels southwards to the better pastures of Tamesna, and so giving them a long-awaited opportunity to recuperate, than about trading large quantities of salt.

The opportunity of meeting the caravans on their return was uppermost in my mind throughout the winter. However, this was not to be. In the spring, before their return, I was once again expelled from Ahaggar, and Algeria. In another month I would have been able to acquire the data I had been awaiting for so long. By the time of my next return to Ahaggar in 1971 the details of these caravans had been forgotten and I was collecting 'impressions', most of which were clouded by the continuation of drought conditions and the fact that although a 'reasonable amount' of millet was brought back it was inadequate for the needs of the camps, and compared very poorly with former caravans.

My one consolation, in retrospect, was that the caravans of 1969 did not have the effect that I was anticipating. During 1968 I had always felt, especially among the Dag Rali, that the renewal of the annual caravans might lead to some form of revivalist movement. But, instead, when caravans were at last allowed to leave Ahaggar they no longer seemed to occupy the dominant place within their value system. Within the cognitive sphere, traditionalism was losing ground to secularization and modernization, while changes in the ecological and commercial aspects of the caravan trade were placing it in a different perspective.

From the ecological point of view the importance of the caravans was shifting towards their transhumant aspect, as a means of moving the emaciated camels to the pastures of Tamesna; while at the commercial level the terms of trade, which in 1965 gave only the smallest advantage to the millet market in Damergou, had turned in favour of Tamanrasset itself. Deteriorating harvests in Niger, particularly during the 1970s, were increasing further the millet price in Damergou, while the reduction and stabilization of prices of all essential commodities in Tamanrasset, particularly since 1966, had been designed to help the poorer elements of the population, such as Harratin and ex-slaves, and the sedentarizing nomad. The distribution of most cereals was regulated through the S.A.P. (Société Agricole de Prévoyance), while O.N.A.C.O. (Office National Algérien de Commercialisation), had cut the price of all essential commodities, such as sugar, oil, etc., by about half,[19] since its inception in 1966.

Moreover, both the traditional 'pull' of the caravans, and their 'escapist' and revivalist elements, which were prominent immediately after independence, were being countered by the processes of modernization, as manifested among the more traditionally orientated Kel Ahaggar, such as the Dag Rali, in their changing values and attitudes towards education, Tamanrasset and the Algerian authorities. Indeed, the re-evaluation of the government even led, among some individuals, to their denying that they had ever been opposed to the government. I remember how I had once commented to a Kel Rela, whom I had known for several years, that it was quite surprising to see so many Kel Ahaggar who had been so resentful of the government now entering Tamanrasset and associating with various government agencies. I was rebuked in the most vehement manner, and told that it was not true that the Kel Ahaggar had ever been opposed to the government, and that I should show more caution before making such suggestions! The identification with Algeria, or, as the government phrased it, the process of 'Algerianization', was manifested in many ways. Perhaps the most striking was the reference of many Kel Ahaggar to themselves as 'Algerians' or 'Algerian Tuareg' as opposed to Tuareg from Niger, Mali or elsewhere. It was also impressed on me most strongly in December–January 1969–70, during the weeks prior to President Boumedienne's visit to Tamanrasset. Although the actual date of his visit was not confirmed until a week or so before his arrival on 29 January, Ahaggar was alive with talk and demands for news and confirmation of the date.

In mid-January I made a most extraordinary journey to one of the most remote settlements in this part of the Sahara, the small basin of Tamdjert in the very heart of the Tassili. A French geological team had given me a lift to the area, but in view of the impenetrability of the terrain I had covered the last twenty miles on foot. On arriving in the basin, which contained three little settlements together numbering only 100 to 200 people, I was given a most hostile reception. The local headman demanded to see my papers and said that I could not stay there without permission from the government! As it was several days' journey over extremely hostile terrain to either Djanet, Ilizi (Fort Polignac), In Salah or Tamanrasset, and as I gathered that the last vehicle to pass through this area had been a French military cartographic team many years ago, I wondered which government he was referring to. To my amazement, the headman produced an Algerian identity card, which appeared to be a legacy of the F.L.N., and said that he had instructions to record and report the details of all strangers entering the area. Who had given him the instructions remained a mystery to me, but it was a most disturbing experience which induced visions of my being held captive in Tamdjert for several months while contact was made with the outside world and my release negotiated! As all my relevant permits had been left with the geological team, I wrote my name on the back of a cigarette packet, suggested to the headman that he took it to Ilizi, and, deciding that caution was the better part of valour, made my retreat from the area while the opportunity still remained. The inhabitants of Tamdjert were predominantly Kel In Tunin, a vassal *tawsit* attached to the Taitok *ettebel*, and I wondered if their belligerent attitude resulted from their loyalty to the chief of the Ahaggar Taitok, Ellou ag Amaray, who was head of the Bureau Politique in Tamanrasset. However, Ellou always refused to discuss the matter with me, saying that the Bureau's affairs were not my business and that the Kel Rela would tell me anything I wanted to know.

It was not surprising that the news of the President's impending visit had not reached Tamdjert, but on the return journey across Amadror to Ideles, and then back through Hirafok, we were stopped repeatedly by villagers and nomads asking for the date of the President's visit and begging us to give them a lift to Tamanrasset to see his arrival. Four and a half years ago, when the President had last visited Tamanrasset, there were barely more than a few hundred onlookers lining the street, and the Kel Ahaggar, with the exception of a few curious bystanders, were noticeable for their absence. On this visit, Tamanrasset was crowded to capacity as thousands thronged into the town to get a glimpse of the President and wave their 'appreciations'.

The main reason, however, that the reopening of the caravan trade was something of an anti-climax, at least for people such as myself who felt that it might lead to some form of nativistic or revivalist movement, was that its timing more or less coincided with the opening of the main SONAREM base at In Eker.

1969 had been a year of rising expectations. Nomads, coming into Tamanrasset, felt that they now had certain rights, especially in their demand for work. Since the closure of In Eker, however, job opportunities had been minimal. Throughout the whole of 1968 the Labour Exchange had registered only 311 work placements. Although there was little improvement in this situation throughout most of 1969, there was at least the rumour of the imminent reopening of In Eker.

The establishment of the main SONAREM base at In Eker in 1969, with a secondary base in Tamanrasset, was the product of Russian technical assistance and preliminary surveys throughout the previous year. However, unlike the development of In Eker by the C.E.A. (Commissariat de l'Énergie Atomique), SONAREM did not require a large unskilled labour force; but for the nomads, In Eker was 'In Eker', and the rumours of its impending reopening, and their expectation of returning to their former employment, as they remembered it under the French, contributed to their increased incursion into Tamanrasset during the autumn.

On Friday 7 November SONAREM opened its doors in Tamanrasset and began signing on labour. Gendarmes were needed to restrain the crowd of several hundreds who jostled outside the temporary recruiting office set up in the Mairie.

The establishment of the SONAREM base was considered by many nomads as the government's response to their demand for work. However, for most of them, optimism quickly turned into the frustration of unfulfilled expectations as the initial labour recruitment was limited to 450 mostly skilled or semi-skilled workers. Nevertheless, this experience served the nomads with an important and immediate lesson. SONAREM was perceived by the nomads as having come from the 'outside', and its management exhibited little interest in or knowledge of local 'human peculiarities'. Labour was not recruited on the basis of ethnic criteria, nor past experience of In Eker, but primarily on the skills it could offer, and in this respect the nomads were sadly lacking. This realization, together with the government's assurance that an increasing number of jobs would become available over the next few years as SONAREM expanded,[20] and the emphasis on the technical nature of the work, was a critical factor in accelerating the nomads' changing attitude to schooling. They had experienced, and seen with their own eyes, how those who had had 'schooling' had been given jobs with SONAREM. Education began to be seen as the prerequisite for guaranteed wage-earning!

Not only was the departure of the caravans overshadowed by the establishment of SONAREM, but the caravans, particularly in their ecological and commercial aspects, could not be readily incorporated into the same value system as the demands of this new development. This had not been true of In Eker (under the C.E.A.), whose demands, particularly during the years after independence, could be absorbed into the traditional value system.

If pasture had been sufficient for the goat herds to provide for the camps and for the camels to carry enough salt to make the caravans a more commercially viable proposition, one wonders if the move towards Tamanrasset, the re-evaluation of the government, and the increasing acceptance of modernizing values associated with education, SONAREM and so forth would have been so pronounced. As it was, many Kel Ahaggar, although not necessarily sedentarizing in cultivation centres, were coming out of their enclave and establishing more permanent camps nearer to or within more easy reach of Tamanrasset. Within Ahaggar this general pattern resulted from the interaction of both 'push' and 'pull' forces. The 'push' was the general impoverishment of pastoral resources, and the 'pull' the increased acceptability of and dependency on Tamanrasset, particularly in the desire for work. A further dimension of this general movement was the return to Ahaggar of Kel Ahaggar who had been resident in Tamesna. The majority of these were Kel Rela, many of whom were actually born in Tamesna but who, unlike the Taitok, had never been officially registered in Niger, and who were now attracted to Tamanrasset by the opportunities for wage-earning and education, and the influential example of the Kel Rela already in Tamanrasset. Many of these families had actually sold their camel herds in Tamesna to finance the building of their own houses in Tamanrasset.[21]

However, although this general pattern of encroachment on Tamanrasset was evident, in varying degree, among most *tawsatin*, we see, amongst the Dag Rali, that it was not characterized either in its overt manifestation or at the cognitive level by any expression of 'totality' or 'finality', but rather by its 'inching' process – a sort of 'three steps forwards two steps backwards' procedure, with the 'backward steps' still firmly rooted in traditional values.

But even within the *tawsatin* this process did not reflect a general uniformity of response, but rather an overall synthesis of action in which there was a danger of losing sight of the extremes. While there was a growing number of individuals, particularly among the younger men, who were becoming increasingly committed to Tamanrasset, there was still a core of nomads who were resistant to any alternative to their traditional nomadic-pastoral existence.

Among the Dag Rali, this 'inching' process was probably best exemplified by the growth of the community at Tagmart during the later sixties and early seventies, which reflected the increasing impoverishment of pastoralism as well as their general aversion to and lack of commitment to sedentarization. Tagmart was not a 'village' or 'cultivation centre' in the customary sense, since it had not been developed by settled Harratin cultivators. The small amount of cultivation that had been practised there had been carried out almost incidentally by the Dag Rali's own slaves, in a similar manner to Terhenanet. It was thus an exclusively Dag Rali community (mostly Kel Tamanrasset), lacking the ethnic plurality characteristic of the other cultivation centres such as Hirafok, Ideles, Tahifet and so forth, in which Kel Ahaggar had been sedentarizing over this period. Furthermore, as a community, it was structurally more akin to a section camp than a village, except that tents had mostly given way to huts (*ekeber*, Arabic *zeriba*), and the bulk of the goat herds were still held in the surrounding camps.

Dag Rali at Tagmart were in easy reach of Tamanrasset, only about twenty kilometres away, and were thus able to make quick visits to the Labour Exchange and be better informed of developments on the labour market and other such opportunities in town. But although within striking distance of Tamanrasset, Tagmart was a traditional sub-area of the Kel Tamanrasset section, so that the progressive 'temporary' settlement there was equated more readily with traditional values than the general process of 'semi-sedentarization' taking place in other centres such as Hirafok.

The convenience of Tagmart as a base from which to raid Tamanrasset, and as a staging-post between Tamanrasset and the nomadic camps, was illustrated by the gradual process of 'temporary' settlement in Tagmart, and the relationship with Tagmart of the members of the Dag Rali camp shown in Fig. 5 (p. 221). Even when this entire camp was resident in Tagmart after at least three or four years of vacillation to and fro between Tagmart and the camp, none of its members regarded the move as permanent and always legitimized it in such terms as 'until rains come' – when they would re-establish their camps in Atakor. However, even during the winter of 1969–70, when all seven tents were pitched in the Oued Amsa close to Taessa so that the goats could benefit from the slight winter pasture, most of the men were making constant trips into Tamanrasset in search of work and other forms of monetary remuneration, and were spending more time at Tagmart than in the camp.

It is also interesting to note that no members of this camp participated in the caravans of 1969, and that all of them, with the exception of Abdullah, who had been contracted by a French tourist organization running camel treks through Ahaggar (mostly on foot in view of the state of the camels!), were in Tamanrasset at the time of SONAREM's recruitment of labour, although none of them were actually signed on.

While this camp typified the pattern of encroachment on Tamanrasset amongst the Dag Rali, there was still a small core of nomads who were resistant to any such move, persisting in their traditional nomadic-pastoral existence. But for these few, nomadic pastoralism had become more of a symbol than a dominant economic activity, with the camps' existence depending for the most part on certain local idiosyncratic conditions. This was true of Sidi Mohammed's camp, which was able to maintain itself largely through its favourable position in the Assekrem area, where a minimal amount of pasture was nearly always available, and where the presence of the 'hermitage' provided a ready tourist market for the sale of such 'traditional artefacts' as sandals, various types of skin bags and so forth. Furthermore, this camp, as we have already seen, like most other remaining nomadic camps was closely related to and partly dependent on its generalized exchange with those section members who had settled and were cultivating gardens in Hirafok and other such villages. Such camps, unlike those in former times, could no longer be regarded as economically self-contained units. Indeed, under the prevailing conditions of pastoral impoverishment, not only was animal husbandry contributing minimally, either directly or indirectly, to the subsistence needs of the camps, but in certain extreme cases, such as Sidi Mohammed's, it had taken on a predominantly symbolic aspect, the economic costs and rationality of which were becoming the subject of scepticism and critical comment among certain younger men.

For Sidi, a man in his fifties, there was no acceptable alternative to the 'camp'. He would, as he himself stated, 'never leave the mountains'. Nevertheless, by 1971, when pastoral conditions were worse than at any other time in the preceding decade, the tenacity with which he persisted in his traditional ways was regarded by some of the younger men as bordering on the foolhardy. All sixteen of his camels in Ahaggar had died during the year, and now in the autumn he was insistent on making the journey to Tamesna to collect some more. Throughout October and November he was preoccupied with his attempts to raise enough cash to hitch a lift south and to purchase enough grain to maintain his camp during his absence. During the few weeks that I stayed in his camp, prior to his eventual departure for Tamesna, he sold a considerable number of 'artefacts' and accumulated at least 300 dinars. I also drove him into Tamanrasset on several occasions to purchase and transport grain back to the camp, as well as to organize his 'laissez-passer' for the journey to

Niger. On one of these trips his twelve-year-old son accompanied us. It was the first time that he had ever visited the town, while his wife, Umeyda, had said that she had visited Tamanrasset once, but had not liked it.

On several occasions I tried to get Sidi to explain why he needed more camels in the camp, and to rationalize the expense of time and money involved in the undertaking. In this latter respect one or two younger men had implied that he was irresponsible, but for Sidi the answer was always in the same tone. He had 'always' had camels. They were the symbolization and justification of his 'nomadic' existence. Camels, so he maintained, were wealth, and provided the basis of his prestige and status! It was a futile and pathetic act upon which some of the younger men, even in his own section, looked with amazement and sometimes ridicule, and even Sidi admitted that the camels might well die within a year or two of being brought back to Ahaggar unless there was a dramatic change in pastoral conditions. But by the end of November, having assured the well-being of his family for the winter, but having disposed of most of his monetary assets, he bade farewell to his camp. I gave him a lift into Tamanrasset, and the last I saw of him was perched on top of a heavily laden truck, clutching a camel saddle and a couple of blankets, as it rumbled south to the frontier at In Guezzam.

I do not know what became of his quixotic mission. He had at least accomplished another 'caravan', his fifteenth, albeit on the back of a truck, and would assumedly have a few camels around his camp for another year or two. But the prestige and status that was associated in former times with the possession of such camels and a successful 'caravan' was no longer universally accorded.

# SIXTEEN
# DIFFERENTIAL RESPONSES OF THE KEL AHAGGAR TO MODERNIZATION

It is time to pull together the strings, and in so doing to focus on the one major question that surrounds much of what we have discussed, namely, why the Dag Rali? Why were the Dag Rali the only *tawsit* not to have sent any children to boarding-school prior to Aktouf's drive through the camps in the autumn of 1968?[1] Was it merely 'coincidence' that the Otoul skirmish was a predominantly Dag Rali affair? And why, following the closure of In Eker and the embargo on caravans, were the Dag Rali noticeably more reluctant to sedentarize and develop various relationships and associations with Tamanrasset and the sedentary community at large? Indeed, why was it that the Dag Rali could be labelled as 'traditionalist', 'conservative', and more resistant to 'modernization' than other Kel Ulli during this period? In more general terms, the question is: How can we explain the difference in the response of various Kel Ulli *tawsatin* to the forces of modernization and Algerianization operative in Ahaggar, particularly during the crucial years between about 1965–6 and 1968–9?

The answer appears to lie in a relatively straightforward ecological–economic explanation. Those *tawsatin* whose territories were less well endowed with pastoral resources and who were consequently less wealthy in livestock, would presumably be less able to maintain themselves in a nomadic-pastoral state in the face of progressive pastoral deterioration and other impediments. This seems to have been the case in the progressive sedentarization of most of the poorer Isekkemaren and Kel Ulli groups in the late 1950s and early 1960s. Indeed, we could postulate that the Dag Rali's greater conservatism and persistence in their traditional ways stemmed from their better endowed and more viable pastoral resource base. With their territory falling predominantly within the Atakor zone, the Dag Rali, more than any other *tawsit*, could at least rely on some annual pasture being available, even during years of minimal rainfall.

Nevertheless, when we compare the Dag Rali and Aguh-en-tehle, we seem to be faced with something of an anomaly, for while their resources, in terms of pasture, accessibility to Tamanrasset, cultivable land and so forth, were comparable,[2] they reflected, within the overall pattern of change in Ahaggar, the two extremes of resistance to and relative acceptance of modernization.

During the critical period 1965–6 – 1968–9, when the nomadic society experienced even more severe deprivations and impediments through the closure of In Eker, the embargo on caravan trade, the continuation of pastoral impoverishment and the final takeover by the Harratin of the gardens that had been formerly cultivated for them on a *khamast* or *aril* system, the Dag Rali's and Aguh-en-tehle's perception of and responses to the alternatives open to them were markedly different. In very general terms the Dag Rali exhibited a greater degree of 'confusion' and lack of cognizance in their perception of the overall situation confronting them, which was manifested in their general resentment and distrust of the administration, their avoidance of Tamanrasset, and their generally more insular and traditionalist response. The Aguh-en-tehle, on the other hand, were less unwilling to sedentarize and cultivate their own gardens, to enter Tamanrasset and send their children to school, and to develop 'economic' relationships with the sedentary community and the newly developed agricultural co-operatives (e.g. Amsel).

However, when we look at the distribution of resources within these two *tawsatin*, we see a noticeable and significant difference. Whereas the four Dag Rali sections are all more or less equally endowed in terms of pastoral resources, cultivable land and so forth, this is not at all the case among the Aguh-en-tehle. The Aguh-en-tehle comprise eight sections, namely the Kel Tarhaouhaout, Kel Twes, Ikenkeren, Kel Tarayin, Kel Azernen (Isandan), Kel Afara-he-hin, Kel Arefsa and the Relaydin.[3] Unlike the Dag Rali sections, the Aguh-en-tehle could be divided into two broad groups: the Kel Azernen and Kel Afara-he-hin (together forming the Isandan) and the Kel Tarayin, whose sub-territories fell within the Atakor and Tarayin zones; and the remaining sections, whose sub-territories extended southwards from the central mountainous area and fell predominantly within the lower Abada zone.[4] While the Abada zone has the best pasture of perennial plants,[5] the rainfall is lower than in Atakor, where annual plants provide the very best fodder. All three zones have their advantages and disadvantages for pastoralism,[6] but in long periods of relative drought, as experienced during the 1960s, it is in the higher Atakor zones, where rainfall is more frequent, that annual fodder is most likely to be found.

Although sections have migratory rights between the various zones, the northernmost Aguh-en-tehle, particularly the Isandan, share more or less identical ecological conditions with the Dag Rali. The Kel Tamanrasset (Dag Rali) and Kel Azernen sections, whose sub-areas are adjacent to each other, have also intermarried.[7] The two sections are thus closely related, both ecologically and affinally, to the extent that the Kel Azernen can be regarded, in terms of their values and attitudes, as being more Dag Rali than Aguh-en-tehle!

The apparent anomaly between the responses of the Aguh-en-tehle and Dag Rali might thus be resolved in terms of these discrete ecological differences between the Agun-en-tehle sections, for the Aguh-en-tehle's greater acceptance of modernization has been manifested predominantly among the southern sections, whereas the response of the more northern Isandan has been similar to that of the Dag Rali. Indeed, the Khalifa of the Kel Azernen section, Ehenu ag Amanrassa, who has married into the Kel Tamanrasset section, was one of the main protagonists of the 'raid' on Otoul.

When we consider the response of the Aguh-en-tehle, not as a uniform group or collective but in terms of these sectional variations, it seems to fit quite satisfactorily into the general ecological–economic explanation – that those groups better endowed with pastoral resources have persisted longer in their traditional ways.

This sort of argument, however, while offering an explanation for the general variation between the responses of the Dag Rali and Aguh-en-tehle to the deprivations and impediments confronting the nomads during this period, does not account satisfactorily for the Aguh-en-tehle's greater awareness of the situation confronting them, particularly in terms of the actions of the Algerian authorities, as opposed to purely 'ecological impediments', and the projected future state.

The explanation, I believe, is to be found in the recognition of another and perhaps more significant variable, namely, the degree of persistence of certain 'relic' or vestigial elements of the traditional *temazlayt* relationship.

I first began to become aware of these elements in Tamanrasset itself. By 1965–6 the population of Kel Ahaggar, consisting mostly of Kel Rela, resident in Tamanrasset was about 100, and several of them had been living there since the mid-1950s. However, what was noticeable during this period, prior to the greater influx of Dag Rali into Tamanrasset around 1969–70, was not only that several Aguh-en-tehle, in contrast to Dag Rali, were entering Tamanrasset quite frequently, but that many of them would visit and even stay the night with certain Kel Rela living in town. In contrast, Dag Rali visited Tamanrasset much less frequently during this period, and when they did they usually stayed in the small house on the edge of town placed at their disposal by the local authorities. It was not for some time that I began to realize that these Aguh-en-tehle visits to Kel Rela were more than just casual social calls but part of a far more complex relationship. In its overt form the relationship was characterized by friendship (I hesitate to use the word 'joking'), relative informality and certain 'economic' transactions. No such relationship appeared to exist between the Dag Rali and Kel Rela. On the contrary, there appeared to be relatively little contact of any kind between them, and their general relationship was characterized by more formal behaviour, bordering at times on 'avoidance' and even occasional hostility.

What was the basis of the relationship between these Aguh-en-tehle and Kel Rela? At the structural level it appeared to be a vestigial element of the traditional *temazlayt* relationship. Although I have found it virtually impossible to collect any reliable data on the composition of former *temazlayt* groups, the way that many individuals explained their relationships led me to believe that they were some sort of remnant or relic feature of the former *temazlayt* relationships. Many of the present relationships seemed to be between members, in the case of some of the older men, or descendants of members of former *temazlayt* groups.

However, unlike the traditional relationship, this relic relationship certainly did not appear to centre around a well-defined group, neither was there any evidence of the continuation of any of the institutionalized rights and obligations associated with the traditional form of the relationship. Indeed, if one was not aware of the traditional *temazlayt* relationship its former existence could hardly have been deduced from this present relationship, which was more 'incidental', occasional and individualistic. Many individuals explained their relationship with various expressions of friendship, saying, for example, that their families had known each other for a long time, or that in the past their camps had often been pitched close together. Although many of these statements implied that their families, or camps, had been related through *temazlayt* ties, the term *temazlayt* was rarely if ever used in these explanations. This lack of reference to the term *temazlayt* raises certain interesting points, focusing perhaps more on my own linguistic limitations, but which nevertheless suggest that the structural relevance of former *temazlayt* groups was more a construct of my own observations and analysis, and of minimal relevance to the individuals involved, at least at the more conscious level.

It was only on discussing the relationship with certain informants with whom I was well acquainted that I was ever able to delve a little deeper into its structural basis and elicit certain details of earlier *temazlayt* involvements. For example, on two or three occasions my visits to Mohammed ag Bubekir[8] coincided with those of two Aguh-en-tehle brothers, Abelgi and Amanrassa ag Ekor. Abelgi, who was eighty-four years old in 1969, was already known to me by name beforehand from the impression he had made on the medical staff in the hospital. The doctor once told me how an extraordinary Tuareg, namely Abelgi, had entered his surgery one day complaining of a headache, and on examining the man he had been confronted with a body, which, in the doctor's own words, 'had been shot through with bullets'! Abelgi's body was certainly a remarkable sight. He had fought in virtually every battle and encounter, on one side or another, from about the time of Tit until the final pacification, during which time he had received six bullet wounds from the French, the scars of which he was only too happy to let me examine. Needless to say, he was one of the finest informants on the detailed history of the many incidents of that period, particularly the Djanet campaigns, where he had received various other wounds (from *takoubas*) fighting alongside Moussa ag Amastane. His younger brother, Amanrassa, who was sixty-five years old, always seemed to be in his attendance, and it always amused me to hear both Mohammed and Abelgi teasing him about being an 'old man' and not being as sprightly as he used to be! Mohammed was particularly affectionate towards the old man, and told me that when he was a boy his family's camp was often pitched close to Abelgi's, for as he stated 'they had a special relationship', which he later qualified with the term *temazlayt*, and that he had always been fascinated by listening to Abelgi recounting the details of these battles.

The actual content of this relationship cannot be described easily. Although certain Kel Rela[9] living in Tamanrasset might be considered 'patrons' in that they held a certain amount of power and influence in the local community and were able to provide various forms of assistance to the nomad, the relationship lacked the institutionalized political symbiosis of the typical patron-client relationship. These Kel Rela encouraged a following, but more with regard to the maintenance of their social status and prestige as nobles than to any real political power.[10]

The concept of 'broker', on the other hand,[11] does provide a more fitting description of the role of the Kel Rela in this relationship. John Perry, in his analysis of local-level brokerage in a rural Lesotho community,[12] recognized five central aspects of brokerage: firstly, that the broker facilitates communication between the peasant and the encapsulating system; secondly, that the broker is a 'fixer'; thirdly, that the broker is a purveyor of information and expertise; fourthly, that the broker exploits his crucial position to enhance his status and achieve power; and, fifthly, that the broker is one of the means by which the local community adapts to the demands of the wider society.

When we look at the Kel Rela living in Tamanrasset we see that most of them fulfilled some of these roles, if not all of them, in varying degrees. But if they saw themselves as 'professional' brokers, we might expect them to have exploited or maximized this role by extending it to as large a clientele as possible. This, however, does not seem to have been the case, for their brokerage was confined largely to their relationship with the Aguh-en-tehle, and in lesser degrees to other *tawsatin*, but minimally, if at all, to the Dag Rali, thus suggesting that its extension was in some way restricted to or limited by the specific structural basis and nature of the relationship that existed between them and the Aguh-en-tehle.

This relationship, while it had its formal, and largely unconscious, structural underpinnings within the *temazlayt* relationship, can be seen to emerge from within the parallel, interstitial or supplementary structure of friendship ties.[13] Within this relationship both types of friendship, 'emotional' and 'instrumental', were operative. The emotional friendship involved a certain sentimental attachment or bond arising from shared past experiences and memories, and may possibly be regarded as an expression of solidarity and a validation of both the traditional order and the necessary transformation of certain aspects of it in the face of the modernizing (Algerian) system.

Instrumental friendship, on the other hand, was manifested in the generalized exchange that characterized the transactional basis of the relationship. The resources of the Kel Rela consisted primarily of their wider network of 'contacts', their greater experience and knowledge of the modernizing system, and their access to relevant information – in short, the resources that enabled them to act as the 'bridgeheads' of the nomadic society in the wider society of Tamanrasset and beyond. The resources of the Aguh-en-tehle, for their part, consisted primarily of the products of, and access to, the nomadic pastoral milieu.

For most Kel Rela living in Tamanrasset, access to the nomadic milieu was important for both commercial, prestigious, and a combination of sentimental, escapist and aesthetic reasons. Although tourism in Ahaggar is increasingly taking the form of package-deal-type, motorized safari tours of varying degrees of sophistication, with a day's camel excursion thrown in somewhere along the way, Tamanrasset has always been the ideal centre[14] for the more energetic and adventurous traveller wanting to organize his own treks and explorations in Ahaggar. Prior to the development of the Syndicat d'Initiative's Tourist Bureau in 1968–9, such travellers, arriving in Tamanrasset and enquiring about the possibilities of hiring camels and guides, would invariably approach, or be introduced or recommended to, certain Kel Rela living in town, who held almost a monopoly over the hiring of camels and guides, for not only were there few other Kel Ahaggar in Tamanrasset but in many cases their reputations were well established through the recommendations of former clients or the experience of Frenchmen who had been stationed in Ahaggar.

However, few of these Kel Rela possessed many camels of their own. Several of them had sold their remaining camels on settling permanently in Tamanrasset, while those who still owned a few could obviously not keep them in Tamanrasset, but tended to leave them in the care of these Aguh-en-tehle. The Kel Rela themselves were therefore rarely able to meet their clients' demands for camels and thus relied heavily on subcontracting both camels and guides, and other necessary equipment such as camel saddles, from the Aguh-en-tehle.

In this particular sphere the relationship between the Kel Rela and Aguh-en-tehle thus assured the Kel Rela of access to the necessary pastoral resources to maintain and develop their prestigious positions within the developing tourist industry in Tamanrasset, while it provided the Aguh-en-tehle with access to, or at least a share in, this relatively lucrative monetary market.

Although it was virtually impossible to ascertain the detailed monetary transactions involved, particularly since most Kel Rela were reluctant to admit their dependence on the Aguh-en-tehle for camels, the benefits to the Aguh-en-tehle were quite considerable. In this respect the Tourist Bureau played a somewhat ambiguous role: it posed, on the one hand, a threat to the Kel Rela's monopoly, but, on the other hand regulation of prices enabled them to increase their rates considerably. The director of the bureau was the vice-President (deputy mayor) of the commune, whose personal commercial interests ramified into most corners of Tamanrasset. Although the intention of the Syndicat was to establish a centralized agency that would regulate the whole haphazard process of hiring camels and guides, as well as other tourist interests, in practice the director exploited his position in the pursuit of his other commercial interests. A fairly common practice was to grant easy credit facilities to those nomads coming into town and visiting his shops, or those of his kinsmen, and then encouraging the nomad to clear his debt by providing camels or acting as a guide for the bureau. Thus, while the individual concerned was indebted, for example, to the amount of fifty dinars, the bureau was charging the tourists concerned at the official rate laid down by the bureau of twenty dinars per camel per day, ten dinars per guide and three dinars per saddle. Not only were there several indications to suggest that such contracts were not officially registered through the bureau, but that the service, not surprisingly since guides were not selected on their professional ability, was far below what the tourist might reasonably expect. Thus, although this practice often cut out the Kel Rela, it enabled them to charge their clients at the official rate.

On one occasion, which illustrates this situation, I had received a letter from friends in the diplomatic corps in Algiers saying that they wanted to spend a week's holiday trekking through Atakor, and asking whether I could arrange camels and guides for them. I asked Beh ag Ahmed, a Kel Rela 'guide' living in Tamanrasset, whether he could arrange the trip. He himself was unable to guide the party as he had already promised his services to a Frenchman and his wife during the same period, but nevertheless guaranteed to provide the six camels and a guide. A few days later Beh brought his chosen guide to meet me, an Aguh-en-tehle called El Litni. However, when Beh and I went to 'register' El Litni at the bureau we were told that six camels were inadequate and that an additional pack camel would be required, and that as one guide could not handle seven camels adequately we would also have to make arrangements for a second cameleer as well as a second pack camel since one pack camel was insufficient for the needs of seven men! The bureau's regulation thus obliged us, quite unnecessarily, to add three more camels and another guide to the party – at an additional cost of seventy-three dinars per day! El Litni arranged for a 'cousin' to provide the additional camels and join the party, and the two men, after five days' jaunt through the mountains, during which time the tourists had provided all their provisions, were paid 1,105 dinars at the bureau's official rate for the hire of camels, guides and saddles.

I was never able to ascertain from Beh what percentage of this payment he had claimed, but believe that he had arranged a 'package deal' with El

Litni, whereby El Litni provided Beh with the camels for his trip with the French couple and took himself whatever proceeds he made from his five-day trek. Although El Litni redistributed this money proportionately among the other Aguh-en-tehle who had provided the camels and saddles for both his and Beh's trips, the sum paid to him was nevertheless a considerable fortune in Ahaggar, sufficient, although such comparisons are meaningless, to maintain an adult male in millet for twelve and a half years![15]

The second dimension of this access to the 'nomadic milieu' was that it provided the Kel Rela with the opportunity for 'weekend nomadism', similar to our 'country weekends'. Kel Rela, desirous to escape from the bustle and urban atmosphere of Tamanrasset, to be with their camels, and to feel the 'freedom' of the camps, would frequently use the opportunity of some errand, such as delivering grain,[16] to spend a day or two in the camps. I remember how, on another occasion, Beh asked me whether I would like to accompany him to the wedding of a Kel Rela girl living amongst the Aguh-en-tehle (Kel Agelella).[17] As the wedding place was two days' ride from Tamanrasset, and as Beh no longer had any camels of his own, he told me that I would have to pay for the hiring of my camel. Our camels were duly provided by an Aguh-en-tehle, whom I paid fifty dinars, and the pair of us set off. With the enthusiasm of a young boy out of school Beh hardly ceased talking, pointing out the minutiae of the landscape and elaborating on a host of recollections of his youth when he was often camped in this part of Ahaggar. We did not follow a direct route, but made a continuous series of deviations as Beh visited almost every Aguh-en-tehle camp and settlement in the area,[18] discussing with them the affairs and news of Tamanrasset and various other snippets of relevant information.

During the two days that we stayed at the wedding Beh remained dignified and aloof, not participating in the camel rides or the *ahal*,[19] which was not surprising as there were only four other senior Kel Rela present in a company of about 300. However, though remaining detached from the public festivities, he spent most of the time being approached by and holding counsel with various Aguh-en-tehle, advising them and discussing certain developments in Tamanrasset.[20]

When we consider the five central aspects of brokerage listed earlier we see that the Kel Rela fulfilled many of them in varying degree, but particularly so in terms of their transmission of information and their facilitation of the Aguh-en-tehle's communication with and understanding of the Algerian order. However, when we consider the Kel Rela as brokers we see that their information was usually given within the context of the broader social relationship, the friendship ties, thus minimizing or reducing the exploitative element of brokerage.

This is apparent when we consider the potentially exploitative position of the Kel Rela vis-à-vis the total nomadic community. Their position in Tamanrasset was in many ways the perfect situation for the professional broker, and one would have expected them to have extended their brokerage to the wider nomadic society. This, however, was not the case, and we must see this role as having grown out of, and being restricted by, the friendship ties that characterized the vestigial *temazlayt* relationship, in which the balance of the exchange was retained by the affective charge of the relationship.

What was the reason for the continuation or development of this relationship between the Kel Rela and Aguh-en-tehle, and not with the Dag Rali? The explanation seems to lie in the possible variations in the specific conditions and processes of disintegration of the *temazlayt* relationship between the Kel Rela and each Kel Ulli *tawsit*.

As we have seen, the internal and external forces operative in Ahaggar during the latter part of the last century and the early part of this century, particularly those generated by the process of pacification, led to a transformation of the relations of dependency between Ihaggaren and Kel Ulli. The Kel Ulli, with their own camels, weapons and so forth, became not only economically independent of the Ihaggaren, but, with the French presence and cessation of raiding, were no longer in need of any form of 'protection'. The Ihaggaren, on the other hand, initially found themselves deprived, not only in terms of the prestige and status acquired as warriors but also in terms of assured access to pastoral resources. As Kel Ulli no longer found justification for the *temazlayt*, so they exercised increasingly their rights of refusal. The balance that had been maintained in former times through the necessary interdependence of the two classes was transformed into a state of imbalance, with the consequent disintegration of the *temazlayt*.

Although we are familiar with this overall situation the almost total lack of reliable source material, both written and oral, relating particularly to the crucial years following pacification prohibits us from commenting on the detailed conditions and processes of this disintegration. Nevertheless, there is no reason to assume that these forces, nor the actual processes of transformation, were either uniform or synchronous among all *tawsatin*. Indeed, if we consider the differential resources of specific groups and areas, the undoubted influence of individual personalities and other idiosyncratic factors, the likelihood of such uniformity is remote.

Thus, although we cannot preclude the possibility that a specific combination of such factors, the details of which are unrecorded and now unknown to us, may have modified the process of disintegration of the *temazlayt* among the Aguh-en-tehle in such a way as to generate or facilitate the emergence of the present relationship,[21] there is an additional consideration, namely their more intense 'joking relationship' with the Kel Rela, which enables us to propose a tentative but more satisfactory form of explanation.

The virtual absence of joking between the Kel Rela and Dag Rali, compared with the intense joking relationship between the Kel Rela and Aguh-en-tehle, may be explained on the grounds that the Dag Rali were commonly regarded as the oldest inhabitant group in Ahaggar – descendants of the Isebeten – compared with the Aguh-en-tehle, who were incorporated into the Kel Rela *ettebel* relatively recently, following their migration into Ahaggar from the In Gal area about two hundred years ago.[22] The Dag Rali's consciousness of this ancestral association with their land rights in Ahaggar seems to have been a relevant factor in the underlying feelings of resentment and antagonism that characterized their rejection of the Kel Rela's *temazlayt* demands. Among the Aguh-en-tehle, however, not only did their subordination to the Kel Rela find justification in this historical reference, but their rejection of the Kel Rela's *temazlayt* demands may have been tempered by their more intense joking relationship – with the result that the more or less complete severance that seems to have characterized the Dag Rali–Kel Rela relationship during this period was avoided, and that some form of social relationship centring around or having its structural underpinnings in the *temazlayt* relationship may have persisted, or at least been more easily activated, in recent times in the form of 'friendship' ties.

The variations in the Dag Rali's and Aguh-en-tehle's perceptions of and responses to the situations confronting them during the 1960s were a reflection of the different stocks of knowledge available to them.

The Aguh-en-tehle's stock of knowledge, through their relationship with the Kel Rela, was not restricted to that of the traditional order, but encompassed and was modified by those cognitions accruing from their relatively closer association with and understanding of the Algerian order. The Dag Rali, on the other hand, without this relationship with the Kel Rela, and the access to and understanding of the Algerian order that it provided, remained relatively isolated and consequently more traditionally orientated in their cognitions of the Algerian order and in their perceptions of and responses to the alternatives open to them.

This suggests that the Kel Rela maintained and accepted the Algerian order, and regarded themselves, or were perhaps regarded, as filling a recognized place within it. We should therefore pause for a moment to reconsider the nature of the Algerian order, particularly its changing definitions and conceptualizations of social reality and a projected future state,[23] as well as the Kel Ahaggar's, especially the Kel Rela's, cognitions of the various phases and dimensions of the imposition of this new order.

For the purposes of analysis it is possible to distinguish two distinct phases of Algerianization,[24] associated with the Ben Bella and Boumedienne governments respectively. Furthermore, the imposition of Algerian socialism and the establishment of a future state involved two dimensions, namely 'replacement' and 'modernization'.

The first phase of Algerian government was characterized by the Algerians' general lack of experience, control and understanding of the region, as well as an absence of any clearly formulated policy as to how the future state would be established, and indeed, even what form this state would take, apart from its having a vaguely defined socialist base. Its policies and actions thus tended to focus, in a piecemeal manner, on the 'replacement', or, in less positive and more realistic terms, on the eradication of the existing order (conceived largely as traditional), or at least those dominant elements of it, such as slavery, *métayage* labour, its land tenure and political systems, that were regarded not only as abhorrent and diametrically opposed to the ideals of the Algerian order but also as impediments to the establishment of such an order.[25] Policy and action were thus essentially negative, and virtually no thought or planning were given to the development and modernization of the region, nor were there any clear conceptions as to how the existing political, economic and social relationships would be restructured.

The second phase, instituted by Boumedienne's coup and Aktouf's appointment to Tamanrasset, was characterized by the government's clearer definition of a projected future state. The previous emphasis on 'replacement' was thus reorientated towards the restructuring of relations and institutions within the framework of a developing and modernizing socialist state, the guidelines for which were laid down in the Ouargla Plan.

These analytical distinctions raise certain fundamental points. Firstly, it can be seen that the replacement process was selective, not being directed towards the existing order in its totality, but to those traditional (and dominant) institutions and relations, such as slavery, that were antithetical to the basic ideals of a socialist order. This leads us to the second and major point, namely that this replacement dimension generated very little change and involved minimal 'restructuring' among the Kel Rela compared with most other Kel Ahaggar, especially the nomads. For most Kel Rela, the 'freeing' of the land was of relatively little consequence, as many of them had already come to a more equitable partnership with their Harratin cultivators, or were in fact cultivating their own garden plots individually and independently. Similarly, many of them were only too glad to be presented with a legitimate means of absolving themselves of their increasingly burdensome obligations to their Iklan.

This is not to imply that the Kel Rela viewed these actions without alarm. On the contrary, the transition to an independent Algerian government and its initial actions were perceived as a dangerous threat to their élitist positions. The removal of the Amenukal from the centre of the political stage and the proposed reconstitution of the entire political system offered new and less ascriptive criteria for entry into the political élite. However, the anxiety of most Kel Rela stemmed not so much from the destruction of the traditional basis of their élitist positions, which was in any case temporarily mitigated by Hadj Moussa's appointment as President of the Special Council and the Amenukal's informal but influential negotiations and compensatory demands, but rather from their inability to conceive the government's intentions with regard to the establishment of a future order in Ahaggar. As several of them told me in later years, they could not understand what the Algerians were intending or planning for Ahaggar – which was in fact a remarkably perceptive assessment of the initial phase of Algerian government! During this initial period there was no clear direction or indication as to what form the new order would take. Algerian policy was orientated towards the eradication of those institutions and relations that were seen to impede the transition to socialism, but the form of this socialism, in terms of the proposed restructuring of these institutions and relations, was left largely to the imagination: liberated slaves were huddled in poverty around Tamanrasset; commune elections were still to be held; and no plan for the future development and modernization of the region had been formulated.

The existing order at the time of independence was characterized, as we have seen, by the growing cleavage between the traditionally orientated and modernizing systems, but their respective élites were fused, somewhat paradoxically, among the Kel Rela. Their positions in Tamanrasset were thus associated primarily with the modernizing structures that were emergent during the initial phases of development in Ahaggar in the previous decade. Their response to the replacement of the traditional order thus amounted to concern for their positions within the 'modernizing élite', which during the first three years of independence were still assured through the continued operation of In Eker and the overall economic depression in Ahaggar. Consequently, the second phase of Algerianization, although more stringent in its replacement policies, was characterized by a clear committal to the development and modernization of the region – an ideal with which the Kel Rela were able to comply and associate themselves more readily. Indeed, in this dimension, the Algerian order, particularly when its projection was more clearly defined and conceived, was not at odds with the modernizing value system that the Kel Rela had already accepted.

This analysis of the Kel Rela introduces a critical dimension into our discussion of such questions as 'the future of the Tuareg' or their 'integration' into the national state, and so forth, for in asking such questions, which are perhaps our dominant concern, we are not talking about the 'integration of an ethnic minority' as a culturally homogeneous group – 'the Tuareg' – but about two quite distinct sub-societies – namely, the urbanized Kel Rela and the nomads.

In the case of the Kel Rela, several of them were already living in or were in the process of establishing themselves in Tamanrasset before independence, and could be considered as 'urbanized' or as 'becoming urbanized'. This process, as we have seen, was a response to two main forces: the increasing difficulty of maintaining themselves in a nomadic-pastoral way of life and, of greater importance, their perception of the threat posed to their pre-eminent social status during the 1950s by the increasing affluence and upward social mobility of their 'dependent classes'. We can thus see that their settlement in Tamanrasset was largely a response to forces generated within the existing order, and not a consequence of coercive policies by the Algerian authorities. Moreover, whereas their entry into the modernizing élite of the existing order had relied predominantly on their ascriptive qualities as Kel Rela, the emphasis of the new order was on achievement. But in this respect the Kel Rela's experience and manipulation of the modernizing structures during the previous decade or so, especially in their positions at In Eker, placed them in a particularly advantageous position, for not only did it provide them with the necessary experience, skills and training to enter the middle levels of the local Algerian 'bureaucratic' élite, in such positions as secretaries in the Mairie, members of the Bureau Politique, foremen of municipality work gangs, and so forth,[26] but it also provided them with the legitimation of their maintenance and acceptance of the new order.

This second aspect is of particular importance, for by seeing themselves or being able to legitimize their positions as 'townsmen', as distinct from 'nomads', in accordance with the ideas and definitions of social reality of the new order, they were in a sense already 'inserted', or provided with a 'place', in the wider society of the national state.

The introduction of the terms 'townsman' (or more specifically 'sedentarist') and 'nomad' in this context touches the heart of the problem of the present transformation, integration, destruction, ruination or whatever will become of the Ahaggar Tuareg within the next generation or so. For in the new Algerian order, the notions of 'sedentarism' and 'nomadism' embody more than a mere categorization and description of 'residency' and a 'way of life'. They are impregnated with political connotations that express the basic ideas and ideology underlying and motivating many of the actions and policies of the Algerian administration in Ahaggar.

In universal terms nomads comprise an ethnic minority marginal or peripheral to the larger settled population of a state. Although their sedentarization may be a natural or spontaneous process resulting from forces generated within their own society, it stems more frequently from the coercion of external forces or the interaction of external and internal forces. In any event, sedentarization usually leads to or is purposefully directed towards their 'integration' and loss of specific ethnic identity within the overall structure of the total national society.

In Ahaggar, government policy towards the nomads has been to coercively encourage their sedentarization and their integration within the structure of the Algerian state. However, for the Algerian administration in Ahaggar, 'nomadism' and 'pastoralism' were synonymous. Nomads are not necessarily pastoralists; neither, of course, are pastoralists necessarily nomadic. But, for the Algerians, 'nomadism' symbolized the domination of the Imuhag.

The replacement or removal of the existing order was thus directed specifically against those institutions and relationships that maintained the political and economic domination of the Imuhag – in short, it aimed at the destruction and denigration, both active and symbolic, of nomadism and the nomadic society. Furthermore, nomadism was also regarded as an impediment to modernization. On the one hand it was seen in somewhat subjective evolutionary terms as 'primitive', 'archaic', the antithesis of modernity, and so forth, in comparison with agriculture. On the other hand, and of greater significance, was the justified belief that as long as the nomads held any vestige of political power and prestige over their former dependants, the latter's entry and integration into a socialist and modernizing state would be retarded.

It was considered that the orientation of a sedentarization policy towards any form of stock-breeding, or towards the maintenance of any of the nomads' traditional pastoral activities, would grant recognition to the nomads' real and symbolic prestige and power over the agriculturalists. The perpetuation and recognition of nomadism through any such policy would have given validation to the traditional order, and would have created the conditions, in spite of the 'freeing of all land' and the restructuring of the social relations of production, in which the nomads could have re-established, through more indirect and subtle means, their economic and political supremacy. It was for these political reasons that the government's sedentarization policy has been directed specifically towards agriculture, to the exclusion of any form of stock-breeding, the potentialities for which are naturally considerable in a region in which pastoralism has traditionally been the dominant economic activity.

The actual sedentarization or 'semi-sedentarization' of nomads during this period has been a response to the interaction of both internal forces, generated primarily by pastoral impoverishment, and coercive action on the part of the Algerian administration. Although we can speculate on how effective such coercion might have been had the decade been one of abundant pasture, we must also realize that 'drought' conditions are part of the Kel Ahaggar's experience and something to which traditional society was adapted. It is therefore not surprising that they perceived the impediments confronting the continuation of their traditional ways as stemming directly from the actions of the Algerian administration. This, of course, was true in the case of the 'liberation of the slaves', the 'freeing' of the land and the subsequent takeover of their *foggaras*, but among several nomads, such as the Dag Rali, the embargo on caravan trade, the closure of In Eker, and at times even the dearth of good rains, were seen as further reprisal actions against them!

The Kel Rela's and nomads' cognitions of the Algerian order were consequently quite different. The Kel Rela's perception of the different phases and dimensions of Algerianization, and their fairly clear and rationally conceived idea of the future, were not shared by most nomads. On the contrary, the shifts in emphasis and direction of policy following Aktouf's appointment to Tamanrasset were to them merely an intensification of the same thing, the only change being one from bad to worse!

As the obstacles to the continuation of the nomadic society's traditional ways mounted, so sedentarization became the most 'rational' and more singular alternative course of action open to them. Sedentarization, however, is not an instantaneous or 'all-or-nothing' process, but tends to be characterized by various stages of 'semi-sedentarization' – stages which are not necessarily defined etymologically in simple geographical, residential or economic terms, but primarily in terms of changing cognitions and perspectives. For sedentarization to be complete or final, the legitimation of the nomad's actions must be confirmed and validated in terms of the ideas and assumptions held by the sedentary society's definition of social reality.

In Ahaggar this reality is that of the Algerian state. Thus, for a nomad to become a sedentarist he must accept and maintain the Algerian order. However, the Dag Rali's perception of this order was limited, being based almost solely on their experience of its 'anti-nomad' policies and actions (seen more as 'anti-Tuareg'). Their persistence in their traditional ways throughout most of this period was thus an attempt to confirm and validate their traditional stock of knowledge and the legitimation of the traditional institutional order.

Within this cognitive framework sedentarization could not be conceived as anything but a partial and reversible process, for otherwise it would merely have resulted in a total disconfirmation of their existing ideas and definitions of social reality. Most nomads, although they sedentarized during this period, could therefore not be regarded as 'sedentarists'; for their settlement, although it took on an air of permanency, did not imply an acceptance of the Algerian order, but was legitimized in terms of the ideas and assumptions of the traditional order, expressed in such statements as 'until the rains come', and manifested, through their attempts to reaffirm and validate their traditional socio-cultural values and traditionally orientated definition of social reality, in their regrouping and encapsulation as a 'sub-society' within the wider sedentary community.

Terhenanet and Tagmart, being exclusively Dag Rali, were extreme and atypical examples of this process. At Hirafok, however, the 'nomads' were grouped in five houses at the extreme eastern end of the village, with their networks extending not so much into the village but predominantly outwards to the nomadic camps of kinsmen and other *tawsit* members. Similarly, in Tamanrasset, the large-scale incursion of nomads into the town since 1968–9 has resulted in a predominantly Dag Rali 'ghetto' being formed in the Tahaggart quarter (village) at the northern end of the town.

Most Aguh-en-tehle,[27] on the other hand, maintained a definition of social reality which, through their relationship with the Kel Rela, was founded on a broader and more objective perspective of both their own situation and the policies of the Algerian administration, and which to some extent shared the Kel Rela's clearer and more rationally conceived idea of the future. This was manifested most clearly in their attitude towards schooling, and particularly in their relations with the sedentary society as a whole.

Not only did Aguh-en-tehle children comprise 40 per cent of the Kel Ahaggar children in the Tamanrasset boarding-house in 1969 (see Fig. 8),[28] but some of their children had been attending school each year since independence. Their relations with the sedentary community were in marked contrast to those of the Dag Rali, particularly at Abalessa, where the Dag Rali have been effectively driven out of the area.[29] Furthermore, Abalessa's prolonged conflict with the Dag Rali made it the most politicized community outside Tamanrasset. Not only did the Party receive strong support in the area,[30] but, as one local official commented, the population of Abalessa was 'la plus sédentaire', as manifested in their adherence to and dependency on agriculture[31] and their rejection, both symbolically and pragmatically, of any association with the nomadic–pastoral milieu. Several cultivation centres, using their own few camels, but usually hiring additional camels and men from the surrounding nomads, had been involved for some years in the caravan trade to Damergou. This was particularly true of Abalessa, but in 1969, when the embargo was lifted, the people of Abalessa demonstrated their political autonomy and their disdain for and independence from the Kel Ahaggar and 'pastoralism' by taking no part whatsoever in the reopened caravan trade.[32]

The pattern of 'semi-sedentarization' among the Aguh-en-tehle during the early and mid-1960s, especially at such centres as Tahifet, In Dalag and Tarhaouhaout, was similar to that among the Dag Rali in such centres as Hirafok, in that the nomads tended to form their own little residential and social nuclei or 'quarters' within the village, with their social and economic ties ranging outwards to the surrounding camps of their *tawsit* section rather than inwards to the village community itself. However, each cultivation centre, as we have seen, has its own peculiarities, arising from historical legacies, geographical factors and such like, so that such generalized comparisons may be dangerously misleading. At Tahifet, for example, the cultivable land is restricted to a series of little 'basins' and sections of terrace strung out among the margins of the *oued*. There is consequently no nucleated village settlement, but rather a chain of little settlement clusters interspersed over several kilometres along the *oued*.[33] New settlement, concentrating predominantly on hitherto unexploited 'basins' or terrace sections, has thus extended this ribbon development of fairly discrete and self-contained communities.[34]

Figure 8 Census of boarders, 1969–70.

| 'Tribe'/Origin | School Year 1 | 2 | 3 | 4 | 5 | 6 | 7 | CEG | Total |
|---|---|---|---|---|---|---|---|---|---|
| 1. Kel Rela | 2 | | 1 | | | | | 1 | 4 |
| 2. Dag Rali | | 9 | | | | | | | 9 |
| 3. Ait Lowayen | 1 | 1 | 3 | 2 | | | | | 7 |
| 4. Aguh-en-tehle | | 5 | 7 | 1 | 1 | 2 | 4 | | 20 |
| 5. Iklan Tawsit | | | 2 | 4 | | | | | 6 |
| 6. Kel Ahnet | 1 | 1 | | | | | | | 2 |
| 7. Isekkemaren | | | | | | | 1 | 1 | } |
| Kel Tazulet | | | | 1 | | | | | } 4 |
| Kel Inrar | | 1 | | | | | | | } |
| 8. Taitok | | 1 | | | | | | | 1 |
| 9. Irregenaten | 4 | 1 | | | | 1 | | | 6 |
| 10. Kel Adrar (Mali) | | | 1 | 1 | | | | | 2 |
| 13. Kel Rezzi | | | | | 1 | 1 | | 2 | } |
| Ahl Azzi | | | | 1 | | | | 2 | } 9 |
| Kel Titi | | | 1 | 1 | | | | | } |
| 11. Iklan | 4 | 5 | 6 | 4 | 1 | | | | 20 |
| 12. Harratin | 2 | 4 | 1 | 7 | | | 3 | 6 | 23 |
| 14. Chaamba | 1 | | | 1 | | | | | 2 |
| 15. Mohala | 1 | | | | | | | | 1 |
| 16. Tamesna | | 1 | | | 1 | | | | 2 |
| 17. Timaiouine | | 1 | | | | | 1 | | 2 |
| 18. Djanet | | 1 | | | | | | | 1 |
| 19. Tin Zaouaten | | 2 | | 1 | | | | | 3 |
| 20. Arab | | 1 | | | 2 | | | | 3 |
| 21. Libya | | | | | 1 | | | | 1 |
| 22. Mertoutek | 3 | | | | | | | | 3 |
| | 16 | 37 | 22 | 24 | 7 | 4 | 9 | 12 | 131 |

In spite of such difficulties in comparing cultivation centres, Amsel shares certain similarities with Abalessa, in that although much smaller than Abalessa[35] it is the administration's 'pilot' co-operative scheme, and is therefore a modernizing and politically aware community that is kept under the watchful eye of the administration. The relationship between

Amsel and the surrounding nomads (Aguh-en-tehle and Tegehe-n-Efis) illustrates the nature of the socio-economic ties that have been maintained and are developing between them. The restructuring of the social relations of production between the Aguh-en-tehle (and Tegehe-n-Efis) and their former cultivators, particularly at Amsel,[36] has shown, in contrast to the situation between the Dag Rali and their former cultivators at Abalessa, a relative lack of conflict and hostility – a factor which seems to have owed much to the Aguh-en-tehle's awareness of the direction and inevitability of change, and their less traditionally orientated definition of social reality. Indeed, the ties that have developed between Amsel and the surrounding nomads may be regarded as the logical and unfettered expression of two complementary economic activities – agriculture and pastoralism.

Whereas the population of Abalessa had dissociated itself completely from the caravan trade and all other associations with nomadism after their conflict with the Dag Rali, the co-operation between nomads and villagers at Amsel in various forms of caravan trade not only continued throughout this period, but appears to have become an increasingly profitable venture for both parties. During the three years when caravans were embargoed, sedentary cultivators in the village, using their own few camels and others hired from the Aguh-en-tehle and Tegehe-n-Efis, had been operating clandestine caravans in partnership with the nomads. In April 1968 a small caravan returned to Amsel with a moderate amount of millet[37] without having been intercepted. After two weeks the same men (mostly Tegehe-n-Efis hired by the cultivators) left for Amadror and returned thirty days later loaded with salt, a small amount of which was sold in Tamanrasset and the rest stockpiled in the village to await the autumn caravans south, regardless of whether or not the embargo was still in force.

A further dimension of this co-operation, which I had suspected but which had always been concealed from me, was revealed quite by chance, when I came across a single Tegehe-n-Efis man about thirty kilometres south of Amsel. He had with him one riding camel, two loaded pack camels and two unladen young camels, and said that he was on his way to Tin Zaouaten (fifteen days' ride) to collect some goats, but was particularly vague about any further details of his mission. We camped together for the night, and my suspicions were confirmed when, on helping him offload the pack camels, I saw that they were carrying in the order of 200 kilos of wheat. Further investigations confirmed that the Tegehe-n-Efis man was just one of several other Tegehe-n-Efis and Aguh-en-tehle who were engaged in such 'business enterprises' with the Amsel co-operative. The President of the co-operative, Mohammed, although a Harratin, had affinal ties with the Aguh-en-tehle[38] and encouraged economic co-operation with them, which in this case involved trading wheat produced by the co-operative for goats from the Tin Zaouaten area. Nomads carried the wheat south and bartered it for goats, which in view of the relatively good pasture in the Tin Zaouaten area[39] were relatively abundant. The goats were then trekked back to Amsel and sold on the Tamanrasset market, where they were in short supply due to pastoral impoverishment in Ahaggar, and the considerable profit on the initial price of the wheat was divided between the nomads and the members of the co-operative. However, most of the individuals concerned were reluctant to admit the existence, let alone the details, of this irregular form of economic enterprise, and I do not know whether the authorities were unaware of it, or merely turned a blind eye, for as Amsel is exhibited as the example of successful co-operative development in Ahaggar, the means of its relative affluence and viability are hardly a matter for scrupulous investigation!

Perhaps, ironically, this developing relationship with the sedentary community, while facilitating their integration into the wider society, has provided the Aguh-en-tehle (and Tegehe-n-Efis) with a limited degree of viability in being able to maintain themselves longer in a more nomadic way of life. Thus, while the Dag Rali were favoured by their relatively better pastoral resources and such other small benefits as the presence of the Frères and the tourist traffic at Assekrem, it may be suggested that the Aguh-en-tehle have been able to maintain some semblance of their traditional way of life through the exploitation of their network of relationships with the Kel Rela in Tamanrasset and the developing cultivation centres such as Amsel.

# SEVENTEEN
# PROBLEMS OF INTEGRATION

There are those who come to Ahaggar to immerse themselves in a 'Tuareg culture', to escape from the pressures of civilization in London, Paris, Frankfurt or wherever, and to search, as if on a pilgrimage, for their ancestral heritage – to experience, temporarily and impossibly, a philosophy and way of life that has been destroyed and denied them – the 'freedom', 'tranquillity' and 'naturalness' of nomadism. The trappings and symbols of civilization, except those that ease the process of immersion (the sunglasses, Ambre Solaire, Entero-vioform, and wrist-watch – and of course the camera, which provides the 'proof' of experience), are discarded self-consciously for the blue gandora, chech and sandals, which, like Polynesian grass skirts, have no meaning outside the tourist culture of Tamanrasset, and which only facilitate the escape into self-delusion, only to meet with the disillusionment of reality. For there are no war-lords of the Sahara, no vassals, only people to whom no homage need be paid – for who are the 'Tuareg'?

There is Assekrem (reoccupied in 1955!), the other peaks of Ahaggar, the tomb of Tin Hinan, some cave-paintings,[1] the bric-à-brac of Tamanrasset, the camels (mostly at the slaughter-house), and 'les soirées folkloriques'. There is no escape, no freedom and tranquillity of 'nomadism' – it must be imagined within the tourist culture and modernity of Tamanrasset.

In Algeria the 'noble savage' is not venerated. The Tuareg have been saved the fate of being cast as museum specimens and placed in a reserve to satisfy the indulgences of tourist cameras and the vanity, consciences and frustrations of their operators, and where their society, cut off from its own dynamism, would only stagnate and die. Ahaggar and its peoples are part of Algeria, in which there is fortunately no place for such museums and reserves.

What then is the future of the Tuareg, and what place will they come to fill within this new state? Prediction is of course dangerous, but since such questions focus primarily on future government policy towards the nomads, particularly their sedentarization, it is only reasonable that we consider, by way of recommendation, how the present policy must necessarily be modified if the nomads are to be successfully integrated, without the total loss and destruction of their cultural and ethnic specificity, and if the inherent development potential of the region and its peoples is to be realized.

The nomads are an ethnic minority in Ahaggar. If their integration into the wider society is to be successful there must first of all be a place for them in that society into which they can be inserted, and in which their ethnic and cultural identity, defined and symbolized as it is in terms of pastoralism, can be accommodated.[2] As long as the government's sedentarization policy is orientated directly towards agriculture, their integration, I believe, will be a long, painful and largely unsuccessful process, for agriculture does not and cannot provide this necessary place and level of insertion.

The social division of labour in Ahaggar, in its broadest perspective, has always been characterized by a division between sedentary cultivators and nomadic pastoralists, between the Izeggaren or Kel Arrem and the Imuhag. This division, in spite of the changing social relations of production over the last decade or two, is still very much a fact – a reality of Ahaggar which cannot be dismissed, and which must be recognized and incorporated in any future sedentarization and development policy.

When nomads despise agriculture as the most menial form of work, and when they know almost nothing of its techniques and methods, the progressive implementation of the present sedentarization policy, orientated as it is towards agriculture, will merely reduce them to a state of dependent marginality.[3] Furthermore, if the transition from nomadic pastoralist to sedentary agriculturalist, as envisaged by the government, is to be complete, it must necessarily entail the abandonment of any form of pastoralism. But in a society in which pastoralism is the dominant ideology, whose social structure and organization are adapted to its demands, and whose cultural and ethnic specificity is defined and expressed primarily in pastoral terms, such an abandonment will not be accomplished readily and without resistance.

We can thus see the dual problem posed by this form of sedentarization policy. On the one hand the nomads find themselves rejected by the wider society, while on the other hand the final outcome of such a policy, if taken to its logical conclusion, will be the total disintegration and destruction of nomadic society – a process which would be resisted in all its phases.

However, this end cannot be attained. Nomads may sedentarize in the purely geographical and residential sense, as they are tending to do, but they will not abandon pastoralism voluntarily. Neither does it seem even remotely possible that the government can bring about such an abandonment by coercive means. The transition cannot be complete. The Dag Rali at Tagmart, Terhenanet, Hirafok, and Tahaggart are not sedentarists in the government's meaning of the term. They are living in these centres for the time being, and may continue to do so, but they are largely excluded from the wider society, and have clustered in encapsulated ghetto-like communities (viz. Tahaggart) from which they view the wider society with a predominantly nomadic perspective.

Here, particularly in Tahaggart, is the clue to our problem. The increased incursion of nomads into Tamanrasset, particularly in the years after 1968–9, their relative acceptance of the boarding-school, the Algerian administration and so forth may be seen as a considerable change in their attitudes, but it is not a change that has led to their successful integration. On the contrary, the settlement of nomads in Tahaggart has been characterized by their encapsulation, and to suggest that this may be otherwise, at least in the forseeable future, is, I believe, to overlook the fundamental nature of this process and its relevance to pastoralism.[4]

The growth of Tahaggart as a nomadic community on the periphery of Tamanrasset was primarily the consequence of the nomads' demands for wage labour and their associated oscillatory drift towards Tamanrasset. This is particularly significant, for wage labour is perceived by the nomads not so much as a 'change' but as an extension of nomadic pastoralism. When we look back to the initial signing on of nomads at In Eker, we see that it was primarily in response to adverse changes in the traditional nomadic-pastoral economy.[5] After independence, In Eker became accepted as almost a part of the nomads' 'traditional way of life' and, with progressive pastoral impoverishment and the intensification of the government's coercive action against nomadism, they became increasingly dependent on its wages to supplement pastoralism. After the closure of In Eker, the demand for wage labour was a response to the intensification of these same forces. Throughout this period wage labour has been perceived by the nomads as the primary means of supplementing pastoralism, as almost a modern-day substitute for raiding as a means of overcoming pastoral impoverishment.

Wage labour, unlike agriculture, does not involve any long-term commitment; its return is almost 'instantaneous'. Neither does it involve any modification or disruption of social and domestic organization, since the absence of men is accommodated in the same way as in former times, when they were away raiding or on caravan. Of crucial significance, however, is the fact that wage-earning enables the nomads to remain relatively independent of agriculture and free of any association, either in practice or symbolically, with the sedentary agricultural society. The settlement of Dag Rali in Tahaggart (and other centres) must be seen in this context. It is perceived in terms of its short-term advantages, and legitimized in terms of the traditional order: it is not only compatible with nomadic pastoralism but essential for its maintenance. The settlement in Tahaggart, although largely a response to the consequences of the government's sedentarization policy, has not made them 'sedentarists', neither will it lead, as we are witnessing, to their successful integration.

This, I believe, is also the case of the most 'modernized' and 'outward-looking' Dag Rali, such as Elwafil, a young man of thirty, who, at first glance, has all the appearance of an agriculturalist, since he has been living and cultivating his own gardens in Hirafok for some years now.

After his father died, when he was barely in his teens, Elwafil continued to live with his mother, three younger sisters and younger brother in the camps of his father's patrilineal kinsmen. With a sense of responsibility towards his younger brother and sisters, and influenced by the Frères at Assekrem, with whom he spent much of his time, and from whom he learnt a reasonable conversational French, he was one of the first Dag Rali to sign on at In Eker. With the closure of the base, and the progressive pastoral impoverishment, he realized that there was little alternative but to cultivate his own land, and around 1966 he settled in Hirafok with his mother and the rest of her children. The goats remained in the camps, tended by one or other of his sisters, while Elwafil worked his own gardens, but always with one eye open for any opportunity for employment, either on the *chantiers* or as a guide/interpreter for tourists.[6]

By 1971 Elwafil had been cultivating his own gardens for about four years. To all intents and purposes he could be regarded as an agriculturalist. At Hirafok, as he explained, 'there is water and good soil, and crops can be guaranteed'. But such statements are merely the expression of his pragmatism. As he continues to talk and justify his existence in Hirafok, his innermost feelings and values – his 'nomadism' – reveal themselves.

> It is many years since there were good rains in Ahaggar. The pasture and the goats are dying. In the past, when there were rains there was pasture – the grass

sprang up. There was *asefar*,[7] *adreilal*,[8] *alkah*,[9] *tamaghé*,[10] *aferhaler*[11] . . . Now there are none of these. There is no *aramas*,[12] there is no rain, the *afezou*[13] is dried up . . . They are all dry.

While such conditions last it is better to live in a house. There is water at Hirafok, and the gardens are reliable. But the work of the Imuhag, above all the Dag Rali, is with camels. If there were camels I'd go on caravans rather than work in the gardens. When there were camels in the camps they went to Amadror to mine salt and then to the Sudan to get millet . . . but now there is very little . . . and then return again to Amadror.[14] If they had guns they killed *mouflon*, for there was always a lot of hunting of *mouflon* and gazelles in the mountains . . . But I prefer to live in the camps, in Ahaggar – at Assekrem. The house is good, but only while such conditions last.

Elwafil probably spends as much time away from Hirafok, mostly in the Assekrem area, as he spends in the village. Most of his kinsmen are still camped in the Assekrem area, and his goats are kept in their camps, but even though he considers that cultivation is a necessity under the prevailing conditions, he prefers working on the *chantiers*, not merely for the money, but because such work is, in his own terms, more suitable for Imuhag than working in the gardens!

This comment, while expressing the traditional division of labour, refers particularly to his own relationship with an Izeggar named Amin. Amin was 'freed' from slavery[15] in the 1950s, and after working on a *chantier* for the French at Ideles, and then at In Eker, returned to settle and cultivate his own gardens in Hirafok. 'Before,' as Elwafil explained, 'he was an Akli, but is now an Izeggar, owning his own land, tools and water – an *elelli* [free man] – like a noble by birth'!

The first time I saw Amin was in Elwafil's garden. When I asked Elwafil who he was, and what he was doing, he replied with an aloofness, designed obviously for my impression, 'You know the Izeggaren. He is just an Izeggar. He puts in the hard work, the physical effort'! From the little that Elwafil told me about his relationship with Amin, I gathered that Amin occasionally helped him in his gardens, particularly with the heavier work and in keeping a general eye on them when Elwafil was away, in exchange for a small share in the harvest, money or certain pastoral products, depending on Elwafil's circumstances at the time.

This particular relationship, as in the case of many others of its kind, was based on a certain sentimentality and friendship derived from earlier associations at In Eker, former bonds of slavery, and so forth, as well as on their perception of the economic benefits to be derived from co-operation and exchange between the agricultural and pastoral spheres; it was primarily an expression of the mutual recognition and complementarity of their respective spheres of specialization and competency.

The significance of this relationship is twofold. Firstly, one sees in it the latent possibility of the Imuhag's re-establishment of their political and economic dominance, albeit through more indirect and subtle means. When pasture regenerates, Elwafil and other nomads, who have been cultivating their own gardens and who have established such relationships with Izeggaren, are more than likely to abandon them in favour of pastoralism, leaving them perhaps in the care of such cultivators as Amin, in exchange for some form of payment in kind – either a share in the harvest or access to pastoral products. Secondly, and of greater significance, is the fact that we are seeing in this relationship the basis of the nomads' acceptability, and their possible level of insertion within the wider society. The basis of co-operation between Elwafil and Amin, as in the relationship between the Aguh-en-tehle, the Tegehe-n-Efis and their former cultivators, is the complementarity of agriculture and pastoralism.

This is also true in the case of the relationship that seems to be developing between several Dag Rali (and other nomads) and their ex-slaves. Several 'liberated' Dag Rali slaves, most noticeably those who have settled in the Ideles area, were beginning in the late 1960s to give small gifts of garden produce to their former masters, which were usually reciprocated with equally small gifts of pastoral produce. Amongst many of these ex-slaves there was a definite desire to re-establish and maintain certain bonds with their former masters. Several female slaves, especially the elder ones, actually remained with their masters after their 'liberation', so that one or two ex-slaves are still to be found in many of the camps. In one such case, which was by no means atypical, an ex-slave by the name of Nati, who was now cultivating his own gardens independently at Ideles, frequently visited his elderly mother who had remained with her master, and spent much time in the camp helping generally with the routine tasks of camp life, and maintaining the same fictive kinship ties that characterized his former slavery. Although the social and sentimental basis of these relationships is usually very strong, it appears that their economic basis is becoming increasingly significant. As with the relationship between Elwafil and Amin, and the Aguh-en-tehle and the population of Amsel, there is a mutual recognition of the complementarity of agriculture and pastoralism, and the benefits to be derived through exchange and co-operation between the two spheres.

The common element in all these relationships is the sedentarist's acceptance and recognition of pastoralism, and we may suggest that the nomads' place in the wider national society lies in the recognition, maintenance and development of pastoralism, for it is pastoralism, not wage labour or agriculture, that provides the necessary place and level of insertion that can ultimately lead to their successful integration.

Pastoralism does not imply nomadism, neither is it incompatible with sedentarization. Indeed, when we consider the 'nomadism' of the Imuhag in former times we can see that it involved little more than an annual movement between the goat camps, which were relatively static for most of the time, and their gardens.

The problem arises when sedentarization is equated with agriculture. If the nomads are to be provided with a place in the wider society, then the present sedentarization policy must be abandoned in favour of one that recognizes the complementarity of pastoralism and agriculture, as well as the fact that sedentarization does not necessarily entail the transformation from pastoral stock-breeding to agriculture. Such a policy must be orientated towards the development of the nomads' dominant ethnic and cultural characteristic, pastoralism, which is the basis of their acceptability.

Such a policy would also realize the full development potential of the region and its peoples. The United Nations Development Programme (U.N.D.P.) feasibility survey of the proposed trans-Saharan highway, carried out in the later 1960s, advocated the development of cattle ranching in the region between In Eker and Tamanrasset, while the idea of sinking bore-holes in the zone between Tin Zaouaten and Timaiouine, to settle the nomads on the basis of some sort of 'pastoral co-operative' along the Algerian side of the frontier, has been aired on several occasions.

How such schemes would be implemented and developed within the framework of the government's socialist policy is another matter. Whereas land can only be a means of production, livestock, on the other hand, as Bourgeot has noted,[16] fulfil two functions simultaneously both as a means of production and as consumable assets. The development of any form of 'pastoral collective' or 'co-operative', unlike that of agricultural co-operatives, faces the problem posed by the contradiction between the need to maintain individual ownership of livestock as consumable assets and the necessary socialization of the means of production.

However this problem is resolved, the development of any such scheme would necessarily entail a shift towards a more regulated movement of livestock within more clearly defined limits, which would in itself stimulate the process of semi-sedentarization and so facilitate the introduction of modern stock-breeding methods, and the more efficient and profitable utilization of both natural and human resources.

The conditions of this transformation must not be imposed coercively, or with the same bureaucratic rigidity that has hitherto characterized the enactment of most government policies. The development of any such scheme, and the transformations that it entails, must be agreed upon through consultation with the nomads, with the initiative coming as far as possible from the nomads themselves, so that some element of self-determination is retained; while all regulations and limitations on live-stock movements and other practices must be sufficiently flexible to accommodate climatic vagaries and other ecological and social constraints.

This overall change from extensive to intensive stock-breeding would destroy the traditional basis of 'Tuareg' society. At the same time, however, it would enable the development of a 'culture' which although new in content was traditional in form, retaining the specificity of nomadic society and facilitating the integration of the nomads into the wider national society that is Algeria – but without their encapsulation and reduction to marginality and, *ipso facto*, their deculturation.

# NOTES

**Introduction**

1. Ahaggar in Tamahak (the language of the Kel Ahaggar); Hoggar in Arabic.
2. Commonly (but incorrectly) referred to as *mouflon*.
3. 'Kel': 'people of'. Kel Ahaggar: people of Ahaggar.
4. Tioueyin was located near the Tefedest massif to the north of Atakor.
5. Quoted by Georg Gerster, *Sahara*, trans. Stewart Thomson, London, 1960, p. 135.
6. Each day goats, in the care of women, leave the camp to graze systematically and water at *gueltas* before returning to the camp at dusk.
7. Nicolaisen, J., *Ecology and Culture of the Pastoral Tuareg*, the National Museum of Copenhagen, 1963, p. 7.
8. Lhote, Henri, *Les Touaregs du Hoggar*, 2nd ed., Paris, 1955, p. 157.
9. Nicolaisen, op. cit., p. 8.
10. Duveyrier, Henri, *Les Touareg du nord*, Paris, 1864, p. 318.
11. See Bourgeot, A., 'Le Contenu sociologique de l'appellation Twareg (Kel Ahaggar): histoire d'un nom', *Revue de l'Occident Musulman et de la Méditerranée.*
12. By 1973–4 the population of Tamanrasset could be estimated as approaching 10,000.
13. During the last two decades, for example (with the exception of certain papers), only two books of academic merit have been published on the Tuareg: Johannes Nicolaisen's *Ecology and Culture of the Pastoral Tuareg* (1963), and Marceau Gast's *Alimentation des populations de l'Ahaggar* (1968). Although both these books are specialist studies, neither are deeply concerned with the history of the Tuareg or the radical changes that are currently taking place in Ahaggar.
14. The Tuareg of the Tassili-n-Ajjer to the east-north-east of Ahaggar.
15. Rodd, Francis Rennell, *People of the Veil*, London, 1926.
16. The Tuareg have no written language, and consequently no written records of their own. A script, known as Tifinagh, exists but is used very limitedly.
17. The term *tawsit*, according to Nicolaisen (op. cit., p. 140), means literally 'a hand root from which fingers issue', which may symbolize some sort of lineage structure. Charles de Foucauld, *Dictionnaire Touareg-Française, dialecte de L'Ahaggar*, I–IV, Paris, 1951–2; III, p. 1533, writes that *tawsit* is 'a mat plaited from afezu grass'. He also states that *tawsit* is synonymous with the term *arref*, but this is not so, for the latter term has the more general meaning of 'people' or 'race'. While

they have been referred to commonly as 'tribes' or 'clans' in most of the literature, they may be described at the most general level as preferentially endogamous, territorially compact, matrilineal descent groups, although as we shall see later their organization, in terms of endogamy and matrilineality, needs closer examination (see Ch. 7).

18. Most Taitok settled in Niger after their expulsion from Ahaggar earlier in this century. By 1971 it was estimated that only about thirty Taitok were living in Ahaggar, although the recent drought conditions in the Sahel have led several of them to return once more to Ahaggar.
19. On the basis of the 1949 census, the Kel Ahaggar (excluding slaves) numbered 4,284: 341 Ihaggaren, 2,423 Kel Ulli and 1,520 Isekkemaren. In traditional times, when the Taitok and Tegehe Mellet were more significant, the proportion of Ihaggaren was probably a little higher (see Appendix I).
20. Terray, E., *Classes and Class Consciousness in the Abron Kingdom of Gyaman*, in Bloch, M. (ed.), *Marxist Analyses and Social Anthropology*, 1975, p. 86.
21. Ibid.
22. See Ernest Gellner's introduction (p. 15) to *Arabs and Berbers* (eds. E. Gellner and C. Micaud), London, 1972.

### Chapter 1 The Early History of the Tuareg and Origins of the Class Division

1. Brahim oult Sidi, in his note to the French geographer, Henri Duveyrier, in the mid-nineteenth century, stated that 'The Imenan or Es Solatin (Sultans) are the true *cheurfas,* half Edrisiens and half Alouyiens, descendants of Sidna Aly' (Duveyrier, 1864).
2. Benhazera, writing at the beginning of this century, considers that the Imenan descended from the first Islamic missionaries who attempted to convert the Tuareg. This could have been as early as the eleventh century AD, for Ibn Khaldoun, writing in the fourteenth century, states that the 'veiled people' had been converted to Islam, after the Arabs' conquest of Spain, by a missionary called Aggag around the eleventh century AD.
3. From Pliny's account of Cornelius Balbus's expedition in 19 BC there is little doubt that the Roman general reached the Fezzan and Ajjer regions, while Lhote's analysis of Pliny's writings leads him to suggest that the Romans not only traversed Ahaggar but reached the Sudan region (Lhote, 1955, 113f.) via a route which the series of rock paintings led him to refer to as the 'Chariot route'.
4. Ibn Abdal-H'Akam, *Conquête de l'Afrique du Nord et de l'Espagne*, texte et traduction de A. Gateau, Bibliothèque Arabe-Française, Alger, 1942.
   Ibn Haukal, *The Oriental Geography of Ebn Haukal, an Arabian Traveller of the Tenth Century*, trans. William Ouseley, London, 1800.
   *Description de l'Afrique*, traduit de l'Arabe par Mac Guckin de Slane, *Journal Asiatique*, 3e. serie, XIII, 1842.
   El Bekri, *Description de l'Afrique septentrionale*, traduit par Mac Guckin de Slane, Paris, 1859.
   —*Das Geographische Worterbuch*, I–II, Gottingen-Paris, 1876–7.

Edrisi, *Géographie d'Edrisi*, traduit par le P. Amedée Jaubert, I–II, Paris, 1836–40.
—*Description de l'Afrique et de l'Espagne*, traduit par R. Dozy et M. J. de Goeje, Leyden, 1866.
Ibn Batutah, *Voyages d'Ibn Batutah*, I–IV, traduit par C. Defremy et B. R. Sanguinetti, Paris, 1853–8.
Ibn Khaldoun, *Histoire des Berbères*, I–IV, traduit par Slane, Alger, 1852–6.
Leo Africanus, *The History and Description of Africa*, trans. John Pory, I–III, London, 1896.

5. Ibn Khaldoun, op. cit., II, p. 104f.
6. Barth, Heinrich, *Reisen und Entdeckungen in Nord- und Central Afrika in den Jahren 1849 bis 1855*, I–V, Gotha, 1857–8 (I, pp. 229–30).
7. Leo Africanus states, contrary to Ibn Khaldoun, that the Lemta, rather than the Targa, formed the western group. This difference may have arisen from the Targa absorbing the Lemta; and this, as Duveyrier suggested (op. cit., pp. 317–28), may account for the fact that the tribe Ilemtin (Ilemtiyen), who descend from the Lemta, have a secondary status in Tuareg society.
8. See also Leo Africanus, op. cit., p. 797f. and Rodd, F. R., op. cit., p. 330f.
9. See Bovill, E. W., *The Golden Trade of the Moors,* O.U.P., 1958; Map III, p. 113, and Map IV, p. 132.
10. Dapper, O., *Beschreibung von Africa*, Amsterdam, 1670, p. 1.
11. See Foucauld's reference to O. Dapper, *Description de l'Afrique*, Amsterdam, 1686: Foucauld, C. de, op. cit., II, p. 534.
12. Ibid., II, p. 533.
13. 'Imrad' are referred to throughout as 'Kel Ulli' (people of the goats).
14. Foucauld, op. cit., II, p. 534.
15. Nicolaisen, op. cit., pp. 409–10.
16. Ibn Khaldoun, op. cit., I, p. 275f.
17. Ibid., I, p. 275f. See also Nicolaisen, op. cit., pp. 409–10.
18. Mercier also considers that the Hawwara were the ancestors of the present day Ahaggar Tuareg (Mercier, Marcel, *L'Histoire de l'Afrique septentrionale*, II, p. 386).
19. Amin, Samir, *The Maghreb in the Modern World,* Penguin, 1970, p. 15.
20. See Alport, E., 'The Mzab', *Man*, 84, 1954, pp. 34–44.
21. Ibn Khaldoun, op. cit., I, p. 191; II, p. 104f.
22. Capot-Rey, Robert, *Le Sahara Français*, Paris, 1953, p. 191f.
23. Nicolaisen, op. cit., p. 306.
24. Ibid., p. 405.
25. Ibid., pp. 479–80.
26. The nature of these descent groups (*tawsatin*, sing. *tawsit*) is discussed more fully in later chapters (see especially Ch. 7).
27. This myth is recorded by Benhazera (op. cit.).
28. Colloque de Sénanque, June 1974. To be published in *Revue de l'Occident Musulman et de la Méditerranée*, No. 21, ler. sem. 1976.
29. See Reygasse, M., *Monuments funéraires préislamiques de l'Afrique du Nord*, Paris, 1950.
30. A further variation states that Takama travelled on foot.

31. See Nicolaisen, op. cit., pp. 406–7; Lehureaux, L., *Sur les pistes du désert*, Paris, 1929; Reygasse, M., op. cit., p. 88f.
32. Benhazera, op. cit., p. 90f.
33. Foucauld, op. cit., II, p. 536.
34. Nicolaisen, op. cit., p. 406.
35. Ibid., p. 405.
36. Foucauld, op. cit., II, p. 536.
37. 'Tribes' refers to *tawsatin* – descent groups.
38. Foucauld, op. cit., II, p. 536.
39. Nicolaisen refers to them as 'tribes'.
40. Foucauld, op. cit., II, p. 533f.
41. Nicolaisen, op. cit., p. 44.
42. Ibid., p. 409.

### Chapter 2 The Division of the Kel Ahaggar into Three Drum Groups

1. See Benhazera, M., *Six Mois chez les Touareg du Ahaggar*, 1908, p. 99f.
2. Even after losing their supreme authority, the Imenan retained the collective title of 'Imenikalen' (sing. Amenukal), which is still used today by their few descendants (see Nicolaisen, 1963, op. cit., p. 393).
3. Nicolaisen, op. cit., p. 393.
4. Duveyrier, op. cit., p. 331; Lhote, op. cit., p. 189; Blanguernon, Claude, *Le Hoggar*, 2nd ed., Paris, 1955, p. 47.
5. Foucauld, op. cit., III, p. 1213f.
6. Verbal information to Nicolaisen (Nicolaisen, op. cit., pp. 393–4).
7. Ibid., p. 394.
8. Reported to Benhazera by Bahammou el Ansari, Khodja of Moussa ag Amastane, the Amenukal of Ahaggar at the time of Benhazera's travels (op. cit., p. 99f.).
9. Duveyrier, op. cit., p. 319.
10. On the basis of the 1949 census, the Kel Ahaggar (excluding slaves) numbered 4284: 341 Ihaggaren, 2,423 Kel Ulli and 1,520 Isekkemaren. In traditional times, when the Taitok and Tegehe Mellet were more significant, the proportion of Ihaggaren was probably higher (see Appendix I).
11. The powerful Arab tribe of Ulad Ba Hammu of Tidikelt claim that the Isekkemaren were originally their vassals.
12. See Benhazera, op. cit., pp. 158–9.

### Chapter 3 Noble–Vassal Relations

1. They are usually killed only at large ceremonial and festive occasions such as wedding feasts.
2. In spite of this, *tiwse* payments were still made, albeit sporadically, by certain groups.
3. Although similar in kind to the payment of other Kel Ulli groups, Dag Rali and

Aguh-en-tehle payments may have been slightly greater in amount than those of other Kel Ulli since they were the two wealthiest Kel Ulli descent groups.

4. Nicolaisen, op. cit., pp. 399–400.
5. These payments were those made after the commencement of caravans to Niger which traded salt for millet (the first such caravan was in 1896).
6. Lhote, op. cit., p. 229.
7. Benhazera, op. cit., p. 148.
8. Another possible reason may have been the disintegration of the *temazlayt* relationship during this century, which meant that the Kel Ulli were no longer giving a considerable amount of their produce to the Ihaggaren, with the result that they retained a greater proportion for themselves and would consequently have been able to afford an increased *tiwse* levy.
9. Benhazera, op. cit., p. 145.
10. Lhote, op. cit., p. 226.
11. Nicolaisen, op. cit., p. 400.
12. The Amenukal (and drum chiefs) normally appointed a number of (two to four usually) Khalifas, who acted as their officially appointed deputies. They were usually kinsmen or heads of prominent sections. Khalifas were appointed, in the same way, by the chiefs (headmen) of all descent groups, whether noble or vassal.
13. Benhazera, op. cit., p. 158.
14. The same Baba who led the raid on Mohammed ben Msis (see Ch. 5).
15. Lhote, op. cit., p. 238.
16. Nicolaisen, op. cit., p. 403.
17. Ibid., pp. 401–2.
18. Ibid., pp. 148–9.
19. The term *amrar* is used for 'drum chiefs', heads of subordinate descent groups and sections, and, by further extension of meaning, is used as a term both of address and reference, as a mark of respect, for any man of senior status (fem. *tamrart*).
20. The Taitok expulsion (see Ch. 5) was of a different order, and, in any case, was not within a drum group.
21. Tenants of areas in which barbary sheep were common often imposed a 'closed season' similar to that placed on pasture.
22. Hunting has declined in importance in recent years, primarily as a result of the progressive destruction of game throughout this century, and also in association with changing needs and the substitution of more readily available products. The diffusion of rifles among the Kel Ahaggar, especially after the Turkish penetration into the central Sahara, and the Ajjer region in particular, has contributed to the gradual diminishment in the numbers, or the extermination, of many species of game. However, it is the French who must be held responsible for the present dearth of wild life. The ostrich became extinct in Ahaggar around the beginning of the century, barbary sheep are now quite rare, and the adax is found only in such remote areas as the mountains around In Azoua. The Algerian government has placed severe restrictions and penalties on hunting, and there are indications that much of the wild life is now increasing.
23. The land-rent (*ehere-n-amadal*) on areas containing specific valuable assets such as barbary sheep was often comprised of such assets. Nicolaisen, with reference

to the Tezza sub-area in Dag Rali territory, which is a valuable hunting ground for barbary sheep, states that the land-rent consisted of one donkey, although it used to be four barbary sheep, while the Dag Rali chief, who formerly received two whole animals, now only receives two hides (op. cit., p. 148). This change in the land-rent was caused by the decimation of barbary sheep and the consequent decline in hunting during this century. It also illustrates how the land-rent was open to modification according to the current assets of any particular area.

24. In more recent times, since the cessation of raiding and warfare, the drum was only beaten to herald extremely important persons, or on the occasion of important proclamations by the Amenukal.
25. See Foucauld, op. cit., IV, pp. 1922–5.
26. Ibid., p. 1965.
27. *Temazlait* (Contrat de protection chez les Kel Ahaggar), *Encyclopédie Berbère*, Édition Provisoire, Cahier No. 7., 10 November 1972, UNESCO, Université de Provence.
28. This summary account of the *temazlayt* is based, with only a few elaborations and modifications, on Gast's note in the *Encyclopédie Berbère* (ibid.).
29. Nicolaisen, op. cit., pp. 403–4.
30. Nicolaisen based this conclusion on the findings of Benhazera (op. cit., 1908), which are not at all clear in that they make no reference to the *temazlayt*, as Nicolaisen seems to imply.
31. Although Lhote (op. cit., p. 194) states that the Ihaggaren received annually a share of the *tiwse* payments made to the Amenukal, we have few details of the redistributive process or means of indirect payment of *tiwse* to individual Ihaggaren, although it appears to have been made predominantly through the granting of usufruct rights over livestock, and more in accordance with the Amenukal's discretion than with any fixed rules or principles. Such grants seem to have served, in some degree, not only as a sanction to maintain the solidarity of the Ihaggaren within the drum group, but also to reinforce the Amenukal's influence over the 'council' (*djemaa*), of which these more important nobles would have been members.
32. See Bourgeot, A., 'Le Contenu sociologique de l'appellation Tuareg (Kel Ahaggar): histoire d'un nom', *Revue de l'Occident Musulman et de la Méditerranée*, No. 11, ler. sem. 1972.
33. See Foucauld, op. cit., II, p. 739.
34. Duveyrier, op. cit., p. 334.
35. Nicolaisen, op. cit., p. 404.
36. This summary account of the various rights and obligations of the *temazlayt* owes much to the studies of Nicolaisen (1963, op. cit.).
37. The question is concerned with 'traditional' times, prior to the arrival of the French. But even acknowledging the dearth of detailed information on this period, it is difficult to cite any instance of conflict between the two classes within any of the drum groups – except, of course, in the case of the election of the two Amenukals (Attici and Mohammed ag Ourzig) at the same time, which may be regarded as exceptional.
38. See Radcliffe-Brown, A. R., *Structure and Function in Primitive Society*, 1952, Chs. 4 and 5.

39. See Nicolaisen, op. cit., p. 402.
40. Ibid. With regard to the Aguh-en-tehle's relatively recent arrival in Ahaggar, their more 'friendly' relationship with the Kel Rela may be explained, in their own terms, by their being 'better off under the Kel Rela' (than under their former nobility in the south).
41. The *tamekchit* relationship is included within this context. Although analytically distinct from the *temazlayt*, its 'function', within the context of a 'communications network', was similar to that of the *temazlayt* in that it afforded the means of social interaction between the two classes.
42. Among the Dag Rali only 5 per cent of marriages over the last three generations have been exogamous to the *tawsit* (see Ch. 7).
43. Cultivation was first introduced in 1841, but was not developed in any way until 1860. Not until after the beginning of this century, however, did the cultivators begin to constitute a significant proportion of the total population.
44. Although the first such caravan was in 1896, they did not become a regular annual event until the 1920s.

### Chapter 4 The Distribution and Changing Balance of Power

1. In such matters he usually consulted and was advised by learned marabouts (religious men), and possibly by a council (discussed later) comprising the more important and influential members of the drum group.
2. This distinction is arbitrary, but is used to differentiate between wars or raiding which involved the whole drum group, as for example in the struggles of the Taitok and Tegehe Mellet against the Kel Rela, and raiding exploits which were organized by individual nobles, particular sections, or *temazlayt* groups.
3. The drum chiefs of the Taitok and the Tegehe Mellet were installed by the Amenukal (who was the drum chief of the Kel Rela), thus symbolizing their subordination to his overall authority over the *tegehe*.
4. Lhote, op. cit., p. 223.
5. By that time there was effectively only one drum group in Ahaggar, namely that of the Kel Rela.
6. See Foucauld, op. cit., II, p. 727, and Benhazera, op. cit., p. 47.
7. Duveyrier, op. cit., p. 334.
8. Heinrich Barth, op. cit., p. 257.
9. Lhote, op. cit., pp. 373–4.
10. Nicolaisen, op. cit., p. 437.
11. Foucauld, op. cit., II, p. 534.
12. He refers specifically to Ag Mama.
13. Lhote, op. cit., p. 192.
14. Gellner, Ernest, *Saints of the Atlas*, London and Chicago, 1969, pp. 89–90. 'To sum up, one can say that Berber jema'as have no sense of corporate identity distinct from that of the group of which they are the jema'a; they have no continuity other than that of the group; they have, of course, no kind of secretariat or records. On the other hand, they can, and generally do when larger groups are involved, consist of people who are delegates, who represent sub-groups. In

dealing with the important matter of the mode of election of chiefs, we are, at the same time, describing the assemblies and hierarchies of assemblies in the fulfilment of their most characteristic and perhaps most important function.' Robert Montagne (*The Berbers*, trans. David Seddon, London, 1973) describes the jema'a as a group of notables; the canton or even tribal council of elders, while Jacques Berque refers to it as 'that basic reality of the whole Maghrib' (Berque, J., *French North Africa. The Maghrib between the Two World Wars*, trans. Jean Stewart, London, 1967, p. 26).

### Chapter 5 Internal Wars and Conquest by France

1. About sixty miles as the crow flies.
2. The Ansar ('supporters') were the Madinese Moslems who gave sanctuary to Mohammed and his few followers of the nascent Islam in al-Madinah. Mohammed's arrival in al-Madinah in 622 marked the end of his flight – the hegira (*hijrah*) – and the official starting point of the Moslem era. After the Ansar's defeat in 692 at the hands of the Syrian caliphate army of Abd-al-Malik, under the command of al-Hajjij, their power was broken and they left al-Madinah and Makkah (Mecca) to join the armies in North Africa. The various communities of Ansar now found scattered across North Africa still regard themselves as the true supporters of the Prophet.
3. Referred to by the Kel Ahaggar as Ibelouien.
4. Bedda of the Tegehe Mellet.
5. The first European to traverse Tuareg country was the Frenchman René Caillé in 1828, crossing the Tanezrouft to the west of Ahaggar from Timbuktu to Morocco. Gordon Laing of the Yorkshire Light Infantry journeyed from Tripoli to Timbuktu in 1824–6 but was murdered at In Arouane, about 200 miles north of Timbuktu. His journey is particularly interesting in that he made contact with Sheikh Othman.
6. *Hyposcyannus muticus.*
7. Lella was a matrilineal granddaughter and consequently *oult ettebel.*
8. Possibly a Kel Ajjer.
9. This is made clear in the letter of M. Feraud to the Minister of Foreign Affairs on 13 May 1881 – quoted by Benhazera (op. cit.).
10. This was the Amrar Safi, who was appointed Kaimakam (a Turkish title) by the Turks on their arrival in Ghat. The position and role of Kaimakam was similar to that of a Sub-Prefect.
11. Schirmer, H., *Le Sahara*, Paris, 1893, p. 393.
12. Bissuel, H., *Les Touareg de l'Ouest*, Alger, 1888.
13. 9 December 1899.
14. Attici was Tegehe Mellet through his father and could thus draw on their support, as it seems he did during the Flatters episode.
15. He died in 1905 at the age of eighty-five.
16. He had a Tuareg mother and a Chaamba father, and became a close friend and informant of Charles de Foucauld.
17. Comprising members of the Ulad Ba Hammu, Ulad Mokhtar, Zoua, Ulad Yakhia

and Ulad Dahane tribes of Tidikelt. See Gast, M., *Alimentation des populations de l'Ahaggar. Étude ethnographique*, Memoires du C.R.A.P.E., Paris, 1968, p. 21.

18. There were also fears for the safety of Ahl Azzi caravans passing through Ahaggar at the time.
19. This frontier was established officially by the Ministry of the Interior and the Colonial Ministry on 7 February 1905.
20. See Richer, A., *Les Oulliminden. Les Touareg du Niger*, Paris, 1924, p. 186–8.
21. These included the exploits of such officers as Gardel and Charlet, after whom the two forts in Ajjer territory were named.
22. This followed the revolt in the Chiati region and the massacre of the garrison at Sebha.
23. Appointed by Si Mohammed Labed.
24. Kaoucen was born near Agades (Ikaskasen *tawsit*) around 1882, but had left his country with the arrival of the French in 1904–5 and participated in the battle of Ain Galakka in the Tibesti. He was a notable anti-French agitator, renowned throughout much of the Sahara for his courage and audacity. During the summer of 1916 he had been in Ghat, but returned to Ayr in the autumn and was offering immunity to all Tuareg who joined him.
25. See, for example, Nicolaisen, op. cit., p. 401.
26. Their chief at this time was Amr'i ag Mohammed, but he was stripped of his authority by the French and replaced by Mohammed ag Mohammed.
27. See Lhote, op. cit., p. 224f.
28. The small erg to the west of Djanet.
29. Dated 30 January.
30. Gast, op. cit., p. 37n.
31. Laarmech, their chief who was responsible for this work, died in 1954. Gast, ibid.

### Chapter 6 Nomadism and Sedentarism

1. For further discussion of this subject see:
   Bourgeot, A., 'Le Contenu sociologique de l'appellation Twareg (Kel Ahaggar): histoire d'un nom', *Revue de l'Occident Musulman et de la Méditerranée*, No. 11, ler. sem. 1972, pp. 71–9.
   Bourgeot, A., 'Idéologies et appellations ethniques: l'exemple Twareg. Analyse des catégories sociales', *Cahiers d'Études Africaines*, No. 48, XII, 4, pp. 533–54.
2. See Nicolaisen, op. cit., p. 10.
3. From the Arabic word *shurfa* (*sherfa, churfa, cheurfa,* etc.), sing. *sharif* – 'a descendant of the Prophet'.
4. Blanguernon, Claude, *Le Hoggar*, Paris, 1955, p. 59.
5. See Lhote, op. cit., p. 210f.; Foucauld, op. cit., III, p. 1300; Nicolaisen, op. cit., p. 18; et. al.
6. See Nicolaisen, 1963, op. cit., and Nicolaisen, J., 'Essai sur la religion et la magie touarègues', *Folk*, 3, Copenhagen, 1961, pp. 113–62 (see especially pp. 134f. and 146).
7. See Nicolas, F., *Tamesna. Les Iullemmeden de l'Est ou Touareg 'Kel Dinnik'*, Paris, 1950, p. 189.

8. Nicolaisen, 1963, op. cit., pp. 443–4.
9. Ibid., p. 440.
10. Ibid., p. 441.
11. Inter-class marriages and the marriage system of the Kel Ahaggar are discussed more fully in Chapter 7.
12. Bourgeot, A., 'Ideologies et appellations ethniques: l'exemple Twareg. Analyse des catégories sociales', Cahiers d'Études Africaines, No. 48, XII, 4, p. 546.
13. Nicolaisen, op. cit., 1963, p. 444.
14. Ibid.
15. Ibid.
16. See Clauzel, J., 'Les Hiérarchies sociales en pays Touareg', *Travaux de l'Institut de Recherches Sahariennes*, Alger, XXI, pt I, 1962, pp. 120–75.
17. The term Harratin is used frequently throughout the book instead of Izeggaren to designate the sedentary agricultural community, in accordance with common but usually incorrect parlance. The Harratin must be distinguished from the Ahl Azzi (Merabtines). Oral traditions of the origin of the Ahl Azzi claim that they originate from Tafilalet and descend from Sidi Embarek el Ambr', who was a contemporary of Mohammed ben Hanifia, the son of Ali ben Abou Taleb, a first cousin of the Prophet. El Ambr' left Tafilalet with his people to settle at Azzi in Touat. Two of his grandsons, Sheikh Abderrahmane ben Hadj Mohammed and his brother Si Belkacem, stopped, on their return from a pilgrimage to Mecca, at Tit in Tidikelt, where they founded a community with the Ksours. The descendants of Si Belkacem settled later at In Salah, forming the quarter known as Ksar el Merabtines. The Ahl Azzi from Tit have maintained themselves as a relatively endogamous society, retaining their Berber traits more than the other Ahl Azzi – a factor which has facilitated their assimilation into Ahaggar. Distinction is thus made between the Kel Tit or Titti, the Kel Touat, and the Ahl Azzi from In Salah – commonly referred to by the Imuhag as Kel Rezzi. Their status and conditions in Ahaggar, although they were predominantly cultivators, were slightly different and more favourable than that of the Harratin.
18. See Foucauld, op. cit., III, p. 1066.
19. Tamahak is the language of the Kel Ahaggar. The script is Tifinagh.
20. Notably Duveyrier, Foucauld, Benhazera and Prasse.
21. Clauzel, op. cit.
22. Within this framework of the inner 'we', the term *ilellan* was used to distinguish 'Tuareg' (i.e. free men) from slaves.
23. Clauzel, op. cit., p. 135.
24. Prasse, K-G., 'L'Origine du mot Amazig', *Acta Orientalia*, Copenhagen, 1959, XXIII, 3–4, pp. 197–200.

### Chapter 7 Descent, Class and Marital Strategies

1. Murdock, G. P., *Africa. Its Peoples and their Culture History*, 1959, p. 408f.
2. This theory was advanced much earlier by Gsell, S., *Histoire ancienne de l'Afrique du Nord*, I–VIII, Paris, 1920–28 (V, p. 38).
3. See Nicolaisen, 1963, op. cit.; Bates, O., *The Eastern Libyans*, London, 1914; Baumann, M., *Volkerkunde von Afrika*, Essen, 1940.

4. Ibn Batutah, during his travels in the fourteenth century, mentions matrilineal traits among the Tuareg. *Voyages d'Ibn Batutah*, traduit par Defremy et Sanguinetti, Paris, 1853–8.
5. This failure to resolve what Barth has referred to as 'the dialectic between cultural aspects and norms, and social reality' (1973), or in Scheffler's terms, the failure to distinguish between 'ideational (cultural) forms and transactional structures or processes' (op. cit., 1966, p. 543), is well seen in Murphy's (1967) analysis of kinship among the Southern Tuareg. Murphy recognizes and tries to explain the lack of fit between the kinship terminology and the social system. Iroquoian terminology, in which parallel cousins are designated by the terms for brother and sister, is congruent with exogamous descent groups in which marriage with the parallel cousin is excluded. However, amongst most Tuareg groups, although the stated marriage preference is with the matrilateral cross-cousin, marriages with parallel cousins are just as common. Murphy's explanation for the presence of the incongruous kin terminology rests on a somewhat questionable diffusionist hypothesis, namely that the ancient matrilineal kin groups were once exogamous, so that marriage with the parallel cousin would have been forbidden, and marriage with the cross-cousin permissible. He considers that endogamy may well have been introduced by Islam, with its preference for marriage with the father's brother's daughter, which could have been extended to the mother's sister's daughter through the pressure of Tuareg matrilineal institutions. If this did happen, it probably occurred early in this millennium when the tribes of Tripolitania came under Arab influence. Murphy's hypothesis to explain the persistence of this kinship nomenclature in the altered social structure beyond the mere question of 'culture lag' is that 'imbalance and dissonance may be the very essence of structure'. The problem with Murphy's analysis and explanations is that his concern for social reality ignores its dominant feature, namely the class structure.

   Barth, F., 'Descent and Marriage Reconsidered', in J. Goody (ed.), the *Character of Kinship*, Cambridge University Press, 1973, pp. 3–19.

   Murphy, R. F., 'Tuareg Kinship', *American Anthropologist*, 69, 1967, pp. 163–70.

   Scheffler, H. W., 'Ancestor Worship in Anthropology: Or, Observations on Descent and Descent Groups', *Current Anthropology*, 1966, pp. 541–51.
6. Today, the few ex-slaves who have chosen to remain with their former masters usually live in their own tents. This was also the case in traditional times.
7. Since 1959 the rainfall in Ahaggar has been particularly low. In only a few years has the rainfall been above the mean annual average, and then it has often been in the form of heavy cloudbursts of short duration, with a considerable amount lost in run-off. Pasture has remained impoverished throughout most of this period, and I have consequently never seen such section camps form.
8. All four are named after the *tawsit* sub-area, or more specifically the main centre in that sub-area, over which they held land rights: viz. Kel Tamanrasset, Kel Terhenanet, Kel Hirafok and Kel Tinhart.
9. Needham, R., 'Remarks on the Analysis of Kinship and Marriages', in Needham, R. (ed.), *Rethinking Kinship and Marriage*, A.S.A. Monograph II, Tavistock, 1971, pp. 1–34.
10. Their matrilineality 'makes sense' in so far as they are not exclusively matrilineal.

As we shall see, matriliny is most pronounced amongst the nobility, who can hardly be called 'pastoralists'.

11. The 'stomach' symbolizes the mother's family and, more specifically, matrilineally related women. (The father's family, and the patriline, are symbolized by the 'back' – *arouri*.)
12. These rules are in accordance with Goody's conclusions on the nature of African descent systems, that 'matrilineal systems of succession and inheritance are intrinsically more lateral, and hence more corporate' (Goody, J., 'Sideways or Downwards? Lateral and Vertical Succession, Inheritance and Descent in Africa and Eurasia', *Man*, 5, No. 4, 1970, pp. 627–38).
13. Nicolaisen, op. cit., 1963, p. 142.
14. The case study which Nicolaisen uses to illustrate these 'rules' (op. cit., 1963, p. 143) is one of the most exceptional amongst the Kel Ahaggar. It examines actual marriages between the two vassal (Kel Ulli) descent groups of the Dag Rali and Aguh-en-tehle. However, over the last three generations there have only been four marriages between these two descent groups, which involved 'exchange' marriages between two families. Indeed, with the exception of two other marriages, these are the only exogamous marriages contracted by members of the Dag Rali during this period. This example is also unusual in that several of the children are 'adopted'. Moreover, Nicolaisen does not make clear whether his 'rules' apply to both classes, although this is implied. They therefore raise such questions (which cannot be answered without much speculation) as whether residency may have been more matrilocally orientated in earlier times, and whether his 'rules' possibly reflect practices that were more common amongst the nobility.
15. Goody, J., op. cit., p. 628.
16. The comments of Marceau Gast and Johannes Nicolaisen, both of whom studied Tuareg pastoral practices extensively, are interesting in this respect. While Gast emphasizes that there is nothing more difficult to calculate among the Tuareg than the sizes and ownership of their herds (op. cit., 1968, p. 126), Nicolaisen warns that statistics concerning the ownership of livestock must always be regarded with suspicion, as it is extremely difficult to obtain data. Even after several weeks in a camp, I have rarely been able to obtain more than a fairly general assessment of individual livestock ownership.
17. The apparent opposition between these two modes of transmission of property rights is largely resolved by the specific marital strategies of the two classes (see below).
18. Labour, through the reproduction of the 'domestic unit' and the means by which slaves are inherited, is thus also transmitted predominantly in this line.
19. The term *anet ma* is also given to the mother's mother's brother's son and the mother's father's brother's son (see Nicolaisen, op. cit., 1963, p. 449), neither of whom may belong to the same matriline as ego. This, however, is in accordance with the merging rules applicable to Iroquoian kinship systems. (The core terminology of the Kel Ahaggar kinship system is Iroquoian.)
20. See: Radcliffe-Brown, A. R., *Structure and Function in Primitive Society*, 1952, Chs. 1, 4 and 5.

    Lévi-Strauss, C., *Structural Anthropology*, 1968, Ch. 2.

Goody, J., 'The Mother's Brother and the Sister's Son in West Africa', *Journal of the Royal Anthropological Institute*, 89, 1959, pp. 61–88.

De Heusch, L., 'The Debt of the Maternal Uncle', *Man*, 9, No. 4, 1974, pp. 609–19.

21. Prescriptive endogamy is rare, and usually found only among large 'groups' such as Jews.
22. This type of marriage does not seem to be forbidden as such, but I have only come across one instance of marriage with the sister's daughter, and this was several generations ago. Similarly, marriage with the daughter of a half-brother or half-sister does not actually seem to be forbidden, although I have never found an instance of such marriage in Ahaggar.
23. The Kel Rela number about 275 and the Dag Rali about 350 to 400. Although the intention was to collect a 100 per cent sample, it is probably nearer 75 per cent. This deficit results from the fact that marriages were taken over three generations, with the inevitable result that kinship ties in higher ascending generations were often forgotten or not easily traced beyond parents and immediate collaterals. Most of the 27·7 per cent of the marriages in this category among the Dag Rali were known to be endogamous within the *tawsit*, while a few of the 22·2 per cent among the Kel Rela were known to be exogamous.
24. The stomach, which symbolizes the mother's family, and the back, which symbolizes the father's family, are said by the Kel Ahaggar 'to be the same thing'!
25. In the case of El Hadj Akhmed's succession, the comments of Duveyrier that 'To establish a successor by right of descent while Ag Mama was still living was not a solution as it would ignite a civil war between all the Kel Rela who had married nieces or even grand-nieces of the living chief', and that 'God alone knows what rival claims will emerge on Ag Mama's death', are particularly pertinent.
26. This strategy is very similar to that of the Tswana nobles, among whom marriage with the father's brother's daughter secures and strengthens certain political advantages. Among the Tswana nobility, 47·9 per cent of cousin marriages are with the father's brother's daughter, while among the commoners 50 per cent of cousin marriages are with the mother's brother's daughter and only 20 per cent with the father's brother's daughter. See Schapera, I., 'Kinship and Marriage among the Tswana', in D. Forde and A. R. Radcliffe-Brown (eds.), *African Systems of Kinship and Marriage*, O.U.P., 1950, pp. 140–65.
27. See Benhazera, op. cit.
28. See Nicolaisen, op. cit., 1963, p. 456f.
29. There was not one single caravan, but a number of smaller caravans which were organized on a *tawsit* and section basis. In most years the total number of camels leaving Ahaggar was nearer 2,000. The total journey to Damergou and back is about 1,000 to 1,200 kilometres (see Chs. 9 and 10).
30. Nicolaisen refers to the *ariwan* as a 'goat camp', and the larger section camp, when all members of the section camped together, as a 'camel camp'. He also noted that when a whole section camped together in this way, the goat herds of each *ariwan* were kept apart.
31. Bloch, M., 'The Long Term and the Short Term: The Economic and Political Significance of the Morality of Kinship', in J. Goody (ed.), *The Character of Kinship*, Cambridge University Press, 1973, pp. 75–87.
32. Ibid.

## Chapter 8 The Symbolic Meaning of the Veil

1. This feature of Tuareg social relations was first recognized by Robert Murphy, working among the Southern Tuareg. See Murphy, R., 'Tuareg Kinship', *American Anthropologist*, 69, 1967, pp. 163–70, for a more detailed discussion.
2. Murphy's expression. Ibid., p. 169.
3. Kin terms and their extended usage may be seen as moral terms. As terms of reference they give a cognitive expression to the general belief system of the culture. Among the Tuareg they are used more for reference than as terms of address. Their usage in address may be usually seen in a tactical or strategic sense, with reference to the moral values attached to the term, to stimulate or evoke a response in the actor's attempt to manipulate the social situation. Restriction in the usage of kin terms adds strength to their tactical implications. (See Bloch, M., 'The Moral and Tactical Meaning of Kinship Terms', *Man*, 6, No. 1, 1971, pp. 79–87.) Among the Tuareg, personal names are used most frequently in addressing all descendants and kinsmen of one's own generation, although cross-cousins (true and classificatory), who maintain a joking relationship, frequently address each other with the respective classificatory kin terms (*ababah/tababaht*). Kinsmen of the second ascending generation may be addressed by the classificatory terms of *anna* or *abba*, as may the brothers and sisters of the parents (except the mother's brother – *anet ma*). These kinsmen may also be addressed by their personal names, depending on the social situation, although most ascendants, particularly those who are considerably older than ego, are usually addressed as *amrar* (fem. *tamrart*). This term is normally used as a sign of respect towards senior kinsmen and other elder persons unrelated to ego, and especially parents-in-law, who are, however, rarely addressed at all in view of the avoidance relationship.
4. The term *litham* (Arabic 'veil'), although used by Oriental Arabs, is unknown among Tuareg groups, and little used among the Maghreb population as a whole, although the term *echchach* (Arabic *chach*) is now used by all Tuareg and indicates the increasing Arab influence.
5. To some extent this is a result of the differential adoption of Arabic traits. See Bourgeot, A., 'Le Costume masculin des Kel Ahaggar', *Libyca*, XVII, 1969, pp. 355–376; Nicolas, F., 'Le Voilement des Twareg – contributions à l'étude de l'air', *Mémoires de l'I.F.A.N.*, No. 10, 1950, pp. 497–503.
6. See Foucauld, op. cit., I, p. 439 (fig.) and Bourgeot, op. cit., 1969. Bourgeot mentions finding an *alechcho* belonging to a noble (Kel Rela) measuring ten metres in length and about sixty centimetres in width, and valued at 500 D.A. (approximately £45): ibid., p. 358.
7. For a more detailed account of the quality and types of material, styles of wearing, etc., as well as an inventory of the relevant Arab and Tamahak terminology, see Bourgeot, op. cit., 1969.
8. Although veiling is an ancient custom, there is an element of uncertainty about the colours and material of the veil prior to the earlier part of this century. Marceau Gast states that the famous indigo veil only became widespread among the Kel Ahaggar quite recently; until 1920, most of them still wore the *tekerheit*, a white woollen veil with coloured bands which came from Tripoli (Gast, M.,

'Premiers Résultats d'une mission ethnographique en Ahaggar', *Libyca*, XIII, 1965, pp. 325–32). Foucauld, writing during the second decade of this century, states, 'Les étoffes employées pour cet usage (le voilement) sont toujours très minces, habituellement de couleur indigo, quelquefois blanches, et très rarement noires' (op. cit., III, p. 1326). Benhazera, writing a decade earlier, is not particularly illuminating on this matter, stating that the veil consists of a single strip of deep blue or black cotton fabric (op. cit., p. 36). He does mention, however, that black material (*kehal*) used for veils was brought from Damergou and Ayr, and that both blue and white cotton material and the white muslin *chach* were brought from Tidikelt and Touat (ibid., pp. 67–8). Black and white cotton veils seem to have been prevalent among the Kel Ajjer in the mid-nineteenth century, for Duveyrier made a distinction between the use of black and white veils and skin colour, saying that the true Tuareg (nobles in particular) preferred the black cotton veil, while men of 'inferior race' (with negroid blood) usually wore the white cotton veil (op. cit., p. 392). If this was true at the time of Duveyrier's writing it is not so today, as veils of both colours are worn by all classes alike, although Francis Rodd, with reference to certain districts in Ayr, makes the same distinction between the wearing of dark indigo or black veils by the nobles, and white veils by servile tribes (Rodd, F., 'The Origin of the Tuareg', *Geographical Journal*, 67, 1926, pp. 27–52). One must therefore conclude that the indigo veil was probably worn predominantly by the noble class. Sudanese indigo cotton has been known in Ayr since ancient times (see Nicolaisen, op. cit., 1963, p. 287), and it is not easy to understand why it did not become widespread in Ahaggar, as Gast comments, until very recently, except that the caravan traffic between the two areas, which became an annual event from the 1920s onwards, certainly opened up and maintained a more regular trade with the south. The greatest impact, however, has been the introduction of industrially manufactured fabrics (notably muslin), which have been promoted through the increasing presence and activity of Arab merchants, especially since about 1920, and the consequent introduction into the vocabulary of Arabic terminology such as *echchach* and *khent* alongside such Berber words as *alechcho*, *tekerheit*, etc., which relate to the traditional artisan level of production. The ascendancy of Arabic influence in the vocabulary thus reflects the transition to another level of technology. (See Bourgeot, A., op. cit., 1969, p. 358.)

9. This was usually marked by his first caravan or, in traditional times, his first raid.
10. Duveyrier, op. cit., p. 392.
11. See Bourgeot, op. cit., 1969, p. 360.
12. Foucauld, op. cit., IV, p. 1329.
13. Lhote, H., 'Au sujet du port du voile chez les Touareg et les Teda', *Notes Africaines*, No. 52, October 1951, pp. 108–11 (see p. 110).
14 Abd el Djalil, R. P., 'Aspects intérieurs de l'Islam', *Bulletin de Liaison Saharienne*, V, No. 16, March 1964, p. 29.
15. Lhote, op. cit., 1951.
16. Bourgeot, op. cit., 1969, p. 361.
17. Nicolaisen, op. cit., 1963, p. 14; Nicolaisen, 'Essai sur la religion et la magie touarègues', *Folk*, 3, 1961, p. 114.
18. E.g. Nicolas, F., op. cit., 1950.

19. Lhote, op. cit., 1951, p. 110.
20. Murphy, R., 'Social Distance and the Veil', *American Anthropologist*, 66, 1964, pp. 1257–74.
21. Goffman, E., 'The Nature of Deference and Demeanor', *American Anthropologist*, 58, 1956, pp. 473–502.
22. Murphy (op. cit., 1964) was the first to recognize this fundamental aspect of the Tuareg veil.
23. Radcliffe-Brown, A. R., *Structure and Function in Primitive Society*, 1952.
24. See Merton, R. K., *Social Theory and Social Structure*, Glencoe, Ill., 1957.
25. See Murphy, op. cit., 1967.
26. Murphy, op. cit., 1964.
27. Ibid.
28. See Goffman, E., *The Presentation of Self in Everyday Life*, Penguin, 1969, p. 220.
29. A man who has made the pilgrimage to Mecca.
30. *Djenoun:* wicked spirits. See Ch. 10.
31. Or *tezama*, a related belief which is prominent in Ayr.
32. Westermarck, E., *Ritual and Belief in Morocco*, I–II, London, 1926, p. 422.
33. Murphy, op. cit., 1964.
34. Bourgeot, op. cit., 1969, p. 360.

## Chapter 9 The Colonial Presence

1. Mostly verbal expressions.
2. Although the role of Khyar ag Heguir and the development of opposed political factions during this period has been emphasized, we should perhaps question the extent to which the French encroachment was critical in the formation of these factions, or whether it merely provided a catalyst and a degree of legitimacy for renewed and increased inter-sectional conflict among the Kel Rela in their internal struggle for power.
3. A vivid picture of the horror of drought was given by Foucauld in his account of the severe drought in Ahaggar and Ahnet in 1882. There was a shortage of milk due to the depletion of the herds, and little wheat as a result of locust attacks. About eight Taitok and Kel Ahnet, accompanied by a few Kel Rela, set off on a raiding expedition in the hope of alleviating the situation and did not return for eight months. During their absence the Taitok and Kel Ahnet women were without milk, meat, grain, and men to go on caravans in search of supplies. Many died of hunger and lack of clothing (Foucauld, C. de, *Poésies touaregues*, vols. I–II, Paris, 1930, p. 59–60). For some idea of the incidence of drought, see:

   Dubief, J., 'Les chronologies des Kel Ahaggar et des Taitoq', *Travaux de l'Institut de Recherches Sahariennes*, I, Alger, 1942, pp. 87–132.

   —'Les Ouraghen des Kel Ajjer. Chronologie et nomadisme', *Travaux de l'Institut de Recherches Sahariennes*, XIV, Alger, 1956, pp. 85–137.

   —'Les Ifoghas de Ghadames. Chronologie et nomadisme', *Revue de l'Institut des Belles-Lettres Arabes*, XI, Tunis, 1948, pp. 141–59.

   —'Les Imanghassaten. Chronologie et migration', *Revue de l'Institut des Belles-Lettres Arabes*, XIII, Tunis, 1950, pp. 23–36.

Dubief, J., 'Les Pluies au Sahara Central', *Travaux de l'Institut de Recherches Sahariennes*, IV, Alger, 1947, pp. 7–23.

4. Gypsum deposits.
5. Many of these artefacts, particularly quern stones, are picked up by the Kel Ahaggar and used again.
6. Fifty miles along the *piste* from Ideles.
7. *Tisemt:* salt.
8. Early references to salt in Ahaggar are found in:

   Lhote, H., 'Les Salines de l'Amadror', *Bulletin de Liaison Saharienne*, No. 14, 1952. The evidence put forward in this paper is derived from El Bekri's *Description de l'Afrique*, traduit par de Slane, Paris, 1859, pp. 340–41.

   Bissuel, H., *Les Touareg de l'Ouest*, Alger, 1888, p. 78.

   Duveyrier, H., *Les Touareg du Nord*, 1864, pp. 290, 376, 412.

   For a detailed description of the uses and appreciation of salt in Ahaggar see Gast, M., *Alimentation des populations de l'Ahaggar*, Mémoires du C.R.A.P.E., VIII, 1968, pp. 170–76. The techniques of extraction of salt at Amadror, its transportation etc., are described by Regnier, J., 'Les Salines de l'Amadror et le trafic caravanier', *Bulletin de Liaison Saharienne*, No. 43, 1961, pp. 234–61. See also:

   Butay, L., 'Les Salines de l'Amadror', *B.L.S.*, No. 12, 1953, pp. 16–17.

   Denis, P., 'Les Salines de l'Amadror en 1958', *B.L.S.*, No. 34, 1959, pp. 178–9.

   Bobo, J., 'Les Salines de l'Amadror', *Travaux de l'Institut de Recherches Sahariennes*, 11, 1954, pp. 141–2.
9. See Dubief, J., op. cit., 1942.
10. It seems that this venture to the Fezzan was not repeated, probably due to hostilities with the Kel Ajjer. See Gast, op. cit., 1968, p. 34.
11. Ibid., p. 34n.
12. There is the unlikely possibility that there were occasional caravans to Damergou during this period of which we have no record.
13. From the report of Captain Florimond, 1938–44, cited by Gast, op. cit., 1968, pp. 33–4.
14. These numbered about 2,000.
15. Benhazera, op. cit., 1908, p. 54 (my translation).
16. The caravan trade from In Salah to Niger tended to diminish as a result of French occupation.
17. Gast, M., 'Evolution de la vie économique et structures sociales en Ahaggar de 1660–1965', *Travaux de l'Institut de Recherches Sahariennes*, XXII, 1965, pp. 129–43.
18. The French military administration moved from Fort Motylinski to Tamanrasset in 1920; the final transfer of the Sahara Company was in 1929. (The Sahara Company was the '*méhariste* (camel-mounted) gendarmerie', comprising a few French officers and sergeants, with Arab soldiers and N.C.O.s – mostly Chaamba.) Ahaggar remained a military Annexe (Annexe du Hoggar) in the Territory of Oasis, administered from Ouargla, until 1957, when with the creation of the Organisation Communes des Régions Sahariennes (O.C.R.S.) – the law creating the O.C.R.S. was gazetted on 10 January 1957 – it became a Cercle Administratif in the arrondissement of Ouargla; the administration was vested in a civil

authority with the installation of a Sub-Prefect in 1960. A Ministry for the Sahara was created, but the confusion over the political and economic prerogatives impeded the start of the O.C.R.S. for about three years. However, the initial political character of the O.C.R.S. and the development of the Algerian War limited the action of the O.C.R.S. to the two Saharan Departments of the Saoura and Oasis.

19. After pacification the installation of the Amenukal took place at Tamanrasset – a move which could be interpreted as symbolizing the subordination of the Amenukal to the French. Two modifications in the process of electing the Amenukal after pacification were the increased influence of the Kel Ulli, evidenced in the letter of Boukhelil ag Douka to the French authorities notifying them of the death of Moussa ag Amastane and the subsequent election of Akhemouk ag Ihemma, and the possible influence of the French administration, for which there is little evidence apart from a few speculative insinuations.
20. In such familial matters he would usually consult with a marabout, who would legislate according to traditional custom.
21. See Appendix I.
22. Chudeau, R., *Sahara soudanais*, Paris, 1909.
23. See Appendix I.
24. Malaurie, J., 'Touareg et noirs au Hoggar. Aspects de la situation actuelle', *Annales Économies, Sociétés, Civilisations*, VIII, 3, 1953, pp. 338–46.
25. Nemo, J., 'Le Régime juridique des terres au Hoggar', *Travaux de l'Institut de Recherches Sahariennes*, XXII, 1963, pp. 123–44 (see p. 132).
26. The whole question of 'ownership' and rights to land in Ahaggar has given rise to countless disputes and problems, particularly during the French period, when the question was never resolved satisfactorily; while since 1962 it has been the focal issue in the Algerian social revolution.
27. *Foggara* is the Arabic term. The Tamahak term is *efeli*, pl. *ifelan*.
28. The most common form of well irrigation was the *tanout* – a sort of bucket hoist operated usually by oxen and occasionally manpower.
29. If the owner of the *foggara* or well did not cultivate his land, he could forbid its cultivation by others, although theoretically he lost all rights to it if it were irrigated by new *foggaras* or wells. See Nemo, J., op. cit., 1963, pp. 133–4.
30. The area irrigated by a *foggara* can vary greatly. The average number of gardens irrigated by a *foggara* is about twelve, although it can be twice or half this number. Similarly the size of gardens varies between about 0·30 and 0·60 hectares, so that a *foggara* system with twelve gardens is thus irrigating an area of between about 3½ and 7 hectares (8½–18 acres). Water from the aqueduct flows into a large basin (*tihemt*), which acts as a regulator from which it is then led out to the gardens. Between the basin and the outflow channel (*tahaft* or *teguhamt*) is a large flat stone (*anefif*) with a hole in the middle. At night, when irrigation is needed, a cotton bung is removed from the hole and water is then led off from the main channel through a series of smaller channels into the gardens. Each garden is divided into small garden beds, surrounded by low earth ridges and narrow irrigation channels. During the day the bung is replaced and the basin refills. (For a more detailed description of these gardens and agricultural methods, see Nicolaisen, op. cit., 1963, p. 186f.).

31. The Kel Ahaggar now hold no such rights to *foggara* systems or to any other type of Harratin-cultivated land, since all forms of *métayage* and slave labour, and the traditional rules of land tenure, have been officially abolished by the Algerian government. It is consequently difficult to determine whether rights over *foggara* gardens were held individually or collectively on a corporate basis by the whole *tawsit* section. Nicolaisen stated that there may not have been kinship bonds between the Tuareg who had gardens at the same *foggara*, and also that when the owner of a *foggara* system, or the individual owners of the gardens, died, there were no fixed rules governing the transference of the gardens, except that they would generally pass to someone in his family (op. cit., 1963, p. 197). Nicolaisen is correct on the first point in so far as some *foggaras* were owned jointly by two different *tawsatin* or *tawsit* sections, with each having rights over a specific number of gardens. For example, the Taramast *foggara* at Abalessa was owned on a fifty-fifty basis by the Cherif of Abalessa and the Dag Rali. Nevertheless statements given to me by Kel Rela, Dag Rali and former *khammes* make me inclined to believe that the principles governing the transmission of gardens, and the *foggara* system itself, were similar to those pertaining to tenant rights over sub-areas. An analysis of the *foggara* systems formerly held by the Dag Rali at Abalessa and Tiffert indicates that the gardens were held on a sort of collective, or rather a corporate basis, by the various *tawsit* sections concerned.
32. Different crops are grown in summer and winter. The most important crop is wheat, and to a lesser extent barley, both of which are sown in autumn and harvested in spring, and require considerable irrigation compared with most summer crops such as tomatoes, millet, sorghum, maize, various types of melons and gourds, and certain vegetables.
33. See Gast, op. cit., 1968, p. 30; Barrère, G., 'Correspondance sur le contrat agricole en Ahaggar', *Travaux de l'Institut de Recherches Sahariennes*, XXIII, Alger, 1964, pp. 187–8.
34. Gast, op. cit., 1968, pp. 30–31.
35. At least not until 1953 when the Amenukal was obliged to modify (or clarify the 'loopholes' of) the traditional system of land tenure.
36. One might also add that the value of agriculture to the Kel Ahaggar increased progressively during the French period, not only in terms of greater total productivity as the size of the sedentary community grew and more land was brought under cultivation, but also relatively compared with other forms of income, especially the caravan trade to Damergou, which became subjected to progressively deteriorating terms of trade.
37. Benhazera, op. cit., p. 57.
38. Gast, op. cit., 1968, p. 36.
39. Lyon, G. F., *A Narrative of Travels in Northern Africa, in the Years 1818, 1819 and 1920*, London, 1821, pp. 101–2.
40. Arabic 'descendant of the Prophet' (sing. *cherif*); Tamahak *echcherifen*. The Imenan had held the title of Echcherifen.
41. For example, the fanatical marabout Abidine activated against the French in the Sahara regions with considerable success for about twenty years.
42. The common name for God is 'Ialla', but the term 'Messinar', implying 'Our Father' or 'Our Maker', is used more frequently. The term 'Amarag' is also used

to designate God, and means 'the one who comes to give help' (the creator of all things). See Foucauld, op. cit., IV, 195–2, p. 1590.

43. See Gellner, E., *Saints of the Atlas*, 1969, p. 12, on the charismatic qualities of *baraka*. Robert Graves associates *baraka* with virtue (*Oxford Addresses on Poetry*, 1961, p. 99f.).
44. Nicolaisen considers that the connection between fertility and *baraka* is seen in the interpretation given by Johannes Pedersen to the conception of *baraka* in the Semitic religions. In Judaism, the mystical force or benediction is, in the first place, the power of reproduction, and the word *baraka* is perhaps related to *boeroek* (knee), which is considered to symbolize the region in the lower part of the abdomen – the centre of the reproductive force. In this context he considers that *tarbit birkija*, amongst the Syrians, means 'the seed of my knee' – or, in other words, 'a son'. Pederson, J., *Israel I–II. Sjaeleliv og Samfunds liv*, 3. udg, Copenhagen, 1958, pp. 157, 407; Nicolaisen, J., 'Essai sur la religion et la magie touarègues', *Folk*, 3, 1961, pp. 113–62 (see p. 121).
45. See Nicolaisen, op. cit., 1963, p. 127.
46. Ibid., pp. 175–80.
47. Although collecting was important, it was as much dependent on climatic conditions as stock-breeding. In periods of drought, when milk yield is low, there are not likely to be many seeds for collecting.
48. There are some exceptions, such as certain domestic animals, notably dogs and donkeys.
49. Kel Ahaggar say that it is not because *baraka* is destroyed by the impurity of the earth, but rather so that people should not walk on *baraka*.
50. Nicolaisen, op. cit., 1961, p. 122.
51. A similar sort of relationship seems to have existed in Morocco, where the Sultan of Morocco was responsible for the *baraka* throughout the whole country (Westermarck, *Ritual and Belief in Morocco*, I, 1926, p. 38f.). Nicolaisen also mentions a similar connection between the responsibilities of the chiefs, notably the Sultan of Agades, concerning the fertility of the land and the maintenance of *baraka* (op. cit., 1961, pp. 120–21).
52. Mortals received *baraka* by praying at the tombs of marabouts. The hands are spread towards the tomb while praying, and a little earth from the tomb is put on the head or in the mouth. Offerings, consisting of pieces of cotton material, are also laid on marabouts' tombs, or are attached to a stone or near-by tree. These pieces of cloth become impregnated with *baraka* and are used by the faithful to wipe their faces while praying.
53. These are often confused with the fiends ('satans') of the Koran. See Buhl, Fr., *Muhammeds Religiose Forkyndelse efter Quranen*, Copenhagen, 1924, p. 102f.; Nicolaisen, op. cit., 1961, p. 124.
54. This statement is a literal translation of a statement made to me by a Kel Rela.
55. It is said that *tandiouin* (sing. *tinde*) – drums – can sometimes be heard here at night, and the following myth was once recounted to me: 'A Tuareg, several thousand years ago, long before the present "tribes" lived in Ahaggar, one night rode alone past Amdelis on his camel. As he passed the mountain the drums started to beat and the sand dunes began to move down the lower part of the mountain until they buried him alive.'

56. *Artemesia judaica*, ssp. *sahariensis*.
57. Foucauld, op. cit., III, 1951–2, p. 1172.
58. This term was occasionally used to describe my position in Ahaggar. My lodging in Tamanrasset was a thatched hut (*ekeber*) belonging to the commune, and described by the Kel Ahaggar as *ekeber-oua-n-amagaren*, meaning literally 'a hut for strangers'.
59. The term *tabauhigen* (sing. *tabauhek*) was used to describe my heavy boots.
60. Benhazera, op. cit., p. 58.
61. Gast, op. cit., 1968, p. 284n.
62. See ibid., p. 284.
63. Literally scribes attached to the *zawiya* (lodges).
64. See Gast, op. cit., 1968, p. 289n.
65. Desparmet, J., *Coutumes, institutions, croyances des indigènes de l'Algérie*, vol. I, Alger, 1939, pp. 110–11.
66. The merchants who came into the region after pacification must also be included within this context. Prior to the French occupation there was no monetary exchange in Ahaggar. With the installation of a French post, however, and the regular payment of the military in money, a few merchants were attracted to the region with one or two setting up shop at Tarhaouhaout (Fort Motylinski) in 1916–17. These shopkeepers were mostly Mozabites from Metllili and the Mzab, and in 1929 six of them had established themselves in Tamanrasset (see Gast, op. cit., 1968, p. 39). Today there are well over sixty such shops in Tamanrasset and several more scattered amongst the other outlying villages. These shopkeepers were concerned with money and not barter, and initially the nomads and sedentary cultivators had little contact with this new means of exchange. Nomads, however, were able to sell their products of milk, butter, grain, etc., to the *méharistes* and the administrative post in exchange for money. The nomad gradually became used to *baylek*, the credit bills that were given in payment to the guides and camel-owners who hired camels to the *méhariste* corps, and which could then be taken to the shops and exchanged for such commodities as manufactured cotton, tea, sugar, grain, domestic utensils, and so forth. (*Baylek* means literally 'administration' or 'authority', and was used as a general term of designation for the French administration.) Nevertheless, the diffusion of monetary exchange was slow and it was a long time before it was readily accepted by the Kel Ahaggar. It was the Kel Rela, through the necessary and increasingly frequent visits of the Amenukal and his entourage to the French administration, who had the greatest contact with Tamanrasset. During the initial period following pacification they remained 'hardened' and 'sulking' in their attitude towards the French, and it was not until the 1930s and 1940s that there was any significant change in this attitude, but with their growing contact with Tamanrasset, they began to show more interest in the benefits of this new form of exchange and commerce. Kel Ulli also began to appreciate the benefits of monetary exchange, but their contact with Tamanrasset and the French administration was much less than that of the Kel Rela.
67. Prior to the sedentarization of the nomads.
68. It seems that the marabouts and *cheurfa* acquired these rights shortly before the Ahl Azzi.

69. 1963, op. cit., p. 22.
70. The increased immigration of these various elements after pacification and the opening up of the region not only accelerated the pluralization of Ahaggar in terms of 'Arabization' and 'islamization', but above all it reorientated the demographic base of the society towards the eventual numerical subordination of the Kel Ahaggar. Lhote (op. cit., 1955, pp. 420–21) actually states that there was a weakening of the Tuareg birthrate following pacification, which was in all probability due to a momentary demoralization, but that the number of births soon increased rapidly to produce a noticeable increase in their population. This may have been true, although the relationship between 'demoralization' and birthrates seems deviously obscure, and suffers, one might suggest, from ethnocentric bias. In any case, one must also consider the possible incidence and interaction of numerous other factors such as drought, prolonged warfare, etc. Whatever Lhote's opinion may be in this respect, the lack of any detailed demographic data makes it quite impossible for us to comment on changing birthrates, deathrates, or any other demographic rates, except in the most generalized way. There certainly appears to be no evidence to support Lhote's statement. All that we can say is that the number of Kel Ahaggar, which at the turn of the century had been about 3,000, had risen to about 6,000 by the end of the French period. During the corresponding period, the sedentary population had grown from a few hundred to about 6,000. But if we exclude the slaves, who numbered between 1,000 and 1,500, and who were included with the Kel Ahaggar, we see that the sedentary community had grown to outnumber the 'Tuareg' even before Algerian independence. This remarkable growth rate must be attributed in large part to their accelerated immigration into the region following pacification and the opening up of Ahaggar.

### Chapter 10 Resistance to Change and the Preservation of the Status Quo

1. See Nemo, J., 'Le Régime juridique des terres au Hoggar', *Travaux de l'Institut de Recherches Sahariennes*, XXII, 1963, pp. 124–44 (see p. 137).
2. Ibid., p. 138. Whatever the basis of these claims, they would have been subject to the customary law that applied to all buildings, which in effect was only a right of enjoyment, or usufruct, without legal ownership as such.
3. Ibid.
4. Translated from Nemo, J., ibid., p. 141f.
5. Bernard, A., *Enquête sur l'habitation des indigènes de l'Algérie*, 1921.
6. Malaurie, J., 'Touareg et noirs du Hoggar: aspects de la situation actuelle', *Annales Économies, Sociétés, Civilisations,* VIII, 3, 1953, pp. 338–46.
7. Ibid., p. 341.
8. Ibid., pp. 341–2.
9. These figures are in metric tonnes. 1 m. tonne = 1,000 kgs. or 2,204 lbs.
10. Galan, P., 'Contribution à l'étude du problème alimentaire au Hoggar', *Archives de l'Institut Pasteur*, XXX, Algérie, 1951, pp. 230–47 (see p. 233).
11. Abalessa 3 per 100; Hirafok 15 per 100; In Amguel 6 per 100; Tamanrasset 5 per 100. Malaurie, op. cit., p. 341.

12. Wheat from their gardens was exchanged for dates at the approximate rate of one measure of wheat for three measures of dates.
13. Information supplied by G. Barrère to Regnier. Regnier, J., 'Les Salines de l'Amadror et le trafic caravanier', *Bulletin de Liaison Saharienne,* No. 43, 1961, pp. 234–61 (see p. 249).
14. Malaurie, op. cit., p. 344.
15. Rognon, P., 'La Confederation des nomades Kel Ahaggar', *Annales Géographiques,* 71, No. 388, 1962, pp. 604–19 (see p. 613).
16. Malaurie estimated 12,000 in 1946 (op. cit., p. 344). The administration, in 1960, estimated the number as 10,000 (see Gast, op. cit., 1968, p. 125). Galan estimated that the total number of camels was 9,000, 7,000 of which were kept in Tamesna (op. cit., pp. 231–2).
17. Gast estimated 90 per cent. Gast, M., 'Aspect de l'artisanat chez les Kel Ahaggar en 1963', *Libyca*, XI, 1963, pp. 221–34 (see p. 232).
18. See Nicolaisen, op. cit., 1963, p. 209f.
19. The development and increase of mechanized transport in the Sahara has led to a general decline in caravan trade, and the caravans from Ahaggar to the oases of Tidikelt and Touat are now almost totally insignificant.
20. This is a more or less literal translation.
21. Transcripted directly from a Dag Rali.
22. Malaurie also gives the Harratin contribution as 197 tonnes. One or other of these figures is presumably a typographic error (op. cit., 1953, p. 344).
23. Galan, op. cit., p. 230.
24. Malaurie, op. cit., p. 345.
25. Attempted between 1930 and 1944.
26. Probably by Harratin from Tidikelt two or three centuries ago.
27. See Nicolaisen, op. cit., 1963, p. 165.
28. See Florimond, Captain, *Annexe du Hoggar. Rapport annuel*, 1938, 200 p. (p. 113); Gast, M., op. cit., 1968, p. 120–21.

**Chapter 11 The Development of the Sahara**

1. Nicolaisen, op. cit., 1963, p. 198.
2. See Gast, M., *Alimentation des populations de l'Ahaggar*, Mémoires du C.R.A.P.E., VIII, 1968, p. 42.
3. Also the Compagnie Générale de Géophysique (C.G.G.).
4. The potential Harratin labour force in Ahaggar was estimated at about 1,500.
5. Blanguernon, C., *Le Hoggar* (2nd ed.), 1955, p. 154.
6. 1951, five months; 1952, short visit; 1953, three months; 1954–5, seven months approximately (op. cit., 1963, pp. 2–4).
7. Nicolaisen, op. cit., 1963, p. 199.
8. Attendance of classes 1947–50:

| | | | | |
|---|---|---|---|---|
| 1947–8 | Class 1 | 15 pupils | M. Blanguernon | 45 pupils |
| | „ 2 | 30 „ | Mme Blanguernon | |
| 1948–9 | „ 1 | 29 „ | | 64 „ |
| | „ 2 | 35 „ | | |

| | | | | |
|---|---|---|---|---|
| 1949–50 | Class 1 | 28 pupils | | 88 pupils |
| | „ 2 | 39 „ | | |
| | „ 3 | 21 „ (girls) Mme Forestier | | |

Source of figures unknown (Inspection Primaire à Constantine?); found in 'archives' left in the old school building in Tamanrasset.

9. See Germani, G., 'Secularisation, Modernisation, and Economic Development', in S. N. Eisenstadt (ed.), *The Protestant Ethic and Modernisation,* 1967, pp. 343–66.
10. Blanguernon, op. cit., 1955, p. 155.
11. One for Tamanrasset and one for the Hoggar.
12. One in the Amenukal's camp at Tiffert near Abalessa, one in Atakor among the Isandan section of the Aguh-en-tehle, and one in Tamesna, near Tin Zaouatene, for the Kel Ahaggar living in that area. A fourth was opened among the Dag Rali in 1961–2 but does not seem to have been operative for more than a few months at the most.
13. Quoted by Malaurie, op. cit., 1953, p. 346n.
14. Gast, op. cit., 1968, p. 41n.
15. Rognon, P., 'La Confederation des nomades Kel Ahaggar', *Annales Géographiques*, 71, No. 388, 1962, pp. 604–19 (see p. 617).
16. Jean-Marie, Henrique, Antoine and Abdullah (Louis Pilate).
17. Blaguernon, op. cit., 1955, p. 161.
18. 723 labourers.
19. Gast, op. cit., 1968, p. 41.
20. Blanguernon gives the number of workers registered from Ahaggar as 1,181, while Gast puts the number at 1,327. This difference may be accounted for by a difference in the periods taken or a differing interpretation of 'non-satisfaits'. The addition of Gast's composite figures gives a total of 1,377, which may be a typographic error or the result of the inclusion of some additional detail from the original report, which I have not been able to consult.
21. Blanguernon, op. cit., 1955, p. 163; Gast, op. cit., 1968, p. 41.
22. The initial processes of development had already led to a fivefold increase in the number of 'shopkeepers' – 100 to 500 during the 1950s, some of whom, such as Laroui, had bought their own trucks and were transporting produce direct from Algiers to Tamanrasset.
23. My estimate.
24. Manual labour was usually referred to as *chantier*! (Fr. 'work-site, construction site', etc.).
25. This practice does not seem to have been developed extensively. It was actively discouraged by the French, and 'interrupted' by independence.
26. This name, and those that follow, are pseudonymous.
27. This conclusion is based on the collection of detailed data of Kel Rela residency. 259 individuals were recorded out of an estimated total number of 300 Kel Rela. (Lhote gives the total number of Kel Rela in 1949 as 275 – op. cit., 1955, p. 224f.)
28. 1949 census. See Lhote, ibid.
29. 322 slaves to 275 Kel Rela.
30. These figures do not include groups belonging formerly to the Taitok drum group, who possessed relatively few slaves.

### Chapter 12 Algerian Independence

1. Arslan Humbaraci, whose assessment of the Algerian Revolution is perhaps overly critical, estimated that one-seventh of the Saharan population lost all forms of income. Humbaraci, A., *Algeria: A Revolution that Failed*, 1966, p. 206.
2. See Gordon, D. C., *The Passing of French Algeria*, 1966, pp. 153–9.
3. Reinforced by the decrees of 18 and 22 March, 1963.
4. *Colon* designates all French settlers in North Africa, both rural and urban. See Gordon, D. C., *North Africa's French Legacy, 1954–1962*, 1964, p. 5n.
5. The director of the Comité de Gestion, although elected by the workers, was appointed by the government.
6. *Le Monde*, 4 July 1963.
7. *Jeune Afrique*, 30 September–6 October, 1963, pp. 6–7.
8. See Gordon, D. C., op. cit., 1966, pp. 154–5.
9. In 1954, 92 per cent of the intellectual cadres and 82 per cent of the technicians occupying subordinate positions were European (Godon, D. C., op. cit., 1966, pp. 81–2).
10. The A.L.N. was founded on 10 October 1954 and reorganized at the meeting of the Conseil National de la Révolution Algérienne on 24 August 1956. After independence the A.L.N. was renamed the Armée Nationale Populaire (A.N.P.).
11. A process that has been referred to as 'Algerianization'.
12. Gast, M., 'Evolution de la vie économique et structures sociales en Ahaggar de 1660–1965', *Travaux de l'Institut de Recherches Sahariennes*, XXII, 1965, pp. 129–43.
13. See Gast, M., *Alimentation des populations de l'Ahaggar*, 1968, p. 42.
14. Moussa has been married twice: firstly to Tenert ult Beuh (deceased), by whom he had one son; and later to Telfensit ult Abukalel, whom he divorced and by whom he had three sons.
15. His brother Ama married an Irregenaten and now lives in Tamesna.
16. Wilayas were provinces established by the A.L.N. during the Revolution. There were six of them, each commanded by a colonel.
17. Wilaya VI was known by the French as the 'Phantom Wilaya', as its activities were almost completely restricted by French aerial reconnaissance over the Sahara.
18. I myself have been guilty of possible exaggeration on this point in an article written before the details of the skirmish became clearer to me (Keenan, J., 'Social Change among the Tuareg', in *Arabs and Berbers* (eds. E. Gellner and C. Micaud), 1972, p. 358.)
19. The injured were taken to separate hospitals, at Tamanrasset and In Eker!
20. The term Harratin is used here to refer to most of the sedentary community, which included several ex-slaves, as well as Ahl Azzi.

### Chapter 13 Drought and Economic Depression in Ahaggar

1. Figures based on the years 1955–64 only.
2. From 1925 onwards.
3. Since the establishment of the Mali frontier in 1905.
4. Gast, op. cit., 1968, p. 126.

5. Nicolaisen, op. cit., 1963, p. 41f.
6. Ibid., p. 146.
7. See Nicolaisen, op. cit., 1963, Fig. 105 on page 146.
8. Literal translation.
9. Nicolaisen mentions that goats may become emaciated if mated too often, and that the long hair of the northern (Ahaggar) variety, which is so important to craft, may not develop fully (op. cit., 1963, p. 38).
10. Ibid., p. 33f.
11. Kids born between these two periods are known as *ameshar* (ibid. p. 39).
12. Ibid., p. 36.
13. See Nicolaisen's study (ibid.) of these techniques for a more detailed account.
14. These two devices are known as *asedras* and *akara* respectively.
15. A technique described by Lhote, whereby the skin of a hedgehog is attached to the kid's head so that it will prick its mother and be kicked away, seems extremely rare, and hardly if ever used (Lhote, H., *La Chasse chez les Touaregs*, Paris, 1951, p. 136).
16. Gast, op. cit., 1968, p. 126.
17. Nicolaisen, op. cit., 1963, p. 42.
18. Meat is not regarded as a 'staple' food.
19. Nicolaisen, op. cit., 1963, p. 40.
20. In addition to these considerations, the meat of very old goats is of inferior quality.
21. Galan, op. cit., 1951, pp. 231.
22. Malaurie, op. cit., 1953, p. 344.
23. Capot-Rey, R., *Le Sahara Français*, Paris, 1953, p. 265.
24. See Nicolaisen's comments, op. cit., 1963, p. 42.
25. Lhote, op. cit., 1951, p. 9.
26. See Nicolaisen, op. cit., 1963, p. 42.
27. Ibid.
28. Gast, op. cit., 1968, p. 126.
29. These visits (in 1964 and 1965) were both in summer, when yields are lower.
30. Gast, op. cit., 1968, p. 71.
31. In 1965–6 the price of both millet and wheat was stabilized by the government and controlled by the Société Agricole de Prévoyance (S.A.P.).
32. Mostly motor-pumps to irrigate their gardens.
33. Bureau de Travail et Main d'Oeuvres.
34. It may be suggested, as several Kel Ahaggar have themselves stated, that the loss of Iklan was partly compensated by there being less mouths to feed!
35. Gast, M., 'Evolution de la vie économique et structures sociales en Ahaggar de 1660–1965', *Travaux de l'Institut de Recherches Sahariennes*, XXII, 1965, pp. 129–43; Gast, M., *Alimentation des populations de l'Ahaggar*, Mémoires du C.R.A.P.E., VIII, 1968.
36. Blanguernon, C., *Le Hoggar* (2nd ed.), 1955.

**Chapter 14 The Preconditions for Socialism**

1. Verbal information.

2. A mechanic, attached to the Sub-Prefecture (agricultural section), visited the co-operatives.
3. These familial dependents may assist in such activities as preparing the land, bird-scaring, harvesting, etc., and the tending of goats and other livestock, which although owned on a family basis are often tethered out to graze on the co-operative land.
4. During recent years the market for dried tomatoes throughout the Sahara has been undermined by the introduction of the tinned variety. The price of dried tomatoes in Tamanrasset in 1970 was 4–5 D.A. per kilo, but since one kilo of dried tomatoes is equivalent to twenty kilos of fresh tomatoes, the effective price of harvested tomatoes is about 0·25 D.A. per kilo – or about 1p. per lb.
5. Aktouf was quite aware of these administrative difficulties and deficiencies, and during his period of office compiled an extremely detailed and penetrative report on the administrative problems and needs of Ahaggar, which is the foundation of the government's present policy of trying to recruit and establish conscientious and sympathetic local administrative and technical cadres within the region.
6. If, for example, a pump breaks down, the mechanic from Tamanrasset is despatched immediately; in other centres a pump may lie idle for weeks.
7. Once a grain exporter, Tazrouk imported forty-five tonnes of grain from Tamanrasset in 1970.
8. By the end of 1971, when I last talked to him, he was extremely pessimistic over the state of affairs and future of Tazrouk. At that time two years had passed without the *oued* flowing, when normally it can be expected to flow up to six times in a year. Also, in 1971, after considerable effort, two tonnes of grapes were harvested and sent to Tamanrasset for sale – only to arrive as a pulverized mass!
9. The particular villager was a Dag Rali!
10. The Director of Education himself could not understand why the villagers, having stated that they wanted schooling for their children, made no attempt to send any of their thirty 'out of school' children to Tamanrasset.
11. Verbal communication.
12. Apparently mislaid in Ouargla.
13. The name 'In Eker' was often used for the employment agency at the base.
14. Nicolaisen, op. cit., 1963, p. 212.
15. On 12 October 1965 the first detachment of *méharistes* graduated from the military college at Ouargla.
16. These figures apply only to the main wheat harvest and do not take into account other 'secondary' crops such as millet, barley, tomatoes, etc.
17. Based on 1964 total wage payments of 300,000 D.A. per month.
18. This amount of millet represented an equivalent monetary value of about 90,000 D.A. (£7,500) based on the Tamanrasset price of 0·60 D.A. per kilo but was obviously of far greater value to the nomads since it involved no initial monetary resources. (This estimate is based on caravans comprising 200 men and about 1,200 camels, which is considerably less than the size of caravans recorded in previous decades – see Ch. 10.)
19. The 197 tonnes of grain contributed to the nomadic economy in 1946 through the *khamast* would have been equivalent to about 120 tonnes under the *aril* system, while the 121 tonnes of wheat harvested in 1950, a bad year, would have

provided a little over 50 tonnes to the nomads on the basis of an *aril* division. This latter estimate makes a small allowance for independent cultivators.

20. The Ait Lowayen also engaged extensively in the southern caravans.
21. Société Nationale de Recherches et d'Exploitations Minières.
22. Prior to independence this man had had eight slaves. He was now left with only one, to whom he paid a monthly wage, and was glad that the others had now gone, for not only had they been a drain on his resources and a constant source of anxiety in terms of his obligations and responsibilities towards them, but without them he could, to use his own expression, 'at last live in peace and quiet'!
23. SONAREM did not establish a base in Ahaggar until 1969.
24. It should be said that Terhenanet and the near-by village of Ilaman (now deserted) are not well suited to cultivation because of their nadequate water supplies.

### Chapter 15 The 'Algerianization' of the Kel Ahaggar

1. Between 1962–3 and 1968–9 inclusive, the number of children attending primary school doubled, while the number at the secondary level tripled; the greatest rate of increase was after 1965.
2. Statement from Ministry of Information.
3. This policy is also aimed at the emancipation of women, who are considered to have an essential role to play in an industrializing state. Between 1962–3 and 1968–9 the number of girls attending school doubled at the primary level and tripled at the secondary level.
4. This excludes the 'écoles nomades' which were closed immediately at independence.
5. This increase was uniform among boys and girls, the ratio between them being about three to one.
6. The Ouargla Plan also recommended the introduction of secondary education at Tamanrasset.
7. Ibn Khaldoun had been opened privately in 1962 by a number of Mozabite, Moulay, and other 'maraboutic' families who wanted their own Koranic school, and who themselves paid for the teacher. In 1964 Ibn Khaldoun was nationalized and renamed Medersa. This, however, involved little immediate change in its organization except that its staffing and management became the responsibility of the municipality. But since the founders of the school had effective control over the municipal council, nationalization merely absolved them from any further personal financial commitment towards the school's maintenance while assuring them effective, albeit 'indirect', control over its management. It is consequently no surprise that by 1965–6 the number of boarders had increased by only four!
8. The boarding-annexe at Tazrouk was never completed.
9. Nine boarders were registered at Tahifet and five at Amsel. There are no records for the number of boarders at either Iglene or Tazrouk as the few nomadic children who entered these schools (mostly Isekkemaren at Tazrouk and Iklan-Tawsit at Iglene) stayed with families living in the villages. These families seem to have had kinship ties with the camps from which the children came.

10. The administration's registration of these children was remarkably vague and inaccurate. The first detailed census of the boarding children was made in 1969. This work was undertaken by myself in collaboration with, and on behalf of, the Director of Education in Tamanrasset. This census, which effectively compiled a 'case-study' of each child, showed that the official government figures were quite meaningless.
11. Heavy rain fell in the summer of 1968, and the total rainfall for the year, 84.7 mm., was above the annual mean average. But rainfall figures for the period show that about half of this rain fell in cloudbursts of short duration, on 31 May (14.7 mm. in 1 hr. 25 min.), 11 June (13 mm. in 1 hr), and 12 September. In such conditions the infiltration capacity of the 'soil' is reached rapidly, so that most of the water runs off into the *oueds*, and is consequently 'lost' to pasture.
12. Of the fourteen Dag Rali children, four were drawn from the camps centred on Terhenanet, eight from the camps centred on Tagmart, and two from the Kel Tinhart section in the Tin Haren area to the north of Ilaman.
13. The fear of 'Kel Asouf' was very real. Staircases, shower closets and so forth were initially regarded with considerable trepidation.
14. The 'guardian' of the boarding-house was a relatively old man, who not only spoke Tamahak but also knew many of the children's families. On several later occasions I came across evidence to suggest that he had played an important part in allaying the nomads' fears and prejudices about the boarding-school by passing on messages to the nomadic community regarding the welfare of their children.
15. It is possible that these particular children (or rather their parents) were not positively motivated in this respect, for Laporte had in fact arranged for transport from these distant centres with prearranged pick-up points along the *pistes*. Nevertheless, as Laporte agreed, it is asking a lot of a 'nomad' to be at a specific point in the middle of the desert at 08.45 hours on a specific day five months' hence!
16. It seems that most of these had in any case been classified by Laporte as 'non-satisfaits' during the previous year, and were thus not encouraged to return.
17. Although there were no confirmed reports of parents removing their children from In Salah, several threatened to do so and expressed their dislike of the scheme. The Sub-Prefect, aware of these feelings and the dangers of continuing with the scheme, obtained authorization for the redevelopment of the boarding-house at Abalessa. Electricity, running water and modern sanitation were installed, and the Abalessa boarding-house was opened for the 1970 school year as an 'annexe' of the central boarding-house in Tamanrasset, under the direction and management of Tamanrasset. The total intake of boarders in 1970 was 220, fifty-six of whom were sent to Abalessa. However, in 1971, because of staffing problems at Abalessa, the 'annexe' was closed (temporarily) and all the children were transferred to Tamanrasset.
18. Deposits of tungsten ore at Laouni, about 200 kilometres south of Tamanrasset, were first exploited by the French around 1964, and were being 'reopened' by SONAREM.
19. The stabilization and maintenance of regional price equivalency on these commodities necessitated the subsidization of their transport costs to Tamanrasset.

20. It was envisaged, optimistically, that 2,000 job opportunities would be created by about 1974.
21. Several of the Kel Ahaggar who had moved back to Tamesna after independence, and particularly after the closure of In Eker, were now returning to Ahaggar.

### Chapter 16 Differential Responses of the Kel Ahaggar to Modernization

1. See Fig. 8. The absence of Kel Ahnet children is accounted for by their inability to attend school after the closure of the 'transit' boarding-houses. This also applies to most other *tawsatin* such as the Ait Lowayen, whose enrolment in the Tamanrasset boarding-house after 1968–9 was low. See p. 309.
2. The Dag Rali were certainly more dependent on In Eker, closer to Assekrem and the influence of the Frères, and probably a little wealthier in terms of livestock.
3. An additional section, the Kel Agelella, lived predominantly outside Aguh-en-tehle territory proper in the Agelella area, which traditionally falls more in the territory of the Tegehe-n-Efis.
4. The three vegetation zones recognized indigenously, Abada, Tarayin and Atakor, conform closely with the vegetation zones recognized by R. Maire (Maire, R., *Études sur la flore et la végètation du Sahara Central*, Mémoires de la Société d'Histoire Naturelle de l'Afrique du Nord, No. 3, Alger, 1933–40), namely: (1) a Tropical Zone up to 1,700–1,800 metres above sea level; (2) a Lower Mediterranean Zone between 1,800 and 2,300–2,400 metres above sea level; (3) an Upper Mediterranean Zone from 2,400 metres upwards. (See also Lhote, op. cit., 1955, p. 41f.; Nicolaisen, op. cit., 1963, pp. 29–31).
5. This perennial pasture consists mostly of acacias, which grow relatively densely in the major valleys. (See Nicolaisen, op. cit., 1963, p. 129).
6. For a full discussion of this subject, see Nicolaisen, op. cit., 1963, p. 130f.
7. These are almost the only exogamous marriages contracted by the Dag Rali. See Table 1, p. 117.
8. Pseudonym.
9. This was also true of other Ihaggaren, such as Ellou ag Amarai of the Taitok, but the number of other Ihaggaren in Tamanrasset was so few that I refer only to the Kel Rela.
10. Hadj Moussa's activities in the years immediately following independence can be regarded as exceptional and are not considered in this context.
11. See Wolf, E. R., 'Aspects of Group Relations in a Complex Society, Mexico', *American Anthropologist*, 58, 1956, pp. 1065–78; Bailey, F. G., *Stratagems and Spoils. A Social Anthropology of Politics*, Oxford, 1969; Perry, J. A. G., 'The Broker in a Rural Lesotho Community', *African Studies*, 32, No. 3, 1973, pp. 137–52; et al.
12. Perry, op. cit., 1973.
13. See Wolf, E. R., 'Kinship, Friendship and Patron-Client Relations in Complex Societies', in M. Banton (ed.), *The Social Anthropology of Complex Societies*, A.S.A. Monograph No. 4., Tavistock, London, 1966.
14. In conjunction with Djanet.

15. Based on adult male consumption of 400 grammes per day. For comments on this estimate and further discussion of the availability and consumption rates of agricultural products, see Nicolaisen, op. cit., 1963, p. 200.
16. Several Kel Rela either owned or had access to motor vehicles.
17. The girl's father's sister had married a Chaamba, whose son had married the sister of Bedi ag Azouri, the son of the Aguh-en-tehle chief. The girl herself was marrying an Iforas man from Timasinin near Fort Flatters.
18. Mostly Kel Agelella, Kel Tarayin and Kel Tarhaouhaout.
19. An *ahal* is an amorous get-together of young men and women (usually unmarried) after dusk, at which women will play the *imzad* (one-string 'violin') and recite poetry. On such occasions as weddings, when many people are gathered together, an *ahal* may continue throughout most of the night. They are a great stimuli to the sensual, aesthetic and intellectual gratification of the Kel Ahaggar, and in many ways are best described as 'institutionalized courting'. Men will often travel great distances to attend an *ahal* held by a woman who is held in high esteem as a great *imzad* player and poetess. For a more detailed description, see Foucauld, C. de, op. cit., II, pp. 559–64.
20. Beh's brother also attended the wedding but drove there in a land-rover, bringing provisions for certain camps.
21. It is also likely that the process of disintegration may have differed between various Aguh-en-tehle sections. Although I have no evidence, this was perhaps the case with some of the Isandan more closely related to the Kel Tamanrasset.
22. The Tegehe-n-Efis, whose territory adjoins that of the Aguh-en-tehle to the west, and who claim to be related to the Aguh-en-tehle as 'cousins', also came from this area at about the same time. It seems that the Aguh-en-tehle's move north to Ahaggar may have been to seek the protection of the nobles of Ahaggar from the tyrannical exactions made upon them in the south. If this was true, it provides us with the historical basis for and 'explanation' of their greater predisposition and 'friendly' attitude towards the Kel Rela in terms of the *temazlayt* relationship, compared with that of the Dag Rali.
23. It is not the order itself that maintains any definition and conceptualizations of social reality, but rather the 'carriers' of that order.
24. 'Algerianization' refers, in this context, to the overall process by which the Algerian order, in all its phases and dimensions, was imposed, and refers specifically to the policies and actions of the Algerian administration.
25. The 'replacement' or 'removal' of these institutions and relations was also symbolic, for the traditional institutional order symbolized the domination and repression of the colonial order. Its persistence was thus a real and a symbolic impediment to the establishment of a socialist order.
26. A few Kel Rela who had gained some specialized training occupied such positions as radio operators, medical orderlies, etc.
27. This excludes those members of the Isandan who were more closely related through socio-economic ties to the Kel Tamanrasset, and perhaps also the Relaydin and other more geographically distant groups.
28. Fig. 8 does not include the four Kel Rela, three of whom were from Tamesna and one from Tazrouk (in the C.E.G.), the Irregenaten, who were predominantly from Tamesna, nor the children listed in categories 16, 17 and 19. It is also a

little misleading, in that many Kel Ahaggar children were attending village schools at this time. For example, there were three Ait Lowayen, two Dag Rali (not collected on Aktouf's drive through the camps) and nine Isekkemaren (Kel Amguid and Kel Tefedest) in the Ideles school. There was also a small number of Aguh-en-tehle children at school in Tahifet. Most Kel Rela children were at school in Tamanrasset. Furthermore, any comparison with the Dag Rali must also take into account the former existence of an 'école nomade' in Aguh-en-tehle territory. Nine of the twenty Aguh-en-tehle children at boarding-school in 1969 had brothers who were or had been at school, and at least two of them had attended the 'école nomade'. Nevertheless, the pattern of selecting Aguh-en-tehle children for school was similar to that of all other nomad groups, among whom children fill an important role in the domestic organization of the camp (unlike cultivators). Aguh-en-tehle children attending school came from families in which there was at least one other unmarried brother living in the camp. The only exception to this pattern was that of an Aguh-en-tehle family which had been settled in Tahifet for some years. The average size of the sibling group (brothers and sisters) of nomadic children attending boarding-school was: Dag Rali 4·1; Aguh-en-tehle 5·5; Irregenaten 5·6; Ait Lowayen 6·0; Iklan Tawsit 6·8.

29. Few Dag Rali will visit Abalessa willingly for fear of the resentful and contemptuous way they are treated. The Dag Rali's rights over Abalessa were vested predominantly in the Kel Tamanrasset and Kel Terhenanet sections. It may be suggested that by being effectively denied access to agricultural land in their major cultivation area, their 'semi-sedentarization' has necessarily been orientated towards Tamanrasset, and the opportunities for wage-earning rather than agriculture.
30. Aktouf himself made two visits to the area after the takeover of the *foggaras*, and stationed a member of the Bureau Politique permanently in the village.
31. See p. 249 regarding increased productivity of *foggaras* after takeover.
32. The increasing dependency on and viability of agriculture at Abalessa is expressed in the relationship between the co-operatives and the *foggara* systems. Although the *foggaras* are worked on a 'family-community' basis, their organization and production is closely integrated with that of the co-operatives. While there is always water available in the *foggaras*, the co-operative pumps may break down or the wells run dry in a bad year. However, most families are represented in both enterprises, so that if there is insufficient water for the co-operatives, its members will assist kinsmen in the cultivation of *foggara* gardens, thus increasing the latter's productivity output to compensate for the decreased productivity of the co-operative.
33. This situation is similar to that of the important Aguh-en-tehle cultivation centre of In Dalag. There, the cultivation 'centre' extends over about fifteen kilometres and comprises a series of little communities (Tehi-n-Oudi, Tin Tsoumar, Tabarakaten, In Tinsi and In Tolouline) dotted down the Oued In Dalag below the main cultivation centre.
34. The relatively low attendance at the Tahifet school is attributed by the Director of Education primarily to the social and geographical problems stemming from this ribbon settlement pattern. On the other hand, it may also be suggested that

this geographical situation has facilitated (socially) the sedentarization of the nomads.

35. The population of Abalessa is approximately 1,000, and that of Amsel about 300–400. The Algerian census of 1966 is particularly misleading, being based on areas surrounding the villages rather the villages themselves. Figures provided for the Department of Education in 1965 (source unknown – probably the Frères) were Abalessa 598, Amsel 242.
36. Although Amsel is located in Tegehe-n-Efis territory, about thirty kilometres south of Tamanrasset, it borders on Aguh-en-tehle territory, particularly that of the Kel Agelella, many of whom camp in the area, especially along the Oued Izernen, which flows through Amsel, and the Oued Tefougigine about five kilometres further east. The Tegehe-n-Efis are a small *tawsit* numbering only about 80 to 100 persons, and their camps are located predominantly in the Oued Tamanrasset downstream of the town, particularly around the small cultivation centre of Tidjenouine. Amsel is thus more or less in-between Aguh-en-tehle and Tegehe-n-Efis territory, and both of them owned gardens there. (The Tegehe-n-Efis, initially attached to the Taitok *ettebel*, later became attached to the Kel Rela.)
37. I was unable to obtain details of the amounts of salt and millet exchanged.
38. No such ties existed between any Dag Rali and their Harratin.
39. This was in the autumn of 1969.

## Chapter 17 Problems of Integration

1. The most significant cave-paintings (the Tassili Frescoes), and the most frequented by tourists, are those in the Djanet area, and not around Tamanrasset.
2. See Bourgeot, A., 'Nomadisme et sédentarisation: le processus d'intégration chez les Kel Ahaggar', *Revue de l'Occident Musulman et de la Méditerranée*, No. 11, ler. sem. 1972, pp. 85–92, for a fuller discussion of this problem.
3. Bourgeot (op. cit., 1972, p. 91) uses the terms 'asociaux' and 'marginaux' in describing this state.
4. Whether encapsulation will become more or less pronounced in the future depends on numerous factors and must be left open to question. As Bourgeot has commented (op. cit., 1972, p. 91), the process of insertion consists first of all of finding a place. But when no such place exists, the process quickly tends towards a conflict situation which is perceived by the 'immigrant' as a rejection by the wider 'adopting' society. For the nomads entering Tamanrasset, such a situation may well become accentuated through the difficulties experienced in their finding employment. In the more distant future, however, when the present generation of children at school have grown up and acquired employment in Tamanrasset or elsewhere, this process may become reversed.
5. In particular, the declining terms of trade on caravans and the shift towards an *aril* system.
6. After about 1968, his younger brother Aflan began to help him more in the cultivation of the gardens, thus allowing Elwafil to spend more time away from the village in search of work.

7. General term for spices and herbal medicines. (See Foucauld, C. de, op. cit., V, 1951–2, p. 1808).
8. *Astragallus vogelii.*
9. Germinating only after rains. (Foucauld, C. de, op. cit., III, 1951–2, p. 1035).
10. *Moricandia arvensis* (wild cabbage).
11. *Verbascum* (?) germinating only after rains. (Foucauld, C. de, op. cit., I, 1951–2, p. 345).
12. *Atriplex halimus.*
13. *Panicum turgidum.*
14. Elwafil himself has never been on a caravan.
15. Amin, as a slave, belonged to Amahis, the wife of the old Kel Hirafok chief, Mohammed el Kamil. Much of his boyhood was spent in Tamesna, where he tended Kel Hirafok camels. After his liberation he worked intermittently on an *aril* basis in Mohammed el Kamil's gardens at Hirafok.
16. Bourgeot, op. cit., 1972, p. 90.

# APPENDIX I

Table A Summary table of Ahaggar population and sources.

| | 1860 | 1909 | 1911 | 1916 | 1938 | 1941–6 | 1948 | 1949 | 1950 | 1959 | 1962 | 1966 |
|---|---|---|---|---|---|---|---|---|---|---|---|---|
| Ahaggar | 3,000 (G) | | | | 6,534 (L) | | 10,288 (FM) | 10,298 (FM) | | 11,606 (G) | 13,000 (G) | 16,124 (Alg) |
| | | | | | 8,000 (est) | | | 10,000 (M) | | | | 15,922 (G) |
| *Nomads* | | | | | | 6,222 (M) | 6,048 (FM) | 6,013 (FM) | 6,253 (L) | 6,069 (G) | 6,500 (G) | |
| Kel Ahaggar | | | | | 3,254 (L) | 4,611 (M) | 4,420 (M) | 4,294 (M) | 4,611 (L) | 4,902* (G) | | |
| Slaves | | | | | | 1,642 (M) | 1,618 (M) | 1,719 (M) | 1,642 (L) | 1,167 (G) | | |
| *Sedentary* | | 697 (L) | 1,203 (V) | 1,310 (L) | 2,280 (L) | | 4,240 (FM) | 4,285 (FM) | 4,093 (L) | 5,536 (G) | 6,500 (G) | |
| Tamanrasset | | 42 (Mot) | 150 (V) | | 686 (T) | | 1,775 (FM) | 1,796 (FM) | 1,600 (T) | 2,300 (G) | 3,000 (G) | 4,060 (Alg) |
| Other centres | | | 1,053 (V) | | 1,399 (T) | | 2,465 (FM) | 2,489 (FM) | 2,493 (L) | 3,236 (G) | 3,500 (G) | |
| (Harratin) | | | | | | (2,558) 1945 (M) | (2,705) 1947 (M) | | | | | |

G – Gast
L – Lhote
T – Archives Tamanrasset
FM – French Military
V – Voinot (see Lhote)
Mot – Motylinski
M – Malaurie
Alg – Algerian Census
* includes Tatiok in Tamesna and Adrar-n-Iforas

Table B Population of Tuareg descent groups in Ahaggar, 1949 (Lhote, 1955, p.224f.; Lhote's spelling).

| | Tuareg | | | | | Slaves | | | | |
|---|---|---|---|---|---|---|---|---|---|---|
| Descent Groups | Men | Women | Boys | Girls | Total | Men | Women | Boys | Girls | Total |
| *Kel Rela* | 71 | 80 | 54 | 70 | 275 | 88 | 109 | 61 | 64 | 322 |
| Dag Rali | 104 | 121 | 80 | 91 | 386 | 125 | 164 | 73 | 64 | 426 |
| Agouh-en-tehle | 118 | 170 | 159 | 138 | 585 | 50 | 60 | 19 | 20 | 149 |
| Ait Lowayen | 82 | 119 | 121 | 81 | 403* | 28 | 37 | 10 | 13 | 88 |
| Relaiddin[1] | | | | | 40 | | | | | |
| Ibargan | 4 | 5 | 9 | 8 | 26 | | | | | |
| Ibettenaten | 36 | 39 | 23 | 31 | 129 | 11 | 8 | 3 | 3 | 25 |
| Iklan Taousit | 117 | 167 | 182 | 134 | 600† | 43 | 15 | 25 | 20 | 113 |
| *Isekkamaren* | | | | | | | | | | |
| Iheiaouen Hada | 46 | 86 | 60 | 61 | 253 | 22 | 48 | 11 | 15 | 96 |
| Kel Inrer | 51 | 50 | 41 | 34 | 176 | 9 | 25 | 8 | 9 | 51 |
| Kel Tefedest | 19 | 22 | 14 | 6 | 61 | 2 | 6 | 2 | 1 | 11 |
| Kel Immidir[2] | 51 | 67 | 25 | 27 | 170‡ | 2 | 6 | 2 | 1 | 11 |
| Kel Tazoulet | 40 | 56 | 37 | 25 | 158 | 15 | 31 | 4 | 7 | 57 |
| Ireguenaten | 107 | 96 | 145 | 91 | 439§ | 49 | 65 | 37 | 21 | 172 |
| *Taitok*[3] | 9 | 10 | 9 | 5 | 33 | 4 | 3 | 1 | 2 | 10 |
| Kel Ahnet | 34 | 38 | 28 | 27 | 127 | 2 | 3 | | | 5 |
| Tegehe-n-Efis | 34 | 38 | 28 | 27 | 127 | 2 | 3 | 12 | 1 | 18 |

| | | | | | | | | | | |
|---|---|---|---|---|---|---|---|---|---|---|
| *Isekkemaren* | | | | | | | | | | |
| Kel I-n-Tounin | | | | | | | | | | |
| Iouarouaren | 9 | 12 | 16 | 10 | 47 | 3 | 4 | | | 7 |
| Ikoutisen | 13 | 24 | 26 | 21 | 84 | 1 | 7 | 5 | 6 | 19 |
| Ikechchemaden[4] | | | | | | | | | | |
| *Tegehe Mellet* | 8 | 11 | 9 | 5 | 33 | | | | | |
| *Isekkemaren* | | | | | | | | | | |
| Kel Terourirt | 20 | 21 | 10 | 11 | 62 | | | | | |
| Kel Ouhet | 17 | 22 | 15 | 16 | 70 | 6 | 7 | 4 | | 17 |
| Kel Torha | | | | | | | | | | |

Iforas (3 fractions) – attached more to Tassili – approximately 150 individuals.

* Lhote totals 400
† „ „ 500
‡ „ „ 179
§ „ „ 435

1. Ralaiddin are part of Agouh-en-tehle.
2. One must add to Kel Immidir the Iselamaten (Tegehe-n-Selama) – fifteen tents.
3. Only counts those Taitok in Ahaggar.
4. Ikechchemaden – no more than fifteen men, and live with Dag Rali.

Table C French military census, 1948–9* (N.B. including slaves).

| Sedentary Population | | | Nomadic Population | | |
|---|---|---|---|---|---|
| Cultivation centres | 1948 | 1949 | Tribes | 1948 | 1949 |
| Tamanrasset | 1,775 | 1,796 | Kel Rela | 605 | 599 |
| Abalessa | 549 | 541 | Tedjehe Mellet | 32 | 38 |
| In did | 66 | 66 | Iforas | 99 | 90 |
| In Dalag | 152 | 159 | Taitoqs | 39 | 43 |
| Iffok | 15 | 15 | Dag Rali | 769 | 812 |
| Tarhaouhaout | 154 | 161 | Adjoun Tehle | 754 | 743 |
| Sileskine | 69 | 69 | Kel In Ghan | 225 | 227 |
| Amsel | 87 | 89 | Ibergan | 24 | 26 |
| Silet | 38 | 38 | Kel Tefedest | 72 | 72 |
| Tiguenouin | 22 | 24 | Ikotessen | 98 | 103 |
| In Amguel | 298 | 295 | Irreguenaten | 600 | 608 |
| Hirafok | 50 | 50 | Kel Imidir | 215 | 225 |
| Ideles | 231 | 231 | Kel Tazulet | 212 | 212 |
| Taguembait | 26 | 28 | Ihaouen Hadda | 328 | 289 |
| In Mertek | 3 | 40 | Iklan Taousit | 638 | 770 |
| Aglil | 24 | 24 | Kel Azziz | — | 104 |
| Tit | 196 | 197 | Irreguenaten | 153 | — |
| Otoul | 35 | 35 | Kel Ahnet | 132 | 128 |
| Mertoutek | 31 | — | Tedjehe nefis | 120 | 120 |
| Tiffert | 164 | 166 | Iouarouaren | 53 | 51 |
| Ait Oklan | 25 | 24 | Ait Lohen | 618 | 488 |
| Tazrouk | 180 | 182 | Kel Ohet | 98 | 84 |
| Tahart | 50 | 50 | Kel Terourirt | 68 | 68 |
| Total | 4,240 | 4,285 | | 6,048 | 6,013 |

* Copied from archives of Director of Education, Tamanrasset. Spelling as in census.

Table D Population of villages (Lhote, 1955, pp. 292–3; Lhote's spelling).

| Village | 1904[1] | 1909[2] | 1911[3] | 1938[4] | 1950[5] | Official census of 1949–50 | | | |
|---|---|---|---|---|---|---|---|---|---|
| | | | | | | Men | Women | Boys | Girls |
| Tamanrasset | | 42 | 150 | 686 | 1,600 | 504 | 447 | 334 | 315 |
| Abalessa | 40 families | 64 | 272 | 250 | 547 | 111 | 125 | 156 | 155 |
| In Amedgel | 40 families | 120 | 180 | 206 | 297 | 76 | 82 | 81 | 58 |
| Iglen | | 19 | | 168 | | | | | |
| Ideles | 20 families | 45 | 70 | 160 | 231 | 76 | 69 | 47 | 39 |
| Tazrouk | 240 persons | 83 | 150 | 148 | | | | | |
| Tit | 40 families | 50 | 75 | 98 | 238 | 63 | 70 | 59 | 47 |
| Tarhaouhaout | | 90 | 140 | 91 | 66 | 11 | 13 | 26 | 16 |
| Amsel | | | 90 | 66 | 73 | 20 | 20 | 19 | 14 |
| Tahifet | | | | 39 | 35 | 9 | 8 | 9 | 9 |
| Tigueneouin | | | 25 | 23 | 22 | 7 | 4 | 6 | 5 |
| Mertoutek | 4–5 families | | | 60 | 38 | 11 | 9 | 7 | 11 |
| Herafoek | 2 families | | | 80 | 195 | 34 | 37 | 73 | 51 |
| Ilaman | | 10 | | 0 | 0 | | | | |
| Tifert | | 12 | | | 155 | 31 | 38 | 45 | 41 |
| Ti-in-Tarabine | 20 families | 41 | 15 | 0 | 0 | | | | |
| Tagrembait | | | | | 19 | 5 | 5 | 6 | 3 |
| Talan-Teidit | | | | | 18 | 5 | 7 | 5 | 1 |
| Aglil | 0 | | | 0 | 24 | 10 | 6 | 1 | 7 |
| I-n-Adjou | | | | | 21 | 7 | 3 | 6 | 5 |
| I-n-Azrou | | | | | 17 | 4 | 1 | 7 | 5 |
| Otoul | | | | 0 | 58 | 17 | 12 | 7 | 12 |
| Ennedid | 0 | | | | 46 | 7 | 10 | 20 | 9 |

Continued on p. 360

Table D—continued from p. 359

| Village | 1904[1] | 1909[2] | 1911[3] | 1938[4] | 1950[5] | Official census of 1949–50 | | | |
|---|---|---|---|---|---|---|---|---|---|
| | | | | | | Men | Women | Boys | Girls |
| Tahart | | | | 0 | 41 | 8 | 9 | 14 | 10 |
| Aitoklane | | | | 0 | 25 | 4 | 9 | 4 | 8 |
| I-n-Daladj | | | | | 191 | 45 | 41 | 60 | 45 |
| Effoq | | | | | 13 | 4 | 5 | 1 | 3 |
| Ti-n-Amensar | 10–15 families | 50 | 36 | 0 | 60 | | | | |
| Essali-Sekin | | 5 | | | | | | | |
| Silet | | | | | (17)? | 3 | 2 | 3 | 5? |
| | | 631 | 1,203 | 2,075 | 4,030 | | | | |

1. Inquiries of Père de Foucauld (approximate figures).
2. Inquiries of Motylinski.
3. Inquiries of Voinot, cited by Chudeau.
4. Archives of Tamanrasset.
5. Archives of Tamanrasset.

These figures illustrate the variation in certain centres, their temporary abandonment, and their renewed activity after a period of favourable rains. Several had become impoverished to the benefit of others, e.g. Tarhaouhaout declined in relation to Tamanrasset with the transfer of the French post. The growing centres around Abalessa have become centres of attraction (Iglen, Tiffert, etc.), and have drawn the population from isolated centres such as Ilaman and Terhenanet. In 1939, some important centres such as Tit, and smaller ones such as Otoul, Tifert, Aitoklane and Talan-Teidit, had been completely abandoned.

The drought of 1950 forced many cultivators to abandon their fields. Thus, only twenty people were resident in Hirafok, when the official census for that same year was 195.

Table E Algerian census, 1966, arondissement of Tamanrasset. (spelling as in census, e.g. Dag Ghali)

| District No. | Name | Population |
|---|---|---|
| 1 | Tamanrasset – Centre ville | 620 |
| 2 | " – Hofra | 484 |
| 3 | " – Kxelfugani | 675 |
| 4 | " – Tahagart (1) | 680 |
| 5 | " –Tahagart (2) | 616 |
| 6 | " – Guatt el Oued | 391 |
| 7 | " – Mechouene | 216 |
| 8 | " – Hadrian | 378 |
| | *Tamanrasset total* | 4,060 |
| 9 | Tazrouk | 599 |
| 10 | Ti-n-Tarabine | 574 |
| 11 | Tahifet | 930 |
| 12 | Tarhawhawt | 687 |
| 13 | Amsel | 491 |
| 14 | In Azrou | 435 |
| 15 | Dag Ghali (Dag Rali) | 542 |
| 16 | | |
| 17 | | |
| 18 | | |
| 19 | | |
| 20 | | |
| 21 | | |
| 22 | Tin Zaouten | 1,041 |
| 23 | Tamiaouene | 554 |
| 24 | Abalessa (1) | 375 |
| 25 | Abalessa (2) | 346 |
| 26 | Iglene | 505 |
| 27 | Ti-n-Amenserh | 610 |
| 28 | Tit | 514 |
| 29 | In Amguel | 987 |
| 30 | Mertoutek | 461 |
| 31 | Amguid | 387 |
| 32 | Meniet | 529 |
| 33 | Hirafok | 473 |
| 34 | Ideles | 669 |
| 35 | Ahnet | 355 |
| | *Total* | 12,064 |
| | *Total for Ahaggar* | 16,124 |

Estimated increase based on national growth rate of 3·2 per cent:

| | | | |
|---|---|---|---|
| 1966 | 16,124 | 1969 | 17,723 |
| 1967 | 16,640 | 1970 | 18,290 |
| 1968 | 17,173 | | |

# APPENDIX II

Dag Rali Land-rent Payments (Nicolaisen, 1963, p. 148).

| Tenants | Name and value of sub-area | Annual land-rent to the Amenukal |
|---|---|---|
| **Danguchi**, chief of the Dag Rali and leader of the Kel Tamanraset section | **Isekram** Hunting of barbary sheep. For every four or five barbary sheep killed one is given to the tenant | two goats |
| **Yeki** of the Kel Tamanraset section | **Tagmart** No particular value | two water bags one rope of goat's hair |
| **Amma** of the Kel Terhenanet section | **Arechchum** No particular value | two water bags one rope of goat's hair |
| **Khabte** of the Kel Tamanraset section and **Akhasen** of the Kel Terhenanet section | **In–Daeag** Hunting of barbary sheep Wild donkeys | one donkey |
| **Afarek** of the Kel Herhafek section | **Akal–Ereren** Hunting of barbary sheep | Unknown |
| **Buskeyas and Demoni**, two brothers of the Kel Tenhart section | **Tahat** Important hunting ground for barbary sheep, which are protected for three months annually. Domestic animals never graze in this sub-area | Formerly three barbary sheep (present rent unknown) |
| **Danguchi**, chief of the Dag Rali representing the two sections Kel Tamanraset and Kel Terhenanet | **Abalessa** A very extended area comprising the village of Abalessa and other agricultural settlements | No land-rent as the Amenukal receives dues for every garden in this area |
| **Danguchi**, chief of the Dag Rali representing the two sections of Kel Tamanraset and Kel Terhenanet. Land-rent is paid collectively by members of the two sections | **Tezza** Important hunting ground for barbary sheep, which are protected for three months annually. Domestic animals never graze in this sub-area | one donkey (formerly four barbary sheep). In this particular case an annual land-rent comprising two hides of barbary sheep (formerly two barbary sheep) are also given to Danguchi as chief of the Dag Rali |

Aguh-en-tehle Land-rent Payments (from Nicolaisen, 1963, p. 149).

| Tenants | Value of sub-area | Annual land-rent to the Amenukal |
|---|---|---|
| **Sama Alatokh**, chief of the Aguh-en-tehle, chief of the Kel Tarhaouhaout section, and leader of the Kel Twes sub-section | Cultivation grounds at Tarhaouhaout and I-n-dalag. Hunting of barbary sheep. Wild donkeys for domestication | two donkeys |
| **Omana**, Khalifa (leader) of the Ikenkeren sub-section of the Kel Tarhaouhaout section | Hunting of barbary sheep. Collecting of wild seeds | three goats |
| **Abergali**, Khalifa of the Kel Tarayin sub-section of the Kel Tarhaouhaout section | Hunting of barbary sheep | two goats |
| **Khofa** of the Kel Tarayin section. No position as leader | Cultivation grounds at I-n-agriwal and I-n-dalag. Hunting of barbary sheep. Wild donkeys | two donkeys |
| **Deyni**, chief of the Kel Arefsa section | No particular value | No land-rent |
| **Akawali**, chief of the Isandan section and leader of the Kel Afara-he hin sub-section | Cultivation grounds at Tahifet. Hunting of barbary sheep. Wild donkeys | one donkey |
| **Hanu**, Khalifa of the Kel Azernen sub-section of the Isandan section | Cultivation grounds at Tamanraset. In the past wild donkeys | one donkey |
| **Khoseni**, Khalifa of the Relayddin now attached to the Aguh-en-tehle | Khoseni is in command of the Relayddin territory to which all members of the Relayddin have equal rights. Each of them gives two goats annually to the Amenukal | |

# APPENDIX III

*School Curriculum Details*

The school curriculum in operation throughout Algeria by the end of the 1960s was as follows:

| Primary Level | Total hours per week |
|---|---|
| 1st year | 20 hours Arabic per week |
| 2nd year | 20 hours Arabic per week |
| 3rd year | 15 hours French per week – reduced to 10 hours per week, the additional 5 being allocated to Arabic |
| 4th year | 15 hours French per week<br>10 hours Arabic per week |
| Secondary Level | All science subjects taught in French. History, civil and moral education taught in Arabic<br>5 lycées are entirely Arabic |

At the level of higher education, the emphasis is on technical and economic training. Such a programme could not be undertaken without sufficient teachers and teacher training colleges. However, the dependency on foreign teachers has been gradually reduced. In 1962–3 there were 7,258 foreign teachers, many of whom were from Syria, in a total number of 20,311 primary school teachers. By 1968–9, the number of foreign teachers had been reduced to 6,040 in a total number of 33,000. At the secondary and higher level of education the proportion of Algerian teachers in 1968–9 was 40 per cent and 50 per cent respectively. (These figures were issued by the Ministry of Education in Algiers.)

# APPENDIX IV

Location and Date of Opening of Schools in Ahaggar

| Location | Date of opening |
| --- | --- |
| Tamanrasset | 1947 } divided into boys and girls |
| Tamanrasset | 1956 } |
| Ideles | 1956 |
| Tazrouk | 1957 |
| In Amguel | 1958–9 |
| Tamanrasset – Medersa (Ibn Khaldoun) | 1962–3 |
| Abalessa | 1962–3 |
| Tit | 1962–3 |
| Iglene | 1965–6 |
| Amsel | 1965–6 |
| Tarhaouhaout | 1965–6 (closed 1967–8) |
| Hadrian | 1966–7 |
| Tamanrasset (Tahaggart) | 1966–7 |
| Hirafok | 1966–7 |
| Tahifet | 1967–8 |
| C.E.A. (Collège de l'Éducation Agricole) | 1967– } secondary schools in Tamanrasset |
| C.E.G. (Collège de l'Éducation Générale) | 1967– } |

# BIBLIOGRAPHY

Abd el Djalil, R. P., 'Aspects intérieurs de l'Islam', *Bulletin de Liaison Saharienne*, Alger, vol. 5., No. 16, 1964.

Alport, E., 'The Mzab', *Man*, vol. 84, 1954, pp. 34–44.

Amin, Samir, *The Maghreb in the Modern World*, Penguin, 1970.

Bailey, F. G., *Stratagems and Spoils. A Social Anthropology of Politics*, Oxford, 1969.

Barrère, G., 'Correspondance sur le contrat agricole en Ahaggar', *Travaux de l'Institut de Recherches Sahariennes*, Alger, XXIII, 1964, pp. 187–8.

Barth, F., 'Descent and Marriage Reconsidered', in J. Goody (ed.), *The Character of Kinship*, Cambridge, 1973, pp. 3–19.

Barth, Heinrich, *Reisen und Entdeckungen in Nord- und Central Afrika in den Jahren 1849 bis 1855*, I–V, Gotha, 1957–8.

Bates, O., *The Eastern Libyans*, London, 1914.

Baumann, M., *Volkerkunde von Afrika*, Essen, 1940.

Benhazera, M., *Six Mois chez les Touareg du Ahaggar*, Alger, 1908.

Bernard, A., *Enquête sur l'habitation des indigènes de l'Algérie*, Alger, 1921.

Berque, J., *French North Africa. The Maghrib between the Two World Wars*, trans. Jean Stewart, London, 1967.

Bissuel, H., *Les Touareg de L'Ouest*, Alger, 1888.

Blanguernon, Claude, *Le Hoggar*, 2nd ed., Paris, 1955.

Bloch, M., 'The Moral and Tactical Meaning of Kinship Terms', *Man*, 6, No. 1, 1971, pp. 79–87.

—, 'The Long Term and the Short Term: The Economic and Political Significance of the Morality of Kinship', in J. Goody (ed.), *The Character of Kinship*, Cambridge, 1973, pp. 75–87.

Bobo, J., 'Les Salines de l'Amadror', *Travaux de l'Institut de Recherches Sahariennes*, Alger, 11, 1954, pp. 141–2.

Bourgeot, André, 'Le Costume masculin des Kel Ahaggar', *Libyca*, XVII, 1969, pp. 355–76.

—, 'Idéologies et appellations ethniques: l'exemple Twareg. Analyse des catégories sociales', *Cahiers d'Études Africaines*, No. 48, XII, 1972, 4e trim.

—, 'Le Contenu sociologique de l'appellation Tuareg (Kel Ahaggar). Histoire

d'un nom', *Revue de l'Occident Musulman et de la Méditerranée*, No. 11, 1er. sem., 1972, pp. 71–9.
Bourgeot, André, 'Nomadisme et sédentarisation, le processus d'intégration chez les Kel Ahaggar', *Revue de l'Occident Musulman et de la Méditerranée*, No. 11, 1er. sem., 1972, pp. 85–92.
Bovill, E. W., *The Golden Trade of the Moors*, O.U.P., 1958.
Buhl, Fr., *Muhammeds Religiose Forkyndelse efter Quranen*, Copenhagen, 1924.
Butay, L., 'Les Salines de l'Amadror', *Bulletin de Liaison Saharienne*, Alger, No. 12, 1953, pp. 16–17.

Capot-Rey, Robert, *Le Sahara français*, Paris, 1953.
Chudeau, R., *Sahara soudanais*, Paris, 1909.
Clauzel, J., 'Les Hiérarchies sociales en pays Touareg', *Travaux de l'Institut de Recherches Sahariennes*, Alger, XXXI, 1962, pt. I, pp. 120–75.

Dapper, O., *Beschreibung von Africa*, Amsterdam, 1670.
—, *Description de l'Afrique*, Amsterdam, 1686.
De Heusch, L., 'The Debt of the Maternal Uncle', *Man*, 9, No. 4, 1974, pp. 609–19.
Denis, P., 'Les Salines de l'Amadror en 1958', *Bulletin de Liaison Saharienne*, Alger, No. 34, 1959, pp. 178–9.
Desparmet, J., *Coutumes, institutions, croyances des indigènes de l'Algérie*, Alger, 1939.
Dubief, J., 'Les chronologies des Kel Ahaggar et des Taitoq', *Travaux de l'Institut de Recherches Sahariennes*, I, Alger, 1942, pp. 87–132.
—, 'Les Pluies au Sahara Central', *Travaux de l'Institut de Recherches Sahariennes*, IV, Alger, 1947, pp. 7–23.
—, 'Les Ifoghas de Ghadames. Chronologie et nomadisme', *Revue de l'Institut des Belles-Lettres Arabes*, XI, Tunis, 1948, pp. 141–59.
—, 'Les Imanghassaten. Chronologie et migration', *Revue de l'Institut des Belles-Lettres Arabes*, XIII, Tunis, 1950, pp. 23–36.
—, 'Les Ouraghen des Kel Ajjer. Chronologie et nomadisme', *Travaux de l'Institut de Recherches Sahariennes*, XIV, Alger, 1956, pp. 85–137.
Duveyrier, Henri, *Les Touareg du Nord*, Paris, 1864.

Edrisi, *Géographie d'Edrisi*, traduit par le P. Amedée Jaubert, I–II, Paris, 1836–40.
—, *Description de l'Afrique et de l'Espagne*, traduit par R. Dozy et M. J. de Goeje, Leyden, 1866.
El Bekri, *Description de l'Afrique Septentrionale*, traduit par Mac Guckin de Slane, Paris, 1859.
—, *Das Geographische Worterbuch*, I–II, Gottingen–Paris, 1876–7.

Florimond, Captain, *Annexe du Hoggar. Rapport annuel*, 1938.

Foucauld, Charles de, *Poésies touaregues*, vol. I–II, Paris, 1930.
—, *Dictionnaire Touareg–Française, dialecte de l'Ahaggar*, I–IV, 1951–2.

Galan, P., 'Contribution à l'étude du problème alimentaire au Hoggar', *Archives de l'Institut Pasteur*, Algérie, XXX, 1951, pp. 230–47.
Gast, Marceau, 'Aspect de l'artisanat chez les Kel Ahaggar en 1963', *Libyca*, XI, 1963, pp. 221–34.
—, 'Evolution de la vie économique et structures sociales en Ahaggar de 1660–1965', *Travaux de l'Institut de Recherches Sahariennes*, Alger, XXII, 1965, pp. 129–43.
—, 'Premiers Résultats d'une mission ethnographique en Ahaggar', *Libyca*, XIII, 1965, pp. 325–32.
—, *Alimentation des populations de l'Ahaggar. Étude ethnographique*, Mémoires du C.R.A.P.E., VIII, Paris, 1958.
—, '*Temazlait* (contrat de protection chez les Kel Ahaggar)', *Encyclopédie Berbère*, Édition Provisoire, Cahier No. 7, UNESCO, Université de Provence, 1972.
Gellner, Ernest, *Saints of the Atlas*, London and Chicago, 1969.
—, Introduction to *Arabs and Berbers* (eds. E. Gellner and C. Micaud), Duckworth, London, 1972.
Germani, G., 'Secularisation, Modernisation, and Economic Development', in S. N. Eisenstadt (ed.), *The Protestant Ethic and Modernisation*, 1967, pp. 343–66.
Goffman, E., 'The Nature of Deference and Demeanor', *American Anthropologist*, 58, 1956, pp. 473–502.
—, *The Presentation of Self in Everyday Life*, Penguin, London, 1969.
Goody, J., 'The Mother's Brother and the Sister's Son in West Africa', *Journal of the Royal Anthropological Institute*, 89, 1959, pp. 61–88.
—, 'Sideways or Downwards? Lateral and Vertical Succession, Inheritance and Descent in Africa and Eurasia', *Man*, 5, No. 4, 1970, pp. 627–38.
Gordon, D. C., *North Africa's French Legacy 1954–1962*, Harvard Middle Eastern Monographs, Cambridge, 1964.
—, *The Passing of French Algeria*, O.U.P., London, 1966.
Graves, Robert, *Oxford Addresses on Poetry*, Cassell, 1961.
Gsell, S., *Histoire ancienne de l'Afrique du Nord*, I–VIII, Paris, 1920–28.

Humbaraci, A., *Algeria: A Revolution that Failed*, Pall Mall, 1966.

Ibn Abdal-H' Akam, *Conquête de l'Afrique du Nord et de l'Espagne*, texte et traduction de A. Gateau, Bibliothèque Arabe-Française, Alger, 1942.
Ibn Batutah, *Voyages d'Ibn Batutah*, I–IV, traduit par C. Defremy et B. R. Sanguinetti, Paris, 1853–8.
Ibn Haukal, *The Oriental Geography of Ebn Haukal, an Arabian Traveller of the Tenth Century*, trans. William Ouseley, London, 1800.

Ibn Haukal, *Description de l'Afrique*, traduit de l'Arabe par Mac Guckin de Slane, *Journal Asiatique*, 3e série, XIII, 1842.
Ibn Khaldoun, *Histoire des Berbères*, I–IV, traduit par de Slane, Alger, 1852–6.

Keenan, J., 'Social Change among the Tuareg', in E. Gellner and C. Micaud (eds.), *Arabs and Berbers*, 1972, pp. 345–60.

Lehureaux, L., *Sur les pistes du désert*, Paris, 1929.
Leo Africanus, *The History and Description of Africa*, trans. John Pory, I–III, London, 1896.
Lévi-Strauss, C., *Structural Anthropology*, London, 1968.
Lhote, Henri, 'Au sujet du port du voile chez les Touareg et les Teda', *Notes Africaines*, No. 52, October, 1951, pp. 108–11.
—, *La Chasse chez les Touaregs*, Paris, 1951.
—, 'Les Salines de l'Amadror', *Bulletin de Liaison Saharienne*, IV, No. 14, 1953, pp. 54–6.
—, *Les Touaregs du Hoggar*, 2nd ed., Paris, 1955.
Lyon, G. F., *A Narrative of Travels in Northern Africa in the Years 1818, 1819 and 1820*, London, 1821.

Maire, R., *Études sur la flore et la végétation du Sahara Central*, Mémoires de la Société d'Histoire Naturelle de l'Afrique du Nord, No. 3, Alger, 1933–40.
Malaurie, J., 'Touareg et noirs au Hoggar. Aspects de la situation actuelle', *Annales Economies, Sociétés, Civilisations*, VIII, 3, 1953, pp. 338–46.
Mercier, Marcel, *L'Histore de L'Afrique septentrionale II*.
Merton, R. K., *Social Theory and Social Structure*, Glencoe, Ill., 1957.
Montagne, Robert, *The Berbers*, trans. David Seddon, London, 1973.
Murdock, G. P., *Africa. Its Peoples and Their Culture History*, New York, Toronto, London, 1959.
Murphy, R. F., 'Social Distance and the Veil', *American Anthropologist*, 66, 1964, pp. 1257–74.
—, 'Tuareg Kinship', *American Anthropologist*, 69, 1967, pp. 163–70.

Needham, R., 'Remarks on the Analysis of Kinship and Marriages', in R. Needham (ed.), *Rethinking Kinship and Marriage*, A.S.A. Monograph II, Tavistock, 1971, pp. 1–34.
Nemo, J., 'Le Régime juridique des terres au Hoggar', *Travaux de l'Institut de Recherches Sahariennes*, Alger, XXII, 1963, pp. 123–44.
Nicolaisen, J., 'Essai sur la religion et la magie touarègues', *Folk*, 3, 1961, pp. 113–62.
—, *Ecology and Culture of the Pastoral Tuareg*, The National Museum of Copenhagen, 1963.
Nicolas, F., *Tamesna. Les lullemmeden de l'Est ou Touareg 'Kel Dinnik'*, Paris, 1950.

—, 'Le Voilement des Tuareg – contributions à l'étude de l'Air', *Mémoires de l'I.F.A.N.*, No. 10, 1950.

Pedersen, J., *Israel I–II. Sjaeleliv og Samfundsliv*, 3. udg, Copenhagen, 1958.

Perry, J. A. G., 'The Broker in a Rural Lesotho Community', *African Studies*, 32, No. 3, 1973, pp. 137–52.

Prasse, K. G., 'L'Origine du mot Amazig', *Acta Orientalia*, Copenhagen, XXIII, 3–4, 1959, pp. 197–200.

Radcliffe-Brown, A. R., *Structure and Function in Primitive Society*, London, 1952.

Regnier, J., 'Les Salines de l'Amadror et le trafic caravanier', *Bulletin de Liaison Saharienne*, XII, No. 43, 1961, pp. 234–61.

Reygasse, M., *Monuments funéraires préislamiques de l'Afrique du Nord*, Paris, 1950.

Richer, A., *Les Oulliminden. Les Touareg du Niger*, Paris, 1924.

Rodd, Francis Rennell, 'The Origin of the Tuareg', *Geographical Journal*, 67, 1926, pp. 27–52.

—, *People of the Veil*, London, 1926.

Rognon, P., 'La confédération des nomads Kel Ahaggar', *Annales Géographiques*, 71, No. 388, 1962, pp. 604–19.

Schapera, I., 'Kinship and Marriage among the Tswana', in D. Forde and A. R. Radcliffe-Brown (eds.), *African Systems of Kinship and Marriage*, Oxford, 1950, pp. 140–65.

Scheffler, H. W., 'Ancestor Worship in Anthropology: Or, Observations on Descent and Descent Groups', *Current Anthropology*, 1966, pp. 541–51.

Schirmer, H., *Le Sahara*, Paris, 1893.

Terray, E., 'Classes and Class Consciousness in the Abron Kingdom of Gyamen', in M. Bloch (ed.), *Marxist Analyses and Social Anthropology*, Malaby, London, 1975, pp. 85–135.

Westermarck, E., *Ritual and Belief in Morocco*, I–II, 1926, London.

Wolf, E. R., 'Aspects of Group Relations in a Complex Society, Mexico', *American Anthropologist*, 58, 1956, pp. 1065–78.

—, 'Kinship, Friendship and Patron-Client Relations in Complex Societies', in M. Banton (ed.), *The Social Anthropology of Complex Societies*, A.S.A. Monograph No. 4, Tavistock, London, 1966.

# INDEX

**List of Authorities**

**Glossary of Tuareg and Arabic Words**

Arabic words are shown in italics

Ababah (pl. ibubah): male cross cousin, 118, 334
Abada: vegetation zone (approx. 1,700–1,800 metres above sea level), 292, 350
Aballag: a form of tribute, 47f.
Abba: father, 97, 334
Achour: religious tax, 155
Adreilal: *Astragalus sp.*, 316
Aferhaler: *Crambe Kralikii*, 316
Afezu: *Panicum turgidum*, 316, 321
Agedellehouf: lower part of veil, 128
Agelmam (guelta); water-hole, 2, 40, 153, 218, 321
Agg ettebel: 43f., 54, 79, 119, 122f., 205, 209; *see* ettebel
Agror: stone enclosure for kids, 228
Ahal: social gathering at night, 107, 299, 351
Aheg: to raid, 103–5
Akafar (pl. ikufar): infidel, i.e. non-Moslem, 6
Akal: land, country, 26
Akara: stick placed in mouths of kids to prevent suckling, 346
Akasa: vegetation of annual plants, rainy season, 227
Alechcho: veil, 128, 334f.
Alkah: *Trichodesma africanum*, 316
Amacheg (Adrar and Sudan): 103–5; *see* Imuhag
Amadal: land, 40
Amagar (pl. amagaren): guest, 147, 154, 168, 179, 341

## Social and Political Groups

**Place Names**

**Personal Names**